Freedom on th

Freedom on the Frontlines

*Afghan Women and the Fallacy
of Liberation*

LINA ABIRAFEH

McFarland & Company, Inc., Publishers
Jefferson, North Carolina

Portions of this work appeared in
Gender and International Aid in Aghanistan (McFarland 2009)

All photographs are from the author's collection.

ISBN (print) 978-1-4766-8942-5
ISBN (ebook) 978-1-4766-4719-7

LIBRARY OF CONGRESS AND BRITISH LIBRARY
CATALOGUING DATA ARE AVAILABLE

Library of Congress Control Number 2022001982

Front cover: A woman stands on an armored personnel carrier
overlooking Kabul (composite image from photographs
by the author and Patrick Seymour)

Printed in the United States of America

*McFarland & Company, Inc., Publishers
Box 611, Jefferson, North Carolina 28640
www.mcfarlandpub.com*

For SARAH *and* AZIZA

*For your freedom
and for women's freedom*

Table of Contents

Acknowledgments

The hardest part to write is this. I am grateful. My heart is full, even as—for Afghanistan—it breaks.

All those I thanked in the 2009 book—I thank you still. Most of you are still in my life—and for that I am blessed. It has been 13 years since I had to write words of acknowledgment, and now there are so many more of you I love. You fill a whole book.

I often say that I live at the intersection of comfort and chaos. The writing of this book proved to be more of the latter, with days and nights at my desk, too much coffee, too little food (popcorn, wine and Sour Skittles notwithstanding).

An array of brilliant minds—and serendipity—birthed this book.

Lucy: you wrote to thank me for helping you with Haiti and ended up giving me the gift that is Rebecca O'Keeffe. Rebecca: there would be no book without you. Together we worked night and day, squeezing in basketball games (yours) and dance (mine) while we crossed time zones (Ireland to New York) and put together something that now looks like a book—in record time. Thank you for agreeing to join me in this madness, and for bringing this book to life. I'm grateful beyond words.

AJ: you joined the chaos as well, and covered the critical little bits. Jessika: you were the starting point and a sounding board—your work laid the foundation. Madeira interns: you fed into this in various ways. "Function in disaster, finish in style," my high school motto told me. I've been doing that ever since.

Gabriella, the one and only Dr. Googs: you keep my academic side solid while I howl into the void. You dropped everything to read this monster, and your support solidified this book.

It takes a (global) village, they say. And I am so grateful for the village that magically appeared when I needed it. For those who fed me, made me laugh, looked after my fur-child, cheered me on, and pulled me back every time I was about to fall—I thank you. You saved me.

Rudy: your food, pup-sitting, and pep talks made the hard parts easy.

Big brothers T&D: for our VillageThree. Mike, legendary triple word score: you combed through, commented, and cheered. And you brought in Cate, who dug diligently for data. "Now breathe and re-enter the world," you told me, on the day the book was done.

My brother Chris: You are safe. And that is enough.

I believe in the strength and solidarity of the sisterhood. And oh am I lucky to have an army of strong women by my side.

StirFrySisters: bitching with you fuels my fire.

SweatSisters: dancing with you feeds my soul.

Myriam, my wonderful workwife: I love the partnership we have, fueled by laughter and sarcasm! Thank you for sharing your Institute with me. And to the AiW Team past and present, you make it happen—simply!

Anayansi, my CitySister fabulous foodie fountain of joy: your smile lights up my city. NYC is not home without you. Devanna, my DDLP: our sisterhood spans continents. We were tied together the day we signed each other's contracts and are forever stuck.

And Salmas, past and present: the legacy of strong women continues.

Writing this book has brought me back to Afghanistan in the most vivid ways. I sit in front of my screen laughing and crying at the memories that have come pouring out of me: the times we provided Kabul with the best (or only?!) chocolate cakes in the city, the time we received a donation of plus-size lingerie from a U.S. shop that was going out of business, the time we had our photos used in the parliamentary election sample ballot (I still have it), the time my passport was "missing" in the ministry for months because it was used to prop up the short leg of a table, the times we invented celebrations for no reason other than being together on the rooftop of the Mustafa Hotel, the times we laughed and danced together for International Women's Day, and many other days. Yes, the times we danced. Those more than anything.

And reconnecting with friends—my family—from those days as we watched Afghanistan fall. We had no words, we kept saying. *No words.*

For all the women in Afghanistan, those I know personally and those I admire from afar, my heart is with you. And you deserve freedom—at last.

B'aman Khoda. I wish you peace.

Preface

An Afghan man once told me:
The world thought they could bring freedom to Afghan women,
but freedom is only won from the inside.

This book is the continuation of a 25-year relationship with Afghanistan. I will start at the beginning. As a graduate student in Washington, D.C., in 1996, I was awarded a fellowship that placed me in a job working on women's human rights. At that point, Afghanistan had fallen to the Taliban—for the first time. I was researching global women's human rights, but the organization asked me to focus only on Afghanistan—"just temporarily," they said, "while we try to figure out what's going on with women over there...."

I stayed with the organization for one year, focusing exclusively on Afghan women's rights, attending briefings on Capitol Hill and reframing all my graduate school writing assignments to reflect my new focus. At that time, Afghanistan seemed so remote to me, but at the same time so very close. I could not let go of what I had learned in that year.

Over the next few years, I carried the story of Afghan women with me as I worked internationally and in Washington, D.C. I followed developments in the country closely. I watched and waited.

An international organization tried to offer me a job in another country. "It's Afghanistan or nothing," I said. Shortly after September 11, that organization said: "OK, it's Afghanistan now." And so it began.

Women for Women International had offered me the job of Country Director for their still-non-existent Afghanistan office. My task was to work with women—training, support, mentoring, financial assistance. I would set up the office, hire the team, and work with them for one year, transitioning to Afghan leadership. In short, I was to work myself out of a job. And I would be the only non–Afghan in the office.

In 2002, I flew to Afghanistan with $20,000 down my pants. I was 27 years old—enthusiastic, naïve, and terrified.

1

I remember that day, climbing down the rickety stairs of the Ariana Airlines flight, dusty summer wind blowing my carefully-positioned veil out of place. An old, bearded man in front of me kneeled and kissed the Afghan earth. He was "home" for the first time in 23 years.

And 23 years of conflict had taken a toll, from Soviet occupation to fighting between Afghan factions to the takeover by the Taliban. And then takeover by an army of aid workers—of which I was one. Expertise-in-abstraction, I remember thinking. *How could I possibly be of use here?*

Despite the country's saturation with international agencies and good intentions, the needs were overwhelming. When I moved to Afghanistan in 2002, it was considered a "post-conflict" country—it was anything but. The needs *for women* were overwhelming and I wanted so desperately to "get it right."

In one year, the office grew to 65 Afghan staff supporting more than 3000 women. And me. Every day, I engaged with Afghan women—and men—listening and learning as they shared their concerns, experiences, and perspectives with me.

I was in a rare and privileged position, with an obligation to treat it respectfully and use it meaningfully, to benefit women. I became conscious of my responsibility to share the understandings that I had acquired in hopes that we might "do better" for women.

I knew that the foundation of Afghan recovery was in these stories. And I knew that we were not listening enough.

In 2003, I started my Ph.D. at the London School of Economics and Political Science so I could "bitch constructively," as I

A doorway in Baagh-i-Babur (Babur's Garden), Kabul.

called it. What I really wanted was to understand what happened, and how we might do it better. I was still working in Afghanistan at the time, and I remained there until 2006.

In 2007, I moved to Sierra Leone, but continued following—and writing on—Afghanistan. Later that year, I moved to Papua New Guinea, carrying Afghanistan with me. I defended my dissertation and received my Ph.D. in 2008. I dubbed myself an "accidental academic" and published a book in 2009 built from my dissertation.

Gender and International Aid in Afghanistan was my attempt to give something back to the country that had given me so much. The commitment—and the writing—traveled the world with me, but with the publication of that book I felt like it could finally return to where it belonged—to Afghanistan.

When the book was published, it wasn't exactly a bestseller. Afghan women were hardly in the media, off the geo-political agenda, and absent from our minds. They were supposedly "liberated," and subsequently forgotten.

In that preface, I wrote, "this book marks the *culmination* of a twelve-year engagement...." Clearly it was not.

I went on to work in nearly 20 other countries—Haiti, Senegal, Lebanon—but Afghanistan remained alive in my mind. I remember still: harrowing flights in and out of Kabul and those majestic mountains, cold nights warming our toes under the *sandalee*, picnics in Paghman on warm summer days, the smell of streetside *kabob* and giant loaves of *naan*, road trips to Bamiyan to climb the caves, imagining where the Buddhas once were. And more stars in the night sky than I've ever seen in my life....

And I stayed in touch with so many during my time there, Afghan and non–Afghan. They had touched my life in ways I could not forget. And with every incident, every bit of news, we would reconnect.

Although Afghanistan never left me, I did not imagine that I would find myself writing about the country again. By 2021, I could not stay quiet. Afghanistan was not doing well, and I needed to process my thoughts. My article "For Afghan women, the U.S. rhetoric of liberation has fallen short" was published in June 2021.

And then the door opened—again. What started as an article lamenting the deterioration and abandonment of the country evolved into the idea to write a second edition of my book. I quickly realized that a "second edition" was not enough; it was going to be a whole new book. This book was written following the Taliban (re)takeover in August 2021, as Afghanistan unraveled. And Afghan women.... I had no words. But I had to find the words.

Ultimately my work was—and has always been—inspired by these women. It is through their lived experiences that progress can be measured and regress can be understood. When I look back on more than two decades of work on women's rights around the world, I see that it always was the women whose voices fueled me—and fueled countries.

Afghanistan is not one of those *other countries, over there*. It is right here. It cannot fall in and out of the news solely based on extreme victories or extreme tragedies. Today the world is watching, but our attention spans are short. *Who pays the price for our short-sightedness?*

What's more, we cannot afford a collective shrug and blanket excuses. "It's their culture," they say. No, it isn't.

Any country can be an Afghanistan. All around the world, women are still fighting for their rights—for choice and voice and freedom—even as those rights are denied or stripped away.

It is for these women, for all women, and for me, that I write this book.

Overview

This new book revisits the 2009 book and continues where it left off to tell the rest of the story through October 2021. The first book started with the premise that the rhetoric of "liberation" was problematic, denying women's agency and sidelining Afghan women.

I argued that the question of women's role in Afghanistan had always been a particularly polarizing part of political discourse, linked to modernity and progress on the one hand and preservation of tradition on the other. Women, politics, and the state have always been intimately connected in Afghanistan, and conflicts have been fueled by attempts to challenge or change women's status. I wrote that Afghan women's experiences are more complex than mere pawns in political struggles. I still believe this.

I also examined the work of the international community, my own community. I said that in terms of rhetoric, Afghanistan is arguably one of the largest gender-focused aid interventions. Everyone, everywhere knows the "story of Afghan women," at least in part. Measuring rhetoric against action, however, the situation was not so clear.

What did we actually achieve?!

Ultimately, Afghan women and men articulated that they felt trapped between their own definitions of progress and strong international agendas. Women said that their cause has been manipulated for political reasons, and external pressures to fast-track *womens rights* and *gender equality* would foment a backlash. They were right.

They argued that the rhetoric of "liberation" lacked the foundations on which real human rights—and women's rights—could be built. And Afghan voices were notably absent from the process. At the same time, Afghan women were used as the barometer to measure social change. All of these things remain true.

But has there been an opportunity for Afghan women and men to find their place in this change? More important: Were they able to determine the direction and pace of this change according to their own priorities and agendas?

The first book was centered on a study of my own community—international aid workers. It is hard to be objective when you study your own community, so the feedback I gathered at that time was to reinforce—or contradict—the self-reflection that I was undertaking in that particular historical moment.

Rather than presenting a critique of aid interventions, this book highlights the voices of Afghan women themselves, how they viewed those interventions, and the physical and ideological occupations they have experienced, particularly in these last two decades.

This new book measures the rhetoric of "liberating" Afghan women—the call that justified the military intervention, which in turn fed into the agenda of the aid intervention—from the perspective of Afghan women. It asks: *If "liberation" was truly the intent, how might we measure today?*

This story is not meant to be exhaustive; there's ample research for that. And there will be more, as we all come to terms with "what happened" over these last two decades. This is not a play-by-play of the Afghan story, of the military story, or of the aid story.

This story is also not intended as an unconstructive critique from an ivory tower academic. Rather, it hopes to be critical and self-reflective in a way that is constructive, written by someone who continues to care for—and believe in—the Afghan people.

Here's what it is: For me, the most important story, the only true measure of progress—or liberation—is through the voices of the Afghan people. What have the changes in Afghanistan meant *to Afghans?*

This work is part of an iterative process spanning four years in the country, and an interest spanning 25 years. And still, it is only a snapshot of a complicated landscape.

This book is equally a reflection of my own growth as a feminist activist and accidental academic. Decades of feminist work—and feminist fire—has changed the way I work, and the way I write. This began as the work of a young feminist aid worker, activist, and academic. It is now the work of someone who desperately wants to see change *today*—not in some distant future. I speak clearly, urgently, and I won't stop fighting—for all women.

Methods

The original study was conducted first through an examination of policy texts and media discourses, then through an investigation of program practice, drawing on the perspectives of the aid community in order to examine the implementation of policies in light of promised transformation for women. Meaning: *Did we do what we said we'd do when we said we'd "liberate" women?!*

Some of this research is featured in the new book, told from a different perspective. Meanwhile, none of this can be divorced from Afghanistan's current reality: poverty, insecurity, inequality. *How can we expect Afghan women to fulfill their potential when they are fighting for their survival?*

For the last two decades, whether I was in the country or not, I remained on the receiving end of communications and comment about our work and our support of Afghan women. *Have we done what we set out to do? What might we have done better?* And—most important: *What could we do now that will help Afghan women find the freedom that has been so elusive to them—on their terms?*

This book is built on feedback from those questions—the voices of more than 100 Afghan women and men, 25 Afghan women leaders, and another 50 aid workers and authorities on Afghanistan over a 20-year period from 2001 to 2021.

Qualitative methods have been used because quantitative data on all things "women" remains incomplete, inaccurate, or an underestimate of reality. While there are some quantitative measures throughout the book, qualitative methods were given priority because the idea was to elevate people's voices and stories. It is through the experiences and perceptions of Afghan women and men that the entire aid intervention of the last 20 years in Afghanistan should be understood.

During my years in Afghanistan, and for the decade that followed, I spoke with a range of aid workers with local and international organizations, people who specialized in women's rights and gender equality as well as those who were leading agencies. I also had a network of authorities on Afghanistan including academics, authors, and experts whose long experience in the country helped me to better understand my own experiences. The following voices are from these conversations.

As both an academic and a practitioner, I have retained the anonymity of individuals and organizations because of codes of confidentiality. Names of Afghan women and men have been changed. Names of prominent or well-known Afghans have not changed, as they are often in public space. Here are the titles I elected to use, for clarity and simplicity:

- *Afghan women leaders* are precisely that. Here, names cannot be used as these women are at risk.
- *Aid workers* are non–Afghans with international organizations— UN, NGO, and other organizations. They range from "gender focal points" to heads of agencies, and more.
- *Authorities on Afghanistan* are published authors and academics with a long experience in the country. Their names are used if/when relevant—with permission.

Segments of this investigation build on previously published analysis that has appeared in a variety of articles and reports. All of these are cited where relevant. Further, these findings have been shared in several international conferences where I have been invited to speak and have benefited from critical feedback. The present conclusions are built from past and present data to offer fresh analysis.

Positionality and Challenges

Why is it important to explain who I am? My position exposes my perspective. The most important thing is this: while I may have lived in Afghanistan, loved Afghanistan, and helped Afghanistan as best I could, I am not Afghan. Meaning that my voice should never drown out local voices. I have spoken now because it was wrong *not* to speak—to provide a counter to the current narrative that Afghan women will "once again" be "victims." And because I have access to stories and perspectives that span more than two decades. So that is why I write.

But who am I?! I recognize that my own identity cannot be abstracted from this process. I am a feminist above all else. I situate myself as a *developing world* feminist because I am Lebanese and Palestinian, raised partly in the Arab region, and mostly in the United States. My feminist consciousness was born out of my own origins and experience, built by academic— and later professional—experience in the United States. I am also an activist, having long fought for women's rights and equality and fundamental freedoms. I am also an aid worker, with experience that spans more than two decades and more than 20 countries. I am also an academic—an "accidental academic" specifically—with research and publications and other academic things behind my name. Since 2015, I have been the Executive Director of the Arab Institute for Women at the Lebanese American University, working at the intersection of academia and activism to advance change for women in the Arab region.

I lived and worked in Afghanistan from 2002 until 2006. Although I am an outsider to the lives of women and men in Afghanistan, I have spent sufficient time working closely on the inside. In my experience in the country, I established strong contacts and made many friends.

I was in a unique position because I was able to gain women's trust through my work. In my four years in the country, I demonstrated my commitment and, to the best of my abilities, delivered on my promises. And Afghan women were honest with me in a way that perhaps other "outsiders" did not experience. In truth, running an organization of 65 staff and 3000 women who were all Afghan meant that I was clearly in the minority. And I greatly benefited from the privilege of experiencing and understanding the Afghan way of things.

In addition, my skin color provided further access and also built trust. As a brown woman, I was initially often mistaken for an Afghan, and therefore in a position of privilege to hear the real story. My special access was not revoked when I corrected the mistake, because I was assumed to be from the region and therefore familiar to them, and familiar with Afghanistan. Because my origins are Arab, it was assumed that I was Muslim. As a result, the women believed that I was also better equipped to explain to others the centrality of Islam to the lives of Afghans.

During my four years in Afghanistan, I was frequently placed in the role of cultural interpreter. I served as a bridge, connecting Afghan perspectives to "outside" policies and plans. I then helped decipher these policies and plans for Afghans. Because I was so closely connected to the inside, I was able to share what I learned about Afghanistan and Afghan women.

There's a tension in being the insider-outsider—but also great value. I recognize that I was part of a moment, but also observing that moment. And existing on both "sides" of a conversation between the international community and Afghanistan that spanned 20 years. In my use of "we" throughout the book, I intend this to mean "the international community," a collection of characters of which I was very much a part.

It is essential to let Afghan voices speak for themselves as these voices are often rendered silent in international circles. I have been the fortunate recipient of many of these voices through my long experience in Afghanistan and my conscious presence of existing on both sides, so to speak, of Afghan women's issues. This isn't a binary, but simply means that I am both an active participant and an observer in this scenario. I've run an organization working to help Afghan women, supporting women on the frontlines. And now I support from the sidelines. In so doing, having worked closely with Afghan women, I have a responsibility to present what I saw, and what they told me.

Translation and language were challenges that I overcame by employing two Afghan research assistants, male and female, who were fluent in

Dari, Pashto, and English. These research assistants were former members of my staff and were therefore very familiar with the issues, accustomed to working with me, and highly credible and capable. These assistants served as my interpreters during conversations and my cultural and contextual interpreters after conversations. They also assisted in translating and transcribing the data. Following the research, my two assistants were married—united by a shared commitment and understanding. We remained in contact, and more than a decade later they were critical advisors and sounding boards for this book.

Structure

Chapter 1 tells the story of "liberation" for Afghan women, starting with Afghan history to illustrate the political nature of all things "women." This is followed by key social indicators, to give us a sense of what things look like now and how things have changed in the last two decades. The chapter then moves on to discuss the most politicized image of all: the *chaddari*, or *bourka*. Bringing all this together, we see that feminism is not incompatible with Afghanistan. In fact, it has always been there—in Afghan women.

Chapter 2 brings in firsthand accounts, the voices of Afghan women and men, to help us understand how they define their own identities. The chapter begins with an exploration of the word "gender" and what it has come to signify. The analysis of Afghan identities builds from this, offering insight into how people see, and define, themselves. Because understanding where we *fit* helps us see where we *fight*.

Chapter 3 adds insight by drawing from Afghan literary history to examine the role of men—either as allies or as gatekeepers—to help us better understand Afghan women's agency. Men play a role in gender politics; they can either advance or oppose women's struggles. And the system of honor helps us understand how social change, especially women's rights, can be received or resisted.

Chapter 4 tells the story of the aid "intervention" and its attempt to "liberate" Afghan women. Measuring aid rhetoric with reality is not straightforward. More important is to measure the perceptions and experiences of the people who are on the receiving end of that aid. Using such stories, this chapter examines some of the major international aid milestones in the last two decades to explain how this approach actually undermined Afghan women's agency and ultimately undercut Afghan abilities to control their own "development."

Chapter 5 provides an example to illustrate aid policy in practice—

the advancing of the so-called gender agenda through its efforts to bring "democracy" and ultimately "peace" to the country. There is a parallel between the quest to deliver democracy and to "liberate" women. This part of the story is told through an inside view to the process as well as through the voices of both Afghans and international aid workers.

Chapter 6 dives deeply into the problem of men's violence against women in Afghanistan, in both public and private space. The chapter shares both figures and perceptions of violence, and also includes a brief overview of documented cases. It argues that no amount of "liberation" is possible as long as there is violence. If women are not safe, no one is safe. And the reality is that Afghan women have never been safe. Women's safety is a critical prerequisite for a stable Afghanistan.

Chapter 7 shows how external influences and the presence of "outsiders" have long had a history in creating tension in Afghanistan. These very interfaces are explored in this chapter bringing the story of "occupations" together to help us understand that anything from the outside will be resisted. Many Afghans made parallels between the international aid community and previous occupiers in Afghanistan's history. And, as history has shown, each occupation has fomented a backlash, playing out on women's rights and women's lives.

Chapter 8 elevates Afghan women's agency and brings in stories of resistance, of individual Afghan women, Afghan women leaders, and Afghan feminist organizations. It reminds us that power exists in the small spaces, and that work is happening—whether we see it or not. This chapter ends with a call to rewrite the narrative in order to ensure that Afghan women define their own freedom.

Chapter 9 tells the story of the unraveling of the country in 2021, told mostly from the perspective of one Afghan woman. This chapter continues—and concludes—with the perspectives of women, the ones who have been, and continue to be, most affected by this story. It is a story that came full circle for Afghanistan. But it is also a story where Afghan women are imagining a new world, one where both freedom and feminism are possible. This final chapter helps us to better understand how freedom is won—from the inside.

CHAPTER 1

The Story of "Liberation" for Afghan Women

Qatra qatra darya mesha
Drop by drop, water becomes a river.

This Afghan expression is used as a saying to advance the women's movement. It advocates slow, gradual change that, over time, will become an undeniable force. Understanding Afghan women's history will help us better understand how Afghan women's rights can be won—drop by drop.

Centering Women in Afghan History

Afghan women's history can be summarized as a story of small progress followed by great regress. This story is characterized by a constant struggle against entrenched patriarchy, often manifesting as misogyny. Despite these forces, Afghan women have always organized and fought for themselves, asserting their agency. While women's rights continue to be delivered and denied by those in power, one fact cannot be refuted: women's rights belong to every Afghan woman, without exception.

Throughout Afghanistan's various conflicts and occupations—by the British, the Soviets, the Mujahideen, the Taliban, the Americans, and now the Taliban again—women's rights have always been highly politicized. Each period brings its own ideas, edicts, and impositions on Afghan women's lives. And each period brings Afghan women activists and feminist movements to the forefront. And each period brings backlashes to women's rights and fundamental freedoms. Despite this rollercoaster of rights won and lost, Afghan women have always found ways to maneuver systems built against them, and push for their freedom. And they will do so again now.

The women's movement marks time in Afghanistan and tells the story of social change in a context where *evolutionary* change is repeatedly

Zia Gul, also known as Khala-jan (Dear Auntie), outside the office of an NGO for women, Kabul.

abandoned for *revolutionary* change.[1] An understanding of Afghan women's history could begin in the 1880s, when Afghan rulers of the period launched one of the earliest attempts at emancipation and social reform in the Muslim world. However, these rulers also proclaimed men as the guardians of women. So begins a story of non-linear movement towards women's rights.

Amidst various contradictory laws concerning women, the protection of women was employed as a call for Afghans to expel the British. It was argued that if these foreigners overran the country, Afghan men would "lose hold over their wives," because British laws gave women freedoms that denied husbands control over their wives.[2] After a long occupation and a series of British-Afghan wars, the British were finally defeated in 1921 and Afghanistan was declared independent. During the 1920s, women's emancipation began to play a prominent role in the nationalist ideology of modernization.[3] In the 1920s, King Amanullah Khan advocated for girls' education, the removal of the veil, and for an end to girl-child and forced marriages. He also began a strategy to use Islamic values—like those that offered certain protections for women in marriage, divorce, inheritance, veiling, and seclusion—as an anchor for progressive policies.

Amanullah's wife, Queen Soraya, was the embodiment of this strategy and the inspiration behind his policies. She was a strong advocate for women's equality, in particular girls' education. She also appeared in public on her own, contrary to the norm. Queen Soraya established the first women's magazine, organization, and theater as well as the first girls' school.[4] She was also outspoken about women's roles, urging women to take part in the building of the nation, as they did "in the early years of Islam." To do this, she explained, women must be as educated as possible in order to "render [their] services to society in the manner of the women of early Islam."[5]

Perceptions of King Amanullah's immorality and excessive Western influence fueled a strong resistance as religious conservatives and the rural population met his attempts at reform with opposition.[6] Violent rebellions began as a conservative backlash to his policies, and violence against women increased in response to calls to abandon veiling and adopt Western attire. It is estimated that 400 women were murdered during this period as a result.[7]

Mullahs, Muslim religious leaders, circulated a rumor that unveiled women's children would be stolen by the Communists and made into soap. *Mullahs*, feeling threatened at the challenge to their religious authority, further instilled fear by claiming that natural disasters would befall Afghanistan due to the sins of liberal women. When an earthquake did occur in 1927, it was blamed on women who had shamed their families and communities by removing their *chaddaris*, or what the Western world knows as the *bourka*, the now-iconic blue garment worn by many women throughout the country.

By 1929, Amanullah was in exile and women had eventually succumbed to the pressure as challenges to social reforms mounted, most notably by the rural population.[8] Women who had removed their *chaddaris* donned them once again to appease religious authorities and regain respect in their communities.[9]

Emancipation continued to be enforced and swiftly challenged. Despite incremental changes, responses to women's rights vacillated between enforced modernity and conservative backlash. Under the leadership of King Zahir Shah, who reigned from 1933 to 1973, women were encouraged to join many professions that were historically solely open to men. His administration granted women the right to vote in 1964 and run for political office. Such measures had a tangible effect, and by 1977, women comprised more than 15 percent of Afghanistan's highest legislative body. It is estimated that by the early 1990s, 70 percent of schoolteachers, 50 percent of government workers and university students, and 40 percent of doctors in Kabul were women.[10] This relatively peaceful period[11] is believed to have established better living conditions for all Afghans and laid the foundations for Afghan women's equal rights in the 1977 Constitution.[12]

And yet, attempts at modernity throughout history have always been imposed from above, without local foundations or popular support, and with little impact on the lives of the majority. Reforms have repeatedly flooded Afghanistan faster than the country can absorb them, should it choose to do so. Such modernity has also been selective: so-called modern contributions such as technology and advanced weapons are accepted, while movements towards women's public participation in Afghan society are not.

The *Saur* (April) Revolution of 1978 overthrew then–President Mohammed Daoud Khan, replacing him with Nur Muhammad Taraki. This period introduced an aggressive program for social change, enforcing such modernizations as women's right to work, serve in the army, and choose their spouses. Mandatory literacy programs for women and the abolition of bride price were viewed as direct attacks on Afghan culture and honor, instigating yet another wave of violence. Many Afghans felt this to be a total disdain for their values, so much so that an Afghan woman I spoke with during my time in the country told me that she believed that the Russians deliberately came to Afghanistan "to play with the dignity of women."[13]

Social change vacillated between incremental progress and considerable regress—measures that appeared to be progressive tended to have undercurrents of contradiction. Taraki was considered progressive in the sense that some of his policy pillars were women's education, literacy, and healthcare.[14] However, his government was repressive in their forced disappearances and killing of more than 20,000 people in imprisonment camps.

Thus, Afghan women once again found themselves at the center of a conflict between Western concepts of modernization and Afghan codes of culture.[15] To most Afghans at that time, the government was perceived to be interfering with Islamic values and disregarding social traditions. It was further encouraging women to engage in public activities which were deemed unladylike, undignified, and detrimental to family honor.[16]

The Soviet invasion of 1979 prompted contradictory changes in the lives of Afghan women; emancipation and greater opportunities for some (a minority, largely urban), and death and destruction for others. The Leftist group in power during the Soviet occupation promised full equality for women but did not deliver on it. Women might have been more visible in Kabul during that time, but they had no real decision-making or power-sharing roles.[17] Soviet decrees were viewed as an unwelcome ideological occupation, labeled as "alien ideological rhetoric" formulated in haste and implemented with great zeal, bringing mass resistance.[18]

Reforms of the 1920s and 1970s teach us one critical lesson: "any legislation enhancing women's status by separating her from her family and community [are] not only met with resistance from the tribal leaders and community but also led to the overthrow of the political regimes sponsoring such legislation."[19] The same could be said for many other periods in Afghan history where social change appears to have been imported and imposed through foreign intervention. Thus efforts to emancipate women "from the outside" are not new, and have never been well received.

In Afghan history, these fluctuations in women's rights—enforced by the state's attempt to exercise centralized control—have actually led to violent, fundamentalist backlashes.[20] As one example, opposition to Soviet reforms for women, and concern for the symbolic value of women's honor, fueled the fundamentalist movement that took hold in refugee camps. This in turn served as the grounds for the Mujahideen opposition to expel the Soviets in the early 1990s, regaining control of Afghanistan, and its women. The Mujahideen (literally holy warriors)—U.S.-sponsored freedom fighters[21]—continued to threaten women's honor by using their bodies as rewards for their wartime victories.[22]

In the 1920s, Afghanistan was a secular country working to extend women's rights, yet by the 1990s the country was a captive of religious fanaticism, tribal patriarchy, and underdevelopment.[23] Indeed, the combination of colonialism, economic dependence, and rapid social change is a recipe for Muslim fundamentalism to flourish. This phenomenon is exacerbated by the international pressure that is exerted at the intersection of Islam, the state, and gender politics. As a result, the place of women becomes "one of the few areas of relative autonomy left to societies whose ties of political and economic dependence severely restrict their choices in every other sphere."[24] Afghanistan repeatedly demonstrates the strong yet volatile link between women's honor and external interventions.

Afghan Women's Agency

Afghan women were not passive victims of these contradictory movements throughout history. At every turning point, women have always demonstrated agency. During the 1970s and 1980s, for instance, they played a huge role in protests, civil unrest, and resistance. Afghan women were on the frontlines of these forces for change, even if history failed to adequately account for them.

In 1970, 5000 women and girls in Kabul protested against men's violence against women, perpetrated by the growing patriarchal powers of fundamentalist groups.[25] Women also marched at the student-led

A woman washes herself by a lake, Bamiyan.

pro-democracy protests in the mid–1970s against King Zahir Shah, in opposition to the regressive policies of seemingly-progressive leaders.

Afghan women continued to position themselves as agents of change. In January 1980, in support of their loved ones, thousands of women stormed the Pul-e-Charkhi prison when President Babrak Karmal failed to meet his promise of granting amnesty to political prisoners. A woman named Najla spoke about her experience on the frontlines in the 1980s where she not only cooked and cleaned, but also provided medical care, taught in school, and participated in military training. She even got married during an aerial assault by the Soviets, with a Kalashnikov in hand.[26] History fails to see Afghan women as freedom fighters in Afghanistan, but nonetheless, women were there defining their own liberation.

The 1992–1996 civil war was characterized by major displacement and destruction. Fighting factions laid landmines throughout the country that would take decades to locate. In fact, Afghanistan continues to be one of the most heavily mined countries in the world. For women, the civil war entailed massive abuses such as rape, abduction, forced prostitution, extremely high maternal mortality rates, unequal access to resources, and unprecedented levels of poverty.[27]

Women's rights activists have been told time and again that national interests trump feminist objectives, and that crimes committed against them should be absolved for the purpose of the nation's stability. Women continue to be trapped in positions of political whiplash—facing violence from men who are one day the enemy, the next day in official positions of power. Rights are made and undone, and justice is scant.

Then came the Taliban.

The Taliban, or students, emerged in the early 1990s in Pakistan, fueled by their own fundamentalist interpretation of Islamic law. They promised peace and security to Afghanistan, to counter the turmoil of the Soviet and civil conflicts.

By 1996, the country was under draconian rule,[28] and women suffered most of all.[29] Girls over the age of eight were banned from schools, televisions banned from homes, women banned from driving. Gender apartheid, it was called.

According to one report, Taliban leaders sent their girls overseas for education[30] while back in Afghanistan, they forced women into temporary "marriages,"[31] or what we might call kidnapping and rape. The so-called Ministry for the Propagation of Virtue and the Prevention of Vice[32] would beat Afghan women[33] if their faces were visible, if their ankles were visible, if their socks were white, if they made noise as they walked, if they spoke to men, if they traveled without a male guardian, if they worked, if they studied. In short—if they lived at all.[34]

At that time, "the extent of female oppression in Afghanistan, for the most part, fell on deaf Western ears."[35] One exception was Emma Bonino, European Commissioner at that time. On a visit to Afghanistan in 1997, she was shocked by the status of women. In 1998, she launched "A Flower for the Women of Kabul,"[36] urging the United Nations to restore women's human rights in the country. At the same time, the Desk Officer for Afghanistan at the U.S. State Department argued that the Taliban's oppression of women was "part of Afghan culture."[37] As Afghan woman leader and former chair of the Afghanistan Independent Human Rights Commission Sima Samar aptly stated, "not only did this further isolate Afghan women, but in hindsight, this incompetence foreshadowed the state of the conflict today."[38]

It is worthwhile to note that men also suffered under the Taliban, although this was hardly noted by the media. In fact, Taliban authority extended beyond women to non–Taliban men as well. Men were not to be seen with women who were not related to them. Homosexuality was punishable by death. Men were required to wear traditional clothes, grow their beards, and behave in a way that was in accordance with their interpretation of Islamic law. Violators would have their faces painted black and nooses hung from their necks, paraded in the streets as an example to others—and a clear indication of who was in power.

Yet again, Afghan women and women's organizations fought back. Women operated secret schools in the basements of their homes and educated themselves and girls who couldn't go to school with minimal resources available to them. They smuggled books and passed them to each other under their *chaddaris*. In this way, Afghan women turned their *chaddaris* into a tool for feminist activism,[39] showing the world what was happening, and hoping the world would respond.

Afghan history is filled with stories of strong women and women's organizations born from struggle, who face the challenge of "liberating" Afghan women on their own terms. One of these is RAWA—the Revolutionary Association of the Women of Afghanistan—best known for their bold efforts to counter the Taliban, and every form of government in Afghanistan. RAWA members and other feminist activists used their *chaddaris* for feminist resistance by smuggling cameras underneath the fabric to take videos of Taliban abuses.[40] It was through the lens of women that the world first saw the Taliban conduct executions in Ghazi Stadium,[41] a venue once used for soccer. The Taliban outlined the following punishments: thieves have limbs amputated,[42] murderers are executed by relatives of the victim, and adulterers are stoned to death.[43] The rest receive public beatings.[44]

A girl in a classroom, Kabul.

Much has been written on women's abuses during this period. The bottom line is this: Afghan women suffered under many regimes in Afghanistan, but women's sphere of influence under the Taliban's reign was virtually annihilated.[45] The Taliban, more than any other regime, were able to manipulate the deeply embedded system linking women to honor, issuing edicts that were nothing short of misogyny disguised as Islam.[46] They remained in control of the country until the

U.S. invasion in 2001, in the aftermath of September 11. And 20 years later, in 2021, the Taliban returned to power. Had they ever left?

A Short-Sighted Agenda

Prior to the fall of Kabul in September 1996, Afghanistan was hardly part of the international community's agenda.[47] Ironically, the Taliban drew world attention to the deteriorating situation in Afghanistan, shedding light on the condition of women's rights (or lack thereof) in the country. This was not uncommon; each invading force has done the same, as a means of occupying Afghanistan to advance their geo-political interests. And so, with the Taliban in power, women's rights became the call to battle around which the Western world would assemble. Despite this attention, an aid worker argued:

> Unprecedented international interest, misinformation, and hysteria have surrounded the situation of women and girls since the Taliban set foot in Kabul. Afghan women have been used by countless media, political, and humanitarian entities, as well as publicity-hungry women's rights groups, to pursue their own objectives.

Nonetheless, international shock at the Taliban's treatment of women took place in a historical vacuum, with little attention paid to pre–Taliban abuses or *chaddari* uses.[48] During this first Taliban period, Afghan women were portrayed one-dimensionally as victims of violence and oppression by the international media. Yet the situation of women in Afghanistan is not simply a product of Taliban policies, and the *chaddari* is not a Taliban invention. Further, the simplistic assumption was that the expulsion of the Taliban would bring women's liberation. Taliban out, women in. Belated discovery of the discrimination of Afghan women—discrimination that passed largely without international comment during previous regimes—is a reflection of both the political agenda and the wider ignorance of the realities of Afghan society.[49]

One such example of international myopia was the U.S.-based Feminist Majority Foundation's Campaign to Stop Gender Apartheid in Afghanistan, launched in 1997 as a counter to the Taliban's misogyny.[50] While this was intended to be an advocacy campaign in support of Afghan women, the discourse was decidedly imperialist, assuming the "benevolence and superiority of the U.S. in establishing gender equality."[51] This same tone would be adopted by the Bush Administration in the call to "save" Afghan women a few years later.

While the Taliban's abuses of women were egregious, women in the country had already suffered in the decades of civil war without vociferous international concern and condemnation. This belated discovery of Afghan women also brought notable silence when it came to certain leaders who, with a history of abuse of women, found themselves in positions of power bolstered by the U.S. government. Short-sighted agendas became the foundation for Feminist Majority's moral perspectives.[52]

Afghan women's groups and global feminists pushed back, asking if such a campaign was really necessary. Would it have been equally compelling to portray Afghan women as they actually were? Would such campaigns have garnered global sympathy if it had been made known "that Afghan women were actively fighting back and simply needed money and moral support, not instructions?"[53]

Activists noted that Afghan women had been neglected for years, only to be discussed on exotic email groups and forlorn internet petitions,[54] the most notorious of which, from a student at Brandeis University in the United States, was the first introduction that many American feminists and activists had to the situation of Afghan women.[55] I received the petition 17 times from different sources in a period of two months in 1999.

The petition stated that "everyone has a right to a tolerable human existence, even if they are women in a Muslim country in a part of the world that Americans do not understand." It went on to say that "Women's Rights is not a small issue anywhere and it is UNACCEPTABLE for women in 1998 to be treated as sub-human and so much as property. Equality and human decency is a RIGHT not a freedom, whether one lives in Afghanistan or the United States."

Few voices expressed concern about the images and stereotypes in this petition and the additional risk this might place on Afghan women. Regardless, the petition had already served its purpose as a political tool. Western feminist media campaigns continued to influence the approach to gender equality in the Afghanistan intervention.

The media is one such interface where we see priorities defined and narratives solidified. It plays a strong part in galvanizing public opinion around selected causes, regardless of the accuracy of events and their interpretations. Focusing on the situation of Afghan women leading up to the U.S. occupation was an effective tactic to manipulate public opinion in the Western world. However, it might appear to Afghans that the sudden feigned devotion to women looked more like political instrumentalization than concern and compassion.

In 1999, Mavis Leno, wife of late-night TV celebrity Jay Leno, galvanized the Hollywood elite to raise funds for the campaign. And so Afghan women became a cause célèbre. The fact that the Taliban owed its strength in part to U.S. foreign policy was carefully omitted.[56] While high-profile campaigning on behalf of Afghan women might serve well in terms of international awareness-raising, it created difficulties for support on the ground.[57] Afghan activists expressed concern with the campaign and the possibility that it could alienate the very women it was trying to help. These Afghan voices were not heard, despite their concern that their opinions were largely absent from campaigns waged on their behalf.[58]

Then on a fateful day in September of 2001, the United States was attacked. President George W. Bush wanted war. First Lady Laura Bush stated that the reason for the war was to "liberate Afghan women"—a compelling plea and call to action, for white Western feminists.[59] And so the Feminist Majority assumed a place of prominence in U.S. plans and policy, attending meetings with high-level State Department officials. It was believed that war and subsequent occupation were the way to freeing Afghan women, with many in the West seeing the *bourka* as the "battle flag" of the invasion.[60] There was an undeniable effect of this rhetoric, drawing on feminist language with savior undertones. The message built on concern for women's rights "over there" with the assumption that these rights had already been achieved in the United States long ago.[61]

Meanwhile, the Bush Administration's vociferous concern for Afghan women's rights as justification for military intervention was undercut by their support of the lawless factions that had repeatedly perpetrated violence against women.[62] As such, the military campaign was launched with little regard for longer-term social consequences on Afghan lives. The military operation was called Enduring Freedom—it is worth asking whose freedom it referred to.

Did Afghan women share the view that they needed "liberation"? Not necessarily. In fact, Afghan feminists and women's rights groups were staunchly opposed. Nonetheless, the United States attacked, and occupied Afghanistan for 20 years. The "Gender Apartheid" campaign was deemed a success with the 2001 "liberation" of Afghanistan—and therefore allegedly of Afghan women—from the Taliban. Many years after the campaign, images of Afghan women as oppressed creatures beneath *chaddaris* still permeated popular perception, although the media's silence led spectators to believe that Afghan women had been liberated and there was no further need to discuss them.

Women's rights did not automatically spring forth following the alleged ousting of the Taliban from power in 2001. In fact, the divide between progressive and conservative ideologies continued, often playing out on women's bodies and lives. Many rural districts were still run, de facto, by the Taliban meaning girls faced great risks in going to school and women continued to exercise caution in their public lives. Underground, however, the legacy of secret schools continued. With scant funding and constant threats they used their *chaddaris* for resistance by smuggling books. Both teachers and students risked their lives for an education. And now with the fall of Afghanistan and the return of the Taliban in 2021, Afghan women are prepared to do so again.

Still, the trajectory of Afghan women's liberation cannot be viewed as a 20-year story. It started long ago. Western intervention did not bring feminism—it was always alive in Afghanistan. Afghan women's history reveals centuries of women's engagement on the frontlines of social reforms. What we saw on the outside was progress interrupted. We were introduced to Afghan women in 1996, but this was an incomplete picture. Decades of war—and decades of resistance—led to this moment. In the last 20 years, Afghan women have reclaimed their space to make great gains in politics, the economy, health, and education. These decades brought greater rights, access, opportunities, mobility, and choice. And they also brought the same challenges as every occupation before it.

The story of progress and regress continues.

Interpreting the Data

In late 2001, Afghan women's human rights and well-being were at the top of the aid agenda. But challenges remained, including lack of available services and adequate support, economic constraints, illiteracy, constricting patriarchal traditions, and violence against women.[63] *Now, 20 years later, how did Afghan women fare after two decades of support? Were the good intentions, strong words, and high expectations met?*

Facts and statistics can only tell part of the story when it comes to determining the freedom, safety, and autonomy of women in Afghanistan. Yet, they are a crucial element in piecing together patterns, showing successes and regresses where applicable, and illustrating that the fight for rights and liberation do not always tell a linear story.

Data presents an important but incomplete picture. Data collection requires funding, infrastructure, and a certain level of security to be able to gather the information required. UN agencies have stated that existing data only reveals a partial picture of the situation in the country with little understanding of women and poverty, access to land and other assets, and prevalence of violence against women, amongst others. For the latter, any available figures, no matter how robust, will always underestimate reality.

The World Bank reported that progress in the first years of the aid intervention was followed by a "slow down, drift, or backsliding—adversely affecting future prospects."[64] Women suffered disproportionately from these adverse effects and, by 2007, Afghan women were among the worst in the world in virtually all aspects of life—health, education, poverty, civil rights, political participation, and protection against violence.[65] Even still in 2019, Afghanistan was ranked the second worst place in the world to be a woman.[66] Using the available data helps us understand progress or regress in these areas over the last two decades.

In 2006, Afghan women's life expectancy was at least 20 years shorter than most other women in the world. Each Afghan woman was calculated as having approximately 6.6 children during her childbearing years, nearly one-third higher than even the least developed countries' average of five children per woman.[67] The most recent data from 2020 however, indicates Afghan women bear on average 4.6 children.[68] Despite this decline, Afghanistan's population is still growing at a rate of 2.34 percent, adding nearly one million new Afghans to the population every year onto an increasingly weakening economic and social infrastructure.[69] Afghanistan has one of the world's youngest populations—63 percent are under the age of 25—and so most of them do not remember life under the Taliban.[70]

Afghanistan's maternal mortality ratio was estimated at 1600 to 1900 maternal deaths per 100,000 live births in 2006—one of the highest in the world.[71] In 2017, the rate was 638 deaths per 100,000 live births.[72] The decreasing maternal mortality rate in Afghanistan can be seen as a success, but even with improvements the country still ranks number 11 for the highest maternal mortality rates in the world. Also alarming, Afghanistan ranks number 1 for infant mortality rates at 107 deaths per 1000 live births.[73] According to a government report in 2020, Afghanistan only had 4.6 doctors, nurses, and midwives and 172 hospitals per 10,000 people. According to the UN, 23 healthcare professionals for every 10,000 is deemed a critical shortage.[74] Out of the 37 million people in the country, only about one third have access to a medical facility within a two-hour vicinity of their homes.[75]

Education has long been held up as a success story of "reconstruction" efforts in Afghanistan. Prior to aid interventions in 2001, only 12 percent of girls of primary school age attended school.[76] By 2015, the figure was approximately 50 percent.[77] While there were massive gains in reducing the education gender gap, enrollment began declining after 2015. In 2017, girls' enrollment decreased in 32 of the 34 provinces, with 206,000 less girls in attendance.[78] As of 2019, in rural and isolated parts of the country, only 36 percent of school-age children were reportedly attending school—79 percent boys and 21 percent girls.[79] In 2020, only 3.7 million (39 percent) of Afghanistan's 9.2 million school-aged children were girls.[80] Moreover, due to insecurity, intermittent conflict, and lack of resources, 65 percent of displaced girls in hard to reach areas were not enrolled in school as of 2020.[81]

Retention rates are crucial to explain how many girls actually continue their education. In 2018, the school life expectancy was approximately 13 years for boys and 8 for girls.[82] Only 67 percent of girls completed primary school, compared to near full completion for boys.[83] This has repercussions for literacy rates and, as of 2018, literacy rates were 56 percent for males and 30 percent for females—meaning 70 percent of Afghan women could not read or write.[84]

From 2001, women and girls returned to higher-level education. In 2003, there were only 7200 female university students in the country but by 2018, this figure jumped to 49,000.[85] According to a 2021 article, female students comprised nearly half of all students in Kabul University, which was established in 1932.[86] Even though this is a major improvement, women's attendance and participation in higher level education has been undone with the return of the Taliban.

School safety is also a factor in ensuring that women and girls have access to education. Attending school has become more dangerous in the years since 2015. Schools have been targets of violence resulting in 26 percent of schools closing because of conflict.[87] COVID-19 put an additional strain on girls attending school, in part because girls are less likely to be able to study from home due to their family duties, and they also face more resistance in access to technology because of gender double standards.[88]

Afghanistan's economy is fragile, struggling, and aid-dependent.[89] A context of prolonged war, continued conflict, and periodic drought has increased poverty and vulnerability. Poverty has brought increased corruption, posing yet another risk to an already precarious and steadily deteriorating security situation. In 2003, the average per capita income was less than $200, and only 14 percent of families had access to a sustainable source of income.[90] In 2018, more than half the population was living on less than $1 a day.[91] In 2021, the average income was approximately $500, and is expected to deteriorate as conditions worsen.

Food insecurity affects about 67 percent of women and 56 percent of men.[92] The 2021 drought has exacerbated these needs, with half of the population now dependent on lifesaving assistance. In 2021, an additional 4.5 million people were in need due to escalating poverty, rising food insecurity, political instability, and widespread conflict.[93] It is estimated that, as of 2021, 50 percent of those in need of humanitarian assistance are women and girls,[94] but the future of aid to the country is unclear as the Taliban affirms its place as the new government.[95]

The number of widows and female-headed households continues to increase. Their situation is far more serious because households with male labor are still better off than those without. Afghanistan is believed to have one of the highest rates of widowhood in the world.[96]

Internally displaced people in Afghanistan went from 724,000 in 2002 to 2,993,000 in 2019.[97] Displacement and urbanization have brought a transition from a largely agricultural economy to one where livelihoods are precarious and daily survival is tantamount. As a result, women continue to enter a variety of fields in order to support their families, the most dangerous of which is opium production.[98]

It is estimated that 76 percent of Afghan women live in rural areas.[99] Rural areas are more heavily affected by conflict and violence. Gains made for women in Afghanistan are more often than not isolated to urban women, and even then to a small segment of urban women. Overall, rural women remain more conservative—and more vulnerable. Rural women are engaged in livestock and agricultural work and micro enterprises, yet they lack access to capital, information, technology, and markets.

In urban areas, Afghans have very little access to basic services and social infrastructure.[100] Resources are limited and those in control are unable or unwilling to meet people's basic needs. As a result, Afghan women's economic participation continues to be relegated to the informal sector. Increased vulnerabilities due to irregular incomes force women to supplement the income, at times through exploitative and hazardous work. Increased poverty has forced more women into sex work.

In 2020, 22 percent of women were in the labor force compared to 75 percent of men.[101] As of early 2021, only 4.1 percent of managerial positions were held by women, and 4.3 percent of middle to senior management positions were held by women.[102] Nonetheless, Afghan women are an underutilized economic force, now imprisoned at home while the Taliban implement stringent policies on what is deemed "acceptable work" for women. The present Afghan leadership will lose a crucial contribution if women are kept out of the workforce.

Despite progress in women's political participation, women are still a minority in public life and are often marginalized in policy-making and decision-making. There is a general lack of awareness of women's rights and certain vestiges of inequality remain in some laws of the country. In 2021, approximately 30 percent of civil servants were women.[103] Thanks to the quota introduced in the 2004 Constitution, women in 2021 occupy 27 percent of parliamentary seats.[104] It is unclear if this will continue under the Taliban.

Throughout two decades of aid intervention, Afghan women continued to experience violence and threats of violence at home and in public spaces. In 2016 there were 104 cases of murder and honor killings, in 2017 there were 176[105] and it is likely that 2021 will see additional cases of femicide. Intimate partner violence and self-immolation continued, although statistics underestimate reality. UN data from 2017 shows that 51 percent of Afghan women experience physical and/or sexual intimate partner violence in their lifetime, and 46 percent had experienced it in that year alone.[106] Adding another layer to the trauma is persistent impunity. In 2017 there were only 31 cases where the perpetrator was convicted and imprisoned.[107]

As of 2018, one in three girls under 18 was forcibly married.[108] These figures will increase as the Taliban consolidate their power. Parents will marry their daughters out of fear or economic necessity, and an entire generation of girls will be denied their rights to an education, and a safe childhood.[109]

Continued insecurity and violence, both at home and in public, have had a role to play in the high rates of suicide. In most of the world, more men commit suicide than women but in Afghanistan, about 80 percent of the suicide attempts (out of approximately 3000) a year are made by women.[110] Many of these attempts are through self-immolation.

The conflict resulted in the loss of more than 47,600 civilian lives over the course of 20 years.[111] If we include the Afghan military and opposition fighters, the number today would be closer to 150,000.[112] The data suggests, once again, that women are most affected by the conflict. For instance, even though there was a slight decrease recorded in civilian casualties in 2012, female civilian casualties increased by 20 percent with 864 casualties in that year alone.[113] This concerning trend continues, with the UN reporting more women and children were killed and wounded in the first half of 2021 than in the first six months of any year since records began in 2009.[114]

Since 2018, Afghanistan has been ranked as the least peaceful country in the world, and has continued to be among the least peaceful countries since 2010. Insecurity consistently ranks as the biggest problem facing Afghans, with 73 percent indicating this in a 2018 survey.[115] Moreover, 79 percent of Afghan respondents reported that they felt less safe in 2019 than they did in 2014.[116] In instances of conflict and high insecurity, violence is a huge risk. According to a 2021 survey, more than 52 percent of Afghans reported suffering or knowing someone suffering serious harm from violent crime.[117]

In terms of the big picture, Afghanistan and Afghan women fall at the bottom of global poverty indices. In 2006, the country was among the lowest in both the Human Development Index and the Gender Development Index and these standings have not shown much improvement over the years.[118] In 2019 Afghanistan was ranked 169 out of 189 countries on the Gender Development Index and in 2020, on the Human Development Index, Afghanistan again was placed 169.[119]

In 2021, Afghanistan ranked 156 out of 156 on the Gender Gap Index, meaning the country has the world's widest gender gap, measured across education, health, economic and political participation.[120] Moreover, the Women, Peace and Security Index incorporates three basic dimensions of women's well-being: inclusion (economic, social, political); justice (formal laws and informal discrimination); and security (at the family, community, and societal levels) and as of the latest 2019–2020 index, Afghanistan ranked 166 out of 167.[121]

Ultimately, it is the opinion of Afghans themselves that holds the most weight. A 2019 Survey of the Afghan people showed that 58 percent believed that the country was moving in the wrong direction, a dramatic increase from the 21 percent who felt this way in 2006.[122]

Zooming out, we understand that safety, security, and survival are the highest priority in Afghanistan—now more than ever. Women's security at home correlates with the security in the country at large.

Both women and men expected more from the reconstruction process, and today those hopes of peace, security, and development have been thwarted. Afghanistan has been, and will likely continue to be, among the worst places in the world to be a woman.[123]

Seeing "Beneath the *Bourka*"

It would be impossible to tell the story of Afghan women without speaking of the *chaddari*. This garment is as politicized as its wearers and has become conflated with Afghan women's rights. I employ the term *chaddari* and not *bourka* because it is the term that Afghans use—therefore it is the correct term for this distinctive garment. It is interesting to note that in conversations, Afghans recognized that the word *bourka* was one that was used more frequently by foreigners. They therefore used the term *bourka* when referring to foreign images of Afghans, but continued to use the more common term *chaddari* in their daily discussions with each other. This distinction shows the extent to which Afghans adapted their language when speaking "for us" rather than amongst themselves. Moreover, *bourka* came to mean something oppressive, while *chaddari* has some ties to Afghan women's resistance.

When Kabul fell to the Taliban in 1996, the sudden, excessive attention paid to Afghan women centered around this particular garment. One journalist described it as a "body-bag for the living," and so the *chaddari* became the international symbol of the Taliban's oppression of women and the galvanizing point for many Western feminist groups.[124]

At that time, Western media portrayed Afghan women as eager to embrace liberation. This rhetoric permeated public perception, leading to a moral imperative to act, and thereby also influencing global perceptions of Afghan women's so-called "liberation." Discourses and images employed by outsiders are often shorthand symbols devoid of context. Nowhere is this more true than with any images of veiling, most notably with Afghan women's iconic blue *chaddari*. An aid worker in the country in 2005 explained that "this is Orientalism and this is racism," elaborating that the media needs symbols that are easily translatable.[125] As a result, images of women in *chaddaris* became the dominant symbol.

In November 1997, following her mission to Afghanistan, the UN Special Advisor on Gender Issues and the Advancement of Women explained that external observers often mistake symptoms and causes, using the *chaddari* as an example. She elaborated that this is not considered a major problem for most Afghan women, but is treated as such by foreigners inside the country and opinion-makers outside the country.[126]

However, the *chaddari* is not a new object of Western obsession. The *chaddari* should be viewed in its socio-political and historical context. A nuanced understanding, one that centers Afghan women, will reveal that the *chaddari* can also be used as a symbol and vehicle of resistance. Its earliest uses by the Pashtun elite provided freedom of mobility and anonymity. During the Taliban era, the *chaddari* was used strategically to transport messages, weapons, cameras, and banned publications in anonymity.[127] Understanding the *chaddari* as a tool of freedom was beyond the Western imagination, including for many who worked in the country. It was far easier to see a one-dimensional vehicle of oppression, further fueling the stereotyped image of Afghan women as "forever enveloped in billowing veils."[128]

The obsession with the *chaddari* obscured other gendered consequences of the Taliban's decrees for men. The Western imagination and political use of this garment helped shape the idea of a battleground featuring Afghan

Chaddaris **dry on a line in front of a house, Kabul.**

men against Afghan women.[129] Simplified understandings of this garment can push women to vehemently defend its use, turning it into a "symbol of resistance to tyrannical Western influences," one aid worker explained. She continued to say that it denies the complexities of gender identities and roles in the country, elaborating that it is "too simplistic to suggest that once women remove their *bourkas* they are free and everything has been made right."

This leads to the assumption that Western attire is progressive, and therefore Western women are "liberated," which is clearly incorrect. It also leads to the assumption that "there will be gender equality when there is no *bourka*," as one aid worker explained.

Despite this assumption, the garment can be credited with bringing much (read: largely Western) attention to Afghanistan. It continues to play a prominent role in Western media and its subsequent collective identity construction of the Afghan woman, producing myriad documentaries, articles, and photographs claiming to offer a glimpse "behind/under/beneath the *bourka*."[130]

This unconstructive image of Afghan women serves only to feed stereotypes and deny Afghan women's agency, fueling the perception that Afghan women are "horribly oppressed and abused—the worst women anywhere in the world," in the words of one aid worker, "the ultimate symbol of the backwardness of Afghanistan." She went on to say that this is, in the eyes of the Western world, the most obvious manifestation of women's inequality. Even as Afghan women disappear from the media, she explained, the story remains the same. "It's still catchy to talk about how oppressed and wretched they are."

Afghan women did not agree. One Afghan woman leader told me that, through Western eyes, the chaddari is a mystery, "they can't understand what it is and why it is worn." But ultimately, their opinion is not the one that counts. She continued to explain that the understanding for Afghan women is much more nuanced. "It is a symbol of their struggle, it hides their emotions, their identity. Can it be humiliating to wear this fabric? Yes, to conceal your identity would appear to be a humiliation. But why does it make them any less worthy in the eyes of Western women?"

It is not unusual for any act of veiling to be misconstrued as a denial of women's agency. Afghanistan is not unique in this case. Many have documented a history of Western obsession with the veil. Despite this obsession, Afghan women repeatedly fail to conform to stereotypical images. Using the *chaddari* as a barometer to measure social change, or lack thereof, is an oversimplification. During the Taliban era I watched videos taken by Afghan women through cameras they smuggled under their *chaddaris*.[131] Women who risked their lives to make recordings called it a "good disguise" and were largely responsible for spurring international outrage for Taliban abuses. These brave women weaponized the anonymity of the *chaddari* to alert the world to their plight.

In my own capacity as an NGO director starting in 2002, I was approached by many journalists about the *chaddari*, to explain why it remains in "post-liberation" Afghanistan. One American journalist told me that, during a five-day visit in early 2002, he estimated that 95 percent of Afghan women were wearing it. He returned for seven days in November 2002 and told me that now perhaps 90 percent of Afghan women still wore the *chaddari*. As a result, he said, he felt that I had "failed" to do my "job" in "liberating" Afghan women. To him, the *chaddari* was the problem, and the aid intervention the solution, the means by which liberation would occur. Therefore, the persistence of the *chaddari* on Afghanistan's streets indicated failure. Some of these women who continued wearing the *chaddari* in the early days of the U.S. invasion suspected that Taliban sympathizers or the ones who couldn't escape were still in disguise and lived in their communities.

This journalist might note with dismay that the *chaddari* persists. And yet, as Afghan men and women will clearly articulate, the presence or absence of this garment does little to indicate liberation. It is more important, however, to distinguish between the transformation of customs—such as veiling and the prevalence of Western clothing—and institutional change in the form of laws and women's sense of their rights and roles.

In fact, one might assume that men have been transformed based on the prevalence of Afghan men in Western dress. The change in men's clothing style does not constitute a Western influence, nor an indication of liberation. There is an assumption that culture is static when it comes to women, and that the sex of the actors is a determining factor in labeling a change Western or not.[132]

The *chaddari* came up repeatedly as the Western symbol for their perceived weakness of Afghan women, and the source of Western pity. One woman explained that the world views Afghan women "just like animals in *bourkas*." Another said: "Foreigners always want to ask about *bourka*. It is the most important thing for them. Afghan women do not see the *bourka*. Foreigners only see *bourka*." During my time in Afghanistan, many Afghan women expressed frustration at our inability to see agency "beneath the *boukra*."

Both Afghan women and men I spoke to at the time felt that the *chaddari* served as a dangerously-dominant image in foreign minds. I wrote the following excerpt in my capacity as NGO director in September 2002 to document my first impressions:

My sense is that Afghan women long for choice. The choice to wear a veil, or a *bourka*, or nothing at all. The issue extends well beyond the actual fabric of the *bourka*. It is more important to address the psychological *bourka*, and its progeny—the fear *bourka* and the poverty *bourka*. Social evolution is a slow process, and our task in this is to offer women the tools with which they can achieve self-sufficiency, a choice, and a voice.

Afghan women repeatedly expressed exasperation with this facile construct, saying that the world thinks "Afghan women are only *bourkas*." As a result of this image, the world felt compelled to save them. An Afghan woman explained that the world thinks of them as "oppressed and weak." This is not accurate, she said, "but the world wants to see us this way." An Afghan man told me he felt pressure to adopt freedoms "like the Western world"—and these freedoms were made visible by the type of clothing worn. Afghan clothes were a symbol of oppression, while Western attire denoted liberation. He said that as long as Afghan women were in traditional clothes, we viewed them as devoid of rights. "This is completely incorrect," he said. "We don't approve of it. Afghan men and women are Muslims and have their own culture and they do what is in their culture."

In 2005, an aid worker told me the following story to illustrate this:

> I remember talking to the public relations person in [the NGO] because I had argued as a policy that we would not show images of women in *bourkas*. They can be in the background but this is not the dominant image. And she said to me "But how else will we know that they're Afghan?"

Many feminists have spoken out against this collapsing of women's identities, reducing their diversity to "a single voiceless image … which in turn made it seem like the only solution for them was to be saved from their own society by Western forces."[133] One author expressed the views of many:

> The veil was probably the clearest example of the perverse nature of media coverage…. The fall of the Taliban has led to the virtual disappearance from the media agenda of the issue of the veil, and indeed of Afghan women in general.[134]

Following the peaks and troughs of public interest and the 2001 "liberation" of Afghan women, the media's attention to Afghanistan—and the cause célèbre of Afghan women—became limited to press-worthy events. Analyses of the change in media focus through different periods of time indicated that press attention on Afghan women abated from late 2001 until discussions of the Afghan Constitution and the Afghan Women's Bill of Rights were proposed in October 2003.[135] This attention was short-lived. Afghan women again hardly appeared in the media until the following year for the presidential election of October 2004. There was silence yet again for another year, until the parliamentary election of September 2005. And, predictably, without the anticipation of major events where women's participation can be showcased, the media continued to highlight only the obvious, easily consumed markers over the past 20 years.

One aid worker reinforced this point, arguing that the international community has the responsibility to correct images that appear in the media that give the impression "that Afghan women are now emancipated and 'de-*bourka*'ed' through international intervention [and therefore] can be forgotten—again." The invisibility and lack of clarity on the quality of life for Afghan women continued in the immediate years after the invasion.

This book focuses on the experiences and perceptions of Afghan women and men, using them as a lens to better understand the story of the last 20 years in Afghanistan. *How did Western—often Orientalist—narratives about women and girls shape the women's rights agenda? And what might we learn from this experience to better support Afghan women today?*

Are We Liberated Yet?

During my time in Afghanistan, I became curious about Afghan perceptions of aid, of media portrayals, and of the women's rights narrative in general.[136] What follows is a summary of my experience and the research, both formal and informal, collected during that time. *What is the view that Afghans think the world has of Afghanistan, and how do they feel about this view?*

Discussions often started with general descriptions of Afghanistan after the Taliban, which were not very positive. What the world saw was *not* Afghanistan. Afghanistan is much more than this. *What about Afghan women? What does the world see?* It was interesting to note the contradiction in each answer. People often conveyed the sense that the past was good, the present is bad—but holds promise. For instance: "Hidden but struggling to better the life of their people."

Images of Afghan women were mixed. Most included the *chaddari*[137] and veil, noting that Afghan women were "oppressed but wanting change." Many felt that the media contributed to whatever negative images they might have had about "helpless women who don't have rights or privileges."

The media "perpetuated negative images of repressed women, veiled unhappy victims," I was told. Another said: "We see images of women under the *bourka* but we hear [former U.S. president] George Bush tell us that women's rights have been restored." The media presented a biased and sensationalized view, victimizing Afghan women further. Afghan women were presented "as either victims, or as victims-turned-success-stories."

Afghans I spoke with felt that there was excessive attention paid to Afghan women in the beginning, but this attention quickly shifted to other issues. With the start of the Iraq war in 2003, the world's focus was elsewhere. The media can be credited with bringing a large degree of attention, and therefore funding, to Afghanistan in the first place. For many Western viewers, this was the only exposure they might have had to the country. According to one aid worker:

> The less there is a focus on women's crisis, the less direct funding there is for women specifically. Without the horrors of the Taliban presence, less attention is paid to the progress being made by women and the support needed for that to continue. It is more or less business as usual.

The cause of Afghan women had been taken up and largely forgotten after the 2001 "liberation." Meanwhile Afghan women continued to struggle under external pressure to defend their feminist activism and their agency alongside their cultural integrity. Afghan women had "good reason to suppose that if their lives were to become the subject of feminist discussion, their own perspectives might be discounted."[138] It is wise to be critical of this sudden interest in the perceived victimization of women in non–Western cultures and the perceived moral obligation that accompanies it. There is arrogance and neocolonialist consequences in the notion that aid organizations know better than the women involved about their needs and interests.

In a 2004 article titled *"Bourka* Politics,"* I wrote the following:

> The media and international agencies only present opposite sides of the spectrum: the few heroines who have attracted the media's fickle eye, and the oppressed masses who remain victims. Even this limited picture of Afghan reality fails to capture media attention today. Isolating Afghan women from the *bourka*-clad to the lipstick-wearer is not the best way to make changes and achieve gains. Focus on Afghan women is lessening, leaving the masses with a false perception that Afghan women have been "liberated" and our task now lies elsewhere. In Iraq, perhaps.[139]

Highlighting individual stories of women's heroic actions in Afghanistan—mostly when they participated in visible professions or activities—continued in the media. The binary depiction of hero and victim stayed alive and reporting ebbed and waned over the years, as if each individual spotlight represented a liberation of a person and therefore a success story for the intervention. Over time, the phrase "women's rights" even became its own buzzword in media discourse (in a similar way that the term "gender" functioned in the aid discourse) and was often narrated by individual stories from women as they became the first to break a glass ceiling or if they joined public sports and activities—identifiable markers of freedom in the West. These stories were used as proof of the military and aid intervention's success, which was inextricable as "the conflict often became synonymous with women's rights," even when the individual stories were rarely put into the context of the systemic issues facing Afghan women.[140] As Afghan women became simplified into a clear victim/hero binary in the media, so too had "women's rights" become a catchall, context-less agenda item. An entity all on its own.

The obsession with the *chaddari* and the way it was spun as the symbol of oppression had further repercussions when it came to Western women in Afghanistan, some of whom would make a point to not adapt their clothing style because they saw themselves as images of emancipation and Western liberation.[141] Many Afghan women saw their behavior as a sign of disrespect. This "politicization of womanhood" widened the gap between Western and Afghan women.[142]

The image of the Afghan woman as an oppressed figure was distilled down to a single image of the *chaddari*. As the United States was making the case for their invasion, guised as a mission for liberation and embodying the notion that "white men are saving brown women from brown men,"[143] women were forced into the role of victim in need of saving. It left little space for complexity or an historically-informed approach, and, more important, for the women of Afghanistan to define themselves. This set a dangerous and consequential precedent for the ways the aid intervention was constructed.

While aid is, in principle, a business built on respect for diversity, the hint of white savior complex did not allow sufficient space for Afghan women to define their own version of liberation. The beginnings of the aid intervention, particularly as they aimed to benefit women and tackle the big issues of women's rights, equality, and freedoms, were flawed from the beginning—the moment Afghan women were excluded from setting their own path forward.

In the Afghanistan of late 2021, as the country collapsed to the Taliban, headings emerged about "*bourka* sales." The fact that this trope remained a legitimate reporting narrative indicated that the image of the *chaddari* as a marker of women's oppression has yet to retire. The presence or absence of this garment cannot be the barometer of liberation.[144] It is true that Taliban edicts enforcing the *chaddari* are a denial of Afghan women's agency. However, the argument needs to be one of choice, where Afghan women do the choosing. Now is not the time to fall back on tired stereotypes of women as one-dimensional characters defined by their wardrobe. Now is the time to understand the complex choices women face, as they recognize how far they've come and determine how far they still want to go.

Afghan women were not—and *are* not—victims in need of saving. This stereotype is undone by a rich history of women's movements, women's autonomy, and women's resistance in Afghanistan. And it is Afghan women themselves who will set this course. As such, this book sets out to chart this rich history of Afghan women's agency and is built on the stories and experiences of Afghans themselves, in order to amplify their voices in a narrative that risks drowning them out.

Women are being forced to make difficult decisions for their futures, with many fleeing their country in fear of what may come. Professional women are burning their diplomas and erasing their accomplishments. They have gone into hiding in fear for their lives. Afghan feminists are saying that there is no international political will to support Afghan women and are worried that whatever emerges will be hollow rhetoric and empty promises.

Meanwhile, Afghan women will do what they have always done: struggle and negotiate the various fluctuations in their social status throughout history to achieve gains on their own terms. Women can be on the receiving end of oppressive and violent actions and can also be agents of their own resistance. Afghan women's historical trajectory defies the assumption that they need "saving." Their story is one of resistance and agency—both then and now.

Feminisms exist everywhere, and Afghan feminism has a long history in Afghanistan. Indigenous feminisms are not alien importations. They evolve like all social movements—in response to issues women face in their own contexts. What's more, Afghan feminists challenge dual oppressions: imperialism and patriarchy.

Afghan women have always been exercising agency—whether the world recognizes it as such is irrelevant. As Afghan history has shown, Afghan women will once again save and liberate themselves.

CHAPTER 2

Where We Fit
Is Where We Fight

*Supporting women was not about understanding social dynamics.
It wasn't about understanding the culture.
It wasn't about the causes of poverty. It was very superficial.*
—Aid worker in Afghanistan

Why delve deeply into stories of who people are and how they see themselves? Because we must understand who people are if we are to know how to help. Stories offer insight to the world, and our role in it. Understanding people's lives and experiences—told through their own voices—ensures that representation is not tokenistic but built on agency and respect. Firsthand accounts help us to learn, to teach, to influence, to inspire and ultimately, they have the power to transform.

Transformation can be seen as an outside imposition resulting in people no longer feeling like the owners of their stories. Stories of oppression, or even of progress, become the stories of the imposer rather than the voices of those who are implicated in those stories. While intending to "do good," some aid interventions can drown out these voices and stories, resulting in the appearance of hollow gestures or—at worst—neocolonialism. This is particularly relevant when aid is accompanied by a military intervention. The missions become conflated and are more likely to be resisted. In Afghanistan, the 2001 Western-led aid and military intervention that used the language of "liberation" is a case in point.

This chapter focuses on an understanding of gender and identities, told first through an exploration of the word "gender" and what it has come to signify. Building from this understanding is an analysis of Afghan identities, helping guide us by offering insight into how people see—and define— themselves. Firsthand accounts bring these analyses to life through the stories of Afghan women and couples.

"Many foreigners who came here chose to do first, and listen later," an Afghan woman leader recently told me. "This is the wrong order. If you

A woman comes to an aid organization seeking support, Kabul.

listened, you would have heard what we are telling you. Are you trying to help or are you trying to leave us with more problems? Ask yourself this next time. If we want your help, then we should be telling you *how* you help. Otherwise it is not help. It is problems."

I started hearing these things in 2002, when I first arrived in Afghanistan. An Afghan woman leader told me throughout the years that she believed the international community had "no interest in understanding these things about Afghanistan." You—meaning the international community—are "not interested in the fundamental social and political changes in Afghanistan," in the way things work, she elaborated, otherwise you would have "passed the process of analyzing the social institutions and their backgrounds and histories for better ways to make changes." She explained that our ignorance of the way things work has fueled a resistance and provoked a backlash. And, she concluded, "we warned you."

An Agenda with a Foreign Name

Some aid workers in the country also recognized the hollow rhetoric and the tendency to "do first, and listen later," as I was told. This "listening later" was made most stark in understandings of the loaded word "gender."

"Gender," in the way that aid workers use it, "seems to be an incestuous topic amongst a group of foreigners, having little to do with the realities on the ground," a colleague told me. She continued to argue that "Afghanistan is not the place to experiment with a Westernized construct of women's liberation."

Within the aid community, all things "gender" became buzzwords that peppered aid reports, policies, and programs. Very often, this erroneously replaced the word women, as if that word itself had become *passé*, hardly relevant in aid programming. It has been argued that "gender" and its discourse was part of the toolkit of the Anglophone aid elite, "never mind that gender did not translate well into many languages."[1]

Both the definition of "gender" and its implications remain under discussion in Afghanistan even now, 20 years later. And yet the term continues to be coupled with other ambiguous words such as "empowerment" and "mainstreaming." "It has never been gender mainstreaming," an Afghan woman leader explained. "It is gender segregation, just highlighting the differences between men and women. Dividing them, not bringing them together." "And that creates a reaction," she continued. "It's the first thing internationals talk about."

Aid organizations are "a bunch of propagandists that have mastered the art of talking for their funders, not for the people they are supposedly here to assist." She argued that we are so embedded in the system, we can no longer see the flaws. And the repercussions are serious and play out on the lives of those we claim to help. Aid organizations, meanwhile, cling to their "overly backwards view of countries in the region" to fit their narrative. We have "gone too far in creating these clichés and now we are stuck with them forever it seems."

Another Afghan woman leader explained it further:

> In Afghanistan, any word which is not part of the patriarchal terminology and is perceived as a Western term and having Western value—even if this word be part of other Islamic concepts and terminologies. Still Afghans will consider it strange and anti-culture and will not be accepted by the majority of people. Gender concept is always strange for the Afghan patriarchal society.... We also should not expect that a great social change in values and norms in a traditional and patriarchal society be warmly welcomed by the society.

"What is 'mainstreaming,' anyway?" one aid worker lamented. "It's a buzzword that makes no sense to me." He explained that we "generously employ lots of buzzwords, like gender." "I don't even know what that means," he admitted, "but I'm told I have to mainstream it. Even our 'gender person,' she sits in her own container on the compound. She's not even physically 'mainstreamed.'"

Regardless, "gender" was the word-du-jour, and the key to international support and therefore, international funding. The language used to justify so-called "gendered interventions" was disempowering, as if we are "here to save the poor victims," as one woman told me. Meanwhile, Afghan women leaders were advancing women's rights, and "doing gender" anyway, using the right words to achieve gains on their terms.

I admired their courage and adaptability. Year after year, I watched Afghan women use these words if they thought it was what foreigners wanted to hear. All the while, they continued working on the ground with women we possibly did not see, and surely could not reach. "We will go about our business as we have always done," an Afghan colleague told me. "You will come and you will go. We are staying," she continued, "and so we have to do 'gender' our way."

Men also used the language of "gender," but mostly to their own ends. I observed this in my work when, on many occasions, I was confronted with men who sought to start NGOs for "women's empowerment" and approached me for funding in the early years of the intervention. An authority on Afghanistan pointed out that "it's the same development we have seen in Western societies. If you push too hard, you make it into something which is politically correct but not accepted and understood by the people."

Communities were sufficiently informed to know that the presence of aid organizations was transitory and that they may need to subscribe to the lingo on paper—*gender equality, women rights,* and so on—in order to attract aid. Regardless of their use of the rhetoric, Afghan groups knew how to apply the terms and how far they could push the gender agenda in their own contexts. "Aid lingo is contagious," one aid worker told me. "You would say the same if it gave you the ability to do the work you know needed doing." She continued:

> Many of the women I encountered wanted their position in society to be improved—through better health, better support—rather than changed. And I wondered whether they used the term *gender* because it was the term used most often by donors.

Despite being able to manipulate the lingo, Afghans nonetheless perceived these terms to be items "in the toolbox of those who were party to Afghanistan's wars."[2] In other words, the discourse took the form of an ideological occupation. As a result, Afghans became resistant to these discourses (not the concepts—an important distinction) because of their perceived ties to Western (largely American) individualism.

The concept of women's rights—and human rights more broadly—are as indigenous to Afghanistan as they are to any other place. They did not need to be imported or delivered. They can be helped or hindered, certainly, but many Afghans perceived this to be more of a hijack than a help.

So it was not about women's rights themselves, but rather the aggressive promotion of the so-called *women's rights agenda*, and the means by which it was transmitted, that generated tensions. Afghan history told us this story before. To many Afghans, the quest for empowerment, for rights, for equality, for liberation felt like a foreign myth. Imposed liberation without input from the communities implicated in that liberation would only leave a vacuum between ideologies, and further distance real people with real issues in need of real support.

Many Afghan women told me of the discomfort they felt in being the center of attention and the "object" of international pity. One woman said that "being a woman is now important in Afghanistan, before it was not." Another woman articulated that being a "woman in Afghanistan is a very popular *object* today." Her use of the word object was deliberate and emphasized. She expressed a sentiment echoed by many, namely that Afghan women were objectified and seen in binary terms in the eyes of foreigners—particularly the media—and that Afghan women were an object of the discourse animating what appeared to be yet another international occupation.

To further complicate matters, there is still no agreed-upon translation of "gender" in Dari and Pashto. To illustrate this point, all of my business cards for positions with gender in the title were written as "gender" in Dari, as if it had become a Dari word. I use the example of my previous position as "Senior Gender Officer" as case in point. "Senior" and "Officer" were translated whereas "Gender" was not. In Dari, the most commonly used word, *jinsiyat*, meaning sexuality, is still heavily disputed and is only used to fill a linguistic void.

"What I see," an Afghan woman leader explained, "is that most people translate things from other languages and bring these things here. In Afghanistan, no one asked what gender means. This word, it is different everywhere. For us, it's important to know and to find out for ourselves what gender means in Afghanistan." The infiltration of English terms contributed to the Afghan perception that their language and culture was under threat.[3]

In one of the many meetings I attended on gender issues, Afghan women made the following points regarding the word gender: (1) The partners in the aid intervention lack a robust understanding of gender in the Afghan context; (2) there has not been an agreed-upon translation; and (3) the word has became loaded with the perception that it is part of a Western-driven agenda and is used when it is believed that it is "what foreigners want to hear." Following the meeting, an update on gender activities was circulated, ending with confirmation of plans "to settle the definition issue." The word *jinsiyat ejtemai*, literally social sex, was created by some gender specialists to fill this void, but there's no connection culturally or linguistically, so it continued to feel foreign and imposed.

Meanwhile, tensions amplified. One woman who worked with me would often tell me what her husband was saying about these allegedly new words. "He is angry with all of these [gender] trainings," she told me. "He says: 'Only training for you and nothing for me. And gender means I sit at home and you go out and do everything. And what are these international agencies doing? And it's a Western idea, and it's bad, and it doesn't respect our culture, and it's not Muslim.'"

Another member of my team added that many international organizations claim that they cannot find an Afghan expert who knows about gender issues, which is ironic, since women leaders and women's rights activists were abundant. She told me that it was not right to bring someone from a different culture to "explain our ways to us." She continued: "What we should do is find those people who know Afghan culture, not another culture, and train them in gender: What does gender mean? What does gender want from the people? What is our responsibility to gender?"

I Become What You Deny

During my time in Afghanistan and for many years afterwards, I was fortunate to hear people's life stories, told to me freely as part of personal and professional conversations. These stories provide a unique window into people's lives. I wanted to better understand how Afghans define themselves, and what *they* thought was important. We can learn so much from these voices, particularly today with the return of the Taliban.

As part of my attempt to understand identities, I had conversations with more than 100 Afghan women and men of diverse ethnic and age groups. I asked them to rank five different aspects of their identity (nationality, religion, ethnicity/tribe, sex, and family) in order of importance to them.[4] The point was to better understand, and learn from, how people perceived their identities at that particular point in time, in the Afghanistan of 2002 to 2009.[5]

Results should not be seen as static, but rather an historical snapshot and a reflection of the priorities at that moment. In other words, their identities could not be divorced from the socio-political tensions in which Afghans found themselves. "So, whatever is important," an Afghan friend told me, "is important possibly because it was *made* to be important." I asked her to elaborate, and she told me this: "I become whatever you try to deny." This is universal; we tend to cling to whatever aspect of our identity appears to be most under threat at any given time.

A woman sits on the edge of Band-i-Amir, Bamiyan.

Identity in Afghanistan, and everywhere, is a fluid concept that can experience shifts over time, especially in response to external influences. Conflict, insecurity, social change, political tensions, and fights for civil rights are a few of these forces which compel us to make choices about our identities, to determine priorities and designate hierarchies, and perhaps to cling to aspects of our identity we feel are under threat at that moment.

Examining various aspects of identities helps us understand how people define themselves and how that changes over time. An understanding of Afghan identities is an important starting point to determine how these identity markers are defined, reinforced, or even resisted. It also helps us understand how better to support people in their own fight for freedom. Ultimately, knowing where we *fit* helps us know where we *fight*.

The term *Afghaniyat* represents the sense of Afghan national identity that evolves in different periods of Afghan history. *Afghaniyat* is not based on the individual. Rather, it is deeply embedded in the collective units of the tribe, clan, and family, reinforcing accepted norms of behavior. In short, these are the economic, political, and cultural markers for what can—or can not—be done.[6] It is this collective nature of *Afghaniyat* that determines Afghans' sense of self and place in the world and how they deal with alien ideologies.

While there might be similarities, there is no uniform situation for Afghan women. When women are singled out as a homogenous group with shared interests, we miss important nuances. Gender roles are not static—they change over time, interconnecting with other aspects of identity and other systems of oppression. Accounting for these differences, in other words, taking an intersectional approach to identity, is paramount.

Globally, gender roles are understood through an overwhelmingly-patriarchal lens evidenced by the fact that no country in the world has actually achieved equality. Afghanistan is now among the worst of these, with the widest gender gaps and the greatest inequalities. But patriarchy alone is a partial picture. Patriarchy in Afghanistan is more tribal than Islamic, with tribal practices often overshadowing Islam, particularly its more progressive messages on gender issues.[7]

In order to gain insight into Afghan women's lives, we need to see the interconnectedness of patriarchy, power, and politics, and where backlashes are fueled with each attempt to emancipate women.[8] Conflict also plays a part in fluctuating identities and in determining how conservative a given group might be at a certain time.[9] Conflicts can amplify certain identities, making them more important than they were in the past. This is particularly true when that identity is under threat.

In order to understand the Afghanistan of 2021, it is important to take a nuanced and contextual look at Afghan notions of identity and gender. Gender identities are embedded in other social categories: family, community, village, tribe. Underlying this is the foundation of Islam—the strongest unifying force in Afghanistan. Even these seemingly-fixed categories have fluctuated over time as a result of various political projects and powers, including outside influences and "occupations."

Khub Musselman Ast

Unsurprisingly, religious identity ranked first for both women (48 percent) and men (60 percent) as the primary social category within which they were more closely affiliated, followed by Afghan identity, ethnicity, sex, and family—in that order. The ranking of religious identity was important as it reflected the prominence Islam has in Afghanistan, and the consequences if Islam is sidelined, threatened, or even perceived to be so, as Afghan history has shown us.[10] The role of religion is therefore deserving of particular focus, given its prominence in the lives of Afghan women and men. Islam provides the parameters by which Afghans live, focusing specifically on relationships between the sexes. Many expressed that they were content within its boundaries, electing freely to abide by its tenets.

"Islam is the primary point of guidance," one woman articulated. "Without it, there cannot be progress." Many men said that their religion was "everything" to them, and therefore those of a different religion were "outside of [Afghan] society's laws." Most women argued that their role in Islam was similar to that of a man, stating that it was the duty of both women and men to be good Muslims. "There is no difference between Allah's creatures," one woman explained. This is not unique to Afghanistan. In many other countries, people with a system of belief often prefer to understand their rights and roles within their religious framework.

Afghan women felt strongly that Islam, more than any other religion, guaranteed equal rights to men and women. "Women have the right to work, to study. Women have lots of rights," they said. "Women have rights in Islam. They can work outside of the house," one woman added. Women explained that they preferred to find ways to defend their rights within an Islamic context. They wanted to search for answers in the Koran, or through another practicing Muslim. And they wanted to know more about Islam and the rights that it afforded them.

It is significant that most of the men and women I spoke with selected religion as their primary identity affiliation, while very few felt that they identified with their sex. This reinforces the importance of Islam in the lives of women and men in Afghanistan—and a channel to make change. In fact, Muslim identity is more than a religious label. It also is an indicator of a person's reputation and a certification that they are credible and trustworthy. The expression *khub musselman ast*, literally meaning "he's a good Muslim," is used for this purpose.[11]

And yet, some felt that there was a lack of clarity on what "being Muslim" means, particularly as the religion has been subjected to various interpretations throughout time, many of which were not particularly progressive for women. One woman explained: "When a baby is born, the family says 'you are Muslim, you are Muslim' but the child is never taught why, so they have a hard time differentiating between the culture and religion."

In Afghanistan, this line is further blurred as tribal customs merge Islam with their own practices. Norms governing women in Afghanistan are often based on tribal codes that trump Islamic laws, particularly in the case of Islam's more enlightened messages on women. A woman explained the dynamic this way: "There are lots of rules for women in Islam, but people weren't educated enough and didn't have much information about their religion. So people preached some wrong words about Islam." This was in reference to the first Taliban period, and it proves to be true again today.

Most men expressed a strong need to safeguard Islam—especially its measures regarding women—from foreign interference and influence. One younger man put it this way: "Religion is an important factor for Muslims.

To defend it they will sacrifice everything." "Islam provides and respects any opportunities for women, but unfortunately a non-respectable culture has been mixed with Islam," one woman said.[12] Many *mullahs* are to blame, they say. "They want to change Islam and mix it with culture and custom."

Religious Afghan men follow the guidance of *mullahs* and adhere to *ghayrat*, the principle of honor. This is a critical socio-cultural value that refers to control and protection of women in a family or extended family. Based on *ghayrat*, men are responsible for keeping female family members pious and obedient, with the understanding that a good Muslim woman obeys the male members of the family. Such "honor" manifests in control of women's sexuality and preserving her virginity, thereby denying her right to make any decisions about her body and sexuality.

Many women and men agreed on one point regarding Islam: they did not feel that the Taliban reflected the true nature of the religion. In fact, they viewed the Taliban as a manifestation of foreign influence that had "soiled" the true nature of Islam. "They tried to act like Muslims and they tried to alter Islam and disrespect the culture of Afghanistan," one woman said. "During the Taliban regime, it was just the name of Islam, but not real Islam. They were like wild animals." "All of their ideas were wrong. They said that women should wear the *chaddari*. They said we must cover. All wrong." "Taliban regime was a dark regime," one woman said. "They forced people to do things that they wanted."

Discussions on the role of Islam in Afghanistan quickly became expressions of duty to safeguard the religion and concern that it could once again be threatened by outside interference, especially ideological occupations. Many felt that aid organizations sought to undermine Islam by their failure to work within a Muslim framework. This was fueled by Afghan perceptions that foreigners view Islam as oppressive—a perfect recipe for resistance. Thus many Afghans saw engagement with the international community as a willful dismissal of Islam. Many women were quick to blame "invading cultures and customs," expressing a dislike for foreign intervention and a desire to regain Afghan autonomy. "Now that we are a little bit free," one woman explained, "I will not be a servant of human beings. I am only a servant of God."

Afghaniyat

The women and men who felt they were Afghan above all else expressed pride in being Afghan, and a strong sense of *Afghaniyat*. Both men and women in this category believed that an Afghan identity is what will bring cohesion to a fragmented society. They expressed a desire to re-invigorate the concept of "being an Afghan" and, as one woman put it, to "try to be as one people." Another woman put it this way: "We are all Afghans first. The rest just divides us." This was a sentiment shared by many in this category. Another older woman said, "being Afghan is what holds us together. It should be our strength."

Of those who identified with being Afghan, many connected their Afghan identity with their ability to drive non–Afghans away. An older man stated that the "importance of being Afghan is because Afghans never want to convert their Afghan identity." Another man reinforced this point by saying: "We don't want to lose our identity and sell ourselves." Many of the men in this category expressed a belief in the strength of Afghans as a force to act in unity against non–Afghans. One man said:

> Afghan also means national unity, brotherhood, balance. The first factor to ful-
> fil all the mentioned aims is to be an Afghan. And our national interests are in
> being an Afghan. It is our responsibility to protect it.

A few of the women who saw themselves as Afghan connected their role as women to their role as keepers of men's honor and therefore, national honor. One woman explained that being Afghan meant that "the women shall be kept at home and no one shall see her. Her role is to do the work of the home and to act as men wish." In many rural areas, women are considered male property and are given monetary value similar to land. The dowry offered to the woman's family is for the bride to be owned by the man, thereby agreeing to be the keeper of his honor.

Another woman expressed it this way: "I put women last because men are the highest degree and women are the lowest. It is more import-ant that we are all Afghans." One woman ranked her Afghan identity low-est, explaining that "Afghan is last because Afghanistan has done nothing good for women." She saw ethnicity as her primary form of identification.

Very few women and men felt that sex was the most salient aspect of their identity. For many, they noted that "being a man or a woman" has only recently become important, since "foreigners started talking about it." Many women and men recognized that sexual politics have destabi-lized Afghanistan at many interfaces in Afghan history, stating that "being a woman is now important in Afghanistan, before it was not." This was not taken as a lack of agency or awareness but rather a reflection on the rheto-ric of the time.

Only one woman—and one man—expressed a more positive and hope-ful sentiment. The woman said she "believe[s] in the strength of Afghan women." The man spoke of "equality" and "rights," explaining that "in recent years, relations between husband and wife—and all men and women—have turned very bad. To remake these relations is an important factor."

Street girls in the city who spend the day on Chicken Street hoping for donations from foreigners, Kabul.

Due to ethnic conflicts and ongoing tensions in Afghanistan, past and present, it is often assumed that ethnicity is the most dominant aspect of *Afghaniyat*. Contrary to these assumptions, the various ethnic groups—Pashtun, Tajik, Hazara, Uzbek, Aimak, Turkmen, Baloch, and others[13]—have evolved into a fairly common culture, psychology, and ethos.[14] The fluidity of ethnic identity is a social and political construct, changing according to the pressure put upon it.[15] When an outside influence forces the adoption of a singular identity above the rest, it can cause social tension and violence.[16] Meaning: *I become what you try to deny.*

Throughout Afghan history, ethnic identity has been manipulated by leaders and foreign invaders to serve their own needs in the country. Today, with the Taliban—who are all Pashtun—again in power, ethnic identity will likely once again become a highly political project to be manipulated for yet another occupation of Afghanistan.

In this particular historical period (2002–2009), very few respondents chose to identify with their ethnic group as this was a divisive issue during the conflict. In fact, one woman put it this way: "During the conflict, ethnicity became the most important thing for us." She explained that she still clung to these views and was not ready to look beyond ethnic lines.

The other respondents—mostly women—guarded these identity markers because, as one young woman explained, "this is how we understand each other, as tribes and groups." Ethnic identity also included tribal affiliation as these are interconnected in Afghanistan.

Another woman reinforced this view, stating that "we are closest to our tribe because this is where we find the most similarities." An older woman explained that she identified with ethnicity because "these are the things that identify us first, not gender roles and relations." I took interest in her use of the word gender as it was the only part of her response that was in English. This emphasized a recurring theme: that gender had become part of the Afghan lexicon, an imported buzzword for use by Afghans in the presence of non–Afghans and a word for which no translation exists.

Many of those who identified with their ethnic group expressed a need to be in a familiar context with their own people. In situations of conflict and displacement, many Afghans found themselves removed from their families, communities, and tribes and without the social safety net that these networks can provide. The expression *mardum-dar* was employed in this regard. This term literally means "having people," having a sense of safety and belonging, for example, within a tribe or clan.[17]

Despite the importance of *mardum-dar*, family affiliation was not a popular answer for women. The men who said they identified firstly with their role as a male member of a family explained it this way: "I am a member of a family first and have an obligation to protect them." Indeed, men who saw family as their primary affiliation likely did so because of their prominent socio-cultural role as head of the family and the sense of duty that this brings. Along with this duty comes the obligation to protect the family honor as it is intimately linked with the man's own honor—and therefore his credibility in the community.

A young man felt that family identity connected him to his ancestors, explaining the prominent role of older generations in forming the young. He put it this way:

> Parents mean responsibility, developing knowledge, culture, humanity, religion. They explain to us what other divisions and identities like ethnic groups, man/woman, and Afghan mean. But parents could also pass on poverty, ignorance, and darkness to their children.

The family, as a social institution, warrants investigation.[18] In such contexts, like in most countries around the world, Afghan women traditionally play the role of wife and mother. They are also a primary conduit through which Islam is passed from one generation to the next. Women carry the legacy of culture and need to be understood for the power they possess in their families and communities. As such, an aid worker explained that her entry point was in supporting the family, and within that, she often found opportunities to "talk gender." Providing support and services for families helped open the door to other conversations.

Similar to other patriarchal societies, gender roles in Afghanistan are shaped by socio-cultural factors largely based on women's role as keepers of the family honor. "Women don't exist in isolation," an Afghan man explained. Attempts to separate women from family and community can be met with strong resistance. Women's identity in Afghanistan has always been part of the collective. Defining women as individual autonomous units can extract them from their social, cultural, and family contexts.[19] One Afghan woman leader had the following to say:

> Gender relations in Afghanistan are complementary and not juxtaposed men against women. This juxtaposition from aid agencies reflects individual rights and a Western capitalist context. This isn't applicable in Afghanistan because traditionally there is coexistence.

I was reminded repeatedly during my time in Afghanistan by Afghan women that they do not see themselves as individuals as much as part of the family and community. *Why not then let them own and control the resources?* A former Minister of Women's Affairs put it best:

> We are from the community. We know our community. We are better at finding the right approaches. We know the problems. We can recognize and identify them better. We know how to transfer the information in the right language, using the right words. We have this advantage. We will work better together than the international community would alone. Reaching the last woman in the farthest place of the country is only possible if international agencies come together in partnership with us.

Identities are political. They evolve and change over time. We all live multi-dimensional intersectional lives, and therefore understandings of who we are present a nuanced understanding of what we need. It is important then that Afghan women be viewed through a combination of identities that they themselves specify and "to explore the diverse experiences of [these] differently positioned women."[20]

When it comes to allocating aid, understanding identities is critical. The way aid is distributed can create divisions or cohesion, depending on how it is done. This is even more challenging in contexts of conflict and insecurity, where identities shift based on politics and power. The argument that aid programming can be divisive is not new or unusual. Aid can be divisive in the context of conflict and reconstruction when it is distributed according to crude divisions in society instead of based on opportunities for peace. It becomes important to recognize where meaningful connections can be made that provide the potential for a sustainable peace. Such choices

can determine whether the effects of such efforts are positive or negative.[21]

Any work on women's rights and gender equality should be grounded
in the local contexts and should understand the history of resistance and
the process of change. Not only in Afghanistan, but perhaps everywhere,
change imposed from the outside is strongly resisted. If we want(ed) to
make gains for women in Afghanistan, we could have worked more closely
within their own understandings of who they are, what their context is, and
how they are connected or disconnected. Ultimately, it is up to the communities themselves—and to the women in those communities, most of all—
to determine how aid should be allocated.

There Is No One Now to Help Us, Even God

I often would ask women I worked with about their lives, and also to
understand what "being a woman" meant at that time. Speaking to women
today, the stories remain very much the same, reflecting a reality that has
not changed. Their words helped me to better understand their lives. It was
their willingness to share their lives with me that laid the foundation for my
research and this book.

As an insider-outsider, I was in some ways a sounding board for them.
When I first arrived in Afghanistan, I noticed that women were happy to
have the opportunity to be in the company of other women, to rebuild their
social safety nets, and to have the luxury to sit and share their stories in a
safe space. These women had not had the time or space to talk about their
lives in order to contextualize their experiences.

Conversations often began with stories of their past as a way to illustrate their challenges in the present and highlight the extent of their desire
for a better future. "I want to tell you about my tragic life," one woman said.
"I've spent days in hunger, nights in the darkness," added another. "Maybe
you know about the life of an Afghan woman, filled with that much pain
and difficulty that I'm not able to express it." There was sadness in these
stories, and a need to process the pain of the past. One woman expressed
her pain strongly: "I have a baby that I can't feed. There is no milk in my
breasts."

The following are life stories from select women who shared with
me.[22] While quantitative investigations are important, they only reveal a
small part of the story. The value of individual stories and accounts is often
missed. Therefore, it is important to let Afghan women speak for themselves, as far too often they have been spoken for. These are their voices and
accounts.

ZACHAHA

Our family consists of 12 people. We are four families who live in one house. We live in one room. Most of our family is women and small children. I am not literate. Because of the war, we moved from one side to another, so I couldn't study. With much difficulty we spent six months in Pakistan. We spent our time knitting rugs so we could provide a little food to keep us alive. I lost a daughter during the war, but now that we have peace in our country I want to live in peace and comfort. I've already suffered a lot.

LAILA

During the fighting between parties, we moved to many different places to escape the violence. We were in Mazar-i-Sharif for about seven years, but we were not comfortable when the Taliban captured the city. They killed people, cut hands and legs, genocide and many more things happened. They also killed one of my sons. Then we secretly left Mazar and came to Kabul City. But unfortunately some other problems came into being … the difficulty of paying for house rent, material, food. Prices got higher because people are coming back to their homeland. I live in one of my relatives' house for free. But life with them is difficult for me. I don't have a house of my own. I live in a room that doesn't have windows. This is only a small part of my painful story.

HABIBA

I want to tell you a little about my life. I hope that you won't get tired of my life story. We have passed very difficult days and severity in Afghanistan. Maybe you have watched it on TV that how difficult was life in Afghanistan. We passed our life with poverty and didn't have anything to eat for many years. I have a son who lost his hand. We Afghan women suffered and passed our lives with many difficulties. Lots of Afghan women are illiterate or not literate enough. There is nobody to help us. I am wondering about the future. I am a woman with many problems in this time. There is no one now to help us, even God.

DIL JAN

I had a good and comfortable life, but all the fightings have destroyed my life. Afghanistan has been a country of war for many years, more than half of its population is living in crisis and poverty. I'm from the poor women of this part of the world. My husband cannot find work. My children are very young. I don't have any breadwinner at all. I need help to make my life better.

NADERA

During 23 years of war, the economic, social, and political situation was not good. We suffered a lot, and we had to live in difficult situation. Now in Kabul City, the situation is getting better, but not in other provinces. There are still warlords and gunmen in other provinces. My economic situation isn't good. I became a widow 16 years ago and my oldest child is 15 years old. I want my children to get educated and also find money to feed them and improve my economic situation so my children serve their country and society, not to destroy it and be away from education.

SOHILA

I am a mother of four children and owner of nothing at all. My husband got lost during the cruel Taliban's regime. Except my four children I have to take care of my husband's old parents. I live only in the hope of my husband's return to home, but there is not any news of him recently. I actually don't know if he is alive or dead. Right now I am the only breadwinner for the family of seven people. Nowadays the rent of the house that I'm living in has increased, I can't afford it.

ROGULL

Now let me tell you about my life. I got married when I was 15 years old, my husband was 25 years older than me. Now that 10 years has passed from my marriage, I haven't seen any good behavior from him. He puts a lot of pressure on me and my children. I am really tired of my life. My sons are seven-year-old twins and my daughter is nine years old. They are all very young. I don't know what to do. Since the day of my marriage I haven't had any comfortable day. I've always worked myself. I am not sure what to do with my life. My husband is very old now and I am 23 years old. I can't live alone now because of my young children. I have to suffer everything. I have a very painful life. He always insults my children. I don't have permission of any thing inside my own home. I don't have any hope for a better life now. What should I do? How should I spend my life like this?

SHIMA

I want to tell you of my tragic stories that happened during the Taliban regime. Before the Taliban, I had a comfortable and peaceful life. I was always satisfied. Some months after the Taliban came, life was no longer easy in Kabul City. Every day they created a new policy for people to accept. We couldn't tolerate it so we left our home and went to Pakistan. We didn't have the comfortable life anymore, and we had to suffer being refugees. But after the Taliban's failure, we immigrated to our beautiful country. We had lost all our life. There was no house left, no things. During these years of war, houses of people were all destroyed. It has harmed people's economics. Since I was born, I have only seen fighting, bombing, destroying, and damaging, nothing else. I haven't felt happiness, peace of mind, and friendship ever. I don't know what it is like. I hope to find all these things in the future. I want to hold true friendship in my arms.

ABIDA

During 23 years of war, our country was destroyed and now American people are helping us to rebuild. All Afghan people spread to everywhere. Most of them went to other countries as refugees. Most of the women lost their husbands and became widows. Children lost their parents and became orphans. People have lots of economic problems. They have lost their homeland. I support my three children. I lived in a place where I could only hear the sound of bombs and rockets. I was very hopeless in life. I hated everyone. Now I know that there are good people living in this world, but in the past I've seen very cruel and bad people. We spend each night to face the day and each day to face the night only in hope of help and kindness. We wait for those who will take weak people's hands in order to help them.

SHEKIBA

I have suffered the war because of the ones who didn't want our country to be in peace. During these wars we couldn't escape from here too because we didn't have enough money to leave and stay in other countries, so we had to suffer and get burnt. I live in Qalai-Musa, a dirty and poor area of Kabul City which has destroyed streets, no electricity, and no water supply. Our house is made of mud and clay. The windows are covered with plastic paper instead of glass.

ROYA

My 15-year-old son is handicapped. We don't have anyone to support and help us. Because of facing sorrow and sadness I can't see very well with my eyes. I was five years old when my father died. I lived with my aunt. When I was 13 years old, my aunt asked me to marry her son. After a few years, my husband left me and married someone else. He ignored my children too. Then, after some time I heard that he had died. Wars and fighting made our life more difficult. But now Allah has shown his kindness and has brought peace to our country. I would like you to convey to the peace-loving women there that Afghan people, particularly women, have faced many hardships. And now they are experiencing the very first freedom and they are learning to struggle for further rights.

KHATOL

I am going to tell you about my life: I am responsible for providing my family expenses. There are five people in our family. I live in a house that has been destroyed by a rocket. I wash clothes to provide some food to feed my fatherless children in order to pass my life. This is the life of an Afghan woman that I am sharing with you.

QANDI

It will be a long time until all the women in pain in Afghanistan are able to live peaceful lives. During these past years we were left from everything. During the dark regime of the Taliban, women didn't have the right to go out of their houses. We were in debt and hungry. And we are still not able to pay the debts. I really want to forget all the past. I want to struggle for a better life. I believe that we are all women and we are able to help each other from anywhere around the world. I'm from a very poor family, but my spirit is always strong, not poor and weak.

KHALIDA

I am single and I live with my old father, two brothers, and one young sister. We are total five people in our family. I couldn't continue my education because of bad economical situation. I live in a rented house. We have a very simple and poor life. I myself sometimes wash clothes in houses to earn living. Now that I have enrolled myself in this organization, I am very happy that I get support. It is like a drop of water that a person pours into the mouth of another who is in a dry desert. That is the drop of water that is going to save her life.

While their stories focused on hardship as a result of decades of conflict, there was also hope. Deeper still, there was a hint of disappointment in the lack of changes in their lives. "You have come to help," one woman said, "but I do not know how." She continued: "We women are wondering how to continue our life."

Many of these women can no longer be reached, but these anecdotes, interviews, and examples confirm that women's lives did not improve as they had expected. Successes were too hard won, too small, and too short-lived. And any gains for women were often subject to swift reversal.

An Afghan woman leader confirmed this, adding that though some women's lives were made marginally better, these improvements were only temporary because women "could not adapt to the culture that was brought to them" through these interventions. "Afghan women's lives orbit around men," she added, "and cannot be treated as independent. Change could have been possile if society as a whole had been the focus."

For most of the women in Afghanistan, the rhetoric of liberation was only ever just that: a myth. Ultimately, Afghan women persist in their struggle for themselves and their families—their survival depends on it.

Inja Afghanistan Ast

Similar to the women, I spoke to men and women together, in their capacity as couples or family members, about their lives. What they shared brought further insights. The oft-repeated phrase, *inja Afghanistan ast* meaning "This is Afghanistan," was used both by men and women frequently to punctuate a phrase. Women used it in exasperation to rationalize "bad things" that happened to them. Men used this line to justify "the situation of women" and as a counter to strong pushes for change and importing alien ideologies. "This is Afghanistan," I was told on many occasions or, in other words, "those things just don't work here." Both women and men conveyed a sense that because "this is Afghanistan" things were not going to change—and certainly not in the way that anyone had expected.

It was important to compare not only women and men as separate entities but also women and men from the same household in order to determine how they define what Afghanistan is within their own households. Analysis at the family level is relevant because it demonstrates the

Hazara men sit near the holes where the Buddha statues once were, Bamiyan.

importance of not extracting women from their families and contexts. The profiles of couples reveal the differing dynamics between men and women animating each household. The research assistant who worked with me at the time said it was unique to compare ideas of men and women within the same household, adding that "there are actually very few couples who are thinking the same."

The following are vignettes from those encounters.

FATIMA AND AMANULLAH, WIFE AND HUSBAND

Fatima was in her early thirties. She had less than two years of education. Amanullah was forty-one years old and had seven years of education. The couple was originally from rural Afghanistan but they moved to Kabul to live with Amanullah's brother in hopes of finding work and providing for their three children. Fatima explained that Amanullah's brother, her brother in-law, was bitter about the extensive focus on women. He was not happy that Fatima attended trainings and tried to convince Amanullah to prevent her from going out. Many fights broke out in the household as a result. Amanullah was beginning to think that participating in trainings was not such a good idea. Neither Fatima nor Amanullah were particularly pleased with the efforts of the aid institutions. Amanullah was concerned that Fatima would start to respect him less with all thes new ideas she was gaining from the training program. Fatima complained:

"You tell me what my rights are, but what is the point if he won't give them to me? He should understand them first!"

MARYAM AND ALAM, WIFE AND HUSBAND

Alam was thirty-seven years old and had several years of education in Kabul. Maryam was thirty-one and completed primary school. They had been married for twelve years. Maryam believed that, according to Afghan culture and traditions, women were respected and protected in Afghanistan, but that things deteriorated in those years. She believed that men are responsible for women and must provide for the family. Alam felt it was a man's duty to guide women. "Women are innocent creatures," he said. "They need protection from other men. Men are in upper level [more] than women." Alam felt that institutions were undermining men's traditional role. He explained that aid institutions were changing "women's minds against their husbands and are encouraging them negatively." Alam further elaborated that aid organizations were interfering in family issues. Maryam was concerned because "not much is done for men." She felt that this could cause problems for her at home.

ZAINAB AND AHMADI, WIFE AND HUSBAND

Zainab and Ahmadi were from central Afghanistan. Their livelihood was based on agriculture. They were not happy to be in Kabul and found that they did not like the direction Afghanistan was moving in those new times. Zainab saw a lot of violence against women around her. She saw this as a new manifestation of an old struggle, but the difference at that moment was the "position of women is better than men in the society. Priority is given to women in every aspect of opportunities." Ahmadi was a day laborer and was able to bring home an irregular income. He was still hopeful that he would find more stable work. As long as he was working, he said he was happy that Zainab was learning a new skill. He saw that other men were cruel and angry, and he did not think this would happen to him.

STORAI AND HEKMAT, DAUGHTER AND FATHER

Storai was Hekmat's daughter. She was twenty-one years old and not yet married. There were concerns that she was getting too old for marriage. Once married, she would have to stop studying and participating in trainings. Storai witnessed how changing regimes have affected gender relations and have led to increased violence at home. It happened in her home. She did not want to get married, she said. Hekmat recognizes that there was more conflict and argument at home those days. He hoped for a day where men and women could return to their Afghan ways and respect their traditions and religion. He was not sure that day would come.

LIDA AND FAWAD, WIFE AND HUSBAND

Both Lida and Fawad were from the countryside. They had no education. Both felt very strongly that Islam provided the answers to managing changes that were taking place in Afghanistan then, particularly those between men and women. Fawad felt that it was his job to support his family and provide for them. He preferred that Lida stay at home. Unfortunately, Lida was participating in a vocational skills training program and he was at home. Although aid institutions provided his family with an opportunity to earn an income, he was not happy with this new international presence. He said that "they have done nothing for men" and he would prefer a return to "Afghan ways" and an Afghan pace of change. Fawad felt that Afghans were not in control of their country, and he was concerned.

SWEETA AND PAYMAN, WIFE AND HUSBAND

Sweeta and Payman were in their thirties. She had a few years of education. Payman had nearly ten years of education and was a teacher by trade, although was unemployed at the time. Sweeta felt that Payman's profession as a teacher helped her to have greater access to education and training. But she knew Payman was unhappy that he was not working. Aid organizations have done nothing for men, she said. "My husband says that they make men angry when they do nothing for them and only offer opportunities to women. He is a teacher so he understands how people think about these things." Sweeta felt that recent changes brought "uproar to families." Payman agreed that he saw an increase in family conflict because women were no longer satisfied "with what men expected from them."

SARA AND WAHEED, DAUGHTER AND FATHER

Sara was eighteen years old. She was not in school, and this upset her. She said that women in Afghanistan still could not study and work, despite what they were told to believe. Her father appeared to be an advocate of education for women and men, but he did not think the current climate was conducive for Sara to go to school. He explained that "since the Americans came, we are told that men and women have freedom and can work outside and learn," but he felt that the situation was still unstable. Both Sara and Waheed felt that things were better for men and women before "the Americans came." Sara said that "some men think that women are being cared for more than men. But the reality is that both men and women suffer."

MASOODA AND FAYZAL, SISTER AND BROTHER

Masooda lived with Fayzal, her older brother, and his family. She was concerned that men were not getting training and were therefore becoming much more rigid and traditional. Her brother was one of those men who could benefit from training "to become open-minded," she said. Fayzal thought that a woman should be satisfied with her role as wife and mother and that women then were asking for too much. Aid institutions encouraged women to leave the house, he explained. These institutions did nothing for men, he said, "only women get training but then they stay at home and it is useless." Women should stay inside for their own protection, he believed. Masooda was his responsibility, and she was getting too many ideas already.

Frozan and Waisuddin, Wife and Husband

Frozan was thirty-five years old. She was illiterate. Her husband, Waisuddin, was more than ten years her senior. He grew up in Jalalabad and attended six years of school. Frozan would receive food aid that she then handed over to Waisuddin to distribute to the family. Her job, she said, was to "make the society by raising good children." She said she would rather not be the only one bringing home food. Waisuddin had become stricter in recent years and said "women must obey what their husbands command." Women were safer under the *chaddari*, he explained. He'd rather that the women in his family not leave the house at all, particularly his wife. Frozan's new role as the breadwinner made her "stand in front of her husband," Waisuddin said.[23] He believed that this new influence took Afghans away from Islam. Aid institutions "keep people away from Islamic prayers since they give them money and they forget to pray."

Safia and Mirwais, Daughter and Father

Safia was nineteen years old and had three years of education. Her father, Mirwais, had eight years of education. Safia saw violence in her family and felt that violence has always been a part of gender relations, but it took different forms in the different periods of history. She explained that "women argue with their husbands because they are not allowed to go outside. That caused their husbands to beat them." Safia said that "the government has set some rules that men can't beat their wives and they no longer have power to be cruel" but she was not sure most men knew about these rules. Mirwais thought that the world did not have a good image of Afghan men. And he felt that aid institutions did not help things at home because "most men think that organizations are creating distance between men and women by encouraging women negatively." He was not sure what the future of Afghanistan holds.

The stories of women and of couples reveal some important findings. Both the women and men that I spoke with felt somewhat out of place at that time. Many believed that the focus on women as independent entities came at the expense of men and their role. Men's "honor" was brought into question due in part to the perception that their values and socio-cultural systems were believed to be compromised by an ideological occupation. Their differences and diversity—as Afghans—were not fully taken into account.

Today, I could not reach the same couples, but did speak to Tahira and Sabir, a couple in their 50s from Kabul. Tahira told me of her job at an NGO as a health care worker while Sabir was unemployed. "He is not working, but he makes the decisions," she told me. He was uncomfortable with his wife earning an income. "It makes him insecure as a man," she said, "because now I am the man." As soon as Tahira was paid, she would offer her salary to her husband, and Sabir would decide how to spend it. This strategy allowed Tahira to continue with her work and still honor her husband as the head of the family. Sabir seemed to be satisfied as long as he was given control of the money.

An old woman waits in line for a distribution, Logar.

These stories remain valid today and are reflections of gender dynamics in societies with conflict and instability, where society is in perpetual transition. This is not unique to Afghanistan.

This Road Leads to Turkestan

"This road leads to Turkestan," one Afghan man told me. This is a well-known Afghan proverb meaning things are useless, going nowhere.[24] This proverb reflects the sentiments of Afghan women and men after decades of development and deterioration.

I took this inquiry a step further and asked women what they thought it meant to be a man in Afghanistan and asked the reverse of men. *How do they perceive each other's roles?* On both sides, many expressed a sense that they were not qualified to answer questions about the other sex. Both men and women emphasized a division of public (male) and private (female) roles common to other patriarchal societies.

Generally, men felt more comfortable answering questions about women than the women were in answering questions about men. When asked questions about women, most men answered using "we"—on behalf of all men. They felt qualified as individuals to express views that they believed were held by all men as a collective. The women, on the other hand, answered questions as individuals. They had difficulty and hesitated at first, but then the responses came quite strongly.

Women compared being a man with being a "lord," possessing power, responsibility, and authority. Some of the women expressed a desire for greater equality and a dislike for men's disproportionate share of power, noting that "men have all the rights they want." One woman said that "men are better than women in all aspects, meaning they can do most of the things that women are not allowed to do." Another recognized that men "have a good position [and] will not give it up."

A few women clearly articulated that inequality was not exclusive to Afghanistan. One expressed it this way: "Not only in Afghanistan, but everywhere from the first day men have been more powerful, strong, and responsible."

During discussions, women's opinions gradually became stronger, often fueled and encouraged by the other women. For example, a widow laughed and said: "A man has to be a caring father, a kind husband, and an active citizen. I do not know how many men fit this image." Men interviewed were far more animated in their responses about what it meant to be a woman in Afghanistan. Men agreed that women were the responsibility of the male members of the household—husband, father, brother, and son—and that they must "obey the commands" issued to them by the men. One man explained that "man means leader, power, principle. And his every order should be accepted by the woman." This sentiment was widely shared.

Women expressed concern that men felt lost in the new Afghanistan, wanting to bring back old ways. Many also felt more comfortable with a reversion to traditional roles, with men in the public sphere. Men's *namoos*, or pride, was under threat, and women felt greater pressure as a result. Afghan women might represent honor, but Afghan men are under obligation to defend it, especially if it is under attack by foreigners.

Men generally felt very strongly about their role as provider and repeatedly defined themselves as such. Many men echoed the sentiment expressed by a man that "a man is responsible to work outside the house and feed his children." A few men expressed fatigue with the responsibility of supporting the family, particularly in the context of ongoing insecurities and the economic challenges they present. One man put it this way: "Man means one who is wandering in search of food 24 hours a day."

Some men felt that the issue of power and rights was a zero-sum game, and that women cannot gain these things without men having to lose them. As a response to various questions, men expressed a sense of feeling lost, less important, and neglected because of women's newly granted power and rights. One man put it this way: "First, there wasn't exactly such a thing as 'woman.' Then, both woman and man did not exist. There was war. Now there isn't such a thing as 'man.'" Most men felt that changes in relations between men and women were not a good thing. They preferred that each understood and respected his/her role as Afghan culture and Islam have prescribed.

Many of the men recognized that circumstances in Afghanistan changed gender relations, and that fluctuations in women's roles have been largely a result of political processes. Another man explained:

> Social customs of different regimes in different periods have negatively influenced the relationship between men and women. It will take time to ignore the ignorant customs that are imposed on society.

Some men expressed willingness to advance toward equality and a recognition that women's roles are changing and expanding, but these men were not in the majority. For example, one man explained:

> It is like a dramatic thing to say that rights of women and men are same. Everybody knows that this is not true. It is too early in Afghanistan to say that. Maybe it takes twenty or thirty years. People are learning now to practice democracy and things like that.

Women held a more cautious view. Some women felt that change must happen at a pace that works for both women and men. She explained that "it is a good thing that relations change, only if they change in a positive way for women. And the change must be slow or men will not be able to follow it." Most women agreed that change should happen slowly, should be led by Afghans, and should fit within the context of Islam.

"Relations are changing because the world is paying attention to Afghan women," one woman told me. "But not all the changes are good. The good changes take a lot of time. In time, we can work with men as equals." She continued:

> Any changes that are too fast are bad. People will not accept them. If the men and women together decide on the changes, they will be good. If someone else from the outside makes the changes, no one will be happy with it.

A few women expressed the view that "relations are not changing the way [they] want" and that "relations change because rules and regulations of government change." This reinforces previously stated sentiments about gender relations as the victim of various regimes and occupying forces.

The male research assistant noted the following in his conversations with men:

> There were men who welcomed me and answered eagerly, while some men tried to avoid the questions. Answering questions about gender didn't make them

Men sit in a line to register for work, Parwan.

happy. They hear too much about this, and they are tired of it. To them, gender means woman. And "woman" means more important than man to the internationals. I am an Afghan man so they told me openly about these things.

The female research assistant explained it this way:

I had discussions with [the male research assistant] and learned many surprising things. During my interviews with women, impressions were different than with men. Most of the women were comfortable in answering questions and did not have trouble addressing issues. Some of them were happy to complain about men! A few of them didn't have answers to some of the questions because they had not thought of those things before.

These conversations offered unique insights not only into the dynamic between men and women but also the differences in perceptions and opinions. Most felt gender relations had changed and subsequently upset the traditional order of the patriarchal society. Not everyone was receptive to these changes, particularly men, and many were left feeling disempowered.

This sense of men losing their identity was expressed by men and women alike. Prolonged insecurity, patterns of aid intervention, and Western "interference" had threatened their honor and sense of masculine identity resulting in anger, resentment, and violence against women (which will be explored more fully in Chapter 6).

Such backlashes countering advances in women's rights and movements towards equality are not unusual. In fact, this is a tension recognized by feminist activists worldwide. Still, for Afghanistan, many Afghans felt if changes had been introduced slowly through a contextual lens, perhaps the last two decades of effort might have been on more solid ground. An Afghan woman leader confirmed this in 2021:

> Even today women are struggling for their rights. Only a minority of women may have experienced change in the past two decades. This change was only possible as a direct effect of security in the country and the fact that some restrictions were lifted and men had a little sense of security so they could allow women have the right to be out and free. Even that had a limitation, women still need a man to travel, especially outside of Kabul. A woman does not have freedom to live alone and be independent.

Now, as women's rights and gender dynamics come under scrutiny once again, these voices might help us better understand how to support Afghans to progress toward more equitable gender relations.

What Else Can We Do but Hope?

In 2006, I had a chance to delve more deeply into these conversations with two Afghan women I knew well. These women, seemingly at opposite ends of the spectrum, spoke at great length about their lives and shared their insights with me.[25]

Mariyam: Waiting for Change

Mariyam was 35 years old. She was a mother of two small children. She couldn't read and hoped that one day she would have enough "free space in [her] head to think of such things." For now she must find a way to support her children because her husband could not. Her family lived in one small room and shared a cooking space with the family in the adjacent room. "This is how our lives have become, in this time of *peace* [emphasis hers]," she said. Her husband was unemployed. He tried to find work as a day laborer but was not able to bring home a steady income. "He is angry," Mariyam explained, "and so he has turned on me, and turned to drugs. What can I do but tolerate this? I am a woman, after all."

Mariyam told the story of how her life had changed:

> My husband was kinder to me during the Taliban time. We were both scared. I felt safer then. We both had no opportunity for work or leaving the house. Life was very difficult but we struggled together. We were equal in our suffering.

Now, she said, in 2006:

> Afghan men are not given chances. But this is not our fault. Afghan women have always been patient, strong, brave, silent. We do what we must do to support our families and feed our children. If I don't go out and take advantage of this [waves hand around organization office], how will we live? He cannot. He wanted to before, but now he is an addict and he is useless to us. But he is my husband and I have no choice.

Mariyam felt that relations between men and women were deteriorating, not just in her household, but in those she saw around her.

> Women are still struggling to make better their relations with men. It is not easy because there is still violence against them. It is a man's job to take care of the family and children financially. In most families that I have seen, relations have gotten worse because of poor economy. It is a bad thing, this change.

Mariyam explained that part of the tension between her and her husband was primarily because she had become the man in the family. Further, she was going out of the house. And, even more serious, she was "involved with foreigners." It was not just her husband, she explained. "Men don't like their women out of the house, especially with foreigners." She elaborated:

> I wish that women would work in local and governmental organizations and schools, not in foreign NGOs. It will cause them problems with the men if they work with foreigners. But I am here because this is where I get money. If there were opportunities for men to work, and for [Afghan] men and women to work together, things will change. But I do not know what opportunities men have. I see many of them without opportunities. Organizations are promising rights that women cannot achieve and cannot understand. On paper, women have been given rights and freedom. But in my mind, women expected more rights because that was what was promised to them.

Mariyam was not unlike other Afghan women she knew in that she was able to make astute observations about the work of aid agencies and the impact their presence and programs have had. She explained:

> Women are the center of interest for everyone. I never imagined I would see a day where foreign people don't stop talking about Afghan women. Every day in this organization some people come, some journalists come, and they want us to tell them that our lives are better. They want us to tell them that we are not wearing *chaddari*, that we are happy. They think we are stupid. And when they go away, we laugh because we have nothing else we can do. The world is watching, and this is what they want to see.

Mariyam had the following to say about the international obsession with the *chaddari*:

> The foreigners say, "remove your bourka, *bourka kharab* [*bourka* is bad]," but I say Afghanistan *kharab*. Afghan men *kharab*. Until we change this—and we will never change it—my *chaddari* protects me. I put it on and "where is Mariyam?" No one knows. And Mariyam comes and Mariyam goes. And Mariyam stays safe. What choice do I have?

Still, Mariyam was able to end on a positive note. "I hope for a bright future," she said. "What else can we do but hope?"

Mariyam might say that hope is harder to find today, as the Taliban return to power and any gains in women's rights are threatened yet again.

General Nazari: Making Change

General Nazari was the Deputy of the Human Rights Department in the Ministry of the Interior. She also represented the Afghan Independent Human Rights Commission in the Ministry. She was tasked with training and assigning women police officers to handle women's security issues. General Nazari also worked to sensitize men in the Ministry to women's human rights and security. Her story was a rare one.

General Nazari had served with the Afghan police for 31 years. In 2002, she became a general. Her father was in the military, and, although he was a liberal man, he did not want his daughter to follow suit. General Nazari recalled her father taking a trip to Turkey and returning with new ideas about women. He began to advocate for women's education, and he expressed opposition to his wife wearing a *chaddari*. At age five, while watching a military parade with her father, General Nazari had decided on her course in life.

General Nazari was serving as a police officer at the beginning of the Soviet invasion. She sent her husband abroad to protect him, while she remained in Afghanistan with their three small children. He returned many years later, but she had decided that she did not want a husband. She continued to invest in her career and served as a role model for women. She expressed concern with the current direction of her country, and asked why organizations were not working with men. She explained: "It is not only women who need help. In Afghanistan you may think that women don't know anything and men do. But this is not the case. Both need help."

When asked about women's security issues and the prevalence of violence against women, she strongly stated that violence against women has increased recently because men are having difficulties dealing with changes in women's rights and status. She elaborated:

In all the world, violence against women is increasing, not just in Afghanistan. But we are Muslim people and we need to study gender issues and women's rights in the context of Islam and society in Afghanistan.

General Nazari explained that the large international presence has prevented women in Afghanistan from defining their rights for themselves:

"Gender" has not had a chance to define itself in Afghanistan. It is unknown here and does not translate. People think gender is brought from other countries and doesn't belong to Afghanistan. But when we say equality of men and women, then the people say "Yes. This is in Islam. Yes. This is in the Constitution." But "gender," this is foreign to us still. In this society, it is difficult for people to accept changes so quickly.

Mariyam and General Nazari present an interesting comparison: one woman is career-driven, successful, and employed in a traditionally-male field in a high-ranking position. She does not represent the norm. The other is uneducated and relies on aid support for her subsistence. The former has chosen to remain without a husband. The latter is burdened by a husband who cannot support her and feels she has suffered more because she lacks male protection. One calls herself a victim, the other a survivor.

These women share some perspectives, however. They both believe that Afghan women can stand on their own and can act on their own behalf, to better their lives. They both believe that an Afghanistan with foreign influence has only obstructed progress for women. They believe that the right pace of social change is one that is instigated by Afghan women and men. And they both believe that the only way Afghanistan—and Afghan women—will achieve liberation is by defining and finding freedom on their own terms.

I do not know where they are today, but I have no doubt that they continue to fight for women, and for themselves.

CHAPTER 3

The Honor of the Nation

Honor for women means respect. Afghan women don't ask for a lot.
They want to be respected by their family and society.
Honor means that even if there is no equality, let there at least be respect.
—Afghan woman leader

Honor is the foundation of Afghan culture. Understanding honor, therefore, is necessary if we are to try and understand the role of gender within Afghan society. As a system of control, "honor" sets parameters concerning proper gender behavior and who is able to enforce this system. In Afghanistan, honor is explicitly tied to the "protection" of women, specifically the protection of women's sexual purity, thus linking women's sexuality to their "honor." The role of protector is allotted to male family members and husbands.

Understanding societal constructions of "honor," therefore, requires that we analyze the various relationships, institutions, and people that uphold and perpetuate this system. "Women don't exist in isolation," one Afghan man explained. In other words, we have to look at the ways that women *and* men are both implicated in this system of honor.

This chapter uses the stories of Afghan men and women, as told to me, and draws from Afghan literary history to examine the role of men— either as allies or as gatekeepers—to help us to better understand women's agency within the Afghan socio-cultural system. In doing so, we recognize the challenges that men face, in particular men's need to search for new identities and to redefine masculinities as society evolves. Understanding men's perceptions provides insights to their own interpretations of reality. Men play a role in gender politics; they can either advance or oppose women's struggles. This helps us better understand how social change—especially women's rights—is received or resisted.

Understandings of honor are built from myth and legend. As such, this chapter begins with a brief look at Afghan stories and poems to better understand the way the code of honor is transmitted through the generations.

Tales of *Ghayrat*

What can stories and poems tell us about culture? So much of culture is transmitted through these tales, passed from one generation to the next. We tell stories to understand, to convey messages, and to denote boundaries. They are a moral compass to guide communities in what is—and is not—acceptable. Literature reflects a nation's history and embodies its culture. Stories and poems speak to both past and present and offer insight into the formation of socio-cultural values. In that spirit, a brief look at Afghan literature and poetry can reveal insights into roles, rights, and the interplay of the system of honor.

Saira Shah, author of *The Storyteller's Daughter* and producer of the documentary *Behind the Veil*, expressed the importance of stories as a special window to understanding Afghanistan:

> Experiences follow patterns, which repeat themselves again and again. In our tradition, stories can help you recognize the shape of an experience, to make sense of and to deal with it…. What you may take for mere snippets of myth and legend encapsulate what you need to know to guide you on your way anywhere among Afghans.[1]

Afghan literature, in particular the short stories of Akram Osman and the *landays*, or short poems, of Pashtun women, offers insight into the family as a social institution and presents a creative interpretation of cultural and social realities.[2]

Akram Osman's story, "Real Men Keep Their Word," uses the term *marda ra qawl* to refer to men of honor who keep their word, a virtue in traditional Afghan culture.[3] The term *ghayrat* from Chapter 2, building on the system of honor to explain "the right to defend one's property and honor by force," also fits this purpose.[4]

Many Afghan expressions exist to depict the state of a man without work, and by extension, without honor. Control of resources is often couched in the language of honor and shame. If men cannot meet those expectations, they report the loss of a sense of integrity and worth causing them great dishonor, or *be-gharyat-i*.[5] In the story "From the Root of a Shrub," a character explains that "a man without a job either fools around or becomes sick," emphasizing need for a man to have work as way to define himself.[6]

It follows then, that lack of honor also means dependence on external aid and "Westernization." In "The Deceptive Object" (1971), one who eats bread without shame "refers to someone who can work but does not work, and eats and lives off others."[7] This sentiment has been expressed by men who feel a growing dependency on international aid, coupled with

Men in Istalif, a town famous for pottery, Parwan.

an inability to achieve self-sufficiency due to lack of opportunity. In "The Brains of the Family," the protagonist laments because "the atmosphere in [his] home became so Westernized that he felt [he] lost his honour, his dark, heavy dignified moustache seemed soiled."[8]

Political leaders such as former president Muhammad Daud Khan linked honor to Afghan sovereignty. Daud, who served between 1973 and 1978 and led a coup against Afghanistan's last king, is also well known for his political poem using the eagle as a "symbol of freedom and indifference towards the dictates and politics of either the West or East."[9] The poem urged Afghans to be "free like eagles," to retain their dignity, and to stop their pleas for assistance from foreign powers.[10] Many stories during the period of Soviet occupation (1979–1989) referred to the tensions, and contradictions, between Afghan and Western ideas.[11]

The *landay* also offers insight to the prominence of honor in Afghan culture. A *landay*—literally meaning "the short one" in Pashto—is a brief poem of two verse lines of nine and 13 syllables, respectively. *Landays* are traditionally written by Pashtun women, meaning that they play a role in dictating Afghan values—through the words of women. These poems are often used to punctuate conversations, to add support or legitimize ideas.[12] As a result, they provide unique insight into the values—and tensions—in Afghan society.[13]

Landays can also be viewed as an act of resistance because they glorify themes that "taste of blood": love, honor, and death.[14] Of these three, emphasis rests on honor, and by extension, the importance of adhering to traditional gender roles, particularly the role of men as protectors of the family and defenders of this honor. These *landays* use battle as a metaphor to represent honor lost or gained:

> May you be found cut to pieces by a trenchant sword,
> But may news of your dishonor never reach my ears![15]
> May you be blackened by gunpowder and dyed in blood;
> But may you not return from the battlefield and in disgrace.[16]
> It is well that you are wounded in battle, my love!
> Now I shall walk proudly.[17]

Mamus Throughout History

Building from the *landays*, we can further explore these values and their impact on women and men in Afghan society. Ultimately, there are no shortcuts to understanding this rich and diverse country, but analyzing these stories, and by extension the voices of Afghan women and men, gives us a good starting point.

Prevalent throughout Afghan literature—and therefore culture and society—is a principle known as *Mamus*. *Mamus* is defined as men's duty to protect and respect women. In this sense it links *nang* (honor) and *namoos* (pride) and can be used to explain gender roles and relations in Afghanistan throughout history. And therefore, *ghayrat,* the principle of honor, is what fuels acts of resistance.

According to an authority on Afghanistan:

> The primary scarce resources remain land, water, livestock, and, in a very real but obviously different sense, women. All four are vital, easily lost, and endlessly troublesome.... It is women, however, who are widely considered the most volatile cause for serious dispute.... With their sexuality generally considered unmanageable, women are secluded as much as possible from all but the narrowest circle of family males. Here they serve as the primal embodiments of masculine honor. A man may suffer the loss of material property and still keep the core of his self-respect intact. Mere suspicion, on the other hand, of illicit access to his women requires an overt response: immediate and extreme.[18]

During my years in Afghanistan, I set out to better understand this resistance in order to support the design of interventions that would be better for Afghan women. I spoke to a range of men and women across different ages, ethnicities, and levels of education. *How did they feel about gender roles and relations in different periods of history? Was it better "before"?*

What might history tell us about today's occupation of Afghanistan?

Women and men agreed that the period before the 1979 Soviet occupation was good for both. They expressed feelings of satisfaction, and a sense that life was "balanced." Most important, women felt that progress was being made toward equality. Even men agreed to this. According to those I spoke to, it was a period characterized by harmony. Everyone seemed to understand "their place," whether that place was progressive or not.

Many men expressed that everyone was generally content and described it as a period of "respect, friendship and love." One man articulated that "both

A woman in traditional clothes for a celebration, Kabul.

men and women had a good position before the war. They were able to come out of their houses and work safely and live to their potential." Another agreed, elaborating that "women could work with men shoulder to shoulder and they could take advantage of their new freedoms." Another man added: "Men and women coordinated with each other and they were solving their problems easily and helping each other in every way."

Some were more critical. One man put it this way: "Women didn't know much about their rights and were satisfied with what men expected from them." A few women noted that this period was more contentious and that "women were beginning to fight for rights, but men were resisting changes." One woman complained: "Women were trying to be equal. People say that there was equality, but I think it was not there and it could not have remained without much resistance."

The period of civil conflict and the first Taliban occupation in Afghanistan (1989–2001) was easier to define. There was general agreement that roles and relations suffered and any progress was undone by the conflict and ensuing violence. They recognized that conflict introduced circumstances that altered gender dynamics, usually to the detriment of women. On the one hand, conflicts can amplify pre-existing vulnerabilities, making women and girls worse off than they were before. However, conflict can also bring opportunities for activism and advancement.

Some of those I spoke with believed that men and women suffered equally, while others—mostly women—believed that the various conflicts affected women more than men. One man explained that "positions were very bad because women and men were living in very deep sorrow because they were put in war unwillingly." Another man put it this way: "During that time there was no difference to be a man or woman—both of them were punished the same." One woman agreed, saying that "things were very bad for women, and even for men." It was generally agreed that the period of conflict destroyed any progress that had been achieved in Afghanistan, particularly in terms of gender roles and relations.

One man explained it this way: "All people were unsheltered, displaced to different parts of the world, and their love changed to violence." Another man reinforced this point, explaining that "during the war, relations between men and women were destroyed because of ignorance and poverty, and instead violence and tortures started."

A few people, both women and men, felt that women suffered more during the conflict. Women stated that "there was much cruelty on women," adding that war stopped all progress between men and women and "women's lives became a prison." Another woman held the view that "all groups took their anger out on women." A man agreed, stating that "women suffered a lot more than men." Another man articulated that women's position deteriorated because "they were living in violence and struggling to survive, and men were oppressing women."

One man explained that during the period of conflict "women didn't have any relations with men, and women were not able to go out and work because they were afraid." And another recognized that women had to take on additional responsibilities, stating that "all women were in search of shelter and protection since male responsibilities came to them because of war." Only one man expressed a preference for women's behavior during the conflict, because "women were more safe under the *bourka*—not like today."

Responses were mixed on the question of gender roles and relations during the period from 2001 until 2021. One woman complained: "Now we are in a situation that we were in before, fighting for rights and men not wanting to give them." Another said: "Only God knows how women will be." And yet another woman reinforced this point: "Today I am not sure which way things will go. Women are struggling for their rights, but that does not mean they will succeed." A man put it this way: "Conditions of the country have a big effect on gender relations. I do not think changing roles and relations is a good thing. In Afghanistan today, destruction is easy, but building is difficult." Only one woman expressed a small sense of optimism amidst frustration: "Laws are now equal for men and women, but we have to realize these laws in our lives."

An Afghan woman leader confirmed this in 2021:

Even today women are struggling for their rights. Only a minority of women may have experienced change in the past two decades. This change was only possible as a direct effect of security in the country and the fact that some restrictions were lifted and men had a little sense of security so they could allow women have the right to be out and free. Even that had a limitation, women still need a man to travel specially outside of Kabul. A woman does not have freedom to live alone and be independent.

For the period after 2001, women generally believed that men sought to cling to power and were resisting change. One woman summed it up:

Women were free in the early days and men were learning to accept women as equals. During the war, both men and women fought for freedom, but war put men in charge again. And now we are told to believe that there is freedom, but men are still wanting to be in charge.

Some men also expressed optimism and saw that change can be positive, although these were the minority. The narratives of two men below illustrate the ambiguity they felt in the years following 2001.

Abdul Ali

Before the war, everyone understood their role. Both men and women wanted, and sought, love between them. Before the war, very few women were in government. Although they were not in the public eye and did not have impact on men, they were content. They did not have violence. During the conflict, violence increased. Not just between men and women, but also homelessness, bad economy, other things. All of this caused corruption. Men and women lost their position. Women had no impact. Violence against them increased. Men didn't have good relations with women. Everyone was lost in his work and grief. After the peace agreement, roles [of women and men] were expected to get better. Contact between men and women increased but we can't see dramatic changes in relations.

Enayat

Before the war, there was not any discussion of rights, but still women's position was getting better day by day. Their relations were good. Both were living with respect and love. Life was good. There was an understanding that men and women's position had to be different. During the war, men's position was good but women's was not, because war converted their ideas completely and their previous ideas were ruined. Their relations were not good because war again had its bad effects. Weak economy and displacement drove them to violence. Now we hope for a better future. We are looking forward to a day when, like before, man and woman will both have a significant place in the society within their traditional positions.

Even though some men recognized change could be possible and positive, the majority of men interviewed were not happy with changes "under the influence of the international community." What's worse, they felt that women were stepping out of their prescribed role and were encouraged by the international community to do so. As a result, many men felt that they were losing their place, as this young man articulated:

During war time, women lost their rights, and their roles in the society, lost their dignity. After peace was built, democracy has given rights to the women which are not part of Islamic rules. And now sometimes violence is coming again.

This sentiment was reinforced by another man who explained that "there must be a difference between man and woman. Woman has her place and man has his."

One woman explained that gender relations have changed throughout Afghan history, but that this particular change was different because women are "protected objects." She shared her perspective:

I think that relations between men and women change because in different periods, the lifestyles of people were different. During the war, men had learned to be the cruel lords and force women to do whatever they liked because the government was supporting them to do so. But now men can't do anything because everyone supports women instead.

I recall a conversation I had with three Afghan men. Alam was a young Pashtun male. When asked about the role of women in Afghanistan, he became visibly uncomfortable but said: "my wife is not working. If she said she wanted to work, it would not be allowed according to tribal regulations. It is this way. I cannot explain it." Alam's wife wore the *chaddari*. He emphasized that this is an important part of the Pashtun tradition.

Aman was in his mid–20s, a Tajik. He worked as a driver and said his wife didn't work but if she did, he would allow it, at which the other men laughed because he did not answer honestly. Ahmadi was a slightly older Hazara man who emphasized the role of religion in Afghanistan and said, "we are Muslim so we respect that. And also the customs of Afghanistan are important to us…. If an elder says that my wife must do something, she must do it." Ahmadi told me the Dari saying "the second mother is our country," meaning Afghans value women in their roles as mothers and wives.

Despite being from different ethnic groups, the men shared the same opinions regarding women and traditional roles. Their wives did not work, and none of them felt that they necessarily had any trouble at home. They agreed that they had unquestioned authority because they are male, and that they were fulfilling their traditional obligations under that role.

"I hope it will get better in the future," Ahmadi said. At that point, it was difficult to predict that the Taliban would return and that things might not exactly "get better in the future."

Dishonor Is Worse Than Death

There has always been a strong link between women's rights and the fate of the nation both in Afghan literature and society. In the same way that men are assigned the role of provider and defender, women become the nation itself—an ideal to be protected. The weight of Afghanistan's honor rests squarely on women's shoulders. As a result, external reforms of gender relations have been met with resistance and are denounced by opponents as un–Islamic, a challenge to faith and family.[19]

To delve deeper, I spoke with a group of only Pashtun women to better understand the concerns of this traditionally-conservative ethnic group. Pashtun women are traditionally bound by the *Pashtunwali,* the unwritten legal cornerstone of their population. In this code, women play a symbolic role as the core of the society and therefore must be protected. The honor of the Pashtuns is therefore intimately linked with—and often entirely dependent on—women's honor. This results in circumscribed movements for women and limited, if any, contact with men. This restriction, known as *purdah,* sets clearly defined rules for women's interactions outside the domestic sphere.[20]

The penalty of transgression of this unwritten code is worse than death: it is dishonor.[21] And death is the only viable alternative to loss of honor. Afghanistan's other ethnic groups have, at varying times throughout history, adopted measures that stem from the *Pashtunwali.* Inaccurate and facile analyses have been made connecting women's oppression to Islamic practices. However, contrary to common understandings of the role of women in Muslim contexts, norms governing women in Afghanistan are based more closely on tribal codes such as the *Pashtunwali.*

The women in this group did express what might be labeled as more conservative ideas and spent the bulk of the conversation discussing the importance of religion and the concepts of *ma'sulyat* and *namoos,* elaborated below. Although this finding might conform to the stereotype of the conservative Pashtun, the label "conservative" is fluid, and relative,

A man sits by a lake, Bamiyan.

depending on who is in power at the time. It is worth noting that while the Taliban are Pashtun, they fuse aspects of their ethnicity with their fundamentalist interpretation of religion to form their own unique brand. Therefore, it is safe to assume that the resurgence of the Taliban in 2021 will adopt a more conservative approach in line with these codes.

Ma'sulyat can be translated as responsibility in Dari, but has much deeper meanings. It refers to a responsibility to abide by codes of honor, including men's control over the honor of women. Women refer to *ma'sulyat* in discussions of men's honor, and their responsibility in safeguarding it. *Ma'sulyat* reflects their understanding of their role and the risks that betraying it may entail.

Namoos (pride) refers to the chastity of women, and implies the duty of men to protect and respect women. The term also refers to men's pride in safeguarding women's chastity. The women explained that they run risks of losing their chastity, or the *perception* that they have lost their chastity, when they are more exposed to the public because they have assumed traditionally male roles.

In Afghanistan, the worst insult for an Afghan man is to call his women *bey-namoos*, without chastity. This distinction reflects the Afghan tradition of strong divisions between the public and private sphere. *Namoos* can also be defined as shame. The term is used by men to exert control over women. It is also used by women to instill fear in other women and to delineate the boundaries of their role. The women used these terms to explain the risks they take in participating in aid programs and the desire they have to not step over these lines.

For these women, the lines are clear: they preferred to remain largely within traditional roles. The context of Islam and its view of gender roles was a frequent reference point. Pashtun women generally viewed their roles as first within the household, with their children. Family is indeed a prominent institution in Afghanistan, and motherhood the preferred role for Afghan women. Since Afghan women view themselves as embedded within the family and society, it should be Afghan society as a whole—not isolated segments—that need to debate human rights in their contexts.[22]

Paradoxically, women found much greater freedom to maneuver when they remained within the confines of these traditional roles. In fact, the women explained that they ran the risk of being further restricted if they tried to assume overly public lives as this negatively affected the public face of the family. More traditional Afghan men believed that work outside the home strips women of their dignity—thereby negatively affecting men's reputations.

These Pashtun women, not unlike other women around the country, preferred that their men were responsible for working, providing for the household, and controlling the domestic resources. Women were conscious of the fact that they could bring shame on the family by assuming this traditionally-male responsibility, becoming like a man or literally, *nar-shedza*, a "man-woman."

Research across history in Afghanistan reveals that when aid organizations showed a distinct preference for women's employment, many men felt diminished, "adding further to male sensitivities about their patriarchal prerogatives." In short, a man with honor provides for his family. A man without work has no honor. When women become the primary breadwinner, and men are dependent on them for survival, the resulting role reversal prompts relationship renegotiations that were often met with tension.[23]

This tension stemmed from an insult to honor and a challenge to a man's "ability to manage and defend his chattel," as it was explained to me. To Afghans, "there are more important things than family or possessions, even than life"—honor.[24]

One woman put it this way: "We don't want men to be unemployed and without dignity. Their dignity will also bring us more freedom." Ultimately, these Pashtun women felt that they were put in a position to advocate for men's engagement as a primary necessity—as a foundation for which they could build their own freedom.

As it turned out, this was not unique to Pashtun women. An Afghan woman leader explained that husbands permitted their wives to participate in aid programs if there was money involved. These husbands would allow them to participate—or even escort them and wait outside. She continued:

> We used to run sessions where women had to attend the trainings and then receive the money. Some women would rush to get the money first and leave, saying their husbands were complaining and saying *If the program is offering aid then what is all the talking about!?* Or they would tell their women to just take the funds and leave, don't stay too long for the training or anything else. The trainers would then tell them that they had to stay if they wanted the money. Many husbands were not happy with this.

She explained that *namoos* came into the picture when women were kept away from home. It was a card to be played when it was convenient, "for show, for the neighbors, for the community," to ensure that "your woman remains within your control." "A man whose wife is in his control is a man with *namoos*."

Dar be Dar

Conversations with many Afghan men revealed that they were not content with the "occupation of the international community," as one said, in particular because aid organizations "did nothing" for them. As a result, he said, they were driven to existing *dar be dar*, or door to door. This Afghan expression describes a man whose circumstances are so desperate, he is forced into a door-to-door existence in order to survive.[25]

One woman explained that "organizations provide opportunities only for women ... so the women have to step out of the house in order for the family to survive." Men's recognition that they were now dependent on their wives for the economic survival of the family brought to light challenges about whose role it was to provide, and how to address the imbalance when this role was negated or denied.

Many men complained to their wives, but they also recognized that their wives were bringing home money, which many of them were receiving and subsequently doling out as they saw fit. One woman explained: "Women are allowed to work. Actually, there are *opportunities* for work. Allowing women to work is up to the husband. But if he cannot find work, he has no choice but to let his wife work." A man confirmed this and said "men were not open minded to let their women work outside but since the Americans came and insisted on this, women are outside. Men only accept so they can solve their economic problems." An Afghan saying expresses this well: "While the rich can afford honor, the poor must 'eat shame.'"[26]

Many Afghan men viewed women's employment as a reflection of their absolute poverty and destitution, an insult to their dignity, and a questioning of their ability to provide. One woman explained that "women get supported in such range that men are falling behind also in the job market, women earn much more and get easier jobs than men." This gets to the core of what it means to be a man in Afghanistan— and in most countries, in fact.

Afghan men articulated that they wanted to feel "as men" yet they were actively denied this because "organizations do not understand men's and

Children in Kabul.

women's place." Afghan women agreed with this view, feeling that the "special bravery of Afghan men" had been compromised, and they were now emasculated. "We don't want [our Afghan men] to stretch the hand of need to anyone in the world," one woman said. She went on to explain that the new "occupying force" has crippled Afghan men's ability to stand on their own.

Women articulated that they would enjoy greater freedom and feel more comfortable with the opportunities they have been given if men were also engaged and employed. "Men need these opportunities also," one young woman explained. "We want our men to have jobs also so that they can allow us to work." Another elaborated: "Men are not working, so women are also kept at home. If all men had wealth and jobs, they would not interfere with the women as much as they do."

The perception that men were neglected fueled greater sensitivity, one woman told me. Men "believe that these organizations train women to stand against the laws and their husbands. Of course this is not true. It is actually what men think."

Research, and Afghan history, has shown that "education and

employment of women at the expense of [men] will once again be perceived as a western ploy and resisted by men."[27] Many women articulated
that they were not comfortable with being in the public eye as they preferred to share opportunities and retain traditional parameters. However,
this did not seem possible because aid organizations single-mindedly pursued their own path, ignoring warnings by many Afghan women that they
faced great risks in taking on these new roles.

These women explained that they took advantage of existing opportunities because there were no opportunities for men to earn a living. Thus
circumstance—not choice—drove their decision. It was out of economic
necessity, rather than a quest for empowerment. In fact, they did not necessarily feel "empowered" by this responsibility, nor were they happy with
their new freedom.

An Afghan woman leader elaborated on this:

> I do not think NGOs for women are such a big help. If an organization comes
> to help men and brings them work and training, it will be better for them—and
> better for women. But we must wait a long time for men to change. Every man
> is old in his head ... [but] give them training and jobs, and then afterwards start
> talking to them about women.

Ultimately, most men were not opposed to changes, "as long as they
are not against what Afghans want." And yet, no one had asked them what
they want. They asked to be respected "as Afghans," within the context of
their culture and religion. When asked about his hope for the future, one
Afghan man said: "I am hoping to be optimistic, but men need some attention still. Changes are harder for them." Another woman reiterated the
same point, adding that "men feel that they have dark futures."

They Just Say, Not Do

Many of the men I spoke with noted that the international community
had promised dramatic life changes for women—"liberation," in fact—but
none of this had materialized. Expectations were raised, and commitments
were not delivered. And when it came to men, "nothing important was
done," one man told me. The work of these organizations is "just symbolic.
They just say, not do."

Many Afghan women activists explained that "talking gender and
doing women" actually undermined efforts towards equality: "It has created a big problem in Afghan society. Men were already sensitive to wom-
en's issues. And now international community is trying to talk about
women. These things will again make men sensitive."

Nuristani men greet the arrival of a helicopter of foreign visitors, Nuristan.

The perception that there was a hardline programmatic separation of men and women was a reflection of a Western-oriented individualistic approach rather than anything grounded in Afghan culture, I was told. In the words of one Afghan woman, the same rights should apply for women and men as human beings: "Do not try to separate them. People are trying to separate them." Reductionist analyses of women as "vulnerable individuals living in a vacuum may eventually isolate rather than reintegrate women."[28]

A dangerous outcome of this separation was that it fueled men's perception that "gender" was a negative word, synonymous with women's power *over* men. An Afghan man explained: "Most of the people, they think that gender is making women in power and decreasing the power of men. Women over men." This belief reinforces the view that rights is a zero-sum game, with men on the losing end. "These organizations, they have done nothing for men," one man told me, "hardly mentioned them. International organizations haven't paid attention to men's rights."

An Afghan woman leader put it this way:

[Gender] is considered as a weapon against men—which is totally against the concept of "gender issues" in the first place. Gender programs should be designed in order to reduce existing problems between men and women. Side effects should be prevented. The way gender issues are undertaken in Afghanistan now will not work. Because gender issues are introduced as women's issues, the whole gender thing is considered to be against the cultural and religious values of the country…. To stop and change the present concept of gender issues in Afghanistan, gender programs need to be transferred to both women and men equally. For successful implementation of gender programs in any country— Afghanistan or not—a few basic things should be considered: religious values, cultural values, social structure of society, level of education, and techniques for implementation. Obviously, a successful gender strategy in the United States cannot be successfully implemented in Afghanistan, and similarly a successful gender strategy in Afghanistan can't be successful in Iraq. And, most importantly, empowerment of both men and women cannot happen by outsiders. Men and women should be able to empower themselves to make choices and decisions. To reach this stage our society needs proper and successful gender programs within the framework of our religion and culture.

One Afghan man argued that "all women's activities … they just talk about democracy and women's rights without any clear vision for changing." Another elaborated: "In the area of importing or bringing foreign culture and tradition, international organizations have bad effect on Afghan women."

A shared sentiment among men was that aid organizations failed to understand Afghan culture "by disrespecting our role and religion," as one man explained. He continued to say that the international community had "unveiled our women, led them away from Islam." One young man expressed the views of many when he said "the world doesn't want a real Islamic regime in Afghanistan and also real Muslim men and women."

Another man added the following:

It can be like a pressure when most of the countries of the world came here and they wanted us to do something regarding women's rights. Before five years a woman was like a machine to work at home and have children. Now it is changing. Of course it takes time. We are not in Europe. This is Afghanistan. Maybe men will say there is equality because they know that this is what they are expected to say. But they know it is not true.

Both men and women attribute this in part due to the image the world has of them, with men constructed as the enemy, and women as victims needing to be saved from their own men by outsiders. The age-old trope of "white men saving brown women from brown men" that was introduced in Chapter 1 speaks to this sentiment.[29]

An Afghan woman explained: "The world thinks that Afghan women need their help and they need to be saved from Afghan men." This might be true for those who subscribe to conservative or fundamentalist ideologies, but her emphasis was on those men who do not.

An Afghan man elaborated that "most people in other countries believe that Afghan men are the ones who have taken the women's rights from them." He added that "they think Afghan man doesn't value Afghan woman, that man doesn't know her as a human." Meanwhile, he continued, it is the world that "looks down upon Afghan women, as if they are oppressed and helpless."

Afghan women further articulated that the juxtaposition of "civilized American men to barbaric Afghan men" was based on the view that Afghan women were mistreated by their own men. As a result, "American men assume the role of the global protector of women, and by extension, civilization."[30]

Another Afghan man explained that the world must have had a bad image of Afghanistan, otherwise their freedoms would not be under foreign control. "They only know Afghan man as a tyrant, extremist, and supporter of terrorism and war but they support woman, peace and construction." A woman added that if the image the world had of Afghans was good, "we would not have so many foreigners coming to say they are helping us."

Facile analyses of women as victims and men as perpetrators serve only to alienate those men who are supporters and who could be mobilized for women's participation. This overly-simplistic image was used, as they explained to me, to justify the design of aid programs that artificially separated women and men, even in cases where they wanted to work together to rebuild the country.

This was reinforced by a young Afghan woman who told me that the high profile placed on women "disrupted the social dynamic in the house." I asked her to explain further. "Everything was coming for her and not for him," she said. And when an outside organization comes in, she continued, and "you don't know how things work in Afghanistan, how Afghans think, and you put women on one side and men on the other side, like cattle. And you distribute benefits unequally, that's not a very smart thing to do."

One man elaborated that "pushing hard for change that is fast and big is not sensible." This pressure has not given room for Afghanistan to advance at its own pace and to foster change that is sustainable. Reductionist labels such as "backwards" erroneously referred to the perhaps slower pace of change that Afghans desired when compared to fast-paced aid interventions.

As a result, many women I worked with and spoke to told me that men were becoming increasingly frustrated as they continued to feel denied the traditional role of provider in the family. They are "more aggressive and angry to women because organizations do not give them any attention," one woman explained to me. Women preferred that men be engaged in aid efforts alongside women, with an emphasis on families—not individuals.

Experts and activists alike cautioned about the shaky foundations on which international aid was laid. If we wanted to better serve women, they argued, we needed to listen to what they were telling us. Ultimately, the perception that men were being excluded put women in danger of violent backlash.[31]

"Be careful not to provoke a backlash," one Afghan activist lamented. "There are examples of this in Afghan history." She argued to instead let the message slowly come from Afghan women themselves, not the international community. She explained that empowering women while ignoring men will cause a backlash—and will bring intimate partner violence. "The more disempowered men feel," she said, "the more resistant they will be to change."

Men expressed concerns that aid organizations were encouraging women to "speak out against their husbands" and therefore deliberately disrupting the established household hierarchy. "Most men are not very satisfied with the organizations," a man explained, "they feel that these organizations are interfering in family issues." Another man felt that "organizations are creating distance between men and women by encouraging women negatively." One man put it this way: "As UN urges, women fight with their husbands for their rights. This is not correct."[32]

An Afghan woman leader (SR) spoke to me (LA) about these tensions:

SR: There are rumors about NGOs being not fair to men.
LA: Why the rumors?
SR: I know a woman whose husband is jobless, he will be trying to find job. He didn't like at first that his women go out at all, but later he had to let his wife join the training.
LA: Because it was the only source of money?
SR: Yes, and from our culture and people's point of view it's considered a shame for the husband to sit and eat the money of the wife.
SR: Though the lady did not point at this issue at all because she was afraid. She is not being treated well because her husband is being more aggressive since he is not working.
LA: Are there more women like her?
SR: Yes. I think women will also not say the truth like that woman, because maybe [they are] afraid to lose the present opportunity of working.
LA: What is the solution?
SR: If there would be equal opportunity, that will be better.

There is a link between this aspect of male identity and resulting violent behavior. Women expressed concern that the lack of support for men has made them increasingly angry, with increased levels of violence as outcomes of this frustration. This is not unusual, in fact this is global. This is explored more fully in Chapter 6.

An aid worker said:

> In Afghanistan women advocated for men and their engagement so they can be protected—to protect themselves. That's their pathway to access any of the opportunities they were given. Afghan women have been living at risk for decades. The progress that has been made is greater awareness that they have rights and can demand rights. But they are so smart, so strategic, that they learned to navigate their wants through the men then slowly taking it in their own course.

Simply put, Afghan women balanced advocating for their own needs and playing by international rules to secure funding and support all while preventing a backlash from the men who had influence over their actions and futures. They were maneuvering to survive.

Help Us First by Trusting Us

Both this chapter and the previous remind us of a critical lesson: In Afghanistan, and anywhere, changes must come from within. Experience throughout the country has shown that "highlighting the boldest changes first or adopting adversarial stances can result in increased conflict."[33] Despite clear warnings from Afghan women themselves, many programs doggedly pursued the approach that warp-speed social change was possible. This provoked a backlash, often accompanied by a retreat to more conservative measures, with the result that *purdah* was more strictly enforced. The international community viewed the reinforcement of *purdah* as a manifestation of Islamic intolerance, rather than a reaction to their own interventions. It more likely signified an attempt to preserve the family—and its dignity—in the context of rapid change beyond their control.[34]

Many women and men counseled that such changes should be made slowly, with small steps. The Dari word *maida* describes this. In the central part of the country, however, *maida* can also be used to mean "broken." "Maida, maida," many Afghan women told me over the years. They wanted to be able to evolve at their own pace, to direct the changes for themselves, to navigate their relationships with their own men, to make gains in the contexts of family and community. These networks do not have to be destroyed in order to improve women's status—but they can be rearranged.[35] As long as women themselves are doing the rearranging.

Meanwhile, changes have not been *maida*. Afghan women have received inconsistent signals from above during the course of history: at one time enforced modernizations and at another a reversion to traditionalism, with little time to negotiate these opposing changes. Today, they have lost the clarity that comes with traditional roles, yet they lack the resources to seize so-called modern opportunities. Gender-focused messages are part of a series of political and social experiments in Afghanistan, granting women rights from above and then subsequently stripping them away. And yet, some women have gained strength through these vacillating initiatives, others as a result of economic necessity. Most Afghan women, however, cannot find their place amidst the new rhetoric that enforces yet another model for women to follow. Their voices were not heard, and these opportunities were lost.

An authority on Afghanistan confirmed these findings and added that "there have been reports that women themselves are not happy about having so much focus upon them, numerous women's projects, freedom from the *bourka*, etc. ... focusing on women is sometimes having a negative effect ... with women themselves feeling uncomfortable about this."

The polarizing of Afghan men and women lacked the nuance inherent in all societies. Had Afghan women engineered the approach, potential pitfalls could have been avoided. This is not to say that a backlash would have been completely averted, but who better to navigate the socio-cultural complexities than Afghan women themselves? Afghan women understood what was at risk from the very beginning. And how they might mitigate that risk.

For Afghan men, as they move beyond the business of warring, they find themselves lost in the new Afghanistan. There was an overarching sentiment that men have been neglected in aid interventions; both women and men shared this view. Those who were unable to find work were feeling threatened by the loss of authority that came with their role as breadwinner. They were further diminished when women assumed this traditionally male role. Men's perceptions that they were neglected could result in a backlash for women and there was a concern that violence was increasing—privately at home and publicly in society.

One authority on Afghanistan put it this way: "The wound of abandonment runs deep in [men]. Afraid to be vulnerable, fiercely independent, they hide their wounds. This is the way they have coped with unspeakable hardship and loss."[36] Another added that we cannot ignore the suffering of men from decades of war, insecurity, and indoctrinated violence. Understanding these dynamics is essential both for women's well-being, and in the interests of men themselves. And there are implications for a society's security as well. She explained:

> In virtually every post-conflict country, the presence of large numbers of unemployed and unskilled men and boys poses a risk to stability. More will have to be done to ensure that Afghan men find constructive means of engagement and employment in society in order to prevent the alienation of men and subsequent backlashes to women's advancement.

Studies show that ignoring the needs of men and focusing exclusively on women's participation can create additional challenges such as male resistance, token female participation, and the continuation of male domination.[37] One expat aid worker explained that when you open doors for women, showing them another reality, if you don't also work with men, it is as if you "close the doors again and she goes back home and probably is less satisfied and less compliant than she was before."

Further, there is huge social pressure on Afghan men to conform to rigid stereotypes of masculinity, with little room to "discuss the positive and negative impact of tradition on their relations with women and girls." They lack both the space and the safety to come to terms with their evolving roles "as gendered beings trying to change gender relations."[38] An aid worker explained it this way:

> Raising a community out of survival mode and into economic stability will be of significant benefit to all members and will thus create a more conducive environment to address gender roles and relations. And more often than not, the community and family will address the subject without external interference!

Communities do address these subjects within their context and culture. This entails congruence with Islam and other social frameworks within which Afghans choose to operate. It is worth noting that an advocate for context is not necessarily an apologist for culture. Culture is one of many dynamic factors that can provide a better understanding of Afghanistan—and better interventions as a result. An understanding of culture might reveal that interventions should be cognizant of the images used and the resulting perceptions that emerge. The perception of an imposed Western agenda coupled with the image of Afghan women as downtrodden creatures beneath *chaddaris* did little to advance the cause of Afghan women, particularly in the context of the Western world's current climate of fear/fascination with women in Islam.

Locally-led approaches that center women and men are critical in order to change gender dynamics and foster sustainable change. The buy-in of powerful societal actors such as religious teachers, imams, and elders can be impactful because "men call on other men to make a change and say why it benefits them."[39] In the words of an Afghan woman NGO leader: "The best way to make gains is to convince men ... get their collaboration and cooperation, [and] any program will be successful." Otherwise, as women's rights activists have argued, they risk a backlash from conservative elements of Afghan society.

Afghanistan may be conservative, but, as one Afghan woman argued, "the stories that are never told are the stories where fathers go on protest when their daughter's schools are shut down, fathers who support their wives to go to work." She went on to say that black and white explanations do a disservice to the country and its people.[40]

No one I spoke with over the last two decades would dispute the focus on Afghan women, but it is women themselves who highlighted the suffering of Afghan men and called out the imbalance in attention. They noted that while the Western focus on Afghan "gender apartheid" centered on women, the role of men was ignored. Non-Taliban men, that is. Men who were—and once again, are—part of the Taliban continue to be a focus of attention. And yet many Afghan men remain opposed to Taliban ideologies. It is far too simplistic to juxtapose men as oppressors against women as victims. Progressive men in Afghanistan are actually a key part of the solution.

I learned from speaking with women that it was in their strategic interest to have men fulfill their provider roles, so that women could focus on their own advancements. The research I conducted in Afghanistan for my doctoral thesis was inspired precisely by the need to explore pathways to make gains for women. "Engaging men," one woman told me, "would give us the room we need to focus on our *own* liberation."

An aid worker elaborated:

> There has not been an overnight revolution, a shift from oppression to liberation. Change does not happen that fast. Also, women are savvy enough to know that the last times there were dramatic and sudden shifts toward a Western model the resultant backlash undid any gains made. There is no need for a revolution, rather for a gradual *evolution* towards more gender equality.

These conversations provide a window into Afghan culture as a pathway to future opportunities. This is an opportunity, in fact, to see Afghan women, and men, as they themselves would like to be seen. Ultimately, the fight for women's rights comes from within, but it can be supported or hindered by external interventions. And understanding how identities and understandings intersect is more than just an intellectual exercise, it is an insight into people's lives. We must know *who* we help before we know *how* to help them.

So where do we go from here? Where we should have started all along: by letting Afghans—Afghan women in particular—determine who they are, what they need, and what we should be doing to support them. "Let us bring it up if, when, and how we want … is it so hard to do that?" an Afghan woman asked me. "And hasn't history shown us," she continued, "that any rapid changes could result in a revolutionary reaction? Help us first by trusting us. We know exactly what we need and how to get it."

CHAPTER 4

Aid as Liberation?

Afghans prefer not to receive aid. We are proud and independent.
We do not easily beg. But now we are absolutely desperate.
We cannot feed our families. We are watching our own children die.
So what is our choice?[1]

Prior to the Taliban takeover and the U.S. withdrawal from Afghanistan in August 2021, approximately 80 percent of Afghanistan's budget was funded by the United States and other international donors.[2] Annually, this amounted to at least $8.6 billion in international aid. The United States alone contributed more than $144 billion to "reconstruction and related activities" in Afghanistan since January 2002.[3]

It may be shocking then, to find a September 2021 UN report warning that "97% of Afghans could sink below the poverty line by 2022."[4] What has 20 years of international aid done for Afghanistan? And how could a country that has received 30 percent of the total U.S. foreign aid budget in economic assistance be positioned to backslide on almost every political, economic and social indicator on "progress" outlined for Afghanistan by the international community?[5]

Numbers obviously do not and cannot tell the whole story of aid in Afghanistan. That is because, despite its claims to the contrary, aid is political. Politics is about the distribution of power—resources and influence—and understanding who gets what, when, and how.[6] But aid interventions are not equipped to address political concerns, even as they make claims to transform and "liberate." Very often, the rhetoric is political, but the implementation is technical—standardized aid packages that are neatly placed from one country to the next. Unfortunately, the situation is never this neat. How, then, do we tell the story of aid to Afghanistan? We can measure what aid organizations *say* and against what they actually *do*. More important is to measure the perceptions and experiences of the people who are on the receiving end of that aid: the same stories that are peppered throughout this book. Using such stories, this chapter will examine some of the major international aid milestones in the last two decades to explain how this approach undermined Afghan women's agency and ultimately undercut Afghan abilities to control their own "development." Worse, women—the most targeted beneficiaries of this international aid—ended up the biggest losers, regardless of how much *gender equality* and *women's rights* were infused into Afghanistan's aid architecture from the beginning.

Following the Money

Measuring the money is one way to compare rhetoric to reality when it comes to international commitments. Money is not easy to track, however, and very often donors themselves cannot account for how much was spent, or where it actually went.

Since 2001, Afghanistan has been the largest recipient of U.S. foreign aid, with $4.89 billion spent in foreign assistance in 2019 alone.[7] Figures are inconsistent, but over the course of 20 years it is estimated that the United States has spent up to $800 million specifically for women's rights in Afghanistan.[8] This is not exclusively a critique of U.S. donor assistance, however. But throughout these two decades, the United States was the leader of both the aid and military operations in the country, and also the loudest voice in the room when it came to women's rights.

U.S. politicians repeatedly pledged that securing women's rights was a central goal of their operations in Afghanistan, and yet this sum represents only .54 percent of $144 billion spent on "reconstruction efforts" between June 2002 and April 2021.[9] That number looks even smaller when compared to the total cost of the war, which some experts place between $934 and $978 billion.[10]

Given the proportion of total aid allocated directly to women's rights programs, perhaps we should not be surprised by the marginal gains on this agenda since 2001. And less surprised even, when reports have repeatedly found that much of this reconstruction money was stolen, wasted, or failed to address the problem it was meant to fix.[11] In fact, the United States, by its own admission, does not know exactly how much it has spent on this mission of "improving the plight of Afghan women."[12] As one Afghan woman leader told me:

> It seemed like there was money everywhere for women. People talking about women's rights. Projects being launched. International agency logos everywhere. Everyone advertised their work for women. I had an organization for women, working in the provinces with women and communities. When we heard of all this money, and all this work, we tried to find some to expand our work and reach even more women. You ask me where the money went? Not to me. I never saw it.

A man with an Afghan flag greets the arrival of foreigners, Nuristan.

Similarly, another Afghan woman leader who ran an organization in the country explained that there was limited funding, and it helped "to an extent." "But," she added, "it was not enough to change women's lives meaningfully or permanently. It was … limited."

Even the Feminist Majority Foundation called this out, noting that rhetoric simply did not match reality when it came to programs and funding for women's rights. In 2003, the Bush Administration was graded "B" for rhetoric and "F" for reality on the Global Women's Issues Scorecard due to high levels of insecurity and low levels of funding to women.[13] The following year, the U.S. president received a "C" for rhetoric and yet another "F" for reality, calling it a "lost opportunity" and a failure to provide security for women. The Administration was accused of mismanaging the situation and "injuring women's rights" by giving too much power to warlords to provide security—the very warlords who were oppressing women.[14]

The fight for "the rights and dignity of women," as former U.S. First Lady Laura Bush called it, was floundering. If accountability to women is measured in aid programs and aid funding, the picture presented was far from promising.

When Soviet-backed President Mohammad Najibullah began his term in 1987, Afghanistan was recovering from almost two decades of civil war.

Approximately one-third of Afghanistan's pre-war population of 15 million had been uprooted and scattered.[15] Eager to rebuild, President Najibullah authorized the operations of international organizations in Afghanistan in 1990,[16] largely to facilitate refugee returns.[17]

When the Taliban assumed power in 1996 following years of armed struggle and severe drought, they faced a choice: they could allow international agencies to continue their domestic operations, providing an influx of higher paying jobs and economic aid, or they could restrict the presence of these organizations and limit unwanted Western influence. For the first three years of their rule, international aid agencies were allowed to continue operations largely undisturbed, save for intermittent security threats. But in the fall of 1999, the UN Security Council passed two resolutions that seemed to sour the Taliban's good auspices: In October, UNSCR 1076 called for "an end to civilian casualties and the discrimination of women and other human rights abuses" and, more significantly, in November UNSCR 1267 froze the Taliban's funds and other financial resources, and limited any member state from providing financial support or assets to any territory under Taliban rule.[18] The policy was amended in December 2002 to allow for humanitarian exceptions, but continues to restrict aid to the new Taliban regime in 2021.[19] This resolution placed a chokehold on international support to Afghanistan during this period, further restricting aid activity.

Women's involvement with international aid was particularly limited under Taliban rule. Over the course of their six year reign, the Taliban produced an estimated 43 documents related to female employment.[20] The series of decrees, edicts and proposals were largely designed to limit female mobility and employment, culminating in the passage of Decree #8 in July 2000, which fully banned women from working in NGOs.[21] Enforcing this was difficult, but the Taliban arrested a U.S. aid worker for employing Afghan women only one day after the law passed, sending a strong signal to feminist allies and employers.[22] Some women elected to disobey Decree #8 and return to work, especially in cases when they were the sole breadwinners in the family and earning relatively high salaries from aid agencies.[23] In these instances, maintaining a salary not only mitigated high male unemployment and scarce resources, but also—in some cases—offered women increased leverage and rights within the family,[24] at least temporarily. This period in Afghanistan was characterized by being stuck between "a development crisis and a human rights crisis,"[25] and many organizations were forced to focus on doing whatever works rather than concerning themselves with women's rights.[26]

The landscape changed again when virtually all international staff were relocated to Pakistan fearing retaliatory attacks after September 11,

2001. The leadership of ongoing aid projects was transferred to Afghan employees. Even UN agencies moved their headquarters out of Kabul, leaving Afghanistan's domestic aid infrastructure more anemic than ever. In the weeks following September 11, Taliban militias raided UN agencies in Afghanistan and warned staff that "if they used [any office equipment] they will face execution."[27]

From Bonn to London

Thus, by the time U.S. president Bush announced "Operation Enduring Freedom" on October 7, 2001, and the first disbursement of $18.1 million in U.S. aid arrived on October 26, 2001,[28] Afghanistan's domestic aid infrastructure had been reduced to a fragile two-tiered structure: with UN agencies and Western NGOs receiving international aid and disbursing it through Afghan partners on the ground, and the U.S. military developing its own aid delivery systems in response to the perceived shortage of operational NGO capacity.[29] In both tracks, foreign diplomats and military officials were positioned to drive the aid agenda, rather than Afghan nationals. This initial distribution of power laid the foundation for Afghanistan's aid infrastructure over the next 20 years: international "experts" setting the agenda and designing donor-worthy programs, supported by Afghan nationals receiving strategy documents and charged with implementing projects on the ground.

In the first weeks of the U.S. invasion in Afghanistan, perhaps Afghans could afford to be hopeful about the influx of funding and new priorities centered on rights. In his first presidential address, President Bush announced that, "as we strike military targets, we'll also drop food, medicine and supplies to the starving and suffering men and women and children of Afghanistan." He then pledged $320 million in humanitarian assistance "to help the innocent people of Afghanistan deal with the coming winter."[30] And a November 2001 U.S. State Department report insisted that "the needs of women are given 'special consideration' in forthcoming aid packages."[31] While this may have sounded promising, the ambiguous language led to some confusion—and a conflation with the military mission. Understandable, when one is on the receiving end of dropped aid *and* dropped bombs.

An early example of such assistance came in the form of the Afghan Women and Children Relief Act of 2001, to provide funds for immunization, education, and "other assistance" targeting "vulnerable women and children."[32] The spokeswoman for the Revolutionary Association of the Women of Afghanistan (RAWA) urged caution and careful monitoring for

the Act to make an impact. "Uplift of women ... is directly linked to political stability," she said, urging the international community not to channel the funds through the government alone, or to leave Afghanistan at the
mercy of warlords. Both of these warnings would be ignored—repeatedly.
President Bush inaugurated the law by saying that "a liberated Afghanistan
must now be rebuilt ... [beginning] by ensuring the essential rights of all
Afghans."[33]

Also in December 2001, U.S. and UN representatives invited 25
Afghans to Bonn, Germany, for the first international conference to determine the future of Afghanistan. The resulting Bonn Agreement was the first
document outlining a timetable for Afghanistan's three-step transition into
a centralized, Western-style democracy. Since that time, there have been
more than a dozen international conferences to discuss strategic priorities and commit donor money to development programs in Afghanistan.
The restoration of human rights and women's rights have been a consistent
theme throughout. At least on paper.

The Bonn Agreement was the first document to codify an institutional commitment to human rights by calling for the establishment of the
Afghan Independent Human Rights Commission and the participation of
women in any future administration.[34] The inclusion of these provisions
signaled the international community's "good intentions" to insert human
rights and women's rights into their vision of Afghanistan's carefully crafted
future.[35] The document also included provisions for the participation of
women in the emergency *Loya Jirga*, Afghanistan's interim grand assembly.

The Bonn Agreement also established the Ministry of Women's Affairs,
the entity that proved to be the weakest link in Afghanistan's national
machinery—much touted but largely marginalized and under-funded. "If
internationals had wanted a strong women's ministry," one Afghan woman
leader told me, "they should have built a strong foundation. Why start it
only to leave it weak?"

To be clear, the Ministry's malnourishment was through no fault of its
own. It continued to be fueled by, and led by, strong women who were committed to bettering women's lives in the country. Champions of the Ministry argued that its existence had "symbolic value," could promote issues
important to women,[36] and helped to "keep the women's agenda alive in
domestic politics."[37] Skeptics doubted that symbolic value was enough, saying that the Ministry's activities had become "limited to token efforts such
as gift ceremonies and organizing International Women's Day," and that the
institution only existed to "appease the international community."[38]

Regardless of its function or dysfunction, resources allocated to the
Ministry were meager, accounting for only 1 percent of the total social
protection sector budget, or .05 percent of the total national budget as of

2016.[39] Even the first grant made in 2002 by United States Agency for International Development seemed cosmetic, offering $64,000 to rehabilitate the building complex in time for an International Women's Day Conference so that the ministry could "carry out ceremonial meetings."[40]

In the words of one Afghan woman leader, "money came at the beginning to the Ministry, there seemed to be a lot of it." But the Ministry's reach was small; it did not extend beyond Kabul. "They were supporting women's economy—training and jobs. This is important, of course, but they could have done much more."

In 2002, donors combined forces to establish the Afghanistan Reconstruction Trust Fund with the aim of coordinating aid to improve lives.[41] The Trust Fund was the "largest single source of funding" for the country, covering a large part of Afghanistan's national budget and, as of 2008, the implementation of Afghanistan's National Development Strategy.[42] The Fund also includes a Gender Working Group which was charged with mainstreaming gender with the recognition that women's empowerment was a fundamental, though increasingly challenging, space.

Following the meeting in Bonn, international donors convened in Tokyo in January 2002 and pledged $4.5 billion in development aid over two and a half years—a small sum when compared to international aid commitments in the Balkans, the Palestine and East Timor, which ranged from $200 to $300 per capita annually.[43] Comparable levels of aid would translate into an annual figure of at least $5 billion for Afghanistan—three times greater than the Tokyo pledges.[44]

More than 60 countries and 20 international organizations took part in the Afghanistan Recovery and Reconstruction Conference, reaffirming their commitment to the Bonn Process, its vision for restoring rights, and its particular commitment to women's rights.[45] The co-chairs' Summary of Conclusions "emphasized the centrality of restoring the rights and addressing the needs of women, who have been the prime victims of conflict and oppression." They added that "women's rights and gender issues should be fully reflected in the reconstruction process."

Another document emerged from the 2002 Tokyo Conference, the National Development Framework, the government's 12-point strategy for promoting growth, generating wealth and reducing poverty—the foundation for the country's development budget.[46] Women's rights received scant mention, with gender identified as a cross-cutting theme that "is critical for all our activities" rather than designating gender as a standalone program area alongside other development priorities like education or health.[47] Global experience has shown that more often than not, when gender is only "cross-cutting," it is crossed off.

Although women continued to be written into Afghanistan's national governing strategy, it was becoming evident that there was a gap between the international community's rhetoric and the socio-cultural realities that Afghan women experienced on the ground. Just one month after the international community finished making additions to the Development Framework, a U.S.-based rights organization published a report based on interviews with Afghans strongly criticizing the top-down nature of the reconstruction process. According to the May 2002 report, Afghan interviewees and aid workers reported "a wide gap between rhetorical commitments and real actions on the ground,"[48] and an international approach to reconstruction that "disregarded Afghan desires to prioritize human rights in actual practice."[49]

When the data was further disaggregated by urban and rural communities, it became clear that Afghanistan's urban population, likely more educated, or at least with more exposure to international rhetoric and aid priorities, thought more favorably of a peace and security agenda. They identified peace as a gateway to securing rights, while Afghanistan's rural respondents named access to food and education as their top concerns. It is possible that the variation in priorities was indicative of their exposure to a Western rights agenda, which if true, suggests that the specific *rhetoric* of rights did not originate from within, but rather was imported from abroad.

This sentiment was echoed by the former chair of Afghanistan's Independent Human Rights Commission, Shaharzad Akbar, who explained that "the language of rights does not feel native [to Afghanistan]. There is a sense that it is something that has been brought from the outside." Even as early as 2002, there were signals emerging that Afghans themselves were starting to feel a gap between the architecture and rhetoric of aid, and their own expertise and agency in shaping the process.

The creation of Provincial Reconstruction Teams in 2002 was yet another gap. Initiated by the U.S. government, these teams fused military and civilian personnel, charged with working across Afghanistan's provinces with local government and leadership. As the concept evolved, other countries took on leadership of these teams, creating confusion in mission and difference in funding.[50] There was never any agreement on if these teams were effective, and if "civilian reconstruction and aid organizations can work in coordination with the military."[51] One result, however, was that working at the sub-national level bypassed the Afghan central government, effectively undermining its efforts to govern the country.[52]

There were a number of national political milestones and international commitments that built upon the frameworks of the Bonn and Tokyo conferences. A new Constitution was adopted in January 2004 by the Afghan Constitutional *Loya Jirga,* enshrining women's rights and equality before the law. Yet human rights and women's rights organizations quickly noted fissures in the document where women's rights vanished.[53]

The Berlin Conference in March 2004 produced Securing Afghanistan's Future: Accomplishments and the Strategic Path Forward, a strategic exercise overseen by then-minister of finance Ashraf Ghani, alongside internal ministers and UN representatives.[54] This "path forward" renewed its commitment to gender issues, and strengthened the discourse to include more aggressive—and elusive—language[55]:

> The gender element is critical, given we are moving from gender apartheid to gender integration, addressing the capabilities of women in the culturally appropriate way requires special attention. However, as shown by the *Loya Jirga*, when women take on these roles they are accepted, the key is not to discuss the role of women in Afghanistan, but to create facts on the ground regarding integration and women's roles.[56]

A key initiative established in this period was the National Solidarity Program, an ambitious undertaking to support 5000 villages in Afghanistan. The $600 million program, funded by the World Bank and bilateral donors, and facilitated by eight national and 21 international NGOs, was the largest ongoing development effort in Afghanistan.[57] Modeled on the principles of community-driven development, this program was supposed to emphasize participatory planning and engagement by local community stakeholders. Since its inception, the Program has established 32,000 Community Development Councils across 361 districts in all of Afghanistan's 34 provinces and has financed nearly 65,000 development projects. However, looking beyond the numbers, a different story appears.[58]

Inaugurated in 2003, the program was specifically intended to "extend the administrative reach of the state, build representative institutions for local governance, and deliver critical services to the rural population."[59] Funding for this program continued, despite emerging reports indicating that the core governing structure, the Community Development Councils, had been relatively ineffective at "changing *de facto* village leadership structures" and that "creating new institutions in parallel to customary structures (*jirga*) may not have the desired effect."[60]

Afghan women quickly encountered barriers to their participation in the newly conceived Community Development Councils. For one, the benchmark for female participation in the Councils was out of sync with local customs, where women are generally restricted from activities outside the household and the threat of violence often limited women's ability to speak or participate freely.[61]

When asked to speak on the subject of women's participation in the Councils, one man said:

Our women are illiterate so they are not allowed to discuss anything.... How can
they become powerful? *Mullahs, sharia* and learned people all say that women
have no brains so we do not share anything with them.[62]

Reports found that the Program succeeded in engaging rural women
in community decision-making "on a modest scale," but was unclear if
these changes would be sustainable.[63] Inequalities at the community level
restrict women's leadership and decision-making and, "in spite of NSP's
commitment to equity; the vast and complex nature of NSP also presents
challenges in isolating these factors and measuring their effects on gender
equity."[64] Further, when women were "given" projects "as passive recipi-
ents," this did not necessarily lead to control over the outcome.[65]

In terms of changing perceptions of women's participation in politics
and local leadership—or even household decision-making—the impacts
were marginal.[66] Reducing constraints limiting female education and
employment were also limited.[67] Nonetheless, while these impacts were not
sustained beyond the duration of the project, reports state that any changes
in gender norms "do not fade."[68] One donor report stated that there should
be "more robust outcome data" in order to determine the benefit to communities, and "whether the decision-making structures established are
making substantive progress in supporting women's empowerment."[69]

More Pledges, More Promises

The London Conference, a 2006 meeting of 66 states and 15 international organizations, was chaired by former British prime minister Tony
Blair to produce a successor to the Bonn Agreement. Although the international community continued to renew its commitment to Afghanistan, the
meetings were always organized and chaired by international politicians
rather than Afghans themselves.

The document produced at this conference, The Afghanistan Compact, followed the same logic that had come to define Afghanistan's national
strategy documents in the first five years of the intervention: opening with
(1) restating a commitment to building "a stable and prosperous Afghanistan, with good governance and human rights protection for all under the
rule of law," continuing with (2) a rhetorical nod to "respecting the pluralistic culture, values and history of Afghanistan, based on Islam," and vaguely
stating that (3) men and women will have equal rights and responsibilities
under all programs. Although these priorities were guided by good intentions, the language lacked cultural context and the implementation lacked
local ownership.

Women wait in line to register for participation in an aid program for women, Logar.

The situation was aptly brought to light for me in a personal communication from an authority on Afghanistan in 2006:

> It is not good—I guess I expected that. What are we all doing with this money and effort? So much goodwill, so many words, but we seem singularly incapable of actually putting ideas and words into practice. We have lost the plot—we observe, commentate, wax lyrical, recommend—then what? Check again, write another report, tie ourselves into bureaucratic knots to make people accountable but sometimes this results in a kind of paralysis. We can't move forward without a radical rethink—or rather redo. As I am writing to you I am feeling so strongly about our failures. I of course include myself in this—but recognition is necessary before you can tackle anything.

At that point, Afghan hearts and minds were certainly not swayed by the paltry aid they received compared to other conflicts. Significant amounts of aid in the first years of post-conflict interventions have brought relative success in other countries. Immediately following their respective conflicts, Bosnia received $679 per capita, followed by Kosovo at $526 and East Timor at $233. According to studies, Afghanistan received a meager $57 per capita in 2006.[70] Other studies say that Afghans have received an even more dismal $42 per capita since 2002.[71]

Both allocations pale not only in comparison to other country allocations, but also in comparison to U.S. commitments under the 1948 Marshall
Plan, which allocated between $100 and $200 per inhabitant per year over a
period of several years, a cumulative total nearing $1000 per person.[72]

This allocation, when compared to other conflicts, contributed to
one ongoing narrative that reconstruction of the war-torn country was
attempted "on the cheap."[73] Through the conflict, the lack of resources
resulted in the sacrifice of long-term priorities to achieve short-term gains.
Malnourishment in the formative years of Afghanistan's reconstruction left
the state on shaky ground, with daunting development challenges and an
accelerating insurgency.[74]

Further studies suggest that Afghanistan was short-changed in its allocation of security forces. Compared to other conflicts since 1993, Afghanistan ranks lowest in terms of peacekeeper support per capita, with 5380
Afghans per peacekeeper in 2003, compared with one peacekeeper for 48
people in Kosovo.[75]

In terms of troop allocation, in 2001 there were 2500 foreign troops
in the country. In 2010, there were 130,500 (of which 90,000 were from the
United States). And in 2019 this figure dropped to 16,600 total troops.[76]
Although Afghan security forces increased, from 6000 in 2003 to 272,500
in 2019, they were ill-equipped to deal with the country's security challenges.[77] In fact, in 2015 the Afghan government controlled 72 percent of
the country, amounting to 70 percent of the population. At that time, 7
percent of the country was controlled by insurgents. In 2018, the situation
deteriorated. The government controlled 54 percent of the country—63
percent of the population—while the insurgents controlled 12 percent.
Thirty-four percent remained "contested."[78]

More important than troop numbers are people's perceptions of their
own safety. In 2006, 40 percent of Afghans surveyed feared for their personal safety. In 2019, this figure climbed to 75 percent.[79] These fears proved
true.

Aid malnourishment would contribute to two decades of sporadic
security, with vast parts of the country in perpetual insecurity. And it
would lead to a re-takeover of the country by the Taliban in 2021. Meanwhile, over the course of two decades, a series of high-profile aid programs
came under widespread criticism for their inefficiency, their exclusion of
Afghan leadership, and their marginalization of Afghan women.

The *Afghan Women Empowerment Act of 2006* presents another
example for a discussion of discourses animating gender interventions in
Afghanistan.[80] The Act, first introduced as the *Afghan Women Security and
Freedom Act* by U.S. senator Barbara Boxer in 2004, sought to authorize
$300 million per year in U.S. funding through 2007 and earmarked funds

for the Ministry of Women's Affairs, the Afghanistan Independent Human Rights Commission, and Afghan women's NGOs.[81] However, the bill was never signed into law. When Barbara Boxer spoke in support of the law, she argued that former Afghan president Karzai himself "admitted that we are falling short on the issue of Afghan women."[82]

The Act was problematic because it began with a denial of Afghan women's agency and assumed a moral imperative to act. It further insisted that funding should focus on the adherence "to international standards for women's rights and human rights" and included a commitment "to disseminate information throughout Afghanistan on the rights of women and on international standards for human rights."[83] Senator Boxer's work reached me through a small distribution list, along with the following preface from an Afghan woman leader: "I hope on the Afghan side this humanitarian money is spent wisely and efficiently in the right spots for the right reason."

The Afghanistan Compact also included a special endorsement for the National Action Plan for Women of Afghanistan (NAPWA) which would be implemented over the coming ten years, 2008–2018.[84] Overseen by the Ministry of Women's Affairs, the National Action Plan for Women included a set of 31 indicators of progress against gender equality goals, and then identified specific ministries and local government units to implement these high-level objectives. In the Ministry's own assessment, only eight of 31 indicators were rated as "achieved" in a 2018 retrospective report, citing "design failures, lack of capacity, political will, budget and an ambiguity of roles" as the headlines responsible for programmatic failures.[85] It also blamed government officials for assuming that the Women's Ministry alone was responsible for the Plan's implementation, a sentiment indicative of the broader issues of lack of coordination and national buy-in. Limited national ownership of an internationally-conceived *national* strategy served to undermine the Plan's potential and reduce its chance of success.

As the implementation of the Afghanistan Compact and its associated programs continued, international policymakers and donors convened for conferences in Rome (2007), Paris (2008)—where donors notably pledged another $15 billion in aid and then-president Hamid Karzai promised to fight government corruption[86]—Moscow (2009), The Hague (2009), and finally in London (2010) to revisit the Compact's goals. Throughout this time, donor funding continued to grow, peaking at $6.75 billion in annual donor commitments in 2011, although it is not clear how much actually reached intended programs in Afghanistan due to corruption, new emergencies, and a general lack of reliable monitoring and evaluation frameworks.[87] And it is even less clear how much actually reached women.

When the U.S. Congress authorized the creation of an office for the Special Inspector General for Afghanistan Reconstruction in 2008, they

committed $11 million to performing an audit of U.S. efforts in Afghani-
stan.[88] The documentation that has come out of this office provides some of
the most concrete data on U.S. shortcomings in Afghanistan. Meanwhile,
others warn that even these scathing and sobering reports present an insufficient picture.

In 2010, Afghanistan reported to the UN on its commitments in fulfilling the Convention on the Elimination of Discrimination Against
Women.[89] Successes included improvement in political participation, education, and health for women, in addition to reporting on women candidates and voters in the country's second parliamentary election. The report
stated that national and international commitments have been crucial to
secure women's achievements, and as the country moves towards peace, it
is vital that these achievements are sustained and women's rights are protected.[90] Meanwhile in 2011, it was reported that "donors spent $503 million
on health care, $256 million on education and $367 million on the 'unclas-
sified' category that includes gender."[91]

In 2013, the United States introduced Promote, "the world's biggest
program ever designed purely for female empowerment" and also "the largest single investment USAID has ever made in its history in the future of
women and girls anywhere in the world."[92] The $280 million program was
designed to help 75,000 Afghan women get jobs, promotions, apprentice-
ships and internships.[93]

Over its five-year duration, Promote's objectives were to strengthen
women's civil society participation, support their economic participation,
and increase their political positions and power.[94] Reports emerged calling
the program "poorly designed and oversold." Then–First Lady of Afghanistan
Rula Ghani was outspoken in her criticism, saying that most of the money
designated for the program was going to American contractors and administrative costs—not to Afghan women.[95] Eighteen percent of the $89 million
disbursed by 2018 was spent on the security costs of the contractors alone.

An understanding of "what happened" proved difficult to obtain.
Reports of results were altered to show positive outcomes. Feedback from
Afghans was compiled, and subsequently omitted, if it did not align with
the program's public face. For example, a large 2016 report omitted "more
than 90% of the people who were interviewed for the project,"[96] a number
that the Washington Post deduced only after twice suing Congress to disclose the full report.[97] Once the complete set of interviews finally became
public in 2019, a Washington Post journalist sifted through the reports that
captured the sentiments of several senior administration officials with
admissions ranging from "every data point was altered to present the best
possible picture" to "the American people were constantly lied to."[98]

"We can't find any good data that they're helping women," the Special

Inspector General for Afghanistan Reconstruction reported, citing the program as "Exhibit A in what's wrong with reconstruction in Afghanistan."[99] Even though USAID officials were celebrating the program's success, the watchdog group that investigated found no data, jobs, trainings, or otherwise to prove this.[100] In the end, $418 billion was spent, yet demonstrating concrete outcomes proved elusive, and Promote was retroactively regarded as less than successful.

These failures are more than just wasted money, they are wasted opportunities. The scarce resources meant that Afghan women's groups would have to compete with each other in order to access funding. With scant resources—or misguided resources—Afghan women have no choice but to sideline their own goals and fight for scraps.

In 2015, Afghanistan reported to the UN on its commitments to women.[101] Successes included increases in women in the armed service and police, as well as advancements in the country's economic empowerment program for women. And yet, security conditions were deteriorating, international interest waned, and funding for women's rights appeared elusive.

A 2017 independent review of the Afghanistan Reconstruction Trust Fund reported "generally slow but incremental progress" along with "a reversal of previous gains" for women. The review stated that gender mainstreaming "has often been weak and patchy" and that gender remains a "second-tier issue for government with little recognition of the fundamental role gender equality plays in building an effective and peaceful state."[102]

Meanwhile, the series of international conferences on Afghanistan continued: Bonn (2011) and London (2014) and Brussels (2016) and Geneva (2020). In Bonn, it was decided that Afghanistan's so-called Process of Transition would be completed by the end of 2014, ushering in Afghanistan's so-called Decade of Transformation (2015–2024), "in which Afghanistan would consolidate its sovereignty by strengthening a fully functioning, sustainable State in the service of its people."[103]

In the United States, as more condemnatory reports emerged and public support for the war in Afghanistan waned, the Obama Administration began to announce troop withdrawals, as well as reductions in funding. The first benchmark on troop withdrawals was set for December 2016, when President Obama promised to drawdown the U.S. presence in Afghanistan to 5500 troops by the end of his presidency.[104] The second benchmark came in January 2021, with President Trump's deadline to cut the presence of American troops in half.[105] Over two decades in Afghanistan, the U.S. Department of Defense spent a total of $837 billion on wargames.[106]

Overall aid efforts in Afghanistan were stymied by the security situation. As security deteriorated over the course of the war, few UN agencies or NGOs placed international staff on the ground. By 2018, humanitarian operations had deemed at least 120 out of Afghanistan's 421 districts to be "hard to reach areas."[107] In these districts, national staff were responsible for implementing internationally-funded aid programs, putting them on the frontline of security threats.

Afghan organizations continued to operate in these districts without security assistance and while dealing with drastic funding cuts. In these districts, women and children were disproportionately affected by insecurity, forcing them to resort to risky measures in order to survive and to support their families. Child labor, girl-child marriage, trafficking, and engagement in illicit business were strategies women were forced to resort to in order to mitigate the effects of increased insecurities.[108]

In 2019, the country once again reported on its commitments to women.[109] Lack of cooperation between ministries and the absence of funding for implementation were cited as major concerns. The report also listed "multiple challenges to the meaningful participation of women ... including patriarchal sensitivities, limited access to education, and the ongoing security and safety threat." The big issue at that time was the inclusion of women in peace negotiations with the Taliban. It was noted that the team was not "inclusive and comprehensive," meaning that "tensions and mistrust in the peace process will continue." Ultimately, the absence of women was "noticeable," with talks failing to "substantively include women."

Still Stuck Between a Development Crisis and a Human Rights Crisis...

As security continued to deteriorate and women's "concerns" continued to be sidelined, U.S. funding was also on the decline, shrinking by more than 85 percent from approximately $8.91 billion at the start of the Obama presidency to $1.03 billion by the end of Trump's term in 2020.[110]

In early 2020, Afghanistan submitted yet another update to the UN on its commitments, raising issues such as increased insecurity, participation in the peace process, inclusion in electoral process, violence against women, access to justice, and so on.[111] Efforts were hampered by lack of cooperation, lack of funding, and lack of accountability.

In mid–2020, Canada's evaluation of assistance to Afghanistan revealed that the Afghan government's priorities and strategies were "influenced by donor priorities at the expense of fully representing the Afghan population's true underlying needs and priorities."[112] What's more, it was noted that "Afghan women were not part of the decision-making process for national gender equality strategies" but rather their needs were determined "by the significantly male-dominated Afghanistan government."[113]

Finally, as part of recommended "learning," the evaluation urged that projects for women "need to be thought through to avoid backlashes and avoid unintended outcomes."[114]

An aid worker reinforced these findings and highlighted the tensions. "Our donor requires more immediate outputs and numbers," she explained, and although she knew the history of the country and understood the pace of social change, she said:

> I often feel that we have to push things a little bit to meet the requirements of our donor. That often means that our monitoring is at a very superficial level—so many women trained, so much money disbursed—and thus does not reflect any potential meaningful change that will continue after our program ends.

In November 2020, ministers from nearly 70 countries and representatives from humanitarian organizations pledged $12 billion in aid to Afghanistan over the next four years,[115] representing a 20 percent decline from the previous four years.[116] The United States pledged $600 million, half of it contingent on the progress of peace talks with the Taliban, with donors stressing that all parties must respect human rights in order to receive their continued monetary support.[117]

In February 2021, the Special Inspector General for Afghanistan Reconstruction issued a report titled *Support for Gender Equality: Lessons from the U.S. Experience in Afghanistan* focused solely on assessing the progress of U.S. efforts to support Afghan women and girls since 2002. Of the 24 gender-related programs that received U.S. funding over this time, the Inspector General reported that the programs displayed "serious shortcomings." Additionally, program design was "based on assumptions that proved to be ill-suited to the Afghan context and the challenges that women and girls faced," and that establishing a correlation between "program activities and related outcomes was not always possible."[118]

As these examples likely show, the story of aid to Afghanistan—and Afghan women in particular—has not been linear. Moreover, the funding committed has not necessarily reached those who need it. Money pledged doesn't usually equate to money disbursed, this is the first discrepancy. Further, money *on* Afghanistan is different from money *in* Afghanistan. Reports show that much of international funding actually leaves the country through "imports, expatriated profits of contractors, and outward remittances."[119] What's more, money disbursed to Afghanistan does not mean money disbursed *to Afghans*. And, worse, money to Afghans does not necessarily mean money *to Afghan women*. There are many discrepancies and disconnects as funding trickles down to women.

Donor funding can help or hinder women. Top-down approaches based on Western blueprints can "effectively [silence] Afghan women in whose name they are operating."[120] *Could donors have done better with their money?* Without a doubt. To start they could have addressed the actual needs of Afghan women, based strongly—solely—on their demands.[121] Afghan women leaders are plenty, as are strong feminist movements. Despite ample rhetoric to the contrary, Afghan women have not been in the lead of the very process that most strongly impacts their lives. Women's rights cannot be "fast-tracked toward swift transformation through external pressure and funding."[122] Rather it must be built by the women themselves with donor assistance in line with women's own priorities.

The following example of support for "women's projects" is one of many accounts of aid missing the mark for Afghan women.

Empowering Women, One Chicken at a Time

"Assistance to women was always a tiny trickle," explained Sippi Azarbaijani-Moghaddam,[123] "until some crisis shone a spotlight on the plight of a specific group and then large funds would be torpedoed in with little sustainable impact."[124]

One way to further understand the impact of aid interventions on Afghan women is to trace this funding. It does not present a complete picture, but it is one way to measure if the rhetoric of investing in women's rights matched the reality. Ultimately, as the story shows, the funding is impossible to track. What we do know is that there were many fissures through which aid to women fell.

In recent years, studies have documented that "gender programming" in Afghanistan is often handed down as "donor requirements," subsequently reduced to a checklist, without sufficient guidance, capacity, funding, or monitoring.[125] Meanwhile, the so-called localization agenda[126] gained prominence, arguing—vaguely—that there is a need to provide greater support and funding to "local" actors. Ironically, women's groups were minimally referenced in the original conception.[127] However, the point was clear: local actors know what they're doing. It is worth noting that this was only established as policy in 2016. "Localization" subsequently became a buzzword—one that was, in practice, as murky as all the others. Despite "localization," it remains very challenging to trace the exact amounts of funding to Afghan women's groups. Ultimately, the most important assessment of this support comes from Afghan women themselves.

However, there are several disconnects that can be traced. Aid to Afghan women perhaps was meager from the beginning because the bulk of funding was swallowed by the so-called "War on Terror." When we define

A woman waits for rope to be tied around her waist before she swims in Band-i-Amir, a lake believed to have healing powers, Bamiyan.

"security" as something to be delivered by armed forces, we automatically lose the alleged "hearts and minds" that needed to be won for the genuine realization of peace and human rights. In short, what we deliver only serves to placate a potentially hostile population.[128]

It has been argued that the true strategy in Afghanistan was that of military objectives under the guise of women's rights. In the words of an Afghan woman leader: "The U.S. government's loud and public promise that they will never again allow Afghan women to be forgotten has done damage. They still funded military operations much more than women's programs." And they risk doing so again.

In addressing insecurity as a purely military matter, we miss out on what is known as "human security," a people-centered focus built on freedom, rights, and dignity. In short, we miss out on women's security. And, we relegate women's issues to so-called "softer" concerns, to be handled *later*. The mythical *later* that fails to arrive.

An Afghan woman leader confirmed this and explained that international priorities, on paper, guided aid interventions which had little relevance to Afghan needs and their own priorities. She expressed the views of many:

The means of aid in Afghanistan, in particular under this fashionable word "gender," is totally focused on international policies and priorities. And these are more to show off to each other in the aid community than to help Afghans. Though most of the fuss has been made about women, even less has been given to them. And even less than that is focused on their needs. So those of us who have to do the work are left trying to sift through the talk and seeking out ways to use the little left in hand as efficiently as possible.

The United States spent somewhere between $459 million and $800 million on programs for women.[129] The figures are inconsistent. More important, audit reports were bleak:

> U.S. agencies struggled to track the extent of U.S. funding to support Afghan women and to measure the impact of programs, and that a failure to anticipate the Afghan cultural context undercut U.S. efforts to support women and girls.[130]

Paltry aid for women's issues was made worse by the knowledge that there was in fact money to spend. Money was disbursed "without reason … [in a] mindless rush to spend," all without adequate planning, or consultation with Afghan civil society.[131] For Afghan women's groups, this presents an opportunity lost. There was never enough money for women, it seemed, even as "women" allegedly helped justify the intervention in the first place.

Another way to understand the impact on aid is through the quality of its programming. The propensity of aid institutions to promote "'feel good,' gimmicky programs with very little analysis" have added little value to women's lives, merely making them present—but no more powerful.[132] To capitalize on the large amount of aid in Afghanistan during the early years, international organizations opted for quick-fix solutions—the road of least resistance. This reinforced women's traditional roles and did little to inspire transformation.

Many of the income generation projects of that time are a good example of this "road of least resistance," emphasizing traditional skills for women and focusing on low-paid, gender-stereotyped occupations. These initiatives and their corresponding trainings were too short, too small-scale, and too little profit-oriented. Income generation is critical, but these projects must be designed with a clear outcome in sight. "Chicken projects," as they were known, were *not* such projects. "It should be obvious from looking at the last twenty years in Afghanistan that six months' funding for a handicraft or chicken-rearing project purporting to transform gender relations is utterly useless."[133]

"Anytime you need to do something for women," an aid worker explained, "it was all about handicrafts and tailoring…. In a way it reinforced the social construction of women's roles … as if there is no other thing that women can do." The market in Kabul at that time was saturated with women tailors who were unable to find employment. "You cannot just have classes and pour in millions of dollars and then have the women go back home. There is no follow-up," an Afghan woman leader stated.

Income generation efforts did not take the time to ask women if they actually wanted to work—or if they were doing it because there was nothing available for men. "You have women who want to be employed," an aid worker explained, "and you have women who say they want their husbands to work instead. It is not always that women are being prevented from such things. It depends."

Chicken Street in Shar-i-now, where one finds carpets, lapis lazuli jewelry, and other Afghan handicrafts—but no chickens, Kabul.

In this case economic necessity proved stronger than other factors. Women claimed the "opportunity" to work, not out of a desire for empowerment, necessarily, but by striking a delicate balance between challenging stereotypes and establishing new gender norms while maintaining behavior that would retain their honor within the family and community.[134]

These types of programs were often created without consultation. "No one asked me if I thought I could feed my family by selling the eggs of a few chickens," one woman said. "I can tell you—I can't." Meanwhile, chicken projects continued. For instance, the Women's Poultry Project in Panjshir province was called "a giant leap forward for the women."[135]

Numbers were used to measure the success of income-generation projects for Afghan women. These indicators drove funding, and projects that achieved their numbers were touted as a success. Programs were designed on a whim, by organizations who constantly reset their priorities based on funding available. Implementers worked to please their donors, not the women they were helping. In a 2006 paper to highlight progress in

Afghanistan, one figure stood out: the training of more than 19,000 women in "improved poultry management."[136] I cannot help but wonder what has happened to these 19,000 women and their chickens now.

Ultimately, it is not about chickens or not, but rather about the market analysis needed to ensure that women are able to earn an income from whatever project they pursue. And that the projects are designed in a way that is meaningful and relevant to women, provided they themselves are designing the projects.

While feedback on the success of income generation projects was mixed, Afghan men expressed their dislike for the initiatives, particularly in their promises for dramatic changes for women. One man expressed the views of many, saying that "Afghan women should not be the clothes-washers of foreigners."[137] An Afghan woman echoed this: "After this much work has been done and promised to women, all women are doing is washing clothing in the offices and that is it."

Peace and Security, as Elusive as Ever

Another major example of missed funding opportunities for Afghan women can be found in the Women, Peace and Security Agenda. This Agenda, launched in 2000 under UN Security Council Resolution 1325, recognized women's critical and non-negotiable participation and leadership in all aspects of peace and security. Part of this Agenda entailed the agreement that countries would adopt a National Action Plan for implementation. These are intended to be robust plans that outline how a country might move from attaining women's meaningful participation in peace and security to achieving women's human security. As such, these Plans are critical, and provide ample opportunities to align donors around funding priorities. If donors wanted to help women in Afghanistan, they could do so through its National Action Plan.

Afghanistan's National Action Plan covered the period between 2008 and 2018. The Plan was envisioned to be all-encompassing, recognizing the importance of women's participation, helping overcome conflict, and creating opportunities—especially in leadership.[138] The Afghan government and the international community reiterated their commitment to the Plan and pledged to support the protection of women through national structures, including the Ministry of Women's Affairs and the Afghanistan Independent Human Rights Commission. In 2010,[139] and again in 2015,[140] commitments were made to increase women's representation in these institutions and across the civil service. Then in 2019, fresh commitments were made to fully engage women in the peace process and in negotiations with the Taliban.

When Afghanistan signed onto the Agenda, it was viewed as a major milestone and a strong affirmation for women's rights and their role in forming the future of their country. In retrospect, however, the reality was not so positive. Women continued to be marginalized at every level, there was a lack of representation of civil society groups and, most noticeably, women were absent from peace talks. The Plan was criticized for being largely symbolic, lacking substantial change, and not reflecting realities on the ground.[141] Moreover, the notable lack of funding, "compounded with the aggravated insecurity situation … hampered implementation and programming."[142]

In the initial adoption of the Plan, international donors built a structure that undermined Afghan women's ability to create their own change. To start, the Ministry of Foreign Affairs, not the Ministry of Women's Affairs, was charged with spearheading implementation, thereby failing to focus in the right direction, namely women's issues *within* Afghanistan. Donors focused heavily on UN agencies and civil society without pushing the government to play a meaningful role.[143]

The structure around the Plan was isolated and did not take a whole-of-government approach but rather was created as a "standalone policy," not integrated into pre-existing plans.[144] Funding, therefore, was also a separate issue and one that caused arguments and project delays. In 2014, there were disagreements about the state of the Plan, and an international consultant was brought in to finish the framework.

As a result of this international effort, the goal metrics that were tracked were easily quantifiable and sound-bite-worthy for donors: women's participation, gender-based violence, economic empowerment. Not to say that these issues are not important—they are critical. However, the influence of international views of Afghan women shaped the agenda and limited their ability to set their own vision.

At the community level, Afghan women's experiences had not changed, "demonstrating a clear breakdown in the NAP's ambition of driving widespread change to benefit all women."[145] Interviews with two donor-country representatives confirmed this, and yet they favored short-term indicators over those that would require long-term engagement, despite knowledge that the latter would be necessary to achieve meaningful change for women.[146] Donors preferred quick, easily digestible, easily quantifiable measures of improvement. Large institutions set the agenda, meaning that by the time aid reached the ground, the limitations and negative consequences were obvious, but the course had already been set. As a result, sustainable change was virtually unattainable.

International organizations were the gatekeepers because donors argued that they had the necessary capacity to respond to donor requirements and therefore are "better suited for serving as intermediaries for donors to disperse funds and manage implementation."[147] The age-old bias that "local organizations can't absorb the money because they don't have the capacity," as I was told on many occasions, still held weight. So international orga- nizations controlled the dollars, but they also controlled program design, meaning they decided if and how they might consult with Afghan women and women's groups. This widened the disconnect between high-level rhet- oric on women's rights and the lived experiences of the majority of Afghan women.

Community activities were relegated to local organizations, who were charged with implementing the Plan without control over the strategy and direction. Afghans viewed this as further evidence of outside intervention that was not aligned with their needs and priorities. In fact, local groups were funded precisely because they prioritized outside expectations over internal needs. National and international groups were put in a position to compete for funding. Some women's groups also found themselves hav- ing to force-fit some of their work into the Plan in order to secure funding. Research done in 2018 found that Afghan women had little to no awareness about the Plan, years into its implementation.[148]

The fragmentation of responsibilities among stakeholders, the ineffec- tive coordination between ministries, and the absence of funding presented significant challenges to implementation.[149] All this was compounded by deteriorating security. Clearly, security was—and is—a critical prerequisite for, and a major obstacle to, accessing aid. *Why then were security consider- ations not a fundamental part of the Plan?*

The plan failed to address disarmament and further failed to connect the proliferation of weapons with women's insecurity and violence against women. As of 2019, Afghanistan was among the top 15 countries in the world with the biggest increase in military expenditure and among the top 30 largest importers of arms.[150]

During this process, Afghanistan was characterized as being in a state of reconstruction and in its "Transformation Decade," which, ironically, left the "peace and security" plan without sufficient attention to *in*security.[151] This was particularly relevant in rural areas, where insecurity is the biggest impediment to accessing aid. The Plan's barometers of success did not take security into account. Meanwhile, the Taliban controlled a sizeable part of the country.[152]

In 2017, after two years of efforts towards implementation, a report[153] was written that read not unlike most other reports of that period. It began by (1) acknowledging successes since the involvement of the international community, followed by (2) explaining the mandate itself, and then (3) point- ing to the failures in design, and continued with (4) strategizing for greater advocacy and cooperation, and concluded with the requisite (5) affirming the historic and contemporary power of Afghan women. This is a common space Afghan women are forced into: middle-women between the priorities of the international community and the needs of their communities—and their own needs, most of all.

Officials maintained the Plan was inclusive, but many women's organizations disagreed. They referred to it as a "wishlist of many dreams," further arguing that it failed to include a diverse range of women leaders and women's organizations for "technical advice as well as more reliable updates about the realities on the ground in areas that are not accessible to government officials."[154] In addition, it created disconnects between other women-focused plans. For instance, the National Action Plan for the Women of Afghanistan created by the Ministry of Women's Affairs was not incorporated into the Women, Peace and Security National Action Plan, despite the fact that these plans were in the same country, and shared the same goal: empowering women.[155]

Ultimately, nothing tells the story of women's lack of engagement in all things "peace" and "security" like the absence of women from peace talks with the Taliban. In those moments, donors can wield political power to ensure that the very principles they claim to espouse are adhered to. The very pillars of the Agenda—the inclusion of women in peace talks, justice, reconciliation—were forgotten. Despite billions of dollars and two decades of rhetoric, women's rights were quickly gambled away once the so-called peace talks began.

So where does that leave Afghan women now? According to a 2020 report, no funding has been allocated by international donors for the Plan's implementation. There remains no agreed-upon financial mechanism.[156] As a result, there can be no effective implementation. The challenges that persisted will now likely worsen.

Poppy Is Better Than Potatoes

It is impossible to build a foundation for equality—or for peace and stability—when the ground is rotten. Corruption has long been a problem in Afghanistan, and these last two decades have seen an increase in corruption—in line with a decrease in security.

Transparency International defines corruption as "the abuse of entrusted power for private gain."[157] Afghanistan is a case study. In 2001, at the start of the intervention, there was insufficient data on the country's level of corruption, but it was recognized as a severe problem—one that could "undermine the Afghan state's legitimacy and drain resources."[158]

In 2005, Afghanistan ranked 117 out of 159 countries on the Corruption Perceptions Index. In 2019, it ranked 173 out of 198.[159] In 2020, Afghanistan ranked 165 out of 180 on the Index.[160] In 2018, 14 percent of the population surveyed believed that corruption was the biggest problem.[161] This is likely to increase under the new Taliban regime of 2021.

The U.S. government claimed zero tolerance, and yet they were well aware of the rampant corruption, and how aid was contributing to it. In 2021, official reports indicated that $19 billion of the total $63 billion that the United States spent on Afghanistan's reconstruction since 2002 was lost to waste, fraud, and abuse.[162] This was due in part to U.S. government funding modalities through U.S. contractors, international organizations, and the military in order to avoid feeding into the corruption of the Afghan government—the very government that the United States had a major hand in creating and sustaining.

And yet, as Richard Boucher, previous Assistant Secretary of State for South Asia during the Bush Administration, said in later interviews: It was better to give funding contracts to Afghans who "would probably take 20 percent for personal use or for their extended families and friends" than give the money to "a bunch of expensive American experts" who would waste 80 to 90 percent of the funds on overhead and profit."[163] Meanwhile, corruption has played a large part in diverting aid money away from its intended use and kept many trapped in a cycle of poverty.

Many U.S. officials now recognize that their "biggest single project … may have been the development of mass corruption"[164] which, as they said, "helped destroy the popular legitimacy of the wobbly Afghan government they were fighting to prop up."[165] We could not have expected otherwise. When foreign powers install warlords in an interim government—warlords guilty of fueling conflict, increasing corruption, and committing crimes against women—these foreign powers have, to some degree, created the political environment they now criticize.

Afghanistan's poppy economy is both cause and effect of the rampant culture of corruption. Increased poverty led many Afghans—including women and girls—into this industry. Women worked as farmers, refiners, or smugglers out of necessity.[166] And, women and girls were under threat from drug traffickers and risked being traded as "opium brides"[167] to repay debts; a practice the Afghan government was aware of, but unable to stop. What's more, it was "not something that government officials are supposed to talk about."[168] There are no statistics on how many girls have been traded as a result of the opium industry.[169]

A USAID program, *IDEA-NEW*, was established in 2009 to create new economic opportunities for poppy farmers and ultimately dissuade them from opium cultivation. The $150 million five-year program collaborated with Afghan government bodies, including the Ministry of Women's Affairs.[170] The initiative was deemed a success, touted as inclusive and consultative at every level. The program claims to have provided business skills training for 15,455 business owners, of which 9,737 were women.[171]

However, from 2009 to 2014, the duration of the project, the total area under opium poppy cultivation increased from 123,000 hectares to 224,000 hectares— an increase of 82 percent.[172] Opium remains Afghanistan's biggest industry. The corruption of this industry has negatively impacted the delivery of aid, obstructing it from its

A man who sells fish on the edge of a lake, Bamiyan.

intended purpose, and intended beneficiaries. Reports revealed that women who grow poppy would have been willing to stop if there had been other opportunities, contradicting the seeming "success" of *IDEA-NEW* in creating training and opportunities.[173]

The long-term toll of corruption has impacted the country's poorest citizens. "After two decades of nation-building and $2.1 trillion [in aid], the economic status of ordinary Afghans has barely changed at all."[174] Ultimately, the Afghan family, as the country's source of strength, has been fractured by the drug trade, in a context of prolonged insecurity, increasing poverty, and rampant violence.[175] "Corruption has sucked away most aid money that could have pulled Afghanistan out of the heroin assembly line."[176] What's more, donors actually *fueled* corruption with the ways they distributed money—excessively and without oversight.[177]

When I was in Afghanistan, poppy production formed a significant part of aid conversations—complicated to understand, impossible to eradicate. I remember learning that the U.S. military nicknamed their operations in Afghanistan "sex, drugs, and rock 'n' roll," meaning gender, poppy, and terrorism. I asked an aid worker why he thought poppy production was impossible to curb. "It makes economic sense," he explained. "Poppy is more lucrative than potatoes." Planting potatoes over poppy can be seen as a decision built on luxury, an option to consider only when the most urgent basic needs are met. The choice was never poppy or potatoes. It was poppy or poverty.

What does this mean for women? While corruption "is an enemy of all Afghans" Sima Samar of the Afghan Independent Human Rights Commission said, "it is a brutal and sworn enemy of women."[178]

Global studies have shown that gender equality helps to curb corruption.[179] When women are represented in all aspects of public and political life—in positions of leadership and decision-making—corruption is controlled. Women in power can be corrupt, of course, but corruption is exacerbated by unequal power dynamics, "limiting women's access to public resources, information and decision-making, thus reinforcing social, cultural, and political discrimination."[180]

Corrupt societies often fuel specific forms of violence against women such as sexual extortion and trafficking. In such contexts, women are robbed of their civil and political rights. Poverty is also linked to corruption, and as Afghanistan—and Afghan women in particular—become more poor, corruption feeds off this poverty, perpetuating a cycle of poverty that becomes increasingly harder to break. Ultimately, corruption in Afghanistan—and everywhere—robs women of their rights and dignity, "impedes their full access to public health, education, and development opportunities, and in many cases threatens their lives."[181] As the Afghanistan of 2021, once again under the Taliban regime, continues to unravel, it is likely that this industry will continue to grow.

In 2005, an aid worker explained the "disillusionment of Afghans because the pace of change to improve their daily existence is too slow, their expectations are dashed, their security is not improved, the cost of living rises and salaries do not." Meanwhile, he continued, there is "massive corruption, the drugs, warlords, criminals and those involved in the most awful atrocities back inside the circle of power. Is it any wonder people are skeptical?"

"Are they really going to adapt to a new system," he asked, "or are they already planning the downfall of this government?" There is so much to do, needs are overwhelming, and "corruption is massive," he lamented. "And women," he concluded, women are "the ones who have to deal with the consequences of all this every day."

What We Should Have Done All Along

At the time of writing in 2021, Afghanistan's economy was set for freefall. The Biden Administration blocked the Taliban's access to Afghanistan's $9.4 billion in international reserves; the World Bank halted all payments to Afghanistan[182]; and the International Monetary Fund suspended plans to distribute more than $400 million in emergency reserves.[183]

The Taliban has been under international sanctions since 1999, although analysts suspect that they will continue to draw funds from other sources, such as drug trafficking, opium production, extortion, kidnapping for ransom, and mineral exploitation—all of which is estimated to pull in $300 million to $1.6 billion in annual revenue, according to a June 2021 UN Security Council report.[184]

Sanctions are a point of leverage, but who pays the price? This go-to political tool obviously has massive economic repercussions, but the economic suffering is not distributed equally and vulnerable groups are more severely impacted. Sanctions impede economic development in addition to delivery of much-needed humanitarian services and support. And, sanctions are gendered, meaning that women will bear the brunt because of their weaker socio-economic and political status. In fact, sanctions have a detrimental effect on women's rights and often exacerbate violence against women.

For a country that relies on international aid for 40 percent of its GDP and three-quarters of its government budget, any reductions to foreign assistance can be devastating.[185] UN agencies have been providing support in the form of lifesaving medical supplies and food assistance. Women and children have been given priority. And donors have peppered their statements with *women's rights* rhetoric—again. As of October 2021, donors have pledged more than $1.2 billion, although only $135 million has been received.[186] Donor reluctance is justifiable under a Taliban regime, but women again stand to be the largest losers.

"If the Taliban has any expectation of acceptance," U.S. secretary of state Blinken stated, "it's going to have to respect

A girl stands in the doorway of the office of a local women's group, Logar.

the rights of women and girls."[187] At the time of writing, it remains unclear if, and how, the Taliban is to be accepted as the legitimate government in the country. It also remains unclear if foreign assistance can compel the Taliban to respect women's rights. Women's lives once again hang in the balance, victims of ideological occupations and military might.

Afghanistan was once described as "a perfect case study of how not to give aid."[188] There have been several disconnects on the complicated road of aid to Afghanistan. Overall, aid lacked a coherent strategy. For two decades, there was never any clarity on what the different donors—particularly the United States—actually wanted to achieve. This was further impeded by unrealistic timelines and expectations, not grounded in Afghanistan's complex reality. The propensity for quick-fix options trumped any long-term strategic planning. On paper, "sustainability" was critical, but in practice implementation was short-term and short-sighted. As a result, whatever was built—government institutions, an Afghan army, an electoral process, or even women's "liberation"—was feeble and naive. The need to "clumsily [force] Western technocratic models onto Afghan ... institutions" likely fueled the very problems they set out to fix.[189]

The story of aid in Afghanistan might prove to be a master-class in how international aid can fall short of its goals. The money spent seems massive, but did the dollars yield results? Funding without impact is destined for failure. We didn't need two decades to tell us this. And women—the international community's most significant targeted beneficiaries—ended up the greatest losers.

Ultimately, aid fell short on its promises and particularly in relation to women's rights. The funding modalities of the last two decades claimed to support women, but more than likely contributed to their marginalization. Aid to women not only ignored local context, it ignored local actors. Afghan women leaders argued time and again that unrealistic goals—measured by numbers of women trained, women elected, women employed—would not bring tangible results. Efforts were measured based on what organizations were *doing* rather than what they were *achieving*.[190]

Work was flawed from the beginning. As one example, USAID did not recognize the need for "gender advisors" in their Afghanistan offices until 2014, 13 years after they established a presence in the country.[191] Women's "issues" in Afghanistan represents the best example of the international community's failed attempt to "usher in an orderly revolution ... [replacing] Afghan social systems with Western or 'modern' systems."[192]

As former Minister of Women's Affairs Hasina Safi said in September 2021: "We would like guarantees. Because the last twenty years you have invested a lot. Do you want to clean up your investment just to erase it? Or as human beings do you want to stand with us?"[193]

"I know what it looks like from abroad," activist Mina Sharif said, "like money has been pumped into Afghanistan for all this time and the international community ... offered this new concept of democracy, and women going to school ... being in the workforce, and we didn't get it."[194]

"Afghan women don't need foreign models of freedom and empowerment," she continued, but rather "a plan to protect their safety after troop withdrawal."[195]

Regardless, "foreign models of freedom and empowerment" were infused into Afghanistan's aid architecture from the beginning. One would imagine, therefore, that the money for women's rights had been bountiful at that time. Unfortunately, it was not.

In recent years, to remedy the problem of misguided money, the principle of feminist funding was established.[196] Funding through a feminist framework entails supporting those who are most impacted, using a contextual and intersectional lens. It demands that we change our funding modalities and focus on supporting and sustaining activists and grassroots groups working for social and political change through flexible, long-term core funding. This was *not* the approach taken. *But, might it be the approach we now take?*

Meanwhile, in recent years, Western funding for Afghan organizations had dwindled. This, even before the Taliban's (re)takeover in 2021. As of late 2021, many international staff evacuated, leaving "development" once again in the hands of Afghans. For women's groups, this means that they will operate skeletal functions, forced to do much more work with much less resources—and much greater risks. With aid to women's organizations having all but disappeared, "we will not achieve what we had hoped," an Afghan woman leader told me, "and now we have to adapt to whatever may come in order to survive."[197]

Adapting and surviving are two things that Afghan women have done for far too long. *How might we now do better in supporting them as they once again struggle to survive?* The answer is in funding Afghan women's organizations—unrestricted funding that enables them to direct the dollars and determine the course of change.

Those of us on the outside can provide technical and organizational support—the tools and resources, and perhaps some inspiration—for Afghan women to direct as they see fit. Now is the time to listen to women leaders—they will tell us what they need. And we need to deliver for them. Afghan women deserve both money and power; they need to be in control of their own priorities. In a way, they always have been.

I asked an Afghan woman leader what we might do now to help. She responded: "Do what you should have done all along. Fund us. And trust us."

CHAPTER 5

Democracy as Liberation?

Women's rights issues have become depoliticized and have been hijacked....
In this context, everybody and everything responsible for gender equality
in Afghanistan equates to nobody and nothing being responsible for putting
women's interests and experiences of injustice on the political agenda.[1]

Starting in 2001, the military invasion and subsequent aid intervention attempted to base its success on the political project of remaking Afghanistan as a democratic and gender-sensitive state.[2] To be clear: there is nothing "foreign" about these values—they exist everywhere. And they exist in Afghanistan. The *concepts* exist, but the *terms* were perceived to be part of a succession of ideological frameworks to create conflict, rather than cohesion.[3]

Democracy fundamentally rests on the principles of equality, security, and participation with the aim of honoring the will of the people through elections, institutions, civil society engagement, and accountability mechanisms.[4] Gender equality, healthcare, education, and access to systems of justice are the ideal cornerstones.

Democracy and gender equality are not uniquely Western products. But the idea that these concepts might have been labeled as "Western" brings a certain resentment and resistance. As we've seen in several intervals throughout its history, Afghanistan has been on the receiving end of values that appear to be imported and imposed from the outside, with little regard for their relevance in the country. This helps to explain why Afghans are reluctant to embrace these ideals when they are not anchored in Afghan values and context. It is not unusual for any message to be resisted when received from outside—even if we subscribe to its contents.

To build a solid foundation for democracy and human rights, specifically women's rights, we would do better to understand the historic progression and the socio-cultural values of the country, and start from there.[5] In this sense, the push for democracy is similar to the push for gender equality in Afghanistan insofar as it *appears* to be in opposition to these societal values.

120

The terms are used liberally, but without meaning and context:

> Democracy based on a Western individualism rather than traditional Afghan Islamic communalism, gender-blind social interaction, and the elevation of the individual above society, do not appear to be part of the emerging.... Afghan worldview.[6]

Afghan women leaders swiftly expressed concern about this agenda. "Let us find our own foundations for democracy and gender equality," an Afghan woman leader told me. "These ideas did not come from you, they are not owned by you. We have been fighting for them all along, even if you did not notice."

Indigenous forms of democracy and gender equality do exist, even if we don't see them from the outside. And there are indigenous foundations upon which these values can stick. What we cannot do is "deliver" democracy, as if it is simply a one-size-fits-all blueprint. What we *can* do is help lay the foundation for it to grow. One aid worker put it this way:

> We might "bring" democracy. You can bring experts and you can organize the elections. And you might have mechanisms for the institution, for the building of democracy. But institutionalizing it is going to take 100 years. We know that from other countries' experiences.

Meanwhile, Afghan women's organizations criticize "the way in which many men frequently bandy the word democracy in a meaningless manner, without implementing these democratic principles within their own families."[7] The outcome is that terms like democracy—and gender—have been saddled with negative baggage, making men increasingly resentful and outcomes for women increasingly deleterious.

An Afghan woman leader expressed the sentiments of many:

> In Afghan history, we have imported policies from other places. This is why it doesn't work. If we want democracy, we have to go step by step, starting from the beginning, and not running. If we run, we will fall down. We should walk slowly and look around us in order to be successful. Again today, just like before, Afghans are running, running after democracy, running after gender. And when we fall down no one will be able to rescue us. Not even the international community.

A Small Step Towards a Hopeful Future

The history of Afghan women's involvement in politics is as much a rollercoaster as the history of Afghanistan itself. Traditionally, political issues in Afghanistan are addressed by *jirga*, an assembly of leaders—usually all male—reaching consensus based on the *Pashtunwali*. As such, women's presence in political life has always been meager.

Women—precisely four of them—contributed to the drafting of the 1964 Constitution, which granted them the right to vote and to seek elected office. This led to the country's first female minister who served in the health department. Three other women served in parliament with her.

The following year, the Soviet-backed People's Democratic Party of Afghanistan was established along with the country's first women's group, the Democratic Organization of Afghan Women. The group set out to eliminate illiteracy among women, ban forced marriages, and eradicate bride price.[8]

Further reforms followed in the late 1970s with an increase in women's education—including at the university level. More women were represented in parliament. Twelve women participated in the next Constitutional *Loya Jirga* in 1977.

One former member of parliament told me about her experience in those days:

In the 1970s, President Daud Khan wanted to reform the constitution and called on all provinces and cities to elect a member that could represent them in the parliament.[9] He wanted to create a constitution that was inclusive and reflects women's voices as well. His goal was that women occupy at least 15 seats in the parliament out of 300 in total, a small step towards a hopeful future. He requested the provincial governors to elect their members and must include female candidates. There were already a few women in Kabul who had been elected, but Daud's plan was to shift the mainstream and bring more women from Afghanistan's rural areas and provinces to the government.

At the time I was the principal of a high school in Kunduz and I was the only woman with a university degree! I was appointed by an open-minded government and elected by the people. My participation alongside other female MPs started the foundation of women in politics and government institutions. We were the pioneers! We women became the voice of all Afghan women in the parliament at a time when women were not offered such opportunities. Most importantly, we women's successes were celebrated in our villages and towns and we were welcomed with open arms.

I remember going back to my province, seeing people from all over Kunduz lined up on both sides of the streets to welcome me as I walked alongside them, shaking their hands and listening to their messages. Most of these people were rice farmers and villagers who had not shaken hands with a woman in public, and yet they approved of me to be their voice!

The power of the People's Democratic Party of Afghanistan increased in the late 1970s as they pushed for rapid social and economic change, including major reforms for women. In 1978 they issued a decree to ensure equal rights for women.[10] The 1970s saw a rise in women representatives in parliament but this so-called "progressive era" led to violent backlash by subsequent governments and a doubling down of "anti–Western ideology."[11]

A poster encouraging women to vote in the 2005 Parliamentary Election, Kabul.

In the years that followed, women's status and participation in authority or governance diminished. From the start of the Civil War in 1992, women were barely present in public service. And during the Taliban period, they were completely invisible.

The Bonn Conference of late 2001 outlined Afghanistan's transition and established an interim government. Only two women were present out of 23 delegates. The resulting Bonn Agreement emphasized that the administration should have "due regard to … the importance of the participation of women" in its effort to create a "broad based, gender-sensitive, multi-ethnic and fully representative government." As such, part of the Bonn "deal" was that women would be active in all political processes.

The next year, the Emergency *Loya Jirga* was held with 220 women out of 1500 delegates.[12] Unfortunately, women's presence was undermined by the presence of warlords. The Constitutional Commission, the body established to consult the people of Afghanistan and produce a draft constitution for the *Loya Jirga*, had seven women out of 35 members. The 2003 Constitutional *Loya Jirga* itself consisted of roughly 20 percent women, a marked improvement.

One female delegate, Malalai Joya, required special security during and after the convention because of her vocal criticism of warlords, saying that they are "responsible for our situation ... they oppress women and have ruined our country."[13] Despite repeated threats, Joya continues to be a well-known Afghan feminist activist. Years later, she said: "They will kill me but they will not kill my voice, because it will be the voice of all Afghan women. You can cut the flower, but you cannot stop the coming of spring."[14]

Also in 2003, Afghanistan signed the Convention on the Elimination of Discrimination Against Women (CEDAW) without reservation. This includes a provision granting women equal participation in political processes. A Women's Bill of Rights was drafted by the NGO Women for Afghan Women in the months prior to the Constitutional *Loya Jirga*, in order to ensure that women's rights would be represented and in line with women's full rights under CEDAW. The Bill, including rights to education, health services, and so on, was presented to President Karzai, who assured the women that their demands would be included, minus one thing: a provision on the legal age of marriage.[15]

Article 22 of Afghanistan's 2004 Constitution states that "the citizens of Afghanistan—whether man or woman—have equal rights and duties before the law."[16] Unfortunately, the Constitution sidelined most of the other demands. It did, however, include quotas for women's political participation: 27 percent of the seats in *Wolesi Jirga* (House of the People) and 25 percent of seats in the Provincial Council were to be reserved for women.[17] Afghan women leaders argued that the Constitution did not sufficiently include women's voices or needs. The Women's Bill of Rights would have assured all of this.

Prior to the 2004 presidential election, a major campaign was launched to bring women to the polls. This entailed a poster campaign, one of which still hangs in my office to this day, but little else. At that time, an aid worker lamented to me: "Women should be called in a meeting forum at a local mosque or school so that they can learn about their rights. From what I know nothing of this sort was ever done." The failure to get women's buy-in through culturally-contextual channels meant that many women would not vote, seeing it as a man's duty to "do politics."

The process was a lengthy one as most women needed to be approached individually and within their own homes. An aid worker elaborated: "Although many women have registered, true representation is a challenge. It is unlikely that women will vote differently from the men in their household, and men will vote to keep themselves secure." Further, proxy voting was common because women did not have photos on their identification cards.[18]

Cultural attitudes have also prevented women from fully participating in the elections. A July 2004 survey found that 88 percent of men and 85 percent of women believed that women need their husband's permission to vote. Furthermore, more than 80 percent of the men surveyed stated that women need a man's advice on who to vote for.[19]

At that time, security risks made voter registration a difficult task. Violence increased in the months leading up to the election, and organizations were reluctant to send staff to rural areas. Women faced threats, targeted attacks, violence, and were harassed during the Emergency *Loya Jirga* (2002), the Constitutional *Loya Jirga* (2003), and the presidential election (2004). Most alarmingly, three female election workers were killed and 12 injured after a bomb targeted a bus full of female election workers.[20] This clearly did not set a good precedent for women's political participation.

During many conversations around this topic, one aid worker told me that "most rural areas have commanders whose word is law, and no one would be likely to vote against the commander's preferred candidate for fear of persecution. In other words, both women and men will do what they are told."[21] In a country with little history of, or faith in, central government, exercising civic duty was not viewed as a priority.

Only one female candidate, Masooda Jalal, ran against the 17 male candidates in the presidential election. She persevered despite harassment and repeated silencing. Her courage paved the way for more than 550 women to run for parliament a few months later.[22] Jalal went on to serve in peace negotiations and was the Minister of Women's Affairs from 2004 to 2006. Some of her legacies include the National Action Plan for the Women of Afghanistan and the draft law to eliminate violence against women, amongst other contributions.

Ultimately, the perception that politics is "Western" and solely the domain of men remained strong. As the following example of the 2005 parliamentary elections will show, it is not the underlying principles of democracy or women's political participation that are in question, but the way the terms are used as part of a Western agenda, leaving Afghans to adopt them publicly but resent them privately.

In discussions of women's role in politics, one Afghan woman asked: "What good is politics? Look at where it has brought Afghanistan."

We Are Just Voting Fodder

As the final step in the Bonn Process, the "free and fair" parliamentary elections of September 2005 were an ambitious and controversial undertaking. Sima Wali, legendary Afghan feminist activist, was one of only three women present. Wali was an inspiration behind the creation of the Ministry for Women's Affairs. Women will play a major part, she said. "We will not go away."[23]

The 27 percent quota was very progressive—only a handful of countries in the world have this in place to ensure women's representation. Such a quota would place Afghanistan as 20th in the world at that time in terms of women's representation in a parliamentary body. The quota itself was hailed as a victory achieved through pressure by Afghan women's groups and the international community, including such countries as the United States, where women held only 14 percent of congressional seats in that same year.[24]

However, while this may seem impressive at first, many of those interviewed expressed skepticism. They were concerned that women were once again being used as window dressing and that this progressive quota served to appease international donors at the expense of laying a foundation for genuine participation. Quotas are critical to advance women's interests, but top-down democracy can bring resistance.

Quotas were used both for the Emergency and Constitutional *Loya Jirgas* to ensure women's participation in the political process. Many felt this was a good start, but it also appeared to be tokenistic. "Right now our women are all over the place, being used for politics, used like dolls," an Afghan woman leader lamented. "Every event they are in front of the TV, the camera. They are being used just to show that women were there." Many Afghans I spoke with felt that, at worst, quotas and external pressure for a male/female balance could run the risk of generating a community backlash. Experience in other countries also reveals that affirmative action measures are perceived to be an external imposition. It is this perception, more than men's fear of lost power, that fuels resistance.[25]

Moreover, the completion of this last step of the Bonn Process was met with fears and rumors that the international community would begin plotting an Afghanistan exit strategy. Researchers and political analysts in Afghanistan cautioned that the country would need many years of continuous international support. Plans for a premature exit of the international community could destabilize, and most likely collapse, the country's tenuous foundation. Elections, with their deadline-driven nature, bring the impression that the work is done when the election has been held. As such, they are the "holy grail of Western transition formulas, providing moral cover for exit."[26]

The parliamentary elections were initially expected to coincide with the October 2004 presidential election. The unstable security situation prompted a delay, and the elections were then scheduled for April 2005. In the months prior to the April election date, there were concerns that the elections would be delayed further. The pervasive sense, according to myriad discussions with organizations, was that the country was ill-prepared for elections. While one arm of the UN system was plowing forth with elections, another arm was counseling caution. The UNDP Human

Development Report warned against conducting elections too soon after conflict and before peacetime politics had a chance to take root. The report clearly stated that "ill-timed, hurried, badly designed or poorly run elections can actually undermine the process of democratization."[27]

The parliamentary elections were finally held on 18 September 2005, despite security issues, threats, and warnings. These elections signified the end of a period of transition and represented a chance not to repeat the breakdowns of state and society that characterized Afghanistan's recent past. In the months leading up to the elections, female candidate participation was widely visible, particularly in Kabul. Campaign posters peppered city walls, and anecdotes of women's participation abounded. For instance, in the northeast of the country, one pregnant female candidate traveled by foot for eight days in order to present her candidacy to the *Wolesi Jirga*.

And so the stories went, liberally employed as evidence of the Afghan people's commitment to democracy. At the same time, while the *kharijis* (foreigners) were congratulating themselves, Afghan women leaders noted the irony. Women's participation in political life in Afghanistan may have been a favorite subject of the international community and the media, but Afghan women themselves had barely broached the topic.

One form of evidence of women's commitment to political processes comes from the numbers of their participation. However, numbers only tell a partial story. Moreover, the figures emerging from elections—particularly the parliamentary elections—were highly contested. This was due in part to suspicions of fraud, ballot stuffing, and unclear procedures in polling stations. The international community might have boasted about the participation of women in elections, but inequalities remained as women continued to have symbolic assignments in the cabinet and other key positions. Too few women were given the opportunity to access higher positions and use their leadership skills to make any substantive input.[28]

Conversations with a range of aid workers at the time revealed concerns that the limitations to women's political participation were not sufficiently addressed. These included lack of security, warlords, and a sense that politics is men's domain. In addition, it was argued that the physical presence of female bodies occupying parliamentary seats would not automatically give them leverage or authority. Women's *presence* doesn't necessarily mean women's *power*.

Most Afghan and international alike agreed that injecting women into all aspects of the democratic process would not automatically address women's interests. Equal numbers do not necessarily translate into equal participation. Afghan women leaders felt strongly that women's participation should be for a purpose, not to appease international donors or to satisfy aid agencies. An Afghan woman captured the views of many:

Why should I vote? ... This election is for you not for us. You will have it and
then you will go, leaving us with a system that has no roots in our country. You
can grow new systems, yes, but it takes time; they need to put down roots. And
the Pashtun women in the countryside, they will be herded like cattle to the voting stations. They will be just voting fodder. What meaning does this have?[29]

An aid worker voiced some of these misgivings, explaining that "the
West is trying to push its own kind of thinking" without factoring in context or prior learnings, built on our "preconceived notions and experiences
... according to what we did in other countries." And we raise expectations
and make promises for a better future, he said, "if you adopt democracy
or 'our way' without explaining [that it] will not happen overnight." In the
end, he said, the burden of this falls on women: "I find it hard to believe that
for most women life has not changed much but the West will still proclaims
'freedom for women.' I wish it were so."

An Insider's View

As an insider to the parliamentary elections process, I often found
myself asking similar questions. In 2005, I worked in some measure on
things "women and gender" for Afghanistan's parliamentary elections. In
assuming the position, I was told by one aid worker that I was just a "warm
body" filling a politically-motivated post that the international community
felt should exist because "this is Afghanistan, and everyone wants to know
about women here." She went on to tell me that gender issues were so contentious in the country, and so much in the spotlight, as a result "everyone
expects that someone will have to do it." There was an obvious pressure to
have someone "do gender," whatever doing gender really meant. In 2005, I
was that *someone*.

At that point, I had already lived in Afghanistan for three years, so I
took this as an opportunity to apply my experience in the country and relative familiarity with the context. I hired a man on my staff to support a campaign working with men to help them better understand the role of women
in the political process. This entailed meetings with *mullahs* and the heads
of Afghan political parties—all men. The challenges that women were facing became clear to me when I was told by a particularly bushy-bearded
political party leader that he would under no circumstances endorse wom-
en's political participation and told me: "Women have no wisdom, women
are 'sick' for seven days of every month. They cannot think. They cannot
judge. Their judgment is impaired. They cannot make decisions for the
country."

This was not a unique sentiment. And this sentiment was not at all

A banner by the Ministry of Women's Affairs in support of the 2005 Parliamentary Election, Kabul.

unique to men. An Afghan woman staff member told me she did not "believe in elections" when I asked her why she did not vote. She had taken the job for financial reasons and felt that the pressure for women to vote was nothing more than an opportunity for journalists to photograph lines of *chaddaris* as evidence of "democracy in action." These sentiments were pervasive. It was believed that the pressure to "get the numbers" outweighed the quality of civic education and participation. A massive campaign was underway to reach the most remote villages, but the result was shallow. In one village, the elder greeted a training team asking: "Are you coming here to tell us the results from the last election?" He was referring to the presidential election of the year before, with no idea if it had taken place or who had won.

In the end, the parliamentary election of 2005 was characterized by a relatively poor voter turnout and a discrepancy in figures that took months to resolve. Regardless, the outward-facing verdict was one of victory. In an international press briefing at the close of election day, a colleague turned to me in surprise and said: "I didn't know the elections were such a 'success'!"

In a discussion with international journalists on gender issues in the elections, I was told that we—the international community—were too smug in our boasting of 27 percent of seats for women. In reality, women outnumber men in the population, and therefore the representation in parliament should reflect this, I was told. This came from one male journalist in a room of 15 European and American journalists—13 of whom were male. It was at that point I realized Afghanistan was being subjected to unrealistic goals and standards that did not even apply in the so-called developed world.

Not too long afterwards, an article appeared asking:

> America has had democracy for 200 years, and during that time no woman has been nominated to the presidency, nor are there large numbers of women in the cabinet ... so why are they imposing on others what they don't have or don't want?[30]

This lesson was again brought home to me one Friday as I listened to the sermon coming from the mosque down the street. "Do not vote, I tell you!" the imam wailed. "These foreigners are trying to strip away your Muslim identity by imposing their 'democracy'!"

Ultimately, "doing gender" proved to be difficult to coordinate with an elections timetable that is deadline—and deliverable—driven. There was little recognition among aid organizations that gender equality is both a product *and* a process, one that requires a long-term investment—not unlike civic education. These entail political consciousness-raising and cannot be brought about through technical solutions and numbers in polling stations. The one-time presence of women at the polls did little more than to appease the international community.

Many women I spoke to felt that the international community unknowingly put women at risk by aggressively promoting their public presence while sidelining Afghan women's groups. Afghan women leaders were, ironically, *not* leading the process.

Women expressed much concern—and fear—when faced with the question of presenting their candidacy. Two women I spoke with had considered running for office but were discouraged by their husbands. Another woman decided not to nominate herself when her husband and brothers learned she would have to be photographed for the ballot. They told her having her photograph taken and displayed publicly would bring shame upon the family. One female candidate told her story:

> I was going to different villages and places when I was doing my campaign. When I was talking to women, it turned more into a "woman gathering" and women started talking to me about their problems. I found out that there is a huge difference between women activists and intellectuals and educated women—and women in those villages and remote areas. There is a need for us to find solutions and ways to help these rural women. There is a huge difference

between village and cities. I noticed that my speech for women was too difficult. They didn't know what I was talking about. They didn't know what was voting and who to vote for. When I noticed that they had difficulties presenting themselves and understanding, I decided to stop my campaign to them and instead spend time talking to them to understand their issues. The result was that in election day, they were going like cattle in a group with a shepherd, leading them to the election and putting them in the centers. They were told what to do. They didn't have any independence or the room to use their right to vote in the way they wanted. What does election mean for these women?

Voter turnout was much lower than expected because of a campaign marked by intimidation—particularly against women candidates and voters. The Afghanistan Independent Human Rights Commission produced three reports in conjunction with the United States Agency for International Development to track progress on the parliamentary elections and raise concerns. These reports, known as the *Joint Verification of Political Rights*, frequently mentioned women and gender issues as primary concerns.[31]

The first report, for the period 19 April to 3 June 2005, noted that "there is a broad perception that intimidation and limitations on political rights are pervasive or will increase." "Female candidates ... have also voiced concerns about their security. In some areas women only registered in the last days of the nomination process to avoid security threats." The report also explained that Afghan society is ambivalent about women's participation in political life, stating that women "internalize these norms and fear bringing dishonor to their families if they expose themselves to public critique by standing as candidates." The pervasive sense in the report was that the country was just not ready for such aggressive change.

The second report for the period 4 June to 16 August did not report improvements.[32] During this period, acts of intimidation against female candidates forced some of them to withdraw. Female candidates continued to feel threatened and were intimidated and attacked. There were also numerous threats and attacks against women election workers. Further, many mosques publicly condemned women's participation, calling it un–Islamic and anti–*Sharia*.[33] The situation continued to deteriorate. The final report, for the period of 17 August to 13 September, reported that four male candidates were killed and that "women candidates have been the target of a number of acts of discrimination, intimidation, and violent attacks."[34] Religious leaders also continued to dissuade people from voting for female candidates and from permitting their wives to participate in the election.

Human Rights Watch was also actively monitoring cases of intimidation of female candidates, stating that security in Afghanistan had deteriorated in conjunction with the elections, particularly in the form of high-profile cases of social and political violence against women.[35] Women

were increasingly targeted, the report elaborated, and they feared that pushing social norms would incur greater retaliation. The report continued:

> Women candidates exposing themselves to public review risk retaliation for dis-
> rupting social norms. Violence and intimidation against these women is highly
> symbolic and sends a chilling message to other Afghan women considering
> expanded roles in public life.

Another article stated that Afghan men believed that women had
become candidates at the "command of Laura Bush"—otherwise it would
never be allowed.[36] It was not only Afghan men who believed that the parliamentary elections were a decree from the Bush family. A more provocative American article stated:

> Females, once considered worth less than scum by Muslim males, are now com-
> ing into their own in Afghanistan, thanks to an ongoing democratic planting.
> There is no other answer but to recognize that it is because of the Bush adminis-
> tration and U.S. assistance in that Muslim country that much progress is being
> made on numerous levels.[37]

I Don't Vote for Women

According to research in 2005, 58 percent of 600 people (525 women,
75 men) surveyed believe that women should not be involved in politics.[38]
In a further survey of 130 women, 85 of them did not feel that women
should be politically active. These findings can be confirmed by research to
gather perspectives of Afghans. Prompted by a concern that Afghan voices
were not heard in the days leading up to the elections, I decided to send my
staff out to collect voices from the street.

A random sample of Afghan men and women was selected and 20
on-site interviews (ten women, ten men) were conducted prior to the elections. Of the ten women, five said they were not in favor of women running
for office. Six of ten men said they do not believe that a woman should have
a role in the public domain, particularly not in political life—a realm traditionally reserved for men. One woman who was interviewed had the following to say:

> I don't vote for women, because I don't want a woman to act as a leader or have
> the authority or power, because women are not capable of playing this role. They
> will lose themselves easily. It is important for women to vote, but they should
> support men candidates more than women. People in Afghanistan don't want
> women to take on prominent roles among the people.... There are many obsta-
> cles for women. And maybe they cannot be removed.

Another woman also shared this view:

Women attending a training session in preparation for the election, Logar.

I'll never vote for a woman. And it has reason, because in Afghanistan women can't do anything without men's permission, so they are not independent and always want to be with men and look to men to support women.

When asked if she thinks it is important for women to vote, the woman explained that these kinds of things are nice to have on paper. "For policy, it is good," she stated. She elaborated that women voting served to appease the international community and fulfills its agenda. "For real work, it is not perfect," she continued. She explained that in reality these things do not work as one would expect. She felt that women are powerless in the home, and therefore they would be powerless in public office. She explained it this way:

Women candidates can't do anything without their husband's permission and can't even make small decisions on their own. And also security is not perfect for women candidates. For example, in some provinces women can't distribute their posters and they are not allowed to go to rural areas and cannot be far from their homes.

She concluded by asking: "What is the point of women in office with all these restrictions? Afghanistan is not ready."

An Afghan woman leader told me that very little changed in the 20

years, and that "keeping women in politics has always been for show only."
She went on to say that the women who were politically active were "symbols of gender equality that were promised to the West." In reality, she said,
"these women were not considered ideal Afghan women in societies, they
were not representatives of Afghan women."

"Being a female politician means keeping the tradition of an Afghan
woman while also competing with men in politics," she told me. "There
hasn't been a balance." Women who entered politics took two routes: they
either "kept their seat and their reputation or they stood up, raised their
voices, and then were shamed."

A man who was interviewed on the street of Kabul expressed concern
that women would not be able to serve the people any better than men:

> In my opinion I won't vote for a woman, because I don't trust that she will work
> more than a man does. Also if we have good men who are very educated and
> more capable than women, why shouldn't I vote for a man?

He recommended that women should vote and had the following to say:
"My advice for women is to vote for men candidates, because as I mentioned men are more powerful than women and they are capable of doing
every type of work."

The man felt that the biggest obstacles to women's participation are
their lack of credibility, security issues, and cultural obstacles. He elaborated:

> There are different issues [between men and women's participation]. As an
> example if a man stands before people in a public area and starts his campaign
> everyone will stand and listen to him. But women can't stand in front of a crowd
> except in some areas because of lack of security and inappropriateness. First
> their families don't allow them, and if their families let them work the society
> is not familiar with that type of situation. It is better for women not to try hard
> because they must keep themselves quiet otherwise they may receive punish-
> ment or harassment.

When asked if he believed that women should be represented in parliament, he had the following to say: "It is good if we have some female representation in parliament and if not it is okay also. We have our men and
they do whatever needs to be done for both men and women."

One man believed that women in Afghanistan are facing fewer obstacles than men—in terms of participation in political, social, and economic
life. He felt that men should be the focus of attention as well as the primary
political actors. One man said he would not vote for a woman because she
would be biased towards women and would thereby rob him of the rights
he now enjoys. The sentiment of political power as a zero-sum game was
heard frequently on the street. Another man said he would rather cut off his

own hand than vote for a woman. He did not feel the need to elaborate any further on his sentiments.

These sentiments have not changed. In 2021, an Afghan man told me that "a woman is always a woman and has to keep her limits. More than her limits, she is shamed." In short, as long as these views were, and continue to be, pervasive, it is difficult to make sustainable gains for women in politics.

Instant Democracy

In a discussion with a former Minister of Women's Affairs on women's participation in the 2005 parliamentary elections, she emphasized the need for female candidates to ground their work in the context of the family. "Without support of their husbands or families, they cannot do this." She illustrated her point using her own example during her campaign:

> My husband often accompanied me to provinces. I did not have guards so he acted as my security too. Sometimes, if I was at a gathering and I was tired after speaking so much, he would speak for me. He said, "She is my wife; she has a lot of experience; she is capable." This is the best endorsement—because he knows me well. Husbands and fathers should be supportive. They should help by going out to speak to male voters.
>
> Ours is a male-dominated society; they have the political power at the level of making decisions—whether in parliament or as head of the family. The best way to tackle the issues is to convince men to give freedom to women and daughters. Local *mullahs* are very influential. If we can secure the cooperation of the religious community, it will have a positive effect on opportunities for women.
>
> It is very important to target men. The programs should contain very primary messages and should encourage men and influentials to come forward and cooperate. It should be done with the target audience in mind—and should speak their language.

These views are reinforced by myriad press articles with quotes from Afghans—candidates and voters—expressing discomfort with the democracy agenda. For instance, in a local paper, a male candidate for the *Wolesi Jirga* claimed that women who hold political office will "eat the rights of men." Another article reported a political party leader as saying: "We will never accept the Western interpretation of democracy in our Islamic republic which they are trying to implement in Afghanistan."[39] Another candidate said: "The rights the West talks about are not the rights we accept. A woman's rights as given in the *Qu'ran* are enough."[40] Yet another article reported that candidates are "not happy" with the quota for women, saying that Afghans were "overdoing things under the pressure of the international community."[41]

Meanwhile in 2005, the weekly publication *Rozgaran* released an article titled "Imposed Parliament" stating: "The Afghan government, the Western world, and the electoral commission had no other objective but to have a parliament for the country no matter of what standards."[42] Indeed, Afghans were not impressed with their new parliament, or with the elections process. In 1980, Louis Dupree, American anthropologist and scholar of Afghan culture, wrote the following prophetic words: "Take dry constitution, combine with fluid elections and stir, and voila, 'instant democracy'—without the agony of generations of development."[43]

In a discussion with an aid worker supporting parliamentarians, he explained that the members of parliament faced death threats if they returned to their constituencies. Even during parliament recess, the parliamentarians feared returning to their provinces of origin because of security. The climate following the election in 2005 was not conducive for an effective parliament, he explained:

> The parliament hasn't made one decision yet. They have nothing to show their constituencies. They have no idea of their own job because it hasn't officially started yet. How can they convince their constituents that democracy works when they have nothing to show for it? No roads, no schools, nothing.

A woman in her courtyard, Paghman.

He continued to say that it was moot to discuss so-called higher issues when basic concerns such as security had not been met. As far as the international community is concerned, the parliament is an old issue. He explained that the parliament received much attention leading up to the elections, but now there was a general sense that "the job is done." As for the international media, if they speak to parliamentarians, "it's only to good-looking women, or warlords."

Indeed, at that time, the "warlord problem" had

yet to be resolved. Many noted the parliament's domination by "warlords, criminals, and discredited politicians responsible for much of Afghanistan's woes since the Soviet invasion in 1979."[44] These very warlords continued to harass female parliamentarians and question their presence in what should be male political space. The presence of these women was meant to signify the starting point of women's political participation, not the end. It is worth speculating whether these women exist merely as "symbolic gestures meant to appease the international community."[45]

A few weeks after the elections, aid workers participated in a post-elections debrief on women's participation. They had promoted the quota aggressively, with little regard for the risks that women would face as a result. In the words of one participant: "There is a security issue we need to consider here. And implications such as violence against women. We might need to rethink this."

One aid worker asked:

Is [the organization] gender-sensitive? Is it the role of elections to do "gender"? What will happen when the international staff leave and no one is there to push the "gender agenda"? Gender receives much attention, it is politically important. But for the next election this attention might fade and then there needs to be more push to get gender on the table. It needs more than a "gender section." It needs a section with authority. Not just calling itself gender because that's what everyone expects.

In an online communication about the future of the Afghan government and its obligation to uphold a "[Western]-engineered Afghan democracy," one Afghan man had the following to say about the presence of the international community and its dictates in Afghanistan: "There is one thing unique about Afghans: we do not appreciate when we are told what to do. Millions of Afghans have died declaring we rather die proud and free than to live a life of bondage."[46]

Gender Politics

The lack of genuine political participation and the pervasiveness of violence against women in political processes persisted after the parliamentary elections. This led to many arguing that former Afghan president Hamid Karzai, who served from 2001 to 2014, reneged on his promise to uphold gender equality and women's rights, believing it was more lip service than action, especially after very little of this materialized in his first few years in office.

Once elected, Karzai began to appeal to conservative policymakers and populations to the detriment of women. For example, during his second term in 2009, Karzai passed the Shia Personal Status Law which Human Rights Watch characterized as, "mak[ing] Shia women second class citizens for electoral gain."[47] This law affected about 15 percent of the population and appeared to be a nod to "the militia men, the strong men and the mullahs and warlords that kind of run the show." The law directly contradicted the constitution and deprived women of equal rights. In it, fathers and grandfathers had sole custody rights, husbands would decide if their wives could work, rapists could pay blood money to avoid prosecution, and if women refused sexual demands, husbands could withhold food.[48] Women protested despite threats they faced. The international community condemned the law, but to no avail. The reversal of any progress made was well underway.

Karzai also reduced the women's quota in provincial and district councils to 20 percent. Although quotas can appear to be an example of hollow political rights, they are a necessary mechanism for increased women's political participation. Research shows that quotas work, not just for women but for the welfare of communities. Conflicts can alter existing gender norms, creating space for women in political life. In such cases, quotas can be introduced by internal efforts, in response to advocacy, or in "an attempt to bargain for foreign aid."[49] While many quotas begin with the appearance of symbolic power, they evolve into actual power for women in politics.

As such, Karzai's action of reducing the quota had massive implications for women's political participation and by 2013, only 8 percent of women held decision-making positions.[50] Even the few women in those positions were subjected to threats, intimidation, and corruption. In 2013, a woman parliamentarian said, "a lot of women MPs are backed by the governor and the chief of police, so they consider their backers' interests, not women's interests, not women's rights."[51] This meant laws sensitive to women's rights and compliant with international standards of human rights had less chance of enactment. In a scathing criticism of Karzai and his failure to fulfill his commitment to women's rights, Masooda Jalal wrote that "he now dances to the music of fundamentalism, drinks from the cups of people who are known butchers of women's rights, and appoints them to positions where they could tear down the foundations of women's rights that were painstakingly built a dozen of years ago."[52]

The gains made in women's rights risked being challenged, revoked, and replaced. Thus, Karzai's actions proved to be an important "lesson" for Afghan women, as they called it. As a result, women parliamentarians once again vowed to unite—and fight. "We cannot take anything for granted. We must always be vigilant," one told me.

Ashraf Ghani was elected president in 2014, having promised to reform policies and institutions with a key focus on women's rights. In line with his commitments to increase women's participation in senior government roles, Ghani announced four women to join his cabinet in 2015 and in the same year appointed Afghanistan's first-ever female Supreme Court judge, Anisa Rasooli, the head of the Afghan Women Judges Association. This sparked both criticism and controversy, and the parliament ultimately rejected the appointment.

Meanwhile, Ghani committed to preserving women's rights in the peace process and told Afghan women that they were a "force of positive change" in a 2019 gathering of more than 2000 women from around the country. The country's "unity and dignity are rooted in the strength of Afghan women," who are "no longer victims of decisions on the future of Afghanistan," he said.[53] In 2020, he announced a new council to safeguard women's rights in response to demands from a coalition of women's rights activists demanding a place in the peace talks. "We will not allow our place and contribution towards rebuilding our country to be erased or reversed," they said.[54]

There was also still reason for cautious optimism in the form of Ghani's wife, Rula Ghani. She was outspoken on women's rights, in contrast to her predecessor, Zeenat Karzai, who rarely made public appearances. The First Lady stated that if there is peace with the Taliban, women "won't lose their rights.... My husband won't allow that." At the same time, however, she could not confirm if women would be at the table.[55]

And so unsurprisingly, women continued to face significant barriers to participation in political processes. A study found some of the main obstacles to women's political participation included violence against women and cultural norms that excluded women from male-dominated spaces.[56] Many women did not run for office out of fear for their lives, and fear of bringing dishonor on the family. Moreover, women regularly experienced manipulation, election-related violence, sexual harassment, voter intimidation, and pressure to vote as they were told. "I have seen by my own eyes," one local elder said, that a man beat his wife because she wanted to vote for someone else, "and he said 'I am your husband and whatever a husband says the wife should obey.'"[57]

As with previous elections, the October 2018 parliamentary elections—originally planned for 2015—were marked by widespread violence. It was believed up to 50 percent of female candidates were subjected to sexual harassment.[58] Further, targeted attacks were carried out on candidates, voters, poll facilities, and roadways, killing or injuring more than 400 civilians.[59]

A higher number of voters were recorded for this third parliamentary election, but serious challenges marred the process, including lack of material and staff. However, many Afghans did not vote, due to fear of violence and increased threats by the Taliban. These concerns likely had a greater impact on women's participation.[60]

While data remains incomplete, reported figures show little change in the percentages of women voters over the years. Women were 44 percent of the voters for the 2004 presidential election, 39 percent for the 2010 parliamentary elections, 36 percent for the 2014 presidential and provincial council elections, and 38 percent for the second round of the 2014 presidential elections.[61] For the 2018 parliamentary elections, only 33 percent of the voters were women.[62] This lower turnout was likely due to the range of threats, risks, and obstacles that continued to keep women from participating in public and political life—both as voters and as candidates. The government committed to creating an enabling environment to strengthen women's participation, but insecurity and continued corruption cast doubts on so-called democratic processes in the country. Moreover, the results were not announced for seven months, seriously undermining the population's trust in "democratic" processes.[63]

Eighteen men—and zero women—ran for president in 2019. Results were once again delayed, and voter turnout was at its lowest point. This was due to escalating attacks and intimidation by the Taliban, resulting in civilian casualties and a loss of faith in electoral processes. The downward trend in women's participation continued and in 2020, women occupied just 6.5 percent of ministerial positions in the country.[64] Since the Taliban's return to power in 2021, *no* women are serving in high-ranking government positions.[65]

In 2019, women received more votes than men and held 28 percent of the parliamentary seats, meaning women won their seats in their own right, exceeding the quota.[66] It also represented a larger proportion than most neighboring countries,[67] and even some so-called "developed" countries such as the United States, which only had 23 percent.[68] However, the numbers started to decrease again in 2020 to the threshold amount.[69] An aid worker said, "the quota system has been interpreted as a cap, rather than as a minimum requirement by those with little interest in seeing women represented in electoral institutions." And even more worryingly, this quota could be threatened with the return of the Taliban in 2021.

Unfortunately, women politicians worldwide experience threats, intimidation, and even violence. Women still lack meaningful participation and the same decision-making power as men have—everywhere. Misogyny plays a role in popular perceptions that women are not "fit" for politics, or lack the experience. Nearly every woman who has fought for her place in political life has proven these assumptions wrong.

In Afghanistan, overcoming these obstacles, particularly for women, would require significant investment and support, including the strengthening of networks between government and women's organizations. Additionally, long-term work focusing on religious and tribal leaders is necessary to change public perceptions of women's role in political life. The greatest challenge remains the lack of security, and under the renewed leadership of the Taliban in 2021, that security seems a long way off.

"Everyone has blood on their hands"[70] is a phrase often employed throughout Afghanistan, but with very different meanings. For some, it denounces the Afghan government's past atrocities and corruption, but for many others, it is utilized as an excuse. In other words, no one's hands are clean, therefore absolving leaders of past crimes with a shrug of indifference, and homogenizing many Afghans who had no part to play in the hostilities. In this way, powerful leaders who are stained with blood can continue to instill fear, create barriers to participation in governance, and obstruct justice processes.

No Peace or Security Without Women

The exclusion of Afghan women from political processes was most noticeable when it came to peace process participation. Afghanistan's transition from conflict to an anticipated peaceful future has been fraught with difficulties. "Transition" in Afghanistan has historically meant going from bad to worse. Afghan women in particular bear the brunt of these consequences.

Rights for civilians and victims have never been prioritized by the Afghan government or the international community in peace processes. As a result, local communities have felt alienated, further fueling their mistrust of international forces. That's why Afghan civil society needs to lead any viable peace process—to ensure that victims and human rights organizations are part of the process. Without women's full inclusion, any peace will be false.[71] Sima Samar, former Minister of Women's Affairs, explained that Afghan women's exclusion from leadership and decision-making is also obvious in the peace process. Without women, she stated, "a sustainable peace is not achievable. Feminism must play a crucial role in paving the way forward for Afghanistan to adopt a long-lasting peace."[72] There should be "no setback on women's rights as part of the peace process," Afghanistan's report to the UN stated in 2020. And yet, commitments to engage women were not met with action.

The Women, Peace and Security Agenda is a good starting point for analyzing why women were excluded from peace processes, despite copious promises and commitments. Signing onto this agenda entailed, amongst

other things, that countries establish National Action Plans to implement the agenda, as already outlined in Chapter 4. Although Afghanistan's
Plan covered the period of 2008 to 2018, implementation began in 2015, for
the period of 2015 to 2022. From the onset, the Plan was not framed in the
usual rhetoric of "rescuing women." Instead, it promised to create opportunities for women as peacemakers in positions of leadership, reminding
the world that "Afghan women are not damsels in distress." While there
is recognition that Afghan women have been victimized, they are not
helpless victims. "They have their own ideas about the needs of women
in their country and must be listened to and supported on their paths to
self-empowerment."[73]

In his introduction to the Plan, Ghani called it "a mechanism for
ensuring the realization of the constitutional rights of Afghan women."[74]
"Bringing lasting change to the lives of our women is the hardest of our
challenges," he went on to write.[75] Amongst other things, the plan committed to women's participation in all aspects of public and political life,
access to an accountable justice system, protection from violence, economic security, education, and special support for women in emergencies.

For the most part, however, the plan remained on paper. It appeared
that there was no trickle-down effect of this policy.[76] The National Action
Plan identified several potential risks, including lack of financial resources,
challenges at the provincial level, low capacity or technical skills, and deteriorating security. To mitigate the latter, the Plan stated that "implementation of new activities in not yet covered areas should be limited or slowed
down and efforts should be increased to support already on-going activities."[77] It is unlikely that this is happening at this stage.

Meanwhile, so-called peace processes in Afghanistan evolved, consist-
ing of a series of events and attempts to stabilize the country. There were
23 rounds of peace talks between 2005 and 2014, yet women were only
included in *two* of the 23.[78] An analysis of Afghan peace agreements in the
last two decades served as further evidence with only 16 percent containing
any reference to women.[79]

The 2010 Peace *Jirga* proved to be another example of women not
being fully included despite promises of consultation, with nine women out
of 70 members.[80] As a result, there were legitimate fears that any agreement would not factor in women's rights. Provincial Peace Committees
were established across 33 provinces, with 71 women peacebuilders. This
was touted as a demonstration of the country's commitment to women in
peace efforts, "recognized as a prerequisite for peace and reconstruction
across the country."[81] In reality, however, it proved to be another example
of a "top-down" process that failed to make a real change in female representation in sub-national institutions, as well as "one that is also failing to

Sunset at a checkpoint on the road to Bagram.

make the impact it seeks beyond a small sub-section of Afghan women who are able to access and participate in high level political processes."[82]

The High Peace Council was dissolved in 2019 "as a result of lack of coordination within the government and people's dissatisfaction with its work."[83] *If it could not deliver on its main goals, how was it ever going to deliver for women's rights?*

In September of 2016, the Afghan government signed a peace treaty with the Hezb-e Islami Gulbuddin, one of the anti–Soviet guerrilla groups who fought against multiple Afghan governments, as well as forming part of the Mujahideen in the 1990s.[84] The peace process once again excluded women as only one woman—Habiba Sarabi—was present.[85] Accepting negotiated settlements from groups like these may well result in "men with guns forgiv[ing] other men with guns for crimes committed against women"—and set the stage for further violations of women's rights.[86]

In early 2019, a series of peace talks began with the Taliban. As these talks evolved, U.S. envoy Zalmay Khalilzad outlined the four elements of the initial agreement with the Taliban: ensuring that Afghanistan will not be a threat to the world or the United States, willingness to change U.S. military posture, dialogue between Afghans, and a permanent ceasefire. Notably absent from the non-negotiable provisions was any mention of human rights or gender equality—two of the headlines often touted as major justifications for the intervention. The very "headlines" that paved the way for international institutions and international funding. Khalilzad agreed to "make sure" that women had a seat, "or several seats at the negotiating table." He went on to say that the success of a society rests on empowering women, built on equality.[87]

Meanwhile, the negotiating team had only three women, and women were excluded from the U.S.-Taliban talks throughout 2019. Despite Khalilzad's promise, women's rights were off the agenda, "leading to widespread concern among Afghan women that their human rights would be compromised for the sake of an agreement."[88] Female delegates felt excluded and women in Assembly were even told "peace has nothing to do with you. Sit down! You should be in the kitchen cooking!"[89]

Wazhma Frogh, co-founder of the Women and Peace Studies Organization in Afghanistan and member of the Afghan Women's Network, criticized the lip service paid to Afghan women by the U.S. envoy.[90] Once again, Afghan women were left to rely on their own informal networks for their rights and security, because they were not granted them through any official channels.[91] It is noteworthy that America's own 2017 Women, Peace and Security Act requires women to be part of peace processes, but Khalilzad and other U.S. diplomats violated this when they agreed to negotiate with the Taliban without protecting the rights of women and girls.[92]

The Afghan government's commitment to women's rights dwindled in response to reduced global focus.[93] This had been obvious for years with discussions of foreign military drawdown and the possibility of peace with the Taliban. The terrorist group that was once a sworn enemy had become a potential partner of peace.[94]

The peace talks culminated in a contentious peace agreement in February 2020 between the United States and the Taliban, calling for the withdrawal of U.S. troops from the country. Tensions increased exponentially following this supposed peace, with frequent insurgent attacks against Afghan security forces and deteriorating security conditions overall.

Talks between the Afghan government and the Taliban started in September 2020 in Doha, Qatar. Despite extensive advocacy work by Afghan women to be included in the peace process, they were largely excluded. The Afghan peace talks in Doha featured only four women negotiators out of the 21-member team: Habiba Sarabi, Fatima Gailani, Sharifa Zurmati Wardak and Fawzia Koofi.[95]

Understandably, this was cause for concern for the future of Afghan women's rights and raised questions about the seriousness of the government and the international community's commitment to safeguarding them.[96] There was a very real fear that gains made in areas of women's education, employment, and political participation would be rolled back.[97]

At the same time, world leaders were lobbying for Afghan women's meaningful participation in the peace process. An open letter with close to 100 signatories stated that not only is women's involvement essential to peace, but peace lasts longer when women are involved.[98] Women's participation is an international security issue, they stated, an understanding that was enshrined in UNSCR 1325 and beyond. Women's inclusion will ensure Afghanistan's stability. They must be at the table, not only on the menu, so to speak. "Peace cannot be made on the backs of Afghan women," they said.[99] Women's meaningful inclusion in all aspects of public and political life cannot be viewed as a "favor" to women, it is a non-negotiable prerequisite for any sustainable peace. As history has shown us, the Doha agreement was not a sustainable peace.

Habiba Sarabi, one of the few women in the peace negotiations, had this to say in one of the meetings where she was the *only* woman:

> Women suffer the most from war, but why are we not considered in meetings such as this? It is unfortunately because we are still not part of a political party and ... we are still not the leader of a military group that has power ... which is why the host countries also don't consider women ... [I am] thus requesting the hosts to take note of this in the future.[100]

"The women of Afghanistan are clear," she said. "Peace must mean peace for all Afghans and must not come at the expense of the rights of the women."[101]

Fatima Gailani said, "Yes, [women] want peace, but they don't want any peace. They want an inclusive peace. They want a peace that women can have a role in."[102]

Meanwhile, as this so-called peace process evolved, security conditions deteriorated. Since the start of the intra–Afghan peace negotiations in September 2020, the UN documented a "46% increase in civilian casualties in comparison to the same nine-month period a year earlier" concluding that "the pursuit of a military solution will only increase the suffering of the Afghan people."[103]

The March 2021 peace talks in Moscow had just one lone woman: Habiba Sarabi. One woman out of a delegation of 12 on the side of the Afghan government. And no women in the ten-man Taliban delegation. The U.S. State Department "wished" there had been more than one.[104] The EU tweeted that "a long-term solution to the conflict requires inclusivity."[105] It didn't mention whose inclusion they were referring to. Unfortunately, wishes and tweets will not create space for Afghan women in political life.

Civilian casualties continued to increase. In May and June of 2021, the UN documented 783 Afghan civilians were killed and 1609 were injured in attacks which was the highest number on record for those two months since 2009.[106] Afghan women leaders and peacebuilders were specifically targeted. In 2021 two female Supreme Court judges were killed amidst increased violence and targeted killings. This was an attack on both women and the justice system as the Taliban sought to "reduce the influence of women in public spaces" and "gain leverage in the peace talks."[107] Ultimately, this attack creates fear for women who defy patriarchal boundaries.

Shaharzad Akbar, chair of the Afghanistan Independent Human Rights Commission, documented the dangers associated with human rights work, describing how colleagues are targeted and murdered. Those who remain have little influence on the peace process as survival is paramount:

> Every day I hear of another friend, journalist, academic, women's rights activist or businessperson leaving the country. Their departures are creating an absence that will take another generation to fill. Those who can't leave feel silenced by fear and have little chance of influencing the peace process.[108]

An Afghan women's group issued a press release on the peace process, stating that women's collective and historical memory is "the only reliable source" and therefore only women, "as the primary victims of the conflict and attacks by the Taliban and other hostile forces," have the right to forgive these criminals. Meaning: a peace without women is no peace at all.[109]

At the same time, some Afghan women leaders warned against presenting Afghan women as a monolith as this would be an oversimplification to assume that their needs are homogenous.[110] These differences are most acute across rural versus urban lines. Rural women have been disproportionately affected by the conflict, an estimated 76 percent have experienced loss, trauma, heightened vulnerability, and greater risks to their survival.[111] Consequently, rural women prioritize the immediate cessation of war and bloodshed, even if that comes with Taliban control. "Peace is the first thing," one rural woman said.[112]

Urban women, on the other hand, do not accept peace at any price. They sought promises from the U.S. and the Afghan government that women's rights would be non-negotiables. Many Afghan women leaders doubted the integrity of the talks, but fought anyway. They believed that the Taliban had an unfair advantage, enabling them to "set the rules and parameters of negotiation," which meant sidelining women.[113]

As of August 2021, any semblance of peace was on hold. Meanwhile, Afghan women continued to fight despite seemingly-insurmountable obstacles and in the face of great risks. Not only does feminism still live in Afghanistan, it warned us of what was to come. Sanam Naraghi Anderlini, founder and CEO of the International Civil Society Action Network articulated that "we have not stood by Afghan women. We have not listened to them. They warned—they have been warning over and over what the Taliban was, what they represent, what's going to happen on the ground."[114]

She continued to say that our intelligence community "didn't think the Afghan forces would fall so fast," while Afghan women were risking their lives to warn the world of this very thing. "They warned repeatedly, and they had solutions," she rightly argued. "Our politicians, our diplomatic community, our media chose not to take it seriously and now everyone is saying, 'oh gosh what happened?' And they're pretending to be surprised by it."[115]

Ultimately, the Women, Peace and Security Agenda was "militarised and women's rights instrumentalised in pursuit of goals of 'countering violent extremism.'"[116] Fionnuala Ní Aoláin, UN Special Rapporteur on the Promotion and Protection of Human Rights and Fundamental Freedoms, put it best: "We've had 20 years plus of the WPS agenda. And if that agenda doesn't mean something now, it's worthless."[117]

Just prior to the Taliban takeover of 2021, Nazila Jamshidi, an Afghan woman, wrote that Afghan women are now "aware of their rights and have been introduced to democracy and freedom." Therefore, the international community, particularly the United States, should stand with Afghan women after the troops withdraw. "Protecting women's rights must be at the top of every agreement."[118]

Ultimately, Afghan women continue to demonstrate their agency. Protecting women's rights cannot be seen as an add-on. It is a critical prerequisite to peace.

Fostering a Feminist Peace

How, then, might we come to understand what peace means to women? Did we miss an opportunity to build the foundation for a feminist peace in Afghanistan?

The Taliban's reclaiming of the country in 2021 has resulted in increased violence against women, leaving little hope of peace in a climate of great insecurity. Ultimately, there's a lesson in this failed peace, a failed peace where Afghan women have been victims, starting with the "American sponsoring of the anti–Soviet Mujahideen that eventually spawned the misogynist Taliban ... the product of a Cold War power play." This in turn led to the unraveling of the already-feeble U.S.-backed Afghan government and the subsequent takeover by the Taliban—again.[119]

There were fissures and failures at several intervals, but the foremost failure was this: a failure to listen to Afghan women, to work with them, to build with them, to follow their lead as they articulated what peace could mean—what peace *should* mean.

A feminist peace is not only possible, it is the only viable peace.

Traditional peace focuses on military and economic issues, just as much as war focuses on force and dominance—both manifestations of masculinity.[120] Waging war in the name of national security, for instance, actually makes people *less* secure.[121] Unsurprisingly, research has repeatedly shown that peace lasts longer when women lead.[122]

While participation of Afghan women in the peace process remained largely symbolic, Afghan women have found creative ways to optimize the space they have. They have had to make their own strategies and to mobilize and advocate on their own behalf. Fatima Gailani said, "there are so many Afghan girls and women worried about the results of these talks, but I hear them, and I am guided by their voices in these talks, this is the voice of the future."[123]

Sima Samar offered "an Afghan-feminist framework to deconstruct the current situation." She explained that we need to critically examine Afghan history—and the history of Afghan women—in order to understand. In so doing, she continued, we can "set concrete foundations for the way forward."[124]

Fostering a feminist peace is about women's voice, agency, dignity. But it is critically about rights, respect, representation, and resources. Women in peace are not the exception—they are the norm, in Afghanistan and elsewhere.

These are the women to whom the international community must be held accountable. In a previous article,[125] I argued that, on paper, we have the right language in the right agreements endorsed by the right actors. But we fall short in our commitments to women in several critical areas:

> Firstly, we liberally claim to support women leaders, women's organizations, feminist organizations, but our funding doesn't measure up to our claims. If we seek a feminist peace, we must fund the organizations that have been pursuing this long before we arrived, and who will be cultivating it long after we leave. This funding must be flexible, long-term, meaningful—with priorities defined by the women leaders themselves.
>
> And, secondly, we continue to fall short in ending violence against women. This is the greatest impediment to peace, progress, prosperity—and to women's participation. Without safety for women, nothing else we do will matter. Again, if we examine the funding allocated to this, we see that it is too slow, too small, too short-term. And yet we know that this is integral to achieving peace and security.
>
> But it's not just about crisis. We need to view every single thing we do through the lens of women's safety. Supporting women and ending violence is the most effective prevention method. We need to revisit our early warning indicators. The bottom line is this: If women are not safe, no one is safe.
>
> And when we refer to women, peace, and security, we've reduced it to a little acronym—WPS. In doing so, we forget the power behind the words. And we

risk turning this work into a sub-category, a sideshow, or an add-on. Imagine if we could just say "peace and security" with the full recognition that women are indispensable to this effort. Globally, there will be no P and no S without W.

And even simply existing as a woman in the world today—that is an emergency. We face a colossal global pushback, making the fight for women's rights harder than ever.

… Women [are] transforming peace as leaders and agents of change, taking charge of their lives and their choices, raising their voices, galvanizing support for peace, and not just claiming a seat at the table—but building their own tables.

These women are not the exception. This is not an add-on or an afterthought. This is the global norm. It is our daily fight—for our very own lives.

Women wage peace everywhere all the time—home, community, country, and at the global level. Women are not just vulnerable in times of war. They have value. The world loses when we fail to acknowledge that value. We need to take these as a small example, a minute acknowledgement of a massive contribution, a contribution that deserves to be fully resourced and respected.

Women worldwide deserve no less.

Women in Afghanistan deserve no less.

CHAPTER 6

War Has Never Been
Over for Them

When poverty walks in through the door,
happiness flies out through the window.
—Afghan proverb indicating that poverty brings trouble
and difficulties at home

Men's violence against women is the most egregious violation of women's human rights. Globally, this remains the most obvious reminder that women are not yet equal because we are not even *safe*. Safety and security, both public and private, are critical prerequisites to any gains and future freedoms. In fact, even if women had equal opportunities—in education, health, politics, the economy—access to those opportunities will be limited as long as violence persists.

Anecdotes and evidence show that the safety of women has always been under threat in Afghanistan. But in 2021, and with the return of the Taliban to power, men's violence against women is only going to increase. Ending violence needs to be the critical first step before all else. But deteriorating security, Taliban violations, and worsening socio-economic conditions are creating a perfect storm for women. Every Afghan woman has warned that we will see more manifestations of men's violence against women in every space in the months and years ahead.

Patriarchal Violence

Afghanistan is not unlike other patriarchal contexts where females are under the authority of males in the family. They suffer restricted freedom of movement and nearly no control over the choices that govern their lives. Most women will not have the opportunity to assert social or economic independence, or enjoy the human rights to which they are entitled.

Men's violence against women manifests as physical, sexual, emotional or economic—all of these are occurring in Afghanistan. Afghan women continue to be abused at home, harassed in public places, married off without their consent, and traded and exchanged to resolve disputes.[1] A girl under their father's authority becomes a woman under her husband's authority. Choice of husband, or even the choice to marry at all, is not up to her. Often, she ends up abused and mistreated in her husband's home. In the worst cases, those who try to escape the abuse are stigmatized, isolated, and possibly imprisoned. Forms of violence in Afghanistan also include practices such as *baad* (giving a female relative to the victim's family to settle a crime) or *badal* (giving a female relative in marriage in return for a bride) as well as exchanging girls for cattle or material goods.

Two women worry as they listen to an aid agency explain its plans, Kabul.

Men's violence against women in Afghanistan also includes intimidation of women in the form of sexual or derogatory comments, harassment, and other means of drawing boundaries and delineating women's place in the patriarchal gender order in both public and private space. Intimate partner violence is common, underreported, and on the rise, particularly in times of insecurity.[2] Physical violence is the most common, and takes many forms including beating, kicking, slapping, hitting as well as burning, poisoning, stabbing, use of weapons, and also dismembering.[3] These forms are severe, severely underreported, and can often result in death. Femicide—the intentional killing of women *because* they are women—continues to take place.

Rape is another common crime against women, taking place in homes, communities and public space. Women can also be raped "as a result of traditional harmful practices to resolve feuds within the family or community."[4] Rapists may also be—or be connected to—powerful men who are, in effect, above the law, and therefore benefit from "immunity from arrest as well as immunity from social condemnation."[5] Communities can also condone—or call for—rape through harmful practices like *baad*, or by forcing the victim to marry her rapist.[6]

So-called crimes of "honor" are also common. Afghan women are viewed as the custodians of the family's honor, as has been previously said. If they experience the crime of sexual violence, the incident is viewed as a "dishonor" to the family, particularly when virginity has been compromised. It is the woman or girl—not the perpetrator—who is then blamed and shamed. She may be ostracized from family and community, or killed. As a result, survivors are reluctant to disclose the crime, because they fear for their lives.

If women choose to report the crime, they can be subjected to so-called virginity tests: "invasive and abusive vaginal and sometimes anal examinations for the purpose of determining virginity."[7] This additional form of violence clearly takes place without her consent and is not limited to specific cases.

Often as a result of these forms of violence, women and girls in Afghanistan will attempt suicide by setting themselves on fire. This practice, known as self-immolation, is common. It can also be forced upon the woman by a member of the family. Self-immolation often, but not always, results in death. If the woman survives, her injuries are severe.

Emotional violence includes threats where the woman or girl is told she will be abandoned, ostracized, or killed. This also includes threats made against her for not bearing children, or *male* children. The man may also make threats against the children or her relatives, including threatening to rape her relatives.[8] Economic violence takes the form of denying a woman control of economic resources as well as taking what may be hers, for instance jewelry, a stipend received from an aid organization, or an income from work. This is fueled by the lack of economic autonomy, but has also made women less willing to take on roles or access opportunities outside of the household, and further contributes to their silence in household decision-making.[9]

All women and girls are at risk, but there are certain vulnerable groups worth highlighting. And violence increases as poverty and insecurity increase, therefore it is likely that there will be more cases in the months and years ahead as vulnerabilities are amplified. Female-headed households and widows are at particular risk, given that they are often on their own and without support. Women working in informal labor or high-risk work face constant threats and lack of protection. Trafficked women and women forced into prostitution are but two examples. Women who are drug users, as well as women living with disabilities, have unique risks and are particularly vulnerable. Young girls and young women are also vulnerable, and face increasing risks of girl-child or forced marriage, magnified in times of crisis. Afghan women leaders, feminists, activists, human rights defenders, women working with "foreigners," or any women who participate in public life are also at risk—now more than ever.

Let us restate the obvious: Not all Afghan women are victims. Not all Afghan men are perpetrators. Not all women are inherently peaceful. And not all men are bellicose. Such constructions reinforce patriarchal models of the gender order and negate patterns of violence practiced by women, and patterns of peace practiced by men.[10] It is important to recognize that not all violence against women is at the hands of men.

There are various examples across cultures and histories to demonstrate that women have the capacity for violence against each other. This ranges from female genital cutting—where young girls are mutilated by the hands of older women— to the violence perpetrated on a new bride by her mother-in-law. In Afghanistan, new brides can face abuse from their female in-laws, particularly if the marriage is the result of *baad* or *badal*. If the bride remains childless, violence can also result. The forms of such violence perpetrated by women are not only physical and often also include emotional or economic abuse.

While it is important to acknowledge such incidents, it is clear that in the majority of cases, women are primarily survivors of violence perpetrated by men. Men's violence against women is a crime that remains too frequent and too readily accepted.

A girl invites us into her home in Khairkhana, where most live in partial tents along a wall, Kabul.

The physical and emotional consequences for the woman are severe and often last a lifetime. There are also deleterious impacts on her family and community. If a woman is not safe, a country is not safe.

Ultimately, men's violence against women is only possible in a context of persistent inequality, fueled by patriarchy built on conservative political and religious forces. In these situations, women's rights are precarious and are quickly "bartered to advance vested interests or issue-specific agendas."[11] Pervasive insecurity and ongoing conflict perpetuate impunity, feeding into a dangerous culture of violence—one that undermines any hope of peace and stability, particularly for women. Men's violence against women is the most heinous example of misogyny, and a constant reminder that we are not yet equal.

In the years following 2001, it was difficult to conduct research and access information on men's violence against women. Available understandings were largely based on anecdotal evidence as data was not widely available. Whatever did exist was unreliable. In the few cases where figures were available, they dramatically underestimated reality. Women said they paid the price of social and political instability. Their words and experiences revealed that men's violence against women became an increasing concern, even in times of so-called peace. Their words outweigh all data.

In Afghanistan, some refused to acknowledge men's violence against women as an issue. Most women—and men—had different definitions of what constitutes violence. Men's violence against women in the private sphere was often not recognized and labeled as such. It was viewed by some women as within the realm of normal gender relations and therefore not assumed to be an abuse of women's human rights. In fact, there was a general perception among these women that violence was a normal part of their lives and that it was unavoidable, even inevitable, perhaps. Many believed that this was what it meant to be a woman in Afghanistan—particularly in violent or insecure times.

Those women who were able to recognize violence against them were still not likely to change or address it. They explained that the recognition, and labeling, of this violence would likely provoke additional violence. Women may have been reluctant to speak publicly about the violence they feared, witnessed, or experienced for fear of being stigmatized. They also risked losing their children, or witnessing abuse inflicted on the children, if they spoke out.

Further, there was a perception that violence against women in the domestic sphere was a private affair that should be addressed within families and not revealed to outsiders. The concern was that such public admissions would bring shame to the family. Men's violence against women was often disguised and denied within the family to retain honor and standing within the community.

In addition to the fear of social stigma and the blame they may have received, women were reluctant to report violence because existing support structures were not equipped to take action and protect them. Reporting the crime may have placed the woman at greater risk. The crime itself may not be recorded or classified as a crime. In Afghanistan, women's complaints of violence were often disregarded by national institutions, such as the Afghan National Police. Thus, women ran the risk of exposing themselves to additional violence from the community and the state—the structures that were built to support them. It was difficult to measure rates of violence accurately, particularly when there was social stigma attached. In a context of changing gender roles and relations, the space created for women brought resentment and backlash, manifesting in an increase from public to private violence. When public violence turns private, it becomes hidden from aid structures and beyond the purview of "development" priorities.

Indeed, the increased levels of men's violence against women were attributed largely to poverty, the ongoing (and evolving) occupation, and frustration around the belief that the international community "failed" to make meaningful changes in their lives. Backlashes against women were not unusual. There is worldwide evidence that violence against women predominates in situations of poverty, particularly where women gain economic independence while men remain unemployed. If such socioeconomic changes provoke men's violence against women, perhaps more caution could have been taken in design of aid programs in order to mitigate this risk.

There is sufficient research and understanding that particular forms of violence against women, especially intimate partner violence, increase after a conflict. In post–2001 Afghanistan, it was not unusual to hear women say that they felt "safer under the Taliban." Men's violence against women was believed to be pervasive in Afghanistan, sustained by a patriarchy that often lends itself to misogyny. Men's violence against women also has significant economic and social costs, impairing women from actively and effectively participating in society and in their own (and ultimately Afghanistan's) development. So, for women, when the national emergency is over, their emergency is just beginning.

No Country Is Safe

It is not unusual for men to use violence against women as a means of establishing and maintaining power relationships. All men's violence

Boys in school, Bamiyan.

against women is caused by power inequality—and an abuse of that power. No country is free from violence against women. *Not one.*

In contexts of conflict, violence against women is amplified and new forms of violence are perpetrated. Sexual violence often increases, where women are deliberately targeted and used as a weapon of war. In addition, women and girls face increased torture, killings, forced marriage, trafficking, and forced prostitution. Women and girls are exchanged and sold as sex slaves for powerful men. Cases of sexual exploitation and abuse increase, and women and girls are forced to provide sexual "favors" in exchange for support. There is a link between conflict, militarized masculinities, and the oppression of women. It is not uncommon to see intimate partner violence as an unfortunate byproduct of the post-conflict culture of violence.

Women's marginalization and exclusion during conflict often motivates aid organizations to focus on women's empowerment, often alienating men.[12] Myriad reports have explained that there are consequences for women when, in the context of conflict and so-called post-conflict, men perceive that they have lost their traditional roles. Instead of finding peaceful alternatives when traditional roles are threatened, many men seek to safeguard the patriarchal gender order and assert masculinity through violence against women. In cases where men employ such violence, women's choices, behavior, and safety are restricted as a result.

Having said all of this, it is worthwhile noting that men's violence against women is not exclusive to contexts such as Afghanistan. So-called third-world violence against women is viewed by those outside as a "death by culture."[13] It is important to think of the context that is lost—and the new one that is gained—when issues of violence against women cross borders and become part of a Western feminist agenda. These *other* issues of *other* women are subsequently adopted, and often hijacked, by academics and feminists and become part of what the West understands "third-world gender issues" to be. If these issues occur in Muslim countries, they then become "Muslim issues" and they continue to be misconstrued and decontextualized with increasing publicity.[14]

Examples from other countries emerging from conflict demonstrate that men's violence against women often increases in the aftermath. This can take many forms, but there is also extensive research and evidence worldwide that intimate partner violence in particular continues following a conflict, in times of supposed peace.[15] In the aftermath, conditions for women risk further deterioration, violence tends to increase, and the potential for future conflict is likely. It is also in this context that international attention and support begins to wane.[16] During a country's reconstruction, violence against women is often ignored or viewed as a low priority compared with other concerns.

The absence of violence against women is not even a precursor for peace. For instance, the Global Peace Index measures a country based on its level of societal safety and security, the extent of ongoing domestic and international conflict, and the degree of militarization.[17] There are a range of indicators under each category, including perceptions of safety and risk. Women—and forms of violence against women—are not mentioned or considered as a line of inquiry. The dangers of men's violence against women continue to be overlooked. And yet, a life free from such violence is a fundamental prerequisite for peace. Meanwhile, the Index ranked Afghanistan as the least peaceful country as of 2021.[18]

The experience of women in Bosnia is an oft-cited case to demonstrate increased violence against women in post-conflict contexts. Violence was inflicted upon Bosnian women at the hands of demobilized soldiers in the form of intimate partner violence. Similarly, in Rwanda, women experienced increased violence following the conflict and became "soft" outlets for men's frustrations. Research on increased violence in post-conflict Guatemala notes that despite a decline in political violence, social violence was increasing.[19] In addition, there was a notable shift to increased urban-based violence coupled with a general sense of lawlessness and disorder.

Afghanistan experienced a similar phenomenon in the years after 2001. Poverty and vulnerability, particularly in urban areas, contributed to a breakdown of social safety nets, increased crime rates, and intimate partner violence.[20] Similarly, in Angola, many men were left unemployed as a result of conflict. Research in Angola revealed that men felt undermined by the fact that they were unable to contribute to the household and that instead women were supporting the families. As a result, men's frustrations led to increased violence against women, coupled with greater drug and alcohol use.[21]

Research in Tanzania revealed striking similarities to Afghanistan. It was noted that efforts to empower women through aid programming had negative effects, with men feeling threatened by the perceived loss of their position as breadwinners and figures of authority. In short, they felt as if aid agencies were "taking their authority and their women from them."[22]

Feelings of loss following a conflict—of lives, livelihoods, homes, social structures, and so on—are played out on gender relations. This can also be a projection of the resentment toward the agency that is attempting to take their women and their masculinity.[23] In the case of Tanzania, some women gave half of their financial support from the agency to their husbands so as not to antagonize them. I noted the same trend in Afghanistan where women presented cash and in-kind earnings to male members of the family to appease them and to secure their continued participation in aid programs. In short, they bought their freedom.

While not in conflict or the aftermath, research in Mexico also bears resemblance to Afghanistan. There, women felt compelled to accept increased men's violence as a reaction to men's own sense of displacement as women were granted greater economic opportunities. When women's economic benefits are offset by increased patriarchal violence, the whole concept of development is thrown into question, "since material 'progress' entails a regression—an escalation in men's violence."[24]

Increased violence against women in the aftermath is not just a phenomenon of the so-called developing world. In fact, research in the United States following Hurricane Katrina in 2005 revealed that American men are just as susceptible to violence in times of uncertainty:

> Especially when so much is out of their control in Katrina's aftermath, men without jobs ... may feel unmasked and unmanly.... Some men will cope through drugs, alcohol, physical aggression or all three, hurting themselves and putting the women and girls around them at risk. We can count on increased reports of violence against women as this is so common in U.S. and international disasters.[25]

The Costs of Social Instability

From 2001 onward, Afghanistan aspired to become a state that was pluralistic, Islamic, prosperous, and peace-loving—but the challenges were great.[26] For the two decades of "development" prior to the 2021 takeover of the Taliban, Afghans argued that violence against women would still continue—and gender inequalities would increase—as long as Afghanistan was under occupation, and as long as aid organizations and the Afghan government failed to make improvements in the lives of the majority of the population.

Afghanistan had, and continues to have, some of the worst social indicators in the world, particularly for women. Ample research shows that women remain oppressed, despite the oft-cited rhetoric of "liberation" of Afghan women. We did not need research to tell us this. No liberation is possible as long as violence persists, and too many Afghan women remain abused or prevented from accessing opportunities and participating in public life.[27]

The UN Special Rapporteur on Violence against Women visited Afghanistan several times during the last two decades to better understand the situation and to recommend measures to end violence against women in the country.[28] The reports from each visit reiterated previous recommendations but also noted the absence of data and therefore the difficulty to obtain a complete picture of the situation of men's violence against women in Afghanistan. Still, the below data and the stories that follow should serve not only as evidence of what transpired, but as ominous predictions of what is likely to come.

The 2004 UN report stated that "the volatile security situation and traditional social and cultural norms continue to limit women's and girls' role in public life and deny them the full enjoyment of their rights."[29] And, there was further evidence of violence against women in the private sphere. A former Minister of Women's

Children living near Kabul Airport.

Affairs was outspoken about the prevalence of violence against women. In a speech on women's rights and security in July 2005, she said:

> It has been more than three years since we embarked on a journey to peace and reconstruction. Our people have embraced peace ... but unfortunately this is not true for many of our women ... real peace has never entered their sphere of life. A different kind of conflict continues to haunt our women.... They live in constant fear of being beaten, harassed, abused verbally, discriminated, denied of rights, robbed of self respect and dignity, exchanged for material goods or for settling conflicts. War has never been over for them.[30]

Studies on livelihoods of the urban poor in Kabul revealed a number of cases of violent conflict between men and women, due to economic deterioration. This deprivation and insecurity had psychological effects on Afghans, particularly those in Kabul who came to the city seeking greater security and economic opportunity. Expectations were raised by promises of large amounts of aid. As a result, many felt frustrated and angry about the absence of improvement in their daily lives—and their inability to access this aid. This displacement of anger is not unusual, as Afghans could generally not point to any improvements in their own lives, and as a result, anger was directed "to the place where they feel they have dominance—their relations with women."[31] Many activists and experts issued warnings: "Hopefully, the aid community will heed the lessons learned over the past decades. Programs are needed to promote the integrity of the family, for one can ignore the family only at the cost of social stability."[32] This isn't unique to Afghanistan.

Reports from the UN and the Ministry of Women's Affairs indicated that in 2007 approximately 60–80 percent of all marriages were forced—many before the age of 16—and occurred frequently as payment for debt or to settle a feud.[33] A child marriage is by definition a forced marriage, because a child cannot have consented freely.[34] A "child" marriage also is, more often than not, a girl-child marriage which, more often than not, entails the marriage of a girl-child to an older man. This, more often than not, entails a sexual relationship. As such, sex between an older man and an underage girl is called rape.

Estimates in 2020 reveal that girl-child marriage remains prevalent, with 35 percent of girls affected.[35] Poverty and insecurity fuels girl-child marriage, but more dangerous is the culture of acceptance by communities, religion and the state. Conservative parliamentarians have driven this by objecting to the concept that forced marriage and girl-child marriage be considered crimes.[36] This can be understood through this expression, used in rural parts of the country: *A girl should have her first period in her husband's house, not her father's house.*

There have been documented increases in intimate partner violence, estimating that one in three Afghan women have been beaten or abused.[37] The Ministry of Women's Affairs recorded 583 reported cases in 2004, with the likelihood of many more.[38] The Afghanistan Independent Human Rights Commission registered more than 1650 cases of violence against women in 2006—and again, many cases went unreported.[39] Intimate partner violence cases continued to be unreported, and in the rare instances where they were reported, they were not properly recorded. Afghan women leaders expressed concern that intimate partner violence was widespread and there remained little public awareness, prevention, or response.

There was little incentive to report as services and support were either unavailable or inaccessible. And access to justice was hardly ever an option. In the first half of 2013, reports from the AIHRC found that only 400 of the cases women brought to the legal system were processed and adjudicated.[40] The absence of effective redress for survivors, whether through informal or formal justice mechanisms, was, and remains, a pervasive human rights problem.

The 2005 UN report noted that violence against women continued to be pervasive in Afghanistan despite intervention.[41] The report cited four reasons for the perpetuation of violence: (1) the traditional patriarchal gender order, (2) the erosion of protective social mechanisms, (3) the lack of rule of law, and (4) poverty and insecurity. Indeed, attempts to improve the status of women were linked with—and often superseded by—the multiple transitions underway in Afghan society.

In this case, it is possible to build on the report by adding a fifth element, the idea raised by many Afghan men and women that aid organizations were provoking a change in gender relations. New forms of violence emerged as a result of women's increased visibility outside the home. Such violence was beyond social, ethnic, religious, tribal, or economic boundaries. The space created for women brought resentment and backlash, driving violence further into the private domain.

Afghanistan's Millennium Development Goals Report for 2005 stated the silent epidemic of men's violence against women was due to the combination of their low status and years of conflict.[42] Men's violence against women in Afghanistan was widespread and ranged from deprivation of education to economic opportunities, through verbal and psychological violence, beatings, sexual violence and killings. Many acts of violence involved traditional practices including the betrothal of young girls in infancy, early marriage and crimes of honor, where a female was punished for having offended custom, tradition or honor.[43]

The 2009 Elimination of Violence Against Women Draft Law was a critical step in ending violence against women, putting responsibility on the state to legally protect women from violence. This law "makes 22 acts of abuse toward women criminal offenses, including rape, battery, forced marriage, preventing women from acquiring property, and prohibiting a woman or girl from going to school or work"[44] and helps facilitate reporting and investigating crimes against women.

In 2013, female parliamentarians pushed for approval to turn this decree into law. The result was a backlash against the law itself and any protections it offered women.[45] The law was seen as a direct attack on patriarchy and "the rules of men [that] have defined Afghan society for a long time."[46] In fact, a 2018 report showed that two-thirds of Afghan men complain that women have too many rights.[47]

Many women were, and still are, unaware of their rights and of the existence of the law. Reporting violence carries stigma and risks ostracization. Shame and blame fall on the woman, and such issues should not be shared outside the family. Understandably, many Afghan women have no faith in the systems of justice or security to protect them. Accessing justice presents huge obstacles as well, such as the costs of travel, the risk of revictimization, and the risks of further violence upon their return. Most Afghan women are financially dependent on men—they cannot file a complaint against the person they depend on for food and shelter.[48] As a result, too few cases were actually tried under this law. Instead of opting for formal justice, most cases were decided by local councils and traditional structures, mainly dominated by strongmen.[49] These structures tend not to rule in favor of women.

If a woman considers reporting the crime, too often the family will force her to withdraw the complaint, or to not report at all. In 2010, the Supreme Court stated that it was a crime for a woman to leave her family for a non-relative's home, even if fleeing abuse, because it was believed to cause a break down in the family structure and cause crimes such as adultery and prostitution, which is unacceptable and against Sharia principles.[50] This led to stigmatization and contributed to women being imprisoned for "moral" crimes as well as an increase in unsubstantiated charges of *zina*, adultery. As of 2018, 50 percent of women and 95 percent of girls in Afghan prisons have been jailed for these so-called "moral crimes."[51]

Despite extensive advocacy from Afghan women's groups, the law was never fully implemented and as of 2021 it remained elusive.[52] The existence of this law is an important step and it must be safeguarded, but moving the law from paper to practice will be a long road. And, the very existence of the law has been compromised since the Taliban regained power.

A provincial council member had this to say on the situation in 2015:

There are many causes of violence against women in our province ... poverty, lack of employment, lack of awareness of women's rights and people selling their girls for ten to forty thousand U.S. dollars. The heavy dowries for girls lead to many murders of women and increase violence cases and sometimes they create tension between two tribes. The provincial council has registered violence against women cases involving forced marriage, running away from home and sometimes murder. These are the majority of cases we deal with ... on a daily basis through family committees in the provincial council.[53]

In 2017, 4340 cases of violence against women were registered, signifying an increase of almost 12 percent in one year.[54] Between 2018–2019, an 8.4 percent increase in reported cases of violence against women was documented, with "beatings" being the most common complaint.[55] The number of women bringing family disputes to court or to the local *Jirga* also increased 21.8 percent in 2018. This can be attributed to the specialized units within the Afghan government dedicated to helping women navigate cases of intimate partner violence and family disputes.[56]

Some other measures have also shown promise or change, albeit slowly. For instance, the traditional practices of *baad* and *badal* have been steadily decreasing. In 2016, 18 percent of those surveyed felt that *baad* was acceptable, and 32 percent continued to support *badal*. In 2018, only 9 percent supported *baad* and 25 percent accepted *badal*.[57] Despite these apparent gains, the data may be misleading. Data collection remains patchy, and implementation of the law remains elusive. Goals set to prevent and respond to men's violence against women were still unattainable. And now perhaps more than ever.

A 2017 review of Afghanistan's gender equality progress found that "women are still victims of discrimination and violation all over the country ... the existing laws are not being duly implemented and the perpetrators of violence, harassment and discrimination against women are not brought to justice."[58] The reality is even more stark for vulnerable women, such as those with disabilities, female-headed households, widows, and many others who face additional forms of violence and discrimination.[59]

In 2017, it was reported that 51 percent of Afghan women experienced intimate partner violence and/or sexual violence at least once in their lifetime, with 46 percent experiencing it in that year alone. These figures were among the worst social indicators for women worldwide.[60] The trend continues, with 19.2 percent of Afghan women ranking intimate partner violence as one of the most significant challenges they faced in 2018.[61]

The high rates of men's violence against women has also been linked to increasing rates of suicide among women. A 2017 report estimated that approximately 3000 Afghans attempt suicide each year. Worldwide, this is more common among men, but in Afghanistan 80 percent of suicides are committed by women.[62] Forced marriage and violence are cited as the main drivers.[63] Too many women prefer death to lives of continued violence.

In just one example, a woman set herself on fire after years of sustaining abuse and violence from her husband. Her husband was arrested for charges of domestic abuse, but his family withheld her son from her and pressured her to tell the police that she had lied about the violence.[64]

In 2017, a survivor of intimate partner violence had this to say on the matter:

> When I went to the police with my father, the police instructed me many times to withdraw the case before it went to the prosecutor. I told them that I would never accept mediation, I want my husband to receive punishment because he beat me for two years. I told the police that many relatives and village residents had tried to mediate the case a hundred times. Now, I want you to forward the case to the prosecution. The police officer told me "we are the police and you are a woman, not my commander." He tried to force me to withdraw my complaint but I resisted and my father supported me. Community leaders and relatives told me that after two months my husband will be released from prison and he will kill me. I told them that he should be punished no matter what happens next. I will kill myself because there is nothing to live for. All of them—police, community leaders and relatives of my husband tried to force me to drop the case but I did not accept their demands.[65]

Despite legal protection—on paper—the security and justice sectors continue to sideline the issue of violence. The decades following 2001 prioritized counter-insurgency over community policing, resulting in a police force that is neither able nor willing to protect women from violence.[66] While the presence of women in the police force increased dramatically during these years, it remained inadequate. In 2010, Afghanistan pledged to increase the number of women in the National Police to more than 5000 by 2015, but fell short of this with only 3000 women serving in national security forces.[67] In 2021, women account for 2.6 percent of the police force—4000 out of an estimated 157,000 person force.[68] While it demonstrates an improvement, it is poor considering the sizable investment from donors and the international community. In addition to the few female police officers, the ones who do exist are marginalized and unable to respond to cases effectively.

A 2020 UN report confirmed that the risk of sexual abuse and exploitation increased and added that a lack of accountability combined with the normalization of violence perpetrated by men and boys also fuels violence against women.[69] The evidence confirmed this, citing 271 cases of violence against women that year.[70] A 2021 report highlighted the barriers women continued to face in reporting intimate partner violence including "family pressure, financial dependence, stigma associated with filing a complaint, and fear of reprisals, including losing their children."[71] This was prior to the country's reoccupation by the Taliban.

Following the Taliban takeover in September of 2021, the Ministry of Women's Affairs was replaced with the Ministry for the Propagation of Virtue and the Prevention of Vice This new ministry includes the Taliban's "Moral Police," responsible for enforcing their interpretation of *Sharia* Law, including a strict dress code, punishable by violence.[72] It is reasonable to be skeptical of what is to come, especially as the Taliban have declared that their new ideology is aligned with their previous reign, fueling Islamic fundamentalism in a manner that Afghan feminists call "misogynist, inhuman, barbaric, reactionary, anti-democracy and anti-progressive."[73]

The situation continues to deteriorate. In addition, the COVID pandemic has resulted in restricted mobility and increased intimate partner violence worldwide—Afghanistan is no exception. All of these challenges, and the risks women face, are now likely far worse. The rights and protections Afghan women fought for in these last decades now risk being completely undone. As the country unravels, so too does the safety of women and the actual—or perceived—freedom they might have had. There is a strong correlation between men's violence against women and conflict. But violence for women does not end when the conflict ends.

In further conversations, the former Minister of Women's Affairs had the following to say:

> Even after years of attention to women, it has not succeeded in making women equal to men. In practical life, at the family and community level, power is still in men's hands. The economy of the home, the economy of the country, all this belongs to men. 100%. Still. So what have we given women?
>
> We have given them opportunities for education. But not for all of them. Only those in urban areas. And even then not all of them. We can open up the gates of schools to them and take away all discriminatory laws—but even then it's not complete because that's only the Constitution and we have other discriminatory laws that are written and unwritten. And we have given them security, generally that has improved but still not fully. Work opportunities, those are limited. Only urban areas again. And we have given them opportunities in political life. We have a number of ministers in the cabinet. But still, all this does not mean equality in their lives. Not at all.
>
> The violence is still going on. It is increasing, even. There has been no positive impact on violence in the last years. It has not decreased, for sure. If we take deaths of women as an indicator, those deaths that have taken place in Herat and other places, self-burning and other things. This happens more than the media reports. I hear these things from the head of the Women's Unit in those places. If we take all this into account, it has increased. Forced marriages are going on, and more than before. Intimate partner violence is more than before.

There is no change in terms of legal protection for women. Small interventions are taking place, but that has had no impact.

So we need to do a lot. For a country where the load of centuries of discrimination is on the shoulders of women, with this little investment it is not possible to give them real equality and freedom and justice.

Evidence of Unintended Effects

Despite the above figures and the concerns they bring, statistics pale in comparison to anecdotal evidence. For this reason, voices, perspectives, and experiences hold great weight.

During conversations with many Afghan women over the years, I exercised caution in explicitly mentioning violence because I did not want to assume that it was occurring, nor did I want to make women uncomfortable. Instead, we talked about their lives at home and how things might be changing. Discussions of violence emerged when the women themselves found it to be an issue that was relevant to the conversation.

Very often, women alluded to violence without specifically stating it. For example, referring to increased verbal abuse, decreased mobility, increased fighting in the family, and statements such as "He makes things more difficult for me now." Terms to connote increased violence included "danger" and "fighting." In Dari, the term for violence, *tashadud*, generally refers to political conflict and violence on a large scale, unless *tashadud aley-he zanaan* (violence against women) is referred to specifically. The more common term for violence against women in the form of intimate partner violence is *khshoonat aley-he zanaan*. The term for conflict, *kash-ma-kash*, was generally not employed for the home. Women used *nezaa* (fighting) more frequently along with words that connote "family problems" or "family concerns." Women also expressed the fear (*tarsidah*) of increased violence in the future and the sense that this was to be anticipated as a result of social tensions at the time. For both men and women, a mention of violence did not always mean that they were personally facing violence in the home. Violence in the home was also put in the context of a general sense of frustration at the continued state of public violence and lawlessness prevalent throughout the country.

Nonetheless, some women were extremely clear in their views and experiences. "Violence is increasing because men are angry," one woman told me. "Apparently men and women's rights are equally distributed but still the violence against women has increased. This talk of rights has just increased the gap between men and women." "Men are more aggressive and angry," another woman added. "Women are fighting with men to secure

First snowfall, Kabul.

their rights, and men are resisting the changes." "Women are trying to have a new life and men don't want it."

Most Afghan men who addressed issues of increased violence did not do so directly, but implied that conflicts at home were becoming an increasing part of their lives. For instance, one man explained that "relations between men and women have gotten worse than in previous periods." Another stated that "fear still exists" between men and women and that "relations are not so good like before." Men referred to difficulties at home and increased pressure. One man even said: "I wish that men should give up irrational discrimination and violence against women." Another man put it this way:

> The international community came here and want to work only for women. And they don't want to improve the status of Afghan men. Therefore Afghan men start making problems for their sister, their mother, their wife. They start making problems.

Conversations with Afghan women leaders and aid workers reinforced the view that violence against women had increased. Intimate partner violence in particular, they argued, was on the rise. The reasons, they said, included the continued availability of weapons, violence that male family members have experienced or meted out, trauma, frustration, and men's inability to access economic opportunities. Afghan history demonstrates that this is not unusual. And, as we've said, this is not just Afghanistan.

Most of those interviewed during the period of 2002 to 2009 did not have the numbers to demonstrate an increase in violence against women, but they expressed concern. There was ample anecdotal evidence to confirm this. In a conversation with an Afghan woman leader, she explained that the best measure of increased violence at the time was from people's individual stories—the voices of women. Many cited concerns of an imminent backlash, or the possibility that the backlash was already underway.

An Afghan woman leader had the following to say:

> There is a kind of negative idea among the people on "gender" that has to be corrected. And some people think that too much goes to women. The communities are sometimes not ready to accept the changes in women's situation. For them it is too much and too fast. One way for men is to use violence. There is a backlash at the speed of change and the focus of foreign aid, women being the focus.

Attacks on women's newly assumed rights and behaviors constitute a postwar backlash against women. UN research cited Afghanistan as a case in point.[74] An Afghan woman leader explained:

> I think that the communities are not ready to accept the new changes in women's situation. They think women expect too much. One way to not give [women] what they want is to use violence against them.

Another woman leader elaborated:

> Men and women are not ready to accept the extent of freedom that Westerners are asking for in their programs in Afghanistan. People become sensitive to the fact that Afghan women are expected to dress in Western style—if they are "liberated"—and to work very closely with men and foreigners. That is the reason violence against women has increased. If the status quo continues, there will be more violence against women. Instead, it should change to a more Afghan— more slow—pace. Change doesn't need to be revolutionary for it to work.

An aid worker shared her experience:

> There were several cases known to me where women were being abused by their husbands for taking classes and participating in women's workshops. Some women became scared and stopped attending. Fathers, brothers, husbands were never involved in any of the programming activities.

Some aid workers attributed the perceived increase in violence against women to a general sense of lawlessness and disorder that characterizes countries in the aftermath. An aid worker told me of the "growing insecurity toward the position of women in the home and community and the fear of Westernization." She explained that there was a backlash "due to Afghanistan opening up to the West, not to mention the sudden and dramatic increase of Western individuals and organizations." While some of this is part of the pushback against women's increased rights and freedoms that we see globally, Afghanistan has some specific constraints. She continued:

> If we compare to other post-conflict countries, it's possible to predict that violence against women is greater here because of the increased power of the mafias and warlords, exacerbated income disparities, the continuously unstable situation, and trauma in men that leads to violence.

Indeed, contributing factors to violence against women include loss of livelihoods, poverty, lawlessness, insecurity, which have in turn eroded social safety nets. An aid worker put it this way:

> There are hardly any reports focusing especially on violence against women from different periods during the conflict. However, I would not be surprised if there was a rise in intimate partner violence as part of post-conflict developments. There seems to have been an increase in kidnappings and trafficking.

The men I spoke with who referred to violence expressed that they felt "anger" against their wives when, after reluctantly agreeing to women's participation in a training program, the women failed to find gainful employment and were unable to provide support for the family. Many men explained that arguments had ensued at home as women tried to convince their husbands to grant permission for trainings and other opportunities offered by aid agencies. This was particularly contentious when it entailed income generation, as this put men's role as provider into question. In the end, economic necessity trumped all other concerns, and certain men agreed to let their wives leave the house. When these trainings did not bring the anticipated results, these men argued that their wives were "useless" (and also told their wives this) and that they were let out of the house "for nothing."

This also bred resentment against the aid organization itself, which was also labeled "useless." Some men went so far as to accuse these organizations of "using women" to fill some kind of quota, without offering substantive training. Men alluded to raised expectations that wives would be able to support the family. Yet when they failed to do so, the wives paid the price through increased verbal and physical violence. The impact on women was severe: they explained that they were afraid to make further demands and less likely to challenge the order at home. Many women articulated that they would feel more comfortable, and more free, to access these opportunities if men were not neglected.

Time and again, women asked me if I could find trainings, opportunities, and work for the men in their lives. "We want dignity for our men, and then they will treat us better," one woman explained. "And we will have more space for us." "Not supporting men directly makes them angry," she added. "All bad things happen when men are not educated and literate," another explained. She continued:

> In some places, men have become "sensitive" about women's organizations. They believe that these organizations train women to stand against the laws and their husbands. Of course this is not true. It is actually what men think.

An aid worker said this:

> There is also a lot of frustration by the men that they cannot find work, which I think leads to resentment when their wives are selected for training. Women around the world struggle with the issues that arise when their husbands earn less, are not working, or feel otherwise inferior—it is not unique to Afghanistan. However, here there are much more violent repercussions against women as the resentment by individual men feeds into a larger group within a cultural context where women are supposed to be taken care of, not supporting the family, and where the culture allows for much more violence in general, and specifically against women. In a gender training that we held for our own staff, the men commented that they would have no problem with women working, as long as jobs for all the men were found first.

Many discussions about violence with women centered around men's frustrations and inability to access opportunities. Women saw this as an explanation for the violence that was newly directed towards them. One elderly woman explained: "My husband didn't have good behavior during the [first] Taliban regime. He was angry because he didn't have a job, so he left me forever." Another was more direct, stating that "men should stop abusing women because of their opportunities." She felt that her husband resented her ability to bring home an income, however meager, and that she would prefer that he work instead.

Some women explained this violence as a result of men's insulted honor. A married woman put it this way: "We don't want our men to be dependent on any other man in the world. It is this that causes violence." She elaborated that Afghan men are feeling dependent on others and as a result their dignity was in question. Both men and women expressed a strong desire for men to be able to stand on their own feet, without the support of others. Another woman reinforced this point, explaining that "men are more aggressive and angry" because they lack employment. A few women were vocal in blaming aid organizations for fostering this imbalance by focusing exclusively on women. One said: "They increased violence between men and women and it will increase more." An Afghan woman elaborated: "The men, they have become more angry, more violent. Much more violent."

A few men, and many women, shared the view that violence against women had increased in the country after 2001. Some felt that this was a continuation of wartime violence, such as this man from rural Afghanistan who said: "Still men are the same. Most men are cruel to their wives and daughters. It might be a cause of the war." This forms part of a post-conflict pattern due in large part to bearing witness to violence during the war and a sense of loss and displacement when the political violence subsides.

Another man blamed the violence on challenges to the patriarchal order, explaining that "fundamentalist ideas have developed because many people feel that the changes happening with gender are obligatory and they are resisting them." This was elaborated by an Afghan woman leader in one of our many conversations on the subject:

> Violence increases when people don't have opportunities. It happens every-where in the world, not just Afghanistan. But in Afghanistan and other third world countries, the women tend to be more domestic. That is the difference. So if they are not given an opportunity to work outside or earn their money, it's not affecting them as much as it would affect a man. And when a woman gets that opportunity and a man doesn't, he becomes frustrated. That is true. And I think it would be true all over the world, not only Afghanistan. Because he cannot work and the woman does. It is a natural thing ... or rather let me say that it is a "nurture-al" thing that men have the ego and sense of being in power and control. So when they see this, they feel that they lose their confidence and they don't feel good about it. And this frustration certainly contributes to the violence against women.

Research in Afghanistan during this period documented men's sense of frustration with their inability to meet the household's basic needs and the violence that they mete out as a result:

> When I had a job, everything was fine; we had good relations in our house. But it was only temporary, and now I am at home and everything gets on my nerves. I am not able to feed my family, and I am angry about that and then I am beating my wife, because she is complaining about that. What can I do? Give me a job, then everything will be good again.[75]

Such accounts were not unusual. Social assets were scarce. Gender roles were changing. Gender relations were strained. Traditional social safety nets were deteriorating. And violence against women was increasing.

Some aid workers urged that we listen to Afghan women. "They know the possible negative implications," they said, ultimately Afghan women themselves will decide "whether they are prepared to take on that fight. At the end, if they are not prepared, nothing is going to happen."

The important message is this: Afghan women recognized the backlash they would inevitably face if they made demands "forcefully" and without the men involved. They warned us that this would happen. And they alerted us when it *did* happen. This backlash often manifested as intimate partner violence, particularly as women appeared to be advocates of changes imposed "from the outside."

The important lesson is that well-intended efforts and interventions may in fact produce unexpected outcomes for women. It would do a great disservice to women in Afghanistan to isolate their suffering and label it an "Afghan problem." Violence against women is not exclusive to Afghanistan, to developing countries, or to conflict and post-conflict countries. It is an epidemic that affects women worldwide and knows no social, cultural, or religious boundaries.

Not only did Afghan women explain all these things, but they also provided solutions. "His work brings my freedom," they told me. Afghan women were ready to claim rights and freedoms, but they needed to maneuver strategically to avoid backlash. They were well aware of the risks in disrupting the patriarchal order. And they were prepared to take on that fight. Our job was to listen as they led us.

I Am Caged in This Corner...

Ultimately there are many factors responsible for the increase in men's violence against women in public and private life. While figures and anecdotes help us understand this dynamic, the bottom line is this: women will not be able to claim rights and freedoms as long as they remain unsafe. Women's safety and freedom from violence is a critical prerequisite. We must assume that violence is happening, and we must take on the responsibility to end it. As has too often been said: Even one case is one too many.

Afghan women's groups continued to voice concern about the increased levels of violence throughout the years—both in public and in private. Meanwhile, insecurity continues in Afghanistan. Nearly every document, speech, and report on Afghanistan, by Afghan and non–Afghan alike, highlighted the need for improved security. No political or social process can be successful or sustainable without a commitment to provide security—starting with security for women. It has been said before but it is now more relevant than ever: If women are not safe, no one is safe.

Even those who work on women's rights and ending violence are at risk. Afghan women continue to be targeted, and killed, for their activism. To save other women, they put their own safety on the line. In 2021, the Taliban are once again attacking women who might be working towards a "Western agenda" or allied with Western organizations. The perception that an Afghan woman is promoting a foreign agenda could lead to the belief that she is "contaminated" by her association with outsiders.[76] In associating with foreigners, it is believed that she has betrayed the trust of the community and thereby undermined her own honor, men's honor, and by extension, Afghanistan's honor.

Afghan women have recognized for decades that they jeopardize their own safety and standing in the community by aligning themselves with foreigners. An Afghan woman formerly employed with an aid organization described how a man on the street blamed her and other women for the return of the Taliban saying, "[women] are becoming too liberal, and too shameless, so that the Taliban have come to discipline [women]."[77]

A young girl looks out over the village, waiting for a truck delivering blankets, Paghman.

In May 2005, three Afghan women were found raped and strangled in Baghlan Province. A note was pinned to their bodies blaming their fate on their involvement with foreign organizations and its resulting "whoredom." As a result, hundreds of women protested in Kabul. Soon after, another woman was stoned in Badakhshan Province, prompting a reaction from Afghan women and resulting in the Declaration of Afghan Women's NGOs. This Declaration demanded investigations to bring the perpetrators to justice and asked for increased security for all Afghan citizens.

These demands for security prompted plans for a protest and an email titled *What you can do about the Backlash*:

> Contact your country representative/embassy in Afghanistan and ask for accountability on how your tax dollars are being spent in Afghanistan. No more empty rhetoric on "national programs and policy"—what are the results on the ground?[78]

Shortly thereafter, *Daily Outlook*, Afghanistan's English language newspaper, noted the increase in violence against women in several front-page articles.[79] In one article, the Minister of Women's Affairs expressed concern with the increase in intimate partner violence and the lack of mechanisms to bring perpetrators to justice. Another article reported a 16-year-old girl who was raped and killed in Kabul. The *Kabul Weekly* ran several articles in English and Dari during that week also. The front page article stated that violence against women continued while the international community "looks on." A subheading of the article stated that the incident revealed "a village uncomfortable with outside interference."

A few months later, Afghanistan was shocked at the murder of Nadia Anjuman, a famed Afghan poet, by her husband. She was 25 years old. According to friends and family, Anjuman was seen as a "disgrace" to her family due to her poetry, which described the oppression of Afghan women:

> I am caged in this corner, full of melancholy and sorrow
> My wings are closed and I cannot fly
> I am an Afghan woman and I must wail

Anjuman's poem, "Soundless Cries," is one of the few that is available in English in its entirety.[80]

> I hear the green paces of the rain
> Here they are coming
> A thirsty few who have come
> With their dusty outfits on
> With their breaths soiled with the
> Deception of mirages
> Paces, dry and dusty
> They arrive here now
> Girls, grown up with hurting soul
> And wounded bodies
> Happiness has escaped their faces
> Hearts, old and cracked
> The word of a smile never written
> In the book of their lips
> Not even a drop of tear can come out
> The dried rivers of their eyes.
> Oh dear God!
> I do not know if their soundless cries
> Reach the clouds, The skies?
> I hear the green paces of the rain.

Her murder was yet another example of the violence that Afghan women continued to face, and the risks they took in speaking out. Two decades on, we see how little has changed.

In 2015, a young woman Farkhunda was beaten and burned to death by an angry mob of men on the streets of Kabul. Her crime? A false accusation that she had burned pages of the Koran. Some Afghan clerics and government authorities felt that her murderers should not be punished. Other Afghan officials went so far as to say that her killing was justified. A few men were arrested and then quietly released, protected by powerful men.

Sippi Azarbaijani-Moghaddam,[81] longtime advocate for women's rights in Afghanistan, discussed this incident with clarity, arguing that Afghan women have felt unsafe long before the Taliban's arrival in 2021. "Farkhunda's fate," she writes, should tell us that "a troubling undercurrent of misogyny" remains "even in the 'new Afghanistan.'" She argued that it stemmed from "the frustration of decades of being told to grudgingly accept women's rights in public … unleashed on one small crumpled body."[82]

Azarbaijani-Moghaddam writes that "Farkhunda was probably emboldened by all the rhetoric on women's rights…. She thought she had a voice. She thought she was safe. But she touched a nerve and didn't understand that she was still in dangerous territory."[83]

She concludes that the fight for women's rights is a long one, and assistance for women has never been sufficient. The way forward is not to forcibly insert women into spaces not ready for them. "It will be fixed," she writes, "by a long-term commitment with humility and understanding about the dangerous uphill journey women and their families had just begun."[84] Farkhunda's story is a stark reminder that Afghan women's safety has always been, and will continue to be, under threat.

On the day of her burial, an Afghan woman leader chased the men away and said: "This is not your dead body. Farkhunda belongs to all of the women of Kabul, of Afghanistan. Her body belongs to all Afghan mothers."[85] When it came time for the body to be transported, the women carried her themselves. Men from Farkhunda's family circled and protected them as they did so. "It was the very first time in Afghanistan—maybe in all the Islamic world—that women took a dead body to the grave."[86] That day, thousands came to protest through the streets of Kabul in the rain with organizers calling it one of the largest demonstrations in Kabul's history.[87] Many men and boys stood as support and protection along the route, heads bowed.

In 2021, with the return of the Taliban, women will increasingly "be targeted not only for issues they cover but also for challenging perceived social norms prohibiting women from being in a public role and working outside the home."[88] The continued existence of violence against women—and even the fear of violence—will remain the most serious obstacle as Afghan women must once again fight forces intent on holding them back. Afghan women will continue to resist, even as they face incredible risks in doing so.

CHAPTER 7

At the Feminist Interface

I have hope, but I have no faith.
—Afghan woman on progress for women in Afghanistan

Our lives are organized around domains, our different arenas with their different sets of cultures, expectations, and ecosystems. Domains help us understand our lives—and our core values.[1] These domains can sometimes clash—the point of clash is called the interface. Afghanistan's interface is one that has played out repeatedly in history—between Afghan and outsiders. The definition of an "outsider" changes, but the view of outsider-as-occupier has not.

Aid is often conflated with radical social change.[2] And radical social change, when brought from "the outside," is resisted. For aid agencies in Afghanistan, this is what they set out to do. The call to "save" Afghan women allegedly fueled the military intervention. This call was translated into a quest to "liberate" Afghan women. Distilling this further, this quest to liberate was interpreted by the aid industry as a need to "empower" Afghan women.

"Empowerment"—meaning people having power and control over their own lives—is, in principle, a radical social change. For women, it is built on feminist principles of power and agency. It is political. And it is powerful. And yet, when translated into aid-speak, this word loses much of its punch. Power and politics are parked neatly to the side, and "empowerment" becomes neutralized, and part of standardized aid programming.

There is no agreement on the meaning of the term or how it is to be brought to fruition, either through acts of government or aid interventions. Despite its centrality to the concept of power, the term is frequently used in a way that strips it of political meaning.[3] Moreover, empowerment manifests as a top-down effort. The underlying assumption is that the present is restrictive, and that women are oppressed and therefore unable to empower themselves.

Aid interventions are hampered by inadequate understandings of the

176

ways gender and power interplay. "Empowerment" has achieved buzzword status, making it somewhat slippery to put into practice. And yet, such buzzwords frame solutions, giving aid policies a sense of purpose and suggesting a world that can be neatly repaired through technical solutions.[4] In reality, buzzwords often give organizations a way to frame their projects on paper with big promises but little strategy or follow through.

Buzzwords are not neutral—they assume meaning when employed in policies which then influences how aid organizations understand what they are doing and why they have a moral imperative to do it. The agenda for transformation brings such a responsibility, and provides the legitimacy to intervene. The empowerment discourse mysteriously becomes stripped of politics and power—its core values—and assumes a depoliticized aid identity that no one can disagree with. As these already context-less buzzwords are applied into local contexts, their meaning becomes increasingly less clear, and less usable.

The empowerment discourse can be seen as emanating from the rights-based development agenda, something to which we are all inherently entitled. However, elements of this discourse are contested on the grounds that they are seen as a Western imposition and an act of moral imperialism, further representing an individualistic worldview that counters the collective identities of patriarchal societies.[5]

The perception that "rights" is a Western import holds much weight in Afghanistan, based largely on the means by which the "rights" message has been delivered. Many theorists have argued this point, particularly with the link between "liberation" of Afghan women and the War on Terror. There is an inherent contradiction between the rhetoric of women's rights and the reality of stealth bombers.[6] The rights agenda is not easily put into practice, and runs the risk of failure when translated into action. The rights discourse needed firstly to be made relevant to Afghan women. This does not compromise its underlying principle of equality. On the contrary, it offers a more solid foundation for sustainability, grounded in local contexts.

Packaged empowerment becomes part of a standardized aid program, measured by program deliverables: *the number of women trained, the number of events organized, the number of chickens per woman.* Meanwhile, real empowerment is a long-term process, working at a deep structural level to address gender inequalities. Empowerment is also more than an outcome; it is a non-linear process built firstly on women's agency and on their own understandings of how they would like to see themselves empowered. Empowerment is transformation. And transformations are not simply introduced by aid interventions but are being negotiated through a complex process that involves all those with something at stake—meaning the people whose lives are implicated in this "empowerment."[7]

How, then, can we measure a fuzzy buzzword? If we lack adequate systems to measure empowerment, how will we know if it has been delivered? Women's participation in the creation and implementation of programs is one way, but presence doesn't necessarily mean power. At the same time, there are clear indicators to the contrary: lack of consultation with communities, rushed design of programs in order to meet deadlines and access conference-related funding, and preparation of documents in English by foreign advisors.[8] *What do the numbers mean if women can't actually determine the direction—or the outcome?*

There is a battle between the "quick-fix" mentality and the time required to make non-cosmetic changes. Since women's rights—and attempts to change them—are highly politicized, this battle plays out in unanticipated ways, with disempowering consequences for women.[9] To reinforce this, an aid worker said: "The general impression I get is that there is a lack of indicators and a lack of quantitative and qualitative tools for measuring change/progress. If you know of any, tell me!" She also expressed strong doubts that interventions had consulted women or felt that they were accountable to women.

Can aid interventions "empower"? Probably not. But they can support or hinder women's potential in achieving transformation through their policies and programs. I do not doubt the sincerity in seeking to facilitate women's rights and ensure their political, social, and economic security—this is what I do, after all—but some efforts lacked a contextualized understanding of gender issues in the country. Missing from the analysis was how to aid Afghan women in their *own* empowerment, and their *own* liberation, rather than claim to do it for them.

The point is not to gauge success or failure of aid interventions but rather to shed light on how this played out in Afghanistan and how international aid came to be seen as yet another interface between outsiders and local communities. It is an understanding of how change can be made—or resisted.

Ultimately, there is a tension between the speed at which aid organizations are expected to operate and the time it takes to understand the dynamics of a particular situation. More often than not, quick fixes are the priority, rather than building a foundation of mutual understanding—especially when it comes to understanding the needs of Afghan women.

One aid worker explained that, even after these years of active engagement, "donors and Western implementers still do not understand the 'mindset' of the women of Afghanistan." She explained that aid efforts, and the people providing, were unable to view Afghanistan through a lens other than their own.

Another aid worker added this:

I find the lack of contextualized analysis to be very true among the international staff. Early after I arrived I actually read a book about women and politics and development in Afghanistan that clearly outlined how difficult it has been to make change in the past, and how negative the reaction was by the Afghans when they felt the changes were being imposed too quickly. It really made me aware of the need to work within the culture and to expect slow change, and only when it was initiated by the community.

An Afghan woman leader explained to me that aid interventions have not addressed the root causes of women's subordination and have therefore failed to affect gender inequality in any significant way. She said that "most mainstreaming approaches to women's development have not been based on analyses of the overall reality of women's lives."

"The international community has to do its homework first before going into a country," another Afghan woman leader explained. "Do homework, and then bring in the project." "Doing homework" entails not only learning about the communities, but also allowing time for the communities themselves to develop trust. "If they don't know where you are from or what you are doing and you set up your office with your flag and you tell them what to do, you see what happens," an Afghan woman leader cautioned. "Better to build on our momentum and what we are already doing. This is better for you. And of course it is better for us."

Meanwhile, many years later, one could argue that Afghan women are neither liberated nor empowered. Interventions that raise expectations of empowerment encourage women to step outside pre-existing gender roles. In so doing, gender and power relations are challenged. Women face greater risk if the environment for social change is seen to be an external imposition. On such shaky ground, advancing women's rights cannot find a solid foundation.

Social change and transformation are not simply introduced by aid interventions, but are longer-term processes operating at a structural level to address gender inequalities—on women's own terms. Such processes are contextual and local. It is not unwise to ask if an international aid-imposed agenda of social change is really the right approach. Further, Afghan women felt that they were not sufficiently consulted on the direction and pace of social change. This demonstrates a denial of women's agency and of their ability to act on their own behalf and achieve their own gains. The risks are great, and backlashes against women are likely when women themselves are not involved in their own change. Empowerment is not a technical tool that can be handed to women. Instead, it must be generated by the women it is meant to serve.[10]

Interventions, Occupations, and Implications

It is problematic to note that many Afghans parallel the "regime" of the international aid community to previous occupiers in Afghanistan's history. The belief that the international community is yet another variation on an occupying force in Afghanistan, with its own ideas and impositions, is not new. Aid has long been a means by which outsiders gain influence in Afghanistan.[11] In fact, Afghanistan's politicized aid history has left the country a graveyard for failed fast-paced efforts by outsiders.[12]

To Afghans, this looks like history repeating. Understanding Afghanistan's legacy of occupation might explain present-day resistance to outside interference. This repeated cultural imperialism fueled Afghan perceptions that "outsiders, no matter how well-intentioned, sit poised, ready to engulf the nation with new sets of foreign values."[13] It is said that the one thing that repeatedly unites a very divisive Afghanistan is the need to drive out occupiers. This opposition to imperialism is voiced most strongly when it relates to women, with each occupier seeking to direct the course of Afghan women's lives.

Feminist movements come from within and are generated in women's own interests, but conflict occurs when the voices of international actors drown out local voices.[14] This starts to look like an "occupation." For Afghan women, this is clearly an issue, one that denies their agency and sidelines their power that already exists. Each occupying regime has tried to control the strings, and each time these strings must be clipped.

For the so-called aid occupation, the impression was that aid interventions would transform Afghan women from their position of subjugation to empowerment and liberation. Implicit in this message is the idea that women are *prevented* from achieving liberation because of socio-cultural constraints, as if it were simply a matter of changing attitudes and values.[15] Such a perspective dislocates women, reinforces victimization, denies agency, and leaves women no role in their own empowerment.

From the very beginning, Afghan women leaders criticized the ways in which the "influx of foreign aid workers" made their "foreign decisions." They needed to be reminded, we were told, that they "know less about the ways and customs and effective solutions than local residents." As such, the liberation agenda denied agency from the start, resting on the premise that (1) Afghan women needed to be saved; (2) Afghan women can't save themselves; and (3) Afghan women needed to be saved *from* Afghan men. Despite these pillars of Western perceptions, Afghan women have always been historical and political actors struggling against patriarchy. International organizations underplayed the leadership roles women have in their own lives and therefore failed to give them leadership roles in allocating their own aid.

A woman sells her handmade blankets on the street, Kabul.

It is wrong to assume that Afghan women need to be liberated, developed, and empowered. *Can aid provide the fuel to drive forward empowerment and liberation?* Yes. But it cannot be the driver. So, women's agency was sidelined while the myth of liberation gained momentum. Such myths served a strategic purpose but often failed to reflect women's realities. When the goal is to liberate without acknowledging agency, it is not liberation.

A researcher on Afghanistan had the following to say:

> What I find interesting is that most foreigners, like many Afghan men, think that Afghan women heard about women's rights through foreigners. There's a gap here. People don't know that women's rights—or at least women fighting for their rights—has been there all along!

One Afghan woman leader reinforced this point, adding:

> Local residents, particularly women, should lead the way. Aid agencies should provide the money and simply document progress to make sure the money is being spent on what it was supposed to be spent on.

"Afghan people do not accept things by power or pressure on them," another Afghan woman leader explained. "If our aim is to change Afghanistan's situation, to change the things that people don't like, we have different ways to reach this goal. We should gain the support of the Afghan communities." It was generally agreed that, in order to be sustainable, the process of social change must come from within.

From without, international experts, advisors, and consultants bring technical knowledge and speak a donor-driven language. But they are expertise-in-abstraction. Better that they—we—provide the tools and resources to Afghan women's groups to amplify the work that is already being done. International actors cannot both set the agenda and determine its success.

A former Minister of Women's Affairs had the following to say:

> The mistakes maybe have been not proper usage of resources. Not proper planning and targeting. Maybe they didn't have enough time to think about the investment that they were doing. Because it was an urgent situation, and emergencies are like that…. In terms of women's status, it is the worst in the world. So in that sense, that is still an emergency. It is like tsunami for women in Afghanistan. But still we need to take the time to think more about what we are doing and where and why we are doing it.

The what, where, and why we were doing it was ambitious, and impossibly so. It therefore failed Afghanistan far more than if less ambitious targets were set and achieved.[16] Meanwhile, would it have been worth asking if "liberation" was possible when most women were struggling for survival?

And when delivered from the top-down, it appeared that Afghan women were a symbol for political gain. Conditions were undeniably political because of the interconnectedness of military objectives. The U.S. policy in Afghanistan—"sex, drugs, and rock'n'roll"[17]—led to a conflation of objectives on the ground, and a sense among Afghans that the liberation of women was merely a byproduct of military action.[18] A report from a U.S. general in Afghanistan clearly exemplifies this confusion, stating that the protection of human rights is a military objective.[19]

The rhetoric used to justify aid interventions stemmed from the language used to justify the ousting of the Taliban—a military intervention. As a result, aid interventions ran the risk of doing a disservice to women by implementing programs and policies that did not take all possible repercussions into account.[20] Aid interventions aiming to empower women inadvertently placed women at increased risk.

Further, in Afghanistan, like other Islamic contexts, international pressure exerted influence on gender priorities, making it difficult for women to demonstrate agency in a context of pre-determined international opinion about the status of women in Islam.[21] The West's view of the Muslim woman as needing to be "saved" was Orientalism.[22] There was a conflicting worldview in the notion that Afghan women were *bourka*'ed damsels in distress awaiting salvation from knights in shining tanks.

Aversions to Islam, particularly pervasive in the U.S. feminist movement, undercut efforts to empower women. The implication was that after "liberation," Afghan women would toss aside their *chaddaris*—along with their Islamic and Afghan identities—and become secular, despite a rich history of negotiating their social status through their Islamic identity.[23] Many Afghan women are still struggling to find the space to act in their own interest. An aid worker explained that "there is a seemingly uncontrollable urge to overlay the experience of 'the Afghan woman' with the Americans' worldview and to create programs that thrust that woman into the American design of what is good and beneficial for them."

Indeed, researchers noted that Afghans felt culturally displaced; forced to place their own identities into a new language in order to receive assistance. This sense of despair was in reality a frustration that while Afghans continued to struggle for physical survival, they risked being overridden by an aid intervention that imposed hasty solutions before giving Afghans time to consider their role in the process.[24]

To further fuel resistance, it was assumed that the corruption and degradation of Afghan women was a fundamental part of the Western cultural imperialist agenda.[25] Afghan history has also demonstrated that the most powerful means by which to destabilize agendas for social change is to label them un–Islamic. Understandings of Afghan socio-cultural contexts inevitably entail recognition of the value and significance of religion in the lives of Afghans. Every Afghan interviewed, woman or man, highlighted the importance of achieving gains within the context of Islam. Among discussions with non–Afghan aid workers, the importance of Islam was often overlooked. Many Afghan aid workers urged that interventions "should do everything with respect to Afghan and Islamic culture," as one Afghan woman leader put it.

For example, many Afghan women have argued that the traditional division between public and private worlds does not necessarily mean that they have no decision-making power. These women prefer to view changes within the contexts of their traditions and religion. An Afghan leader urged "gender experts [to] follow a gender perspective in Afghanistan *through Afghan eyes*. This means taking into consideration the prevailing customs and traditions."

Not taking prevailing customs into consideration also manifested itself in the form of parties, pornography, and alcohol with the perception that this was a direct, deliberate onslaught on Afghan values.[26] This was demonstrated by the "no Afghan" door policy in Kabul restaurants that served alcohol at the time, or the myriad brothels masquerading as restaurants. A colleague put it this way:

There are reports circulating on internet groups of the anger amongst Kabu-
lis when they hear and see international lavish parties and self-congratulatory
news of their contribution to the development effort when the city and the
country as a whole is still teeming with a half-starved, ill-serviced, growing
population.

These recreational activities appeared to Afghans to be an attack
against their *Afghaniyat*, or sense of Afghan identity. The perception was
that men were under threat by outside forces who did not understand the
social fabric, who were coming in and seemingly treating men as threats
against Afghan women. More than the aid agenda, the presence of internationals made the feeling of threat more palpable. The influx of non–Afghans
from different countries brought customs and traditions that appeared
to be threatening or challenging to Afghan ways. Indeed, this ideological
occupation took the form of perceived imposition of an alien culture. It
has been argued that the U.S. invasion in particular resulted in increased
poverty, crime, drug addiction, unemployment, and the imposition of an
alien culture—factors that contribute to the breakdown of social relations
as the Afghan safety net.[27] This imposition, coupled with the lack of meaningful changes in the lives of Afghans, has resulted in Afghans adopting
more conservative views.[28]

Traditionally, these conservative views were thought to be isolated in
rural areas. At several periods of interface in Afghanistan's history, hostility toward modernization was led by those largely in rural areas against a
government or military. However, in the last two decades, this interface is
manifesting in open clashes in urban areas. The urban population increased
dramatically since 2002 as refugees and internally displaced persons were
lured to Kabul and other Afghan cities to access the opportunities of urban
life and benefit from greater aid.

The floundering of aid efforts and questionable track record of supporting women's rights was not simply due to a contradiction between
modernity and tradition. It was in fact a widening of the gap between the
urban elite and the rural majority.[29] This was, firstly, because the aid community was centered in urban areas. And, even more noteworthy, the rural
population had been displaced to the cities. It was in the cities that the dramatic social changes have been received or resisted. And it was in the cities
where, historically, Afghan women have been both delivered and stripped
of their rights.

The old urban elite who applauded strong pushes for social change
in the past have largely left Afghanistan. Today, the population of Kabul
is predominantly comprised of Afghans of rural origins. Once a liberal
urban center, Kabul has become a site of violence and therefore, an interface where a brand of patriarchy rooted in misogyny has taken hold. It is

difficult and counterproductive to lay blame on any sole factor, but many Afghan women have expressed concern that this new urban dynamic has led to increased harassment on the street. "On one level such sexual aggression is almost the inevitable product of the Taliban years ... on another level it is clearly a statement of what many Afghans think about the takeover of their capital by foreigners."[30] Forces of change have been played out in the cities, and the first discussions of women's rights and roles began in Kabul and continue to transpire largely in the capital. Thus, urban women face a particular challenge even if they only comprise a small percentage of Afghan women.

Liberation from Above

Many people I spoke with during my years in the country referred to this interface as an ideological "occupation." They often took this a step further, aligning three "occupiers" namely the Soviet Union, the Taliban, and the international community due to their similar quests to restructure gender roles and relations.

A RAWA article explained:

> The Taliban used the "women's question" to enforce its own agenda. The imperialist occupation forces have also used the agenda of gender equality to ultimately pursue their own interests: the occupation of Afghanistan for strategic geo-political reasons. In the eyes of many people, the ministry of women is associated with the occupation.[31]

One woman told me this:

> Before the war men and women were under the government's control. During the war they were under the control of different regimes. Now again men and women are under control—this time it is the control of the international organizations.

Other Afghan women reiterated this, emphasizing the need to operate on Afghan terms. In a conversation on the consequences of external pushes for progress, women often used examples from Afghan history to illustrate their sentiments and to demonstrate the Afghan population's reaction to enforced social change. "In the Soviet time, when they started to establish literacy classes for women in the villages," one woman told me, "everyone reacted very strongly. Village leaders warned everyone not to have it, period." The conversation continued:

> **LA:** "Only because it came from the outside?"
> **Sweeta:** "Yes. Exactly."

LA: "So it wasn't about literacy at all?"

SWEETA: "It didn't matter what it was about, only that it came from the outside..."

Another woman added: "To you and other foreigners, I always insist on the fact that we cannot copy any other modernity to our country. We need to translate international ways into our own language, into our own context, and into our own culture. Or it will not take hold."

Many men I spoke with took this concern a step further, arguing that the international community promoted change that was contrary to Islam. This sentiment is dangerous because, whether grounded in reality or based on perception, it has the power to undermine any efforts toward progress. Simply arguing that something is anti–Islamic is the trump card that, when played, silences all arguments to the contrary.

Some women agreed, stating that the hidden agenda of interventions was "to change what is Afghan culture" and to focus on "rights that are not in Islam." These women argued that their rights were in fact safeguarded in Islam and that they were not for the international community to give. One man believed that institutions are "unveiling our women." Another man explained: "In the area of importing or bringing foreign culture and tradition, international organizations have bad effect on Afghan women."

Men expressed concern with the influence the international community has had on Afghan culture. They felt that the interventions deliberately sought to enforce Western codes of culture as superior to Afghan ways. "Aid organizations inspired foreign culture on our men. They introduced Afghan man incorrectly. And also they brought down their role in the family and society, so it caused difficulties and violences between men and women," one man explained.

A young boy with an AK-47 looks out over the city, Kabul.

Many men cited a lack of respect and the perception that they were "under the authority of others." Another frequent response was the concern that the rest of the world did not want to support a free and stable Afghanistan, but was looking to occupy the country to meet their own needs.

"We want a free Afghanistan without the intervention of foreigners," one man explained. He was not alone in his opinion. Many Afghan men felt strongly that they should be the ones to decide the direction of the new Afghanistan, and that the international community should align with their views. Another man put it this way: "For Afghanistan I wish peace, safety, Islam, Afghan-ness, freedom. A complete free country which shouldn't be occupied by others."

An elderly man had this to say: "I do not know what image the world has but somehow they think we are not good and this is why some of our freedoms are under their control."

The author of a book on Afghan women said this to me:

> I think you would probably see the same dilemmas I do as I think about how to "translate" many of the Western notions that underlie the field into something that is progressive and possible and built from indigenous Afghan thought.

She shared the view that we lack a shared language of respect when we speak of liberation and who delivers it. She agreed that women's liberation, and women's agency, are negatively impacted by what she called "liberation from above." This, she argued, "destroys the sense of agency, empowerment and community control by and for women that was found at the grassroots level. While some women have seen improvement, many have seen none and others have lost informal, community opportunities for agency as elites, 'experts,' and government and international controls are put in place."

At that time, in 2009, our concern was the brewing backlash against women's rights and fundamental freedoms. Desires for immediate, visible, and externally-evident signs of progress in women's lives will only foment a backlash, and she and I agreed that the repercussions were stronger than ever. She followed it up with this advice:

> Special plea: Take it easy, at least publicly, on "Afghan women's leadership." The whole country is on the brink of collapse in a manner not altogether unlike what happened in the late 1920s and late 1980s. The main attack comes from ultra-conservatives. I worry that post–9/11 gains for Afghan women could be reversed as happened after the fall of Amanullah and then Najibullah. Foregrounding women's issues at the moment risks severe backlash.

Disaggregating women from their communities will only repeat the past. Those attempts failed because they lacked a base of community support, drawing instead on development models that were pasted from other contexts, without adaptation to the socio-political and cultural realities of Afghanistan.[32]

In the words of one Afghan woman leader:

> I do not need to remind you that imposing an idea on Afghans is impossible. You know this. To bring positive change, the idea should be fixed in an Afghan cultural framework. Gender is the most valid example of this.... But we have not yet learned from history and we still try to do things the wrong way. Backwards.

The risk of not doing so is serious: changes will not be accepted. Worse, they will be rejected outright. And any indigenous movement for change will risk appearing to be aligned with an external agenda, meaning we put Afghan women leaders at greater risk, even as we try to "help" them. And we put them in a position of having to defend a supposedly sacred cultural ground, one that many of them have spent decades reforming on their own. This risk should not be underestimated, and can be life-threatening. At a minimum, it will result in backsliding of any gains made. In short, if we really wanted to help Afghan women, we should have followed their lead from the very beginning.

Aid interventions for empowerment bring their own message that people lack the ability to empower themselves, and therefore this must be delivered from the outside. More problematically, aid agencies lack the accountability to actually deliver on empowerment. *What is the cost of not empowering—and who pays that price?* The only adequate measure for me is the voices of those who were meant to be "empowered" in the first place. Allowing space for Afghan feminists to advocate for structural change in their own contexts is the only way to acknowledge Afghan women's agency.

Ultimately, the message is clear: Afghan women, in all their diversity, must be viewed within the socio-cultural context in which they exist. There are entry points for support, and there are Afghan women already doing the work. An interview with an Afghan woman named Zohra in the book *Women of Afghanistan Under the Taliban* expressed the sentiments of many:

> Of what I have read in history ... and what I have experienced in 46 years of my life, one thing has been confirmed to be right, that if there is foreign handling of our affairs, our people will never see a progressing Afghanistan. And I must say that our people throughout history have proved their opposition to the foreigner and never have accepted any kind of slavery. I have a piece of advice for the U.S., Pakistan, Iran and Saudi Arabia that before taking any decision on Afghanistan, spend a few minutes and flick through the pages of Afghanistan's history, I am sure they would find some useful materials. The twenty years of wars have struck our innocent nation severe blows that they are incapable to speak out against the external and internal aggressors, but a time will come when our people will stand on their feet and sweep out the enemies of Afghanistan.[33]

A Brewing Backlash

An understanding of Afghan history demonstrates that backlashes are not new. Attempts to force women's rights have resulted in violent backlashes, leaving women worse off than they were before. In light of this, an understanding of the Afghan historical trajectory—particularly regarding gender politics—could illuminate patterns and problems that might pose obstacles in present attempts to restructure gender relations. This was elaborated in Chapter 1.

Experts counsel against taking shortcuts to historically and sociologically informed analyses of the context and transformations of Afghan society.[34] This is the foundation for understanding gender issues in Afghanistan. More profound analyses of and engagement with Afghan society could prevent women from being addressed in a social and historical vacuum, creating interventions that complement—rather than contradict—women's realities.

During my years in Afghanistan, it became more and more apparent that a backlash was brewing. Aid workers were vocal in expressing concern about the way aid was allocated, and what effects it might have. This brewing backlash would play out negatively for women, this much we knew. Even the UN articulated their concern, stating that Afghan history repeatedly demonstrates that "efforts to strengthen women's status inherently carry the danger of a backlash."[35]

And yet, we continued.

One aid worker put it this way:

> The current and seemingly deteriorating situation in Afghanistan makes the gender discussion even more critical. We do so much relatively high-profile work with women, I've begun to be concerned about what kind of negative attention we could be in for in the future.

Many people, Afghan and non–Afghan alike, agreed that there were many well-intended initiatives, but sustainability was in question. Moreover, in the words of one aid worker:

> Aid agencies pose a barrier to progress in that they take on all the responsibility and decision-making forgetting to pass the baton to the "developees" ... giving up control is not easy to do ... allowing people to make mistakes in your presence is even harder ... it is so much easier to just tell people what to do!

It was agreed that "doing gender" in Afghanistan wasn't as easy as was expected. And, alarmingly, Afghan women leaders were facing increased risks because of their work, particularly if it was associated with the international community. Following the tragic murder of three Afghan women working for an international NGO, a colleague said this:

After that terrible incident ... we probably have to rethink gender and how we understand and facilitate it in the communities. In doing gender work in areas of high insecurity, am I jeopardizing the women that I work with?

Former Afghan president Professor Burhanuddin Rabbani,[36] an outspoken critic of Western cultural imperialism, argued that the goal was to corrupt Islam and obstruct Afghanistan's development as an independent country. He put his views this way:

We consider this a conspiracy against our religion, our freedom and security. They talk about women's issues, while thousands of women die, and nobody cares for them. But that does not stop them from talking about "moral corruption." They haven't come here for the reconstruction of Afghanistan, but they have come here to corrupt us.... The regime that rules our country stands against the wishes of the entire nation.... In Afghanistan, our policies should be defined by our nation, not by any foreign country. The current Afghan government's policies are not acceptable to the Afghan people. We must protect our freedom. If a foreign country gives aid, that should be without any strings attached. If the donors put conditions, we should not accept such aid.[37]

His influence over Afghan public opinion should not be underestimated, nor should his understanding of it. Rabbani's thoughts might have been provocative, but his words resonated with many Afghans.

This frustration had been brewing in Afghanistan starting in late 2002 when Afghans began to articulate dissatisfaction with the army of international aid organizations—and their international standards of living—that were failing to make visible and sustainable changes in Afghanistan.

This anger moved from the streets to the Afghan cabinet with the appointment of Dr. Ramazan Bashardost as Minister of Planning in 2004. Bashardost coined the now oft-cited term *NGO-ism* to describe the failure of the international community to assist Afghanistan, opting instead to foster corruption and increase their own wealth. Bashardost further accused NGOs of "economic terrorism" and blamed them for the misuse of the country's scant development funding.[38]

On another occasion he went on to say that the aid community was a mafia, and that they had "killed a golden and historic chance to foster cooperation between a Muslim country and a Western country." His words played well to the Afghan public, particularly in Kabul, and continued to be replayed to fuel the overall hostility towards aid institutions.

In May 2005, an article in *Kabul Weekly*—a paper written in English and Dari by Afghan authors—also reinforced this point.[39] It is relevant that the authors were Afghan and the text was English because the messages conveyed were geared to the international community. The article "NGO-Union Founded to Create Self Sustainability: NGOs in Afghanistan Take a Step Towards Ending Reliance on International Funds" told the

Pashtun men, Kabul.

story of Afghan NGOs wanting to dictate their own agenda and end their "dependence." The subheading read: "Afghan NGOs seeking to rid themselves of international funds" and elaborated that foreign organizations are "attempting to project the values and norms of foreign civil societies on Afghanistan … [bringing] negative results."

The article also stated that "experts believe that NGOs' activities are not useful unless they find national financial sources and organize their programs according to the priorities of the nation's needs." One Afghan NGO-Union member said: "Their meetings and activities are commanded by foreigners, who are of no use to Afghanistan." He continued to say that NGOs should be free of foreign donors so that they can be allowed to implement projects in line with the values of Afghanistan: "Only then can they release themselves from the bondage of strangers."[40]

The significance of the Afghan perception of being occupied by yet another regime cannot be overstated. It is expressed most clearly in this "Open Letter to Expatriates in Afghanistan," written by Sanjar Qiam and sent to various distribution lists in 2006. Segments of this letter follow:

The historical irony of this phenomenon never ceases to amaze me. Both post and pre Taliban eras are marked by oligarchic order: warlordism rooted out whatever was left of state infrastructure and committed all sorts of atrocities. The post

Taliban period is marked by Expatlordism—a new type of oligarchy.... There is an increasing concentration of the means of communication at the top, this is due to communication culture, instruments, language and tendencies in foreign organization.... Organizational oligarchy has brought about societal oligarchy. Just like everything else a society can absorb a certain dose of foreigners over a certain period of time. Afghanistan can take a very small dosage of foreigners as they are allergic to them. Every page of history witnesses the low "absorption capacity"— if I may borrow the term from the EU.... I am making a reference to the history of a proud and individualistic man who defends his way of life.... My point is for one reason or another we are all protective. Except the difference is in your network every one should play by your rules, which is fine. But you play by your rules in my network too. You don't have the faintest idea of my network and you even don't try to acquire some. You never think of shifting your stand, and redesigning your aims and your way of work. You tend to make Afghanistan feel like home. But Afghanistan is not your home. The more you try to live your life the more Afghans would hate you.

Yours truly, Sanjar

In June 2006, BBC aired a special report titled "Afghanistan: Losing the Aid Game." This report took place within a discouraging political climate in Afghanistan where frustrations and disillusionment were higher than they had been in previous years. This report was aired following the May 2006 riots in Kabul, ignited by a traffic accident between Afghan vehicles and a U.S. military convoy, leaving more than 14 people dead and nearly 150 injured.

A volcanic reservoir of discontent overflowed into the city, directed at "the outsiders." Myriad news articles reported on the sense of frustration felt by Afghans at the lack of progress in their country. "Underlying it all is the fact that young men have not seen any tangible change in their lives in terms of either jobs or basic services," explained an aid worker.[41] Another article quoted an Afghan security officer who said: "Many people hate the NGOs because they see all this money coming into the country and they have not been able to get jobs. They were waiting for a day like today."[42]

These riots followed the killing of four Afghan aid workers with an international organization in Jawzjan Province. Aid workers, both Afghan and international, were increasingly at risk. In 2003, 12 aid workers had been killed. This number more than doubled in 2006 and tripled in 2008.[43] Targeted attacks continued, and every year of the 20-year intervention, Afghanistan was ranked as one of the most violent countries for aid workers.[44] While these examples appear to be old, they are in no way outdated. The sentiment remains. In fact, it proliferated as security deteriorated and quality of life seemed elusive for most Afghans. Many speculated Afghanistan's likely return to war. With the reoccupation of the country by the Taliban in 2021, attacks increased exponentially as the Taliban gained ground across the country and the United States began its withdrawal. While there is no data yet to confirm, it is likely that 2021 was the most violent year on record for aid workers in the country. It remains unclear what will happen, but the prognosis is not good.

Meanwhile, in 2006, the situation continued to deteriorate. I was invited to join a working group called "Post-Conflict and Negative Attention" to explore these issues further. The group consisted of Afghan women leaders and international aid workers. *How could we ensure community acceptance in Afghanistan? What do we do about the increasing resistance to our work and our presence in general?*

It was agreed that the lack of coordination, funding difficulties, short term focus, and desire for "quick-fix solutions" were key problems. The group raised the importance of understanding people's perceptions—whether or not they match reality—and what impact the rhetoric we used might have on communities. The rhetoric of "liberation" was a case in point. Such language is problematic, it was agreed. It raises expectations and results in unmet promises and disillusioned people. Further, it comes with the dangerous assumption that a savior is going to deliver liberation. None of this is suitable in Afghanistan. Or anywhere.

One woman explained that "we were not at all prepared to deliver on what we're saying, and if we don't, we are creating new tensions." The language used and the promises made fostered a rhetoric fatigue, fueled by a renewed dislike for foreign occupation and alien ideologies.

Afghans I spoke with felt that it was a convenient excuse to blame Afghan culture for resistance to women's "liberation," but this only reflected a failure to adequately understand Afghan society. Though there may be pockets of resistance, feminism remains very much alive. This is true in Afghanistan. And everywhere.

The group emphasized the importance of understanding Afghan history and the ways in which social change has been received or resisted. This history, one Afghan woman explained, could have revealed that in the 1920s, for instance, the women's issue brought down a monarchy, resulting in many years of regressions in terms of women's rights. This was the result of an aggressive program for social change led by an urban minority with little relation to rural communities. She elaborated that "we need a more in-depth analysis and we need to look at what we're doing and turn it around before a backlash becomes inevitable."

One aid worker added:

> We don't spend enough time understanding. We need to build trust, we didn't do that. Go back to history and see what went wrong. They went out aggressively to bring reform with women whatever regime it is, Soviet, American, and so on.

Many of those interviewed, particularly Afghan women, expressed strong sentiments against using radical language and tactics for fear of a backlash. This also included adopting a seemingly-Western approach to working with women. One woman elaborated: "It was clear that the policy that was set for the U.S. to free Afghanistan was to 'liberate' Afghan women from the *bourka*. No Afghan is going to align themselves with that."

And yet there were repercussions. "Why are girls' schools being burned? Are we facing a situation that is creating new tensions?" one woman asked. There was a backlash, another woman explained, to what we, the international community, believed was the appropriate response to the so-called *women's rights issue*. It was agreed that this environment never was post-conflict, firstly because the tensions never really subsided, and "because new tensions have been created."

Afghan women leaders also expressed concern with keeping up with international aid priorities. *Was it income generation? Women's leadership? Economic empowerment? Rights education?* "What trend are we supposed to follow today?" one leader asked me. "We are chasing you and your ideas so we can get the money we need to do the work we know. Sometimes you are hard to follow."

These fluctuations in aid priorities occurred faster than Afghan women's organizations could follow, and yet they were supposed to implement these programs if they expected to receive money. Their priorities often fell off the radar as donor dictates drove agency priorities that were then handed down to local organizations. Ultimately, Afghan women and men paid the price, with no time to consider their roles in the process and no space to set the direction of the interventions.

So it was agreed that we didn't understand the history, we didn't listen to the people we were supposedly there to help, and we didn't listen to Afghan women, who had warned us. "When we assume that Afghan women's voices are not heard," one woman explained, "it is because they are not heard by *us*."

And finally, an American women's rights activist had the following to say about the situation:

> Sadly, what we've seen is that U.S. rhetoric on "liberating Afghan women" was completely devoid of substance. We saw this from the beginning with the willingness of the U.S. to cooperate with the Mujahideen groups whose gender ideology was just as restrictive as the Taliban's. Reports from Afghanistan are uniformly bad on women's rights issues; violence against women is still common and women are still being intimidated out of participating in public life. In my opinion, the Bush administration used Afghan women—used them by focusing on their real suffering under the Taliban to get what they wanted i.e., support for U.S. military action against Afghanistan, and then never putting

in any real effort towards improving their lives. You ask if there have been any unexpected outcomes—I'm sorry to say that I expected this outcome from the beginning.

I Am Told We Are Equal Now...

Afghan women and men frequently stated in the early years of the intervention that they were not pleased with the progress made by the international community. Many felt that the money could have been better spent and with farther-reaching effects. Afghans generally felt resentment for aid interventions. One Afghan man said: "We are really angry at all these foreign NGOs ... they conduct lots of surveys but nothing happens. There are more NGOs than people in Afghanistan. They should either work harder or ... go ... home."[45] Indeed, many of those I spoke with shared this sentiment.

Many felt that aid progress was limited, and that promises had not been met. "They haven't done that much anyway," one elderly woman stated. "To make real progress will take much more time." The little that had been done was "only in a very symbolic way." One woman explained that if she measured against promises made, "the future is in ruin." Another elaborated that "women have opportunities presented like treats, but they cannot access them." One old woman lamented: "I am told that we are equal now, but I am not sure yet." This sentiment was reinforced by another woman who asked: "Now women have rights on paper, but what do they do with them?"

Other women expressed feelings of deception, seeing a very different implementation of aid programs than what was promised. Women saw organizations being established in the name of women but then only working to advance their own professional goals. The attention to women's rights was clear on paper but despite big promises, there was no indication that this was being applied in real life.

Indeed, the theme of empty promises was oft-repeated. One man expressed it this way: "They haven't done very good things yet, just promises of complete freedom. They prepared the opportunities for working. And now we wait. The rights which have to be given unfortunately haven't been given." Another added that aid organizations have "done their work hypocritically." Another stated that the Afghan government "should be based on its people, not on international organizations."

Many men felt that the international community had misused and withheld funds from Afghanistan. One older man put it this way: "We want those donations which the world is giving to Afghanistan today to be given

Women at work, Bamiyan.

to the people that are entitled to it, not to their agents." By agents, he was referring to aid organizations.

Despite report after report calling for greater funding for local organizations, Afghan women were left without the support they were promised from the very beginning. Afghan women viewed this as a failure of the international community. One aid worker recently explained: "It is the UN system that is flawed. The UN system and the donors need to ask themselves what they are doing to the women's movement, pitting women's organizations against each other. Making them fight each other for the scraps. For their survival."

"They only saw one layer of society," one man explained. It was therefore not a surprise that promised changes would not reach the people who needed them most. Another woman elaborated: "I do not think the world cares about Afghanistan anymore. They are tired of saving them and now look elsewhere." These women generally agreed that aid entered Afghanistan with much fanfare, re-arranged things, and subsequently made a swift exit. Indeed, for many years Afghanistan, and Afghan women, were not on the global agenda—until August of 2021.

Meanwhile, Afghan women put their lives and their futures on the line while they watched their cause fade from the headlines. "The world does not want to know of Afghan women now," one woman told me. The harshest words were on the notion of freedom: "We all fought for freedom, and now we are told to believe that there is freedom." If only it were so.

The Personal Is Still Political

The discourse of liberation is inherently political and fraught with dangerous political implications, as Afghan history has shown. There's a fundamental contradiction in the role aid organizations play: On the one hand, they set out to achieve social change, but on the other, they aren't supposed to be political. Social change *is* political, and within that, nothing is more political than women's rights.[46] As a result, aid organizations are political actors "whose actions have political impacts whether they like it or not."[47]

It is worthwhile advocating for a renewed understanding of the connection between personal and political—particularly as this plays out in aid "occupations." This reconnection fuses an Afghan feminism—inherently contextual and political—with international opportunities for support grounded in Afghan women's own priorities. But this has not been the path taken.

Are lessons learned—as we like to say?[48] The term is a peculiar piece of aid lingo. We know the lessons, but we neither learn nor apply them. The idea of lessons learned is actually a misnomer. Perhaps we can hope to do no harm—or possibly do *less* harm—by learning from past efforts. We cannot claim ignorance, and yet we fail to implement changes to our practices.

Women's rights are, and have always been, the most highly charged and politicized interface in Afghanistan. They are the stage on which internal and external tensions have played out in Afghan history, used by political groups to rally support one way or another, and by foreign occupiers to interfere in Afghan politics. An Afghan man put it this way:

> When foreign intervention or influences are seen as the catalyst for reform in women's rights, rather than allowing the reforms to grow from within, the changes are not long-lasting. Conservatives and traditionalists inevitably use the issue of women's rights to link the ruling government with foreign interests or to accuse the government of running counter to Afghan culture or tribal customs. These accusations are then used to build popular support against the government and its reforms. In many cases, these foreign interests have been successful in hampering developments in women's rights…. If the issue of women's rights is regarded solely as an agenda to appease pro–Western influences, conservative groups are likely to use the issue to build popular support against the government that brings about such changes.[49]

Even following unsuccessful interventions, the resulting consensus on what ought to be done has not led to change. Gender policies do not operate in a socio-political vacuum. Afghan history demonstrates that externally-enforced social reforms have been resisted time and again. Attempts at engineering a social transformation will continue to have serious repercussions for women as long as their agency is denied in the process.

"We don't learn, we just repeat," an Afghan woman leader explained. "When we talk about women in Afghanistan, there is a list of important things showing what we did wrong. And we are still doing it. And we have not learned … yet." And now, we have an opportunity to rectify past wrongs and support Afghan women in the way that *they* would like us to.

In a discussion of the failure of redistributive reforms in Soviet-occupied Afghanistan, Barnett Rubin, a leading authority on Afghanistan, cites four lines of argument that could easily be applied to attempts to "liberate" women[50]:

1. The reforms failed because the reformers had insufficient knowledge of the society they were trying to reform.
2. The Afghan state did not have the capacity to carry out the reforms.
3. External intervention deprived the government of the chance to correct its "mistakes."
4. Finally … the reforms failed because the government that carried them out lacked legitimacy.

These lines of argument fit well with the questions that launched my own investigation. We did not fully understand the socio-cultural context. The state, as the duty-bearer, nonetheless lacked the capacity and legitimacy to address the issue on its own. And external intervention hijacked the issue, but failed to adequately address it.

In late 2021, Barnett Rubin argued strongly that:

> The main victims of this scam were the Afghan people. While the U.S. forces were there, some Afghans benefited from the foreign aid and the freedoms that came with it. These were real gains, for as long as they lasted, but there was no plan to make them last … [giving] a false sense of security to the elites who gained power and the new professional class, especially the women, who gained unheard of freedoms. To those parts of the population decimated by U.S. bombs those promises always rang false. Eventually the U.S. betrayed the Afghans who had supported its presence, claiming it never really meant those promises of a better life—it had come only to fight terrorism aimed at the U.S. Those who broke the impossible promises bear some of the responsibility, but those who made those reckless promises bear more.[51]

Looking back, both Afghan women and men warned of this interface and the results it might have. Here's the critical piece we missed: Afghan women leaders were there all along, telling us how to get it done.

We need to place our understanding of "what happened" in Afghanistan in the context of increased violence and conflict, and a deteriorating political and economic situation. In other words, we could have seen this coming. We have systematic ways to predict and prepare, in fact. There are a range of "early warning indicators" that give us signal of approaching conflict, things like increased petty crime, high unemployment, political instability or discontent, restricted civil and political rights, increased militarization, a breakdown in law and order, ethnic dominance, rural insecurity, and so on.

I also use women as an indicator. After all, who knows better what is really happening on the ground? *Are women present in public spaces? Are they in markets? Are they safe?* And so on. And when these conditions change, it becomes clear that security conditions are deteriorating.

One might argue that we saw this coming—we've seen this coming for almost two decades.

There are also indicators that are critical prerequisites for strong, stable, secure societies such as safety, government accountability, participation and inclusion, peaceful regional relationships, supportive institutions, and so on. And women. I think that the greatest indicator of a society's success can be found in women's rights. Research reinforces this: the best hope a country has of peace, prosperity, progress is not in the type of government nor the state of the economy—it is in how the country treats its women.[52] And today, under Taliban 2.0, how might Afghanistan fare? How might *Afghan women* fare?

It has been stated that Afghanistan is one of international development's largest failings.[53] Disillusionment with the government and the international community led to two decades of speculations of a likely revival of conflict. Afghanistan's semblance of freedom is fragile, we were continuously told. This was prior to the takeover by the Taliban in 2021.

Critiques were vociferous and valid. We were warned that good intentions and solid plans did not translate on the ground. And despite these intentions and plans, there was an absence of action, although an abundance of consultants. Throughout these two decades, critiques frequently surfaced about the military and aid interventions. *Where was the money going? What were the foreigners doing? Why were Afghans still suffering? Was any of this actually working?!*

Today, Afghanistan feels like an opportunity lost. And yet the country could have been a positive example of what a concerted international effort can accomplish. Ultimately the lesson is this: Afghans will not embrace changes, particularly those involving women, as long as they are believed to be aligned with foreign interests. Meanwhile, the international community missed a history lesson by not anticipating the resentment that would ensue when "outsiders" try to meddle with "their women." Afghan history aptly demonstrates the deep and pervasive dislike of foreign intervention.

Indeed, there exists an invisible corrective to foreign engagement in Afghanistan—a force of nature, dragging Afghanistan back to its roots.[54] It might be argued that the tensions that played out over the last two decades at this interface contributed to the Taliban's strength and their subsequent takeover of the country in 2021.

During my years in Afghanistan, I distinctly remember brief periods of hope and even a sense of victory, albeit naive and premature. At that time, Afghanistan was hardly in the news, unless there was a noteworthy tragedy or a unique success story with international appeal. The sense, at least from the outside, was that Afghanistan was OK. And that Afghan women were well on their way to being OK as well. Anyway, the world had turned its short attention spans elsewhere. In March 2003 they faced Iraq, where a new war was launched. And so Afghanistan swiftly fell off the geo-political agenda.

In mid–2021, we once again turned to face Afghanistan. We thought it was OK when in fact, it was not—nor had it ever been—OK.

I argued at the beginning of this writing that "liberating" Afghan women was the call that initiated the military intervention, which in turn fed into the agenda of the aid intervention. If that was truly the intent, how might we measure today? This is not a judgment on whether the military or aid interventions succeeded or failed. Rather, it asks: *If the women's rights agenda was indeed the ultimate benchmark, what did two decades do? And—what now?!*

Am I arguing that the U.S. withdrawal was a mistake? No. Granted, it was hastily executed and showed little concern for Afghanistan's stability or for the lives of Afghan women, the very lives they sought to "liberate" in the first place. Ultimately, Afghanistan's future depends on Afghans— and a viable Afghan government—not U.S. soldiers.[55] An Afghan woman leader put it well, thanking the international community for their support but also acknowledging that "Afghans do not like to have foreign troops in their country."[56] Ultimately, this could have been done better, laying a stronger foundation for peace. At the end, she said, "nations are built by its own people and we Afghans have been trying to be self-reliant and self-sufficient for some time."[57]

Her answer reminds us that the solution is political, and peace is— or could have been—possible. A gradual political and economic transition could have been put in place, centering the security of Afghan civilians. The security of women.

One year after the fall of the Taliban in 2001, *Malalai*,[58] the women's magazine, asked what has changed for Afghan women one year on. The lead article, titled "Freedom for Women: Only Words," argued that "the freedom which now exists for women is a freedom with little meaning."[59] A "flame of hope has been kept alive ... [albeit through] endless speeches

A man stands on an old tank overlooking the city, Kabul.

about the tragic lives of women and the importance of paying attention to them." But Afghan women and men alike were increasingly disillusioned with the reconstruction process and believed that it was indeed only words.

"We need more than words," I wrote in a statement on International Women's Day, 8 March, in 2003:

> We must follow through with action. But we must also be prepared to be patient. This will not be a "quick impact project." What is needed is social evo-lution. Just a glance at the history of Afghanistan shows that rapid social change has resulted in serious consequences. Efforts to improve women's lives will be worthwhile in the long term if we remain sensitive to the culture and history of the country and if we operate with a clear sense of where Afghan women themselves want their future to be. Essential to starting this process is recogni-tion and awareness that women are essential to the rebuilding of Afghanistan and should be given an active role in all development efforts. Women across Afghanistan want to participate meaningfully in the reconstruction of their community.[60]

I could have written the same thing 18 years later. In fact, I am—it is this book.

CHAPTER 8

Women's Agency and Resistance

Put your head against the wall and push.
You will either break your head or break the wall.
—Afghan expression meaning keep pushing,
fighting, moving forward

Afghan women's history is filled with examples of feminist activists who have not only fought against their own oppression, but have galvanized forces that have inspired generations. Afghan women have led protests, organized movements, pushed boundaries, and fought for freedom. They do so again today. And yet, agency and resistance are not always public displays. They transpire in small, private spaces, and in discreet but powerful ways.

Afghan women have always found ways to maneuver, first and foremost for their own survival and safety, but also for their rights and freedoms. Fighting for survival is the primary foundation of resistance. Politics start with the individual, and the daily practices of many Afghan women demonstrate an acute awareness of the conditions and constraints—and how to get around them. They practice public self-regulation in order to create a barrier for their protection and a guise for their work. They chip away at the fractures in patriarchal power at home and in public spaces. This is a life-long (re)negotiation, especially in contexts where public defiance can be life-threatening. What might look like "provoking, avoiding, and enduring" from the outside is marked by "apparent victories, contradictions, assertions, regrets, and re-evaluations"[1] from the inside.

Power lives in the small spaces. The daily lives of women—*all* women—are micro-displays of autonomy in whatever sphere they occupy, with whatever tools they wield, and for whatever issues they influence. In Afghanistan, the home is a stage for these movements. Many Afghan activists have advocated for greater focus on the private sphere, or at least recognition that it can be the tinder to ignite a larger flame.

Additionally, when women defy patriarchy at home, even in small ways, they create space for their daughters to do so. And their sons as

202

well. And eventually, an older generation of men who are traditionally the household power-holders:

> When fathers, brothers, husbands, mothers, sisters, in-laws, clergy, workplace supervisors and colleagues and so on provide relational support to women who act in defiance of gendered power, they participate in refusing to provide consent to gendered power. In fact, that relational support is key in taking the first step to resist openly, especially in a context where the consequences of resistance are violent.[2]

Every woman I met in Afghanistan expressed confidence in her own strength, and a determined ability to act in her own best interest, on her own behalf. These women continued to demonstrate agency across all aspects of their lives—whether or not outsiders viewed it as such. In fact, many Afghan women felt that they have always exercised agency, despite foreign perceptions that they are oppressed.

Afghan feminism exists. "Can I not be both at once, just as you are?" an Afghan woman leader asked me. "Our feminism responds to our context—it is home-grown." Afghan women did not need to be saved. They have always exercised agency—and "saved" themselves. Their feminist movement, like all indigenous feminisms, evolves out of a need to challenge present circumstances to create better alternatives. Afghan women have struggled and negotiated the various fluctuations in their social status throughout history, using long-established mechanisms to achieve gains on their own terms.

Another Afghan woman leader put it this way: "*Kharijis* [foreigners] cannot try and change Afghan culture. If they do, it will bring more problems for women. It has brought more violence upon women. Women will ask for changes when they are ready."

"No foreigner can help me," she went on to say. "I will help myself."

We Want to Direct the Changes...

Who has been defining "liberation" for Afghan women?

From the perspective of the international media, the *chaddari* has often taken on a symbolic role as the barometer of social change. The liberation discourse in international media was instrumental in creating a particular image of Afghan women. This image served to create a picture of an oppressed Afghan woman beneath a *chaddari*, in turn contributing to the design of programs and aid interventions. Such an image denied agency and did not resonate with Afghan women and men, as was said in Chapter 1. The *chaddari*, or any act of veiling, must not be confused with, or made to stand for, a lack of women's agency.[3] Unfortunately, international liberation discourse favored visible transformations—prevalence of a veil or *chaddari*, or meetings of men and women—over institutional changes such as laws and improvement in status.[4]

Conversations with Afghan women suggest that gender inequalities have not been rectified by engagement in aid activities as they had expected, based on aid rhetoric. The promise of transformation, as it were, did not materialize. In fact, these women were quite vocal about what they saw as a deteriorating situation regarding gender equality. They expressed concern about the high-profile focus from the international community and the media, and felt that facile analyses regarding the *chaddari* and their low social status were misguided and did not reflect Afghan realities. "With a veil on her head, no Afghan woman has ever stopped herself from letting her voice be heard, and frequently is it she who has the last word."[5]

Some Afghan women went so far as to say that they were beginning to see themselves through the eyes of the world, not as the strong and resilient women they felt themselves to be. They recognized that they were being measured against standards that did little to reflect their realities. As a result, they also felt anger at having been underestimated. These women were extremely vocal and articulate in discussions of their own agency. Many women, Afghan and non–Afghan, demonstrate their own agency in ways that outsiders cannot see and therefore, are not able to judge.

One woman explained it to me this way:

> The world did not think well of Afghan women, thinking we are only oppressed and weak! This is not accurate, but the world wants to see us this way. This image influenced work on women in Afghanistan. That is why they wanted to help and they thought they could save us. They thought we could not struggle for our rights without their help. We are happy for help, but we want to direct the changes. Afghan women are stronger than outsiders know.

Another woman added: "The world thought Afghan women were prisoners. In a way this was true, but we are able to survive as we have over the years. We are not only victims." Afghan women articulated strongly that they want to be the ones to decide on the images. "One day we will have the power to change this image and people will listen!" one woman stated.

These women felt strongly that the pervasive images were "through the eyes of other countries" and had little to do with Afghan priorities. "Their images are their own and we do not interfere," one woman explained. "But as we see it, they are far away from the truth." This image, many women explained, should be one that reflects who Afghan women are, what they want, and how they would like to see their society.

Many women expressed that they feel solidarity with their Afghan

Two young performers celebrate Afghan Independence Day (19 August), Kabul.

brothers and would prefer that women not be viewed as needing "saving from Afghan men." "We don't want our men to be owned by anyone," one woman stated. Most women felt that they were artificially juxtaposed against men. Simplistic analyses of women as unhappy victims and men as tyrants and terrorists were hard to combat.

"Tell the world that Afghan women are very strong and they will do anything for the future of their country and their children," one woman demanded of me. "Tell them who we are. You have seen us, now you know us!" One woman eloquently expressed sentiments that were echoed by other women: "I think other countries pity us, pity Afghan women. You should tell them that if there had been peace in Afghanistan, our country and people would be just as educated and successful as any other."

Meanwhile, Afghan women argue that they have not been given the space to determine their own course. An Afghan woman leader told me that her activism, and her organization, was born from her own conviction. And yet, the context of perpetual insecurity has given her—and other women leaders—little time to reflect. "It's very important to be given some chances to look at what we're doing," she told me. "In the West, people plan their year. Here we plan our day. We cannot look beyond the day." The daily need to survive has been detrimental to the Afghan women's movement.

"This causes lack of coordination," she continued. "We just run behind opportunities. We don't have our own strategies. Unfortunately, we run after anything. There is no cultural-sensitive and context-specific strategy for this country," she concluded.

In spaces of solidarity and within women's networks, women's displays of strength would also be coupled with sharing challenges and co-creating strategies to make gains on their own terms. I watched this time and again in every space where women were able to congregate. Difficulties at home or resistance from male members of the household were addressed in strategic and creative ways, ensuring that nothing would stand in the way of their quest to better their lives and that of their families.

One woman told of the negotiations she regularly undertook with her husband in order to have permission to attend trainings. She explained that, at first, he gave her permission because there was no other source of income for the family. But a few months later, his increased frustration and feelings of uselessness had taken a toll on her. She then made arrangements to split the financial assistance she received as support from the organization with her husband in order to buy his compliance. The women who heard this story agreed that, while this was not ideal, it was a strategic temporary measure in order to gain space—space that she would use to her advantage.

Another woman shared her story, explaining that her 11-year-old son forbade her to leave the house, saying it would shame him if she were to be seen "wandering in the streets." She was a widow, and, left without a father, the 11 year old was now the man of the house. She argued with him, explaining that there was no alternative and in order to support the family and provide food, she must take advantage of the only opportunity available to her. His response was "If you want to leave the house, you'll have to kill me first." She respected his wishes and delayed her participation in the program until her son was enrolled in school. Even then, many months into her participation, he did not think she left the house during the day.

One woman returned to Afghanistan after a scholarship took her to the United States for her master's degree. She returned to her community to teach at the nearest university. She also managed to start an organization to help women and girls learn English as a second language. All this until the Taliban's recent takeover forced her to leave her home. She is now in hiding as her work has put her at risk. She told me this: "I have done everything I can for other women with the opportunities I have been given. I know I have been a role model for many women and girls in my community for spreading knowledge and teaching what I have learned to those who have never travelled outside Afghanistan's borders."

Yet another woman I spoke to told me that she acquired skills in alteration and design as a refugee in Pakistan in the 1990s. She returned to Kabul after 2001 and started her own business, renting a workshop near her home to teach designing and sewing. She manages 15 to 20 female students at a time and also opened her own clothing boutique. She said: "I am young, but I consider myself an entrepreneur." She recognizes the challenges women entrepreneurs face and she is committed to not only continuing her business, but also giving back to her community. "Not only have I managed to run the business by myself, I also earned enough to buy a house for my parents in Kabul and also sent my brother to Turkey to complete his education."

These are but a few of many stories depicting subtle acts of resistance with radical, transformative potential. As seen throughout this book, Afghan women have always gone about the business of liberating themselves. It would be impossible to do justice to all of these women. They represent *every* woman. Their power lies in the extraordinary ordinariness of their movements, and in their will to survive.

Power in the Small Spaces

How can "liberation" be measured? Not through development indicators or matrices. They are measured in the stories of Afghan women's resistance. Some of this resistance has also fueled fires and ignited movements. These are but a few:

In 1999, during the Taliban's first reign, Shukriya Barakzai violated Taliban rules and was badly beaten.[6] Her crime was leaving the house without a *mahram*, or male guardian, in order to seek medical attention. She had shaved her two-year-old daughter's head, dressed her in boys' clothing to pass her off as her guardian, and went to the doctor. Taliban militants from the Ministry for the Propagation of Virtue and Prevention of Vice, who circled Kabul in pickup trucks in search of Afghans to publicly shame and punish for violating their moral code, found her and beat her.

Prior to this, Barakzai was a student at Kabul University—until women were forced to leave. As a result of this encounter with the Taliban, she began to organize underground classes for girls. She then went on to assist in the drafting of Afghanistan's Constitution, and also to serve two terms in Parliament.

Khawar Amiri was the Head of the Literacy Department of her province's Directorate of Education. She is a mediator for women's issues, an education advocate, and a human rights defender. Her province, Khost, has very low levels of literacy. Amiri conducts literacy courses and also defends women's rights through the local council. In Khost, women and girls are exposed to a great deal of discrimination and violence. Girls are educated until grade six, and then they are often forced into marriage. Amiri has intervened in many abuse cases, despite being threatened and attacked for her activism. Her commitment is to support women and girls in their quest for independence, for security, for equal opportunities for education, and for a life free from violence.

Fawzia Koofi was a member of parliament from 2005 to 2019 and also served as vice president of the National Assembly. We met Koofi in Chapter 5, as a member of the Afghan delegation negotiating peace with the Taliban. The day she was born, she was left out to die—because she was a girl. She survived, and was the only girl in her family to attend school, going on to establish a network of secret girls' schools in the 1990s. These stories and more appear in her 2012 memoir *The Favored Daughter*. She is a fighter and a survivor, having survived two assassination attempts by the Taliban.[7]

In an interview with Al Jazeera in September 2021,[8] she spoke strongly against the international community, especially the United States, for fueling a corrupt government. But she said that there is a transformed generation in the country, a young generation, fighting for their rights and demanding to be included. "What I have gone through as a woman gave me the reason to change things for us … it is always the women who have to pay the highest price." She went on to say that "every woman that carried the burden of what's going on in the country, [they] kept me moving forward…."[9]

Nadia Ghulam's story is also the stuff of legend.[10] Starting when she was 11, she took on the identity of her dead brother for ten years in order to survive, working alongside men in order to feed her family. Her truth was never revealed. She knew that if she was discovered, the Taliban would kill her. "I assumed that one day I would die," she said. "In that moment, I knew I had no choice."[11] Ghulam's story is reflected in her book *The Secret of My Turban* and was the basis for the 2003 film *Osama*. She said that being a man was the only way to survive Afghanistan under the Taliban. She now resides in Spain. In 2016, Ghulam published her second novel, *The First Star of the Night*, recounting the lives of Afghan women who have fought for more than 40 years for their freedom.

Wazhma Frogh founded the Women and Peace Studies Organization in 2015 to elevate women's voices in peace processes and fill in gaps such as establishing a watchdog operation to foster greater transparency in government and training young women in tactics of conflict resolution.[12] Frogh also worked with religious and tribal leaders, trained women police officers, and published research and reports on peace and security. Additionally, Frogh uses motherhood as a space for resistance. She established groups to bring mothers together to prevent their sons from gravitating into extremist activity—the most extreme of which is suicide bombing. She taught mothers what to look out for, how to speak to their sons, and how to foster peace. Through her mothers group, she has prevented many suicide bombings. Frogh is a peace-builder who uses every available platform for change.

Aziza Aman has always been a voice for the education of women and girls. Her education began in Kunduz, her hometown in northern Afghanistan, a very progressive city at that time. She studied literature at Kabul University, then returned to Kunduz as a Dari language teacher and eventually became director of her high school. Her women's rights activism was born at that time. She defied gender stereotypes by taking high school girls on field trips and organizing girls' volleyball tournaments.

In 1975, Aman ran for the Constitutional *Loya Jirga* to draw up a new national constitution, and was elected as one of six women representatives in the country—the first women to ever occupy such positions. In 1989, due to deteriorating security, she moved to Pakistan where she spent 15 years as a refugee. During that time, she worked on education and human rights, supporting other Afghan women refugees who had escaped the Taliban to find opportunities for education and work. And in 2002, she returned to Kabul to establish the Afghan Women's Resource Center. With a career and commitment that spans generations, Aman has never stopped advocating for change.

Afghan women are also building the next generation of feminists who will carry on the fight. "Inaction is not an option," an Afghan friend told me. "Or hopelessness."[13]

I spoke to her after the Taliban takeover in August 2021 to ask how she was managing the crisis in Afghanistan. *As a mother of young children, how did she explain the situation to them?*

"Kids right now don't know what is happening and are asking questions. Why can't we go to school? Why can't we ride our bikes anymore?" my friend told me.

"Why are we covering our faces?" the young girls ask. "Why are we inside all day?!"

Being a child in Afghanistan now means learning the horrors of the past—horrors the older generation believed were truly in the past. But now, these horrors have come to their doorstep. *What do you tell an Afghan girl who has never seen violence like this?*

In a personal communication, an Afghan woman told me:

Today, Afghan mothers are telling their children not to look the Taliban in the eye. Mothers are concerned about their children's safety, and their unknown future in a land that was only just beginning to be free. These kids, they may not be able to continue with their education. And girls, they now have the sense that they are unequal, less-than. We fought so hard to rid them of this very feeling.

> I tell my children about what is happening in the world even if it is too terrifying. The more they know, the more prepared they will be to face the world.

The young generation in Afghanistan were raised with relative freedom, and a sense that the story of the Taliban was becoming a part of Afghan history.

"Here is what I tell my daughter," my Afghan friend told me. "I tell her: *Tonight, we wait. And tomorrow, we fight.*"

These stories of resistance hardly scratch the surface. Afghan women throughout the country risk their lives every day to ensure that their girls go to school, their neighbors are protected from violent partners, their sisters are able to read and write, and their allies are supported as they speak out for women's rights. There are countless stories like these, and I could not possibly do them justice here.

In October 2021, activist Sahar Sahil Nabizada said, "It's possible that I die … basically we accept risks in order to pave way for the generations to come, at least they will be proud of us."[14]

Afghan women leaders continue to take incredible risks in order to secure their hard-won gains, even as strong forces work against them.[15] At the organizational level, the story is very much the same. Afghan civil society is filled with strong women's groups, started by everyday women galvanized into action. Below are a small sample of these groups.

Boys in a classroom, Bamiyan.

Afghan Women's Network

The Afghan Women's Network is a coalition organization that was founded in the wake of the Beijing Conference for Women in 1995 and have now built themselves up to a network of 126 organizations around the country. Their work focuses on peace and security—even before this became a UN acronym. The group was instrumental in bringing this to UN attention and garnering support for the inclusion of women in all aspects of security and, in particular, understanding security through a feminist lens. In 2020, they led a door-to-door campaign asking women what the peace process meant to them in order to bring women's otherwise-absent voices to the negotiating table with the Taliban.[16]

Their founder, Mahbooba Seraj, was imprisoned by the Communist Party in 1978 and lived in exile in the United States for 25 years.[17] She now resides in Afghanistan and says she is not going anywhere, refusing to hide from anyone. In 2021, as the Taliban took over the country yet again, she said that she would do anything for Afghanistan and for its women and children. "The world left us like a hot potato," she lamented. "They dropped us and now we are where we are. So now we should do it. We should stand for what we believe and really work hard. I feel so abandoned by the United States.... I cannot even talk about it without wanting to scream."[18] She said that the Taliban cannot ignore Afghanistan's 18 million women.[19] They will *not* be ignored.

"What is at stake now?" she lamented in October 2021. "Everything that we knew, everything that we built. Especially for the women."

Afghan Women's Resource Center

Despite patriarchal barriers and many other restrictions in Pakistan, the Afghan Women's Resource Center (AWRC) was founded in response to the need to serve Afghan women refugees. In August of 1989, a group of Afghan women activists in Pakistan accepted this challenge, creating an organization that would be run by Afghan women, in service of Afghan women.

Since its inception, AWRC worked with thousands of Afghan women and children in Pakistan, and was established in Afghanistan in 2002. In Afghanistan, AWRC focuses on livelihood opportunities through vocational skills trainings and micro-finance loan programs, literacy programs, preventive health education, and professional capacity building programs. AWRC's work has had great success advocating for Afghan women as well as changing society's perceptions of Afghan women.

Revolutionary Association of the Women of Afghanistan

If there is one Afghan women's organization that has captivated our imaginations, it would be the Revolutionary Association of the Women of

Afghanistan. RAWA describes itself as "the oldest political/social organization of Afghan women struggling for peace, freedom, democracy and women's rights in fundamentalism-blighted Afghanistan."[20] An unapologetic feminist and nationalist organization that promotes women's rights and secular democracy,[21] RAWA was founded in 1977 by Meena Keshwar Kamal when she was 21. Meena established schools, hospitals, and training centers for Afghan refugee women and children and also launched the women's magazine *Payam-e-Zan*, Women's Message. The organization grew by word of mouth and consisted of both public and private acts of defiance, including marches and protests. RAWA soon began covertly distributing anti–Soviet and pro-women political leaflets either under the *chaddari* or concealed amongst clothes in their laundry bundles. Every moment was seen as an opportunity for liberation.

Meena was assassinated in 1987 by Soviet agents for her work as an activist and human rights defender.[22] Through the Soviet occupation, civil war, and Taliban years in Afghanistan, RAWA was bold in their efforts. RAWA gained international notoriety through their secret schools as well as their staunch opposition to every Afghan government in the last four decades. In 2001, when a journalist asked a RAWA member what she did when the Taliban came after them with sticks, she responded: "We hit them right back…. We have sticks too."[23]

RAWA continues to be a fearless champion for women's rights and today they remain as vocal as ever. They are calling on global feminist support to advance their cause: "If you are freedom-loving and anti-fundamentalist, you are with RAWA."[24]

MyRedLine

In March of 2019, a group of Afghan women leaders coined the phrase that would launch a movement. There was concern during the Doha peace talks of 2019 between the United States, the Afghan government, and the Taliban that women were not going to be fully represented. Farahnaz Forotan and Ferdous Samim co-founded the campaign as a way to bring Afghan women's voices to the table. MyRedLine is a social media campaign that became an accessible way for women in all provinces and of all ethnicities to announce their personal "red lines"—in other words, the non-negotiables for their future. Women were asked to post short video clips that were then aired during the talks.[25]

This campaign was created and sustained by Afghan women, for Afghan women, with a call to action, asking women "What is your Red-Line?" Following its success, tensions ensued between the founders and a UN agency regarding the UN's co-opting of this movement along with its refusal to provide support. The irony is there. A key tagline of aid agencies is their commitment to supporting and amplifying "local voices" which includes providing adequate resources to fuel their movements. And yet, this was not the case. The *rhetoric* of support for women's rights was prioritized over actual work on the ground. And an opportunity for real support was missed, presenting an unfortunate example of aid agencies' potential to hinder movements created on Afghan women's own terms. Unfortunately, MyRedLine is not unique in this experience.

Raising the Voices of Afghan Women

> Afghan women will push forward no matter what. The only question is how bad it will get for them…. Is there a chance the world will be there to support them diplomatically, politically and economically as they live on the front lines of extremism and fight for their futures and their country's? Right now the answer looks to be no. And that is a loss for all of us.[26]

Afghan women continue to define their own liberation, taking on public roles to defend human rights and communicate with the world. However, this is not without grave risk. Journalists, and particularly female journalists, continuously find themselves the targets of threats and attacks causing many to leave the profession, or leave Afghanistan altogether. In January 2020, there were 1900 female journalists. By November 2020, 200 had left the profession. In a four-month period, six journalists were murdered.[27]

The absence of Afghan women from both Afghan and foreign media outlets based in Afghanistan meant the international media did not amplify Afghan voices and often portrayed Afghan women in simplistic, binary terms—as either heroes or as victims in need of saving. To counter this, Zahra Joya founded Afghanistan's first feminist news agency, Rukhshana Media, in December 2020 following a decade of work as a journalist. At the time, Joya was also Deputy Director of Communications at the Kabul Municipal Government. She established Rukhshana to provide a counter-narrative, to elevate women's voices, and to provide a national news source for all Afghan women.

"This is your space," she would tell Afghan women. "A place where we will tell your stories and the stories of all our sisters across Afghanistan."[28] Joya partnered with *The Guardian* on the Women Report Afghanistan project, using her network of female journalists around the country to report on the situation as the Taliban began its takeover. The journalists are all young women, "so brave and so fearless," Joya said.[29] And all of them are now at risk because of their work. As of September 2021, Rukhshana reporters have either been evacuated or are in hiding. Barely a fraction of female journalists remain.

Sahar Speaks is another example of women-led resistance through journalism. Founded in 2015 by Amie Ferris-Rotman, Sahar Speaks trains, mentors, and publishes Afghan female journalists, centering Afghan women's experience and needs.[30] Initially, alumnae flourished and many went on to work for international media. However, over the years, the number of Afghan women journalists reduced drastically in Kabul, usually corresponding to the deteriorating conditions. And with the Taliban back in power the risk is even greater to Afghan women and more specifically, the women who can't get out:

> If these women, some of the best educated their country has to offer, with access to gratifying jobs and relative freedom over their personal lives, chose to leave at the first opportunity, what did that mean for the rest of Afghan women?[31]

Farahnaz Forotan is an Afghan journalist who was reporting from conflict areas in the country and also hosted a popular segment on TV, "Kabul Debate." Her visible presence in the media was a victory for women's representation, ensuring the inclusion of women's voices and perspectives in the shaping of Afghan society. At the same time, her journey was far from easy. In her early years, she was restricted both by men in her media company and security forces for being a woman reporting from conflict zones.[32] Eventually, her position became life-threatening. After she interviewed a Taliban member in Doha during one of the peace talks, she was put on a hit list and had to leave the country and seek safety abroad.

During the interview, she was not wearing a headscarf—like many young Afghan women at that time. She explained that the Talib "couldn't hide his disdain at my presence and set about to ignore me." Forotan stood her ground and "refused to be invisible," courageously insisting that the interview continue. "Afghan women live with a sense of being invisible," she said. "Our voices go unheard, our existence barely registered." She noted the irony: "Our presence in any public space is celebrated as gender equality in and outside Afghanistan, but all we experience in daily life is inequality and discrimination. It filled me with rage."[33]

Female journalists are a particular target not only for the issues they cover but also for their public roles, in defiance of perceived social norms. These journalists receive threatening letters, known as *shabnama*, from the Taliban telling them of their moral violations and demanding that they stop working. "If you continue," one letter said, "then you have no right to complain" about the consequences.[34]

In recent years, there was a spike in targeted attacks and killings of journalists: 14 women working for media outlets were threatened or violently attacked in 2020.[35] The Taliban often deny involvement but also "welcomed the killings of journalists on social media, calling these killings in many cases a religious duty."[36] The Afghan Journalists Safety Committee 2020 report explained that

> Taliban supporters accuse journalists of being agents of Western countries, and corrupted by Western values, thereby legitimizing any violence against journalists and the media as not only being permissible but a key part of their war.[37]

These stories are important because women's journalism was touted as a "win" over the last two decades. Now these journalists are the faces on the frontlines of Taliban restrictions. The women who were once visible on television, whose articles were read, whose voices were heard, whose opinions had influence, have been sending their identity records and work to foreign embassies for safekeeping before eliminating any trace of their existence.[38] One said: "For many years, I worked as a journalist ... to raise the voice of Afghans, especially Afghan women, but now our identity is being destroyed and nothing has been done by us to deserve this."

And yet, Afghan women persist in protecting the gains made from the last 20 years. As Zahra Joya said, "The Taliban can use their guns and their rules to try to break the spirit of Afghan women, but they cannot silence us all. I will never stop resisting."[39] They continue to also find hope in the new generation of Afghan women who did not live under the Taliban. Shukriya Barakzai pointed out how "they are full of energy, hope, and dreams ... they're more alert. They're communicating with the world." The Taliban may be taking territory "but not the hearts and minds of people."[40]

Educating Women Is the Only Hope...

In Islam, a high value is placed on education, so much so that "the first order from Allah is 'Iqra,' which means 'Read.'"[41] Therefore, it is not even possible to ban education on Islamic grounds, but female education continues to face setbacks in Afghanistan.[42] For the Taliban and other conservative groups, girls' education was viewed as similar to women's political participation, or any participation in general. It was not only a threat to their power and order, it was an imposition of Western culture. In conservative rural areas, women and girls were long accustomed to restricted mobility, including denial of the right to education, regardless of Taliban presence.

During the Taliban rule from 1996 to 2001, girls were actively banned from school. As a result, education became a foundation for women's agency and resistance. Women fought back with each setback, finding

Girls on the street asking for food, Kabul.

creative yet risky ways to continue to educate themselves and their daughters. In some parts of Afghanistan, the Taliban turned a blind eye to girls' primary schools. And in other areas, the communities challenged Taliban edicts. Girls in one district actually went on a hunger strike to defend their education—and they won.[43] But for most of the country, girls were either at home or educated in secret underground schools, established by courageous women who valued education—even over their own lives. Teaching girls became an act of resistance, and seeking education turned into a risky gamble.

Following the ousting of the Taliban, the international community invested billions into the education sector in Afghanistan. The sector is said to be one of the greatest success stories of Afghanistan's reconstruction.[44] It is the most visible, and easily quantifiable, measure of "progress." In 2001, only 5000 Afghan girls were enrolled in schools. By 2020, girls made up almost 39 percent of students in the country, meaning 3.7 million girls were in school.[45] Education for girls has increased at every level, including in higher education.

There are successes, undoubtedly, but also setbacks. In reality, the backlash continued and, in many places, increased. A study in 2016 revealed that, despite the rhetoric of success, schools were struggling even after the Taliban as deteriorating security conditions, weak governance, and systemic corruption continued to plague the education sector.[46]

This example shows the extent of insecurity that remained in education, and in any activities focused on women and girls:

> This is to warn all the teachers and those employees who work with companies to stop working with them. We have warned you earlier and this time we give you a three days ultimatum to stop working. If you do not stop, you are to blame yourself[47] [Taliban *Shabnama* from Zabul].

Shabnama, or Night Letters, are threatening letters left in public places or on the doors of individual homes at night. This tactic was frequently employed during the parliamentary elections to intimidate female candidates. Female teachers and civil servants often receive *shabnama*, at times bearing the seal of the area's shadow Taliban governor, warning them to leave their jobs. Other working women face similar threats. Many have been killed.

Shabnama frequently make the case that those Afghans who are "associating with infidels" are thereby "betraying Islam and Afghan culture" and will be punished:

> Muslim Brothers: Understand that the person who helps launch an attack with infidels is no longer a member of the Muslim community. Therefore, punishment of those who cooperate with infidels is the same as the [punishment of] infidels themselves. You should not cooperate in any way—neither with words, nor with money nor with your efforts. Watch out not to exchange your honor and courage for power and dollar[48] [Taliban *Shabnama* from Helmand].

Historically, schools in Afghanistan have been at the frontline of hostilities that are directed at the central government and at perceived foreign interference. During Soviet occupation, for instance, a female literacy program in Helmand province was met with so much local resistance that teachers had their throats slit.[49]

"We always have to be careful," one Afghan woman educator explained, so that women are not targeted. "Something that can take a month may take us four to five months because we have to be so careful. This makes us look bad to someone in Washington.... But it is the insurgency that hampers us from moving faster."[50]

Groups opposed to girls' education have used threats of violence as a deterrent, keeping an increasing number of girls out of school every year. Indeed, it is not unlike the force to keep women out of public office. The forces against girls' education are often stronger than the communities' will to resist them. A member of a women's group in Kandahar explained it this way: "Culture is an issue, [but] security is more important because even those people who want to break tradition are not able to."[51]

Even as access to education improved, parents continued to be afraid to send their daughters to school. Teachers and women leaders spent years advocating in rural communities, working with tribal and religious leaders and parents to encourage them to allow the education of their daughters. Today, much of this work stands to be lost. Recent figures record approximately 60 percent of out-of-school children are girls and the downward pattern is expected to continue with the return of the Taliban.[52]

In the Human Rights Watch report *Attacks on Education in Afghanistan*, research was conducted on violence and threats against the education sector. One hundred and ten attacks against schools, teachers, and students took place between 1 January and 21 June 2006—barely a six-month period.[53] These threats only increased, and a 2021 report classified Afghanistan among the countries most heavily affected by attacks on education.[54] More than 300 attacks on schools were identified, injuring or killing at least 410 students, teachers, or education workers between 2017 and 2019.[55]

Attacks on education disproportionately impact women and girls, and put both female students *and* female educators at risk. These attacks led to the closure of more than 1000 schools in a two-year period, which not only denied half a million children their right to education, but also highlighted the continued resistance to girls' education. Even as many Afghan women and girls embraced new freedoms and opportunities, the fears remained.

As security in the country continued to deteriorate, funding for education was rerouted into the defense and security sectors. In 2020, the Ministry of Higher Education communicated to all public universities across the country that the government would need to withdraw $10 million from the Ministry's development budget to be channeled into defense and security. At the same time, girls' schools faced continued risks, teachers received threats in the form of *shabnama*, and ultimately, violence and insecurity prevented many women and girls from an education. Female education has long been impeded by a lack of available schools, security concerns, poverty, discrimination and gender inequality. In rural areas, many women and girls were only able to benefit from education if the men in their lives approved or were willing to protect them from scrutiny or violence.

Meanwhile, girls' education essentially became the benchmark for advances towards equality over the last 20 years. Aid reports and world leaders used education as evidence of success despite the reality on the ground. Boris Johnson, Prime Minister of the UK, claimed some credit for the two million girls in school across the country, adding that "if you want to point out one crowning achievement of the toil and valour of our servicemen and women, look no further than the Afghan girls who now have the chance to go to school."[56]

With the Taliban's return to power in 2021, girls have been banned from secondary education, but boys are permitted to return to school.[57] This edict makes Afghanistan the only country in the world to deny an education to half of its population. Further, male teachers are no longer allowed to teach female classes, crippling women's opportunities in higher education due to the shortage of female teachers. This is expected to deteriorate further as evidenced by their segregation policy already enforced across university classrooms.[58]

The Taliban organizes weekly committee meetings on education, but only for men. At the time of writing, they stated that "some form" of education will be permitted for girls, but it is unclear what that form might take. If girls' education resumes, they will be required to wear an "Islamic hijab" in school, but this too can mean many things.

One Afghan woman leader told me this: "The new frontline is women's education, especially for the new generation. Taliban has banned schools because they know the more educated people become, the harder it will be to oppress them."

At the same time, women leaders and Afghan organizations like Pen Path are preparing to fight back.[59] Educating women is the only hope for a better Afghanistan—and the strongest tool of liberation for women. Pen Path's founder, Matiullah Wesa, helped reopen hundreds of schools across Afghanistan, campaigning for girls' right to an education through door-to-door visits. He builds libraries in rural areas, fueled by a network of 2400 volunteers around the country. Many have faced risks in doing this work. Pen Path has provided 57,000 children with access to education, reopened 100 schools, and provided literacy classes at home for 1400 girls—girls who live in communities without schools. He calls girls' education his red line, and has said he will continue his work "regardless who comes into power." Wesa, like many Afghan fathers and brothers, will fight alongside women and girls for their right to an education.

The 2019 Survey of the Afghan People showed an increase in support for women's education: 87 percent, up from 84 percent in 2018.[60] What's more, 43 percent of Afghans surveyed cited lack of educational opportunities as the biggest problem facing women.[61] The will for change exists.

In 2021, international support is more crucial than ever. Afghanistan is dependent on donor assistance to fund its education system but if this comes under strain, the obstacles to education will be exacerbated and any progress made will be undone.[62] Additional aid needs to be channeled to the women's organizations who are, and always have been, doing the work. They will need support for underground schools, for secure networks, for supplies, for their own safety.

The future of female students and their female teachers remains unclear. There is a generation of girls who have been raised to believe that they have a right to education. "We have become educated, strong women," one Afghan university student told me. "We are not going back to dark days. I will risk my life to study. And I will teach other girls. If they cannot get to school, I will get to them."

Teacher Atifa Watanyar refused to stop teaching, despite Taliban restrictions.[63] In October 2021, she said: "It's just the thing that we can do for our children, for our daughters, for our girls."

An Afghan woman leader told me this in late 2021:

> Educating women is the only hope for a better Afghanistan. Education will liberate Afghan women from oppression, whether it is Taliban or the patriarchy embedded in Afghan culture. It is time for Afghanistan to move forward and pace with the rest of the world. Afghan women can not do this alone. They will need international attention, and the world can not forget Afghanistan—at least not now.

We Know What Freedom We Want

Education serves as an example of women's resistance, despite risks and restrictions. But this is not the only one. Many who worked in Afghanistan saw, and learned from, the ample examples of strong indigenous movements for women's rights, even prior to the Taliban. Women and women's groups who, in the words of one aid worker have been "consistently working on altering the social and political fabric of their lives," and doing so with little to no assistance.

Throughout the two decades of support, we failed to adequately support these groups. We cannot fail them now. "They still need support," she continued, "now more than ever." In the past, we overlooked these groups unless they fully subscribed to our agenda. The aid worker added that "no one, or very few, of those in international gender development are seeking out these existing relationships because they have their own agendas or programs or ways of 'doing gender.'"

As we have argued, our ways of "doing gender" are not the ones that will work. Another aid worker reinforced this in a recent conversation with me:

> You know this is how it went … the women, they did all the real work. And they did it without any resources. And then we came in, trying to exploit their expertise without giving them any credit. Or any resources. Most of all the resources. That's the problem, we gave them nothing.

She continued to explain that the scant funding that was allocated to women's groups was only to fill our own programmatic needs and gaps.

On a hill overlooking Kabul.

"We denied their political considerations, their feminist intent." In the end, our support was in the form of "small, short, underfunded programs. Insulting. Destined for failure."

"It is the system that is flawed," one aid worker added. "The UN system and the donors need to ask themselves what they are doing to the women's movement by pitting women's organizations against each other. Making them fight each other for the scraps. For their survival."

Another aid worker added that, in her experience, it was always the so-called experts who continued to speak on behalf of women. "We sidelined them even as we knew their voices to be strong," she said. We are not the experts, we never were. Women's organizations always existed in Afghanistan. Feminist movements were active even before the Taliban. "They were there before any of us were there. Before any of us even heard of Afghanistan," she said. "And they will remain when we are all gone."

And now the Taliban have returned. "We knew this would happen," one of the aid workers said, "but great women leaders exist, and even more will emerge. They have the will to survive." "Afghan women will rise on their own terms," another one added. "They always do."

Afghan women have, unfortunately, long been accustomed to living with and navigating risk. But they have made progress in smart, strategic, and contextualized ways. "We can help them advance this progress, build on what they are doing, support what they want to do," the aid worker argued. She continued:

We should take our cue from them regarding their needs and what approach we should take. Especially now as things deteriorate so rapidly. We can make sure that the pipeline of access to resources will be open legally or through clandestine operations, which may be more effective. Without security, what is the point of anything else? Security first. And *women's* security first.

Attacks and targeting of human rights defenders, specifically women's rights activists, have increased since 2020. A 2021 attack by insurgents targeted Afghans working for an international aid organization exposed how members of the Taliban are "going door to door, looking for specific government officials and people who had cooperated with the United States."[64] An Afghan woman formerly employed by an aid organization expanded on this:

> The Taliban have said that they'll have no place in the new government for those who cooperated with the occupying powers or international organizations … they've searched many women-led organizations and NGOs in Afghanistan, so they have information and can easily find people and punish them.[65]

One Afghan woman leader shared her fear for herself and her family: "Because I work at a Western NGO, my colleagues and I thought that we would be helped … if worst came to worst, the NGO would protect me. Now I think they have forgotten me."[66]

"Here is what I want everyone to know," one of the aid workers said. "This time, we do it right. This time, the global women's movement should step up. We must prepare to provide *real* support. A collective response of networks to support Afghan women, based entirely on what *they* need." For the Afghan women who have been taken out of the country, they will need support as well, she continued. They are the women leaders who "galvanize strong movements outside the country to channel to their Afghan sisters."

Meanwhile, as we rally to support Afghan women, one aid worker lamented about a high-level conference on Afghanistan in September 2021 where she lobbied for days to have women's voices included. All the rhetoric on Afghan women and we still have to argue for their inclusion. She told the story:

> Advocates for women's rights in the UN system constantly question the impact of their work, recounting endless stories or behind the scenes advocacy and lobbying at all levels of the system to give space and voice to women in displacement, including for Afghan women. The results of such advocacy? A two-minute video of women's voices in a four-hour high level conference with over 80 member states and UN speakers. Is that a win or simply tragic that such a basic low-level "outcome" could even be viewed as a "win"? Why didn't any of the member states—who all spoke about women's rights and participation—ask if women's voices were going to be included? Why didn't any of them make that ask? To fight tooth and nail down to the last minute, all for a two-minute video.

And when did they screen this precious two minutes? In the third hour of the event. So, for all the rhetoric of women's voice and participation, two minutes was too much. We all failed Afghan women. I failed. It would have been better to not fight for this tokenistic inclusion.

With that story in mind, I reached out to another former colleague in Afghanistan to ask what she thought:

Let me tell you what I think about Afghanistan right now.... I have spent thirty years working on this country, living in this country. I know this country. I married into it. It is my family. Firstly we talk of urgent needs. Humanitarian aid for all Afghans. Every third Afghan now suffers from hunger. And then, don't quit don't leave don't give up, but rather engage with the country, and stay engaged, and do so with a long breath. Media attention will go away soon. We must not go away! For women, we must continue to evacuate those women who are at highest risk as their lives are at stake but also engage with all Afghan women on the ground, those who will stay, especially Afghan women activists. We must do this with their safety as our top priority. They cannot be exposed on social media as it puts them at greater risk. In any future talks with the Taliban, the international community should stress equal rights for women as a prerequisite for financial support and any recognition of the Taliban government. And we should not forget Afghanistan—surely not Afghan women. We must show solidarity with them and support them in all the spaces we occupy, with whatever platforms or influence we may have.

"Ultimately, it's this," one aid worker told me. "We women activists from outside of Afghanistan," she continued, "*we* are the ones who need to prepare. The Afghan women are already prepared. They always have been."

Who better to speak to this than Afghan women themselves? In late 2021, I reached out to some additional activists and women leaders in the country. Here are their words.

Fariha

I am an activist! I have been fighting for women's rights since the 1970s. Afghan women are survivors! They learn how to adapt and survive the day they are born from their mothers. They pass down their legacy to their daughters and to the generations after. They have always found a solution and a way out in the worst of times. This time is no different. The Taliban can not break us. They WILL NOT break us. They will not undo what we have achieved all these years.

Masooda

We brought our own freedom, our own liberation. Yes, the international community helped, but we Afghan women have always been helping ourselves, much more than anyone has been able to help us. But now, what happens? We are back to zero, it seems. But it is not zero. We know freedom. We know how to fight for freedom. And foreigners can finally help us in that fight for freedom. Listen to us. We know what we need, and we know what freedom we want.

KHALIDA

You ask us what now for Afghan women? I see my sisters on the street, protesting to get their status back and be able to continue with higher education alongside men in a co-education system. They want the world to be involved and to remember them. Even media coverage in the West showing what they are going through could put the Taliban under pressure. Taliban want recognition and are watching to see if the world approves of them. If no one speaks about women's rights and their involvement in the new government, they will ignore it. Every time there is a protest by women on the streets, there is small progress. The world is watching now. And that visibility means the Taliban is under scrutiny. Initially they had asked women to stay home, today they announced that universities will open for women as long as male and female campuses are separated. So that is something....

KHATERA

The world should keep watching, putting pressure. But don't just watch. Advocate, support, fundraise. There will eventually be a way to get money to Afghan women's groups so do that! Get ready for it. Also support Afghan women in not missing out on their lives; distance learning is an option. Whatever they can do online, bring them in and let them do it. Create space for them to keep going ... give them the tools and resources they need to keep going.

SARAH

I see women, many women, who managed to succeed in their lives during the last twenty years. Overall, most of these women have obtained social status and success through education. Women have empowered themselves by getting university degrees and secure jobs in the government or private firms. They have gained personal control of their lives more than their predecessors.

During the past decade, women have been offered scholarships to travel out of the country and study abroad which was not common and permitted even pre–Taliban era. Afghan women have evolved in so many ways. The younger generation have seen the outside world and they are single-minded and stronger.

I know so many scholarship students who went to the United States and pursued degrees and despite knowing what may come upon them, returned to their homes and started working to bring a change; to slowly change the mentality of their own families and gradually the entire community. They have stood up for their rights and said no to arranged marriages.

To some extent the society had adapted to their new social status. Women were seen on the screens of TV and media channels not wearing any head coverings. They were legal experts, judges, musicians, and artists. They had come a long way to get there.

What will they do now?

Most are still in shock. They hadn't realized how far they had come and what the cost of losing it all could be. To them, freedom is to live a normal everyday

A woman speculates on why greater changes have not been made since "liberation," Paghman.

life now. A simple routine to go to work or school in the morning and hang out in social circles seems impossible now. Most of the women who have been protesting against the Taliban do not fear them anymore. They also believe that the world is watching through social media and the Taliban may not harm them because they are in the spotlight. International attention may protect them—while they have it.

Time to Rewrite the Narrative

In 2001, we heard the call to "liberate" Afghan women. In our efforts to liberate, we forgot that Afghan women's agency is, and has always been, alive in Afghanistan. *How might our efforts in 2021 be different? And how might we measure what's working?*

It is wise to rethink how we measure progress—for rights, for democracy, for liberation, and for development more broadly—and what the effects of our efforts might be. *By whose standards are we working?* The only true measure of progress, I've argued, is through the voices of the Afghan people, for whom the progress was intended in the first place.

Agency comes from within. And it can be found in the small spaces, spaces where we often fail to look. Over the last two decades, our work in Afghanistan fell short in three critical ways: we were perceived as an outside intervention and thus not fully accepted, we spoke of "liberating" Afghan women but our resources failed to match our rhetoric, and we undermined Afghan women's agency in the process.

Meanwhile, Afghan women have been speaking, advocating, and fighting all along. Despite constant challenges, Afghan women have always been pushing for change—no matter how challenging the environment or how great the risks to their own safety. Afghan women are the authors of their own stories. They should be—and always should have been—the leaders of their own agendas and the creators of the strategies to bring about the futures they want.

This story is not as simple as a "failed" aid intervention or a "failed" military intervention. It has not been clear—or linear. History will be the judge of these interventions. What we now know is that Afghanistan has once again fallen to the Taliban—and that women will pay a heavy price for this fall. Now we've been given an unfortunate opportunity to change the narrative. *How might we respond this time?*

And the critical question now becomes: *Are we ready to (re)commit to Afghan women—to help them fight for their own liberation?* Perhaps at last we are aware of the limitations of our role, but also of its value. We can provide funding and support, ideas and inspiration. We are doing so already, but we can do more. We can serve as a fueling station for Afghan feminists. The global feminist movement is mobilizing, and perhaps this time our promise to Afghan women will be fulfilled.

In June of 2021, I wrote[67]:

> I believe that Afghan women are the face and the force of their country's future. The research says the same; a country's chances of peace, prosperity and progress rest not on the fiscal or legislative but on the way in which it treats its women. But Afghanistan's women will continue to need support—resources, tools, access to opportunities—in order to build the Afghanistan that they deserve. The U.S. might be withdrawing, but direct funding for frontline women's groups must continue. In fact, it must increase. And women must be included in every aspect of leadership and decision-making at every level. It is the best chance Afghanistan has.

I still believe this to be true. Simply existing as a woman in Afghanistan, or anywhere, is an act of resistance.

In September of 2021, an Afghan friend told me this:

> We did not want a second round of this. We did not need to once again fight—for space, for rights, for freedom. We did not need to put our strength to the test. We did not want to show the world our "resilience," as you put it. We did

not want these things. We wanted space, movement, joy, rights, opportunities, education, laughter, air, music…. We wanted our *lives*. And we did not want to ask for help—again. We did not want to be a "cause" or a charity or a pity. We did not want to be a media story, a sad story. No one wants these things. But now we *are* these things. And you, you can help us by listening. Listen to us and—if you want to help—we will tell you how to help.

CHAPTER 9

Freedom Is Only Won
from the Inside

There is something in this world that is to me, in my eyes,
worth dying and living for and standing by, and one of them
is the rights of the women of Afghanistan.[1]
—Mahbooba Seraj, October 2021

I wrote this closing chapter on September 11, 2021—the 20th anniversary of the fateful day that changed the lives of so many, for the worse. This opened the door that would lead me to Afghanistan a few months later.

We relive that day again and again. And yet, what have we learned?

My friend and former colleague Deborah Alexander, PhD, who spent a decade in Afghanistan as U.S. Department of State senior political advisor wrote this:

Today I relive 9/11 over and over.

Those towers in smoke and flame, that gut punch hole in the Pentagon, the burned field in Pennsylvania….

Or is it seeing on screen the same Taliban faces (or their sons) in power I saw on screen 20 years ago. Or reliving the blunder of Iraq and its theft of years from the Afghanistan mission. Reliving the fall of Kabul just a few weeks ago. Or the scenes of thousands rushing to hang on planes in flight. Images yesterday of journalists beaten in Kabul. Or the Taliban with their whips, lashing women protestors.

Which is worse?

Twenty years later. Thousands of lives taken. Two trillion dollars. A lot of miles covered, minutes lost, money spent, oceans of tears cried.

So why does it feel like time froze? That we've gone forward to the past?

How Did We Get Here?

I will not repeat the story of how Afghanistan, after two decades of aid and military support, numerous elections, unfathomable amounts of

Eidgaah mosque at sunset, Kabul.

money, and many feeble attempts at peace, returned in 2021 to where it had been in 2001—under the suffocating rule of a regime known as the Taliban. I will, however, continue to tell the story from the perspective of women, the ones who have been—and continue to be—most affected by this story. Here, we will begin with a so-called peace deal that betrayed women, bargaining their rights away. A deal made between men, all with blood on their hands. It is a story that, for Afghan women, came full circle. But Afghan women are imagining a new world, one where both freedom and feminism are possible. A world that is not about occupation, but about collaboration. A world that doesn't import "liberation," but rather builds on existing agency to form a new freedom.

The world is watching—today. But by the time this book is published, our attentions will be elsewhere. Who pays the price for our short-sightedness? Will Afghanistan be forgotten, just like Afghan women were forgotten in the wars men started? This time, we can't afford to look away. Ultimately, this book is a snapshot of an historical moment, a complicated landscape, one in which we are all, to some degree, complicit.

This book *is* about "liberation"—what it means, and on whose terms it is. It will perhaps help those of us on the "outside" understand what a renewed fight for "liberation" might look like in Afghanistan today, and on whose terms it will now be.

This part of the story starts on International Women's Day in March of 2021, with the Revolutionary Association of the Women of Afghanistan lamenting the costs Afghanistan will now pay for the betrayal of Afghan women—and all of Afghanistan, in fact—in the so-called peace. The lesson is clear, they wrote, "our people have realized that the U.S.' claims of democracy, women's rights and progress in any country, including Afghanistan, is a blatant lie."[2]

"I feel a little like history is repeating itself," said Afghan women's rights activist Sima Samar later that month, expressing concern that the gains in women's rights over the last two decades are fragile.[3]

The following month, in April, U.S. president Joe Biden announced that it was "time to end America's longest war" and withdraw U.S. troops. This "longest war" had cost the government trillions of dollars and far too many lives—especially Afghan lives.

Biden said that the withdrawal would begin in May and conclude in time for the 20th anniversary of September 11. The day that prompted the invasion of Afghanistan in the first place. Biden later changed the withdrawal deadline to 31 August.

In May, U.S. troops began their withdrawal as planned. Immediately, the Taliban mobilized. In fact, they had remained powerful throughout the 20-year period. Afghans were fearful. Their faith in U.S. support—and in their own government—wavered.

By the end of the month, the Taliban had attacked and captured a range of provinces, starting in rural areas that were already under militant control, and moving into the government-controlled cities. The Taliban claimed a quarter of the country in a matter of weeks[4]—so much for "security" and "sustainability." Gains were striking and speedy. Still, the withdrawal remained on schedule.

Also in May, Afghan and international groups sent a letter to President Biden calling for a UN peacekeeping force "to ensure that the cost of U.S. military withdrawal from Afghanistan is not paid for in the lives of schoolgirls."[5]

In June, Deborah Lyons, the UN Special Envoy for Afghanistan, told the Security Council that "preserving the rights of women remains a paramount concern and must not be used as a bargaining chip at the negotiating table."[6]

On 11 June, I contacted my friend Aziza, women's rights leader and partner from my time in Afghanistan. I asked how she was, and how the women's movement would fare. She wrote:

> I am speaking to some women in my circle. They believe that things are not going to get any better. We feel stuck in a vicious cycle and fear from this precarious situation. Aid has ended and NGOs have long been closed. We will not have achieved what we had hoped. What we set out to do. What we started to do. And now we have to adapt to whatever that may come in order to survive.

On 16 June, I published a piece on CNN[7] arguing that the U.S. rhetoric of liberation that animated their invasion nearly 20 years ago had fallen short of its goal. This built on an argument I made in my 2008 doctoral thesis and later in my 2009 book, *Gender and International Aid in Afghanistan*.[8] There, and again here, I argued that the status of Afghan women was used as the barometer to assess social change, and that the promise of freedom had fallen short. That book and the CNN article have now formed the basis of this new book.

In the CNN piece, I explained that the $780 million spent by the United States to promote women's rights in Afghanistan would have gone to waste as this hasty withdrawal would likely lead to greater human rights violations, more school closures and increased violence against women. The voices I heard from Afghanistan were fearful. Women's rights were hanging in the balance. Again.

Two decades of investment in women undoubtedly did achieve many goals: schools reopened for girls, giving them access to education, including university.[9] Women had access to employment. They worked, flew planes,[10] joined the military,[11] became government ministers ,[12] and more.

But gains were patchy.[13] Progress was perpetually met by major backlashes,[14] a resurgence[15] of a fundamentalist order, and more violence against women.[16] Rural women still lived in Taliban-controlled areas, under severe restrictions.[17] They did not benefit from these improvements. Opportunities for work,[18] health care,[19] education[20] never reached them.

On 22 June, Aziza told me this:

> We could have predicted this. Patriarchy is so embedded in the culture and roots. There is need for gender awareness, education and prolonged efforts to change what generations of men in power have created. The work that was done during the last two decades was not enough to change the fundamentals. It provided a short-term relief to what women had suffered during Taliban, but it could get worse when there is no more intervention.
>
> I believe with troops gone, women may not keep their seats in the parliament or any other powerful seat—if there will even be a government left at all.

In early July, the United States vacated Bagram, its biggest airbase that once housed tens of thousands of U.S. troops. Afghans claimed this happened without their prior knowledge. The United States argued otherwise. In leaving Bagram, the United States left behind aircraft, armored vehicles, and sophisticated equipment worth tens of millions of dollars to add to the Taliban's military arsenal.

Taliban gains continued. Afghanistan was unraveling. And Biden remained recalcitrant. What's worse, he stated that a Taliban takeover was "highly unlikely," despite all intelligence to the contrary.

On 24 June, I was invited to speak on CNN, building from my article. I was asked how serious things were for Afghan women. Very serious, I explained. At that point we had already heard of greater human rights violations, more school closures, increased violence against women. It was just getting started—things would get worse.

I said that despite gains made, two-thirds of girls remained out of school, 70 percent of Afghan women and girls still cannot read or write, and more than 80 percent of Afghan women and girls have experienced abuse. Most of this has taken place in the home. Women's security in the home is a reflection of the security in the country. If women cannot be safe at home, they're not safe at all. And if women are not safe, then no one is safe. This, I have long argued, should be the barometer by which the entire intervention is judged.

I explained that yes, Afghan women are incredibly strong. They have always demonstrated that strength, along with incredible courage and resilience. They always had strong voices and the ability to use them. But, are we listening? Did we listen then—and do we listen now? They have powerful voices, but they have no microphone. Did we do all we could to amplify their voices as they articulated their own needs? Did we even meet those needs?

When asked about women's engagement in the so-called peace process, I responded that my global experience has shown that when women are not engaged in every aspect of peace, it is no peace. It is a peace on shaky ground. When women are involved, any peace is better, stronger and lasts longer. Where were Afghan women when a so-called peace was negotiated? A peace with the Taliban is no peace, certainly not for women.

"I'm sad," said former U.S. president George Bush, in July.[21]

"If the U.S. doesn't learn from the past, Afghan women and girls will pay the price," Sima Samar wrote in August, just a few days before the Taliban reclaimed power.[22] At the same time, Mahbooba Seraj issued her message for the international community: "All of these men of the world in power ... they are destroying something we worked so hard for. What is happening in Afghanistan today is going to put us 200 years back."[23]

On 10 August, U.S. intelligence warned that it would take 30–90 days for the Taliban to topple the government and occupy Kabul. The city fell five days later.

We Adapt to Survive

Aziza wrote to me:

When I think of women's situation before and now, I think that the international intervention since 2001 only changed a specific group of women, those who came from open minded families and were empowered in their communities. They were allowed by their male counterparts or fathers or sons to get education or work but their freedom was limited because of Taliban prior to 2001. Things changed for them as soon as Taliban were defeated. They were the first who entered the workforce, first to ditch the bourka and hijab, first to raise their voices for their rights. The NGOs further empowered them. But they were already powerful! All along they had the support of the men in their families who had allowed them to reach their potential. They are also the ones who are fearful the most right now. They will lose everything they have built and will fall victim to Taliban abuse.

On the other hand, there are Afghan women who have always lived under abuse in male-dominant communities. As a matter of fact, those communities are already seized by Taliban because the men voluntarily handed them the power as it happened in Kunduz. The international and American intervention after 2001 did not make a huge difference for these women. The financial aid may have fed their families but the patriarchy remained. Some of those women got financial freedom temporarily by finding jobs that were only available for women thanks to women NGOs like sewing and things. But it didn't last long enough to lift them from the grassroots. Today they are under the same abuse—or even worse.

On 14 August, the Taliban had taken most of the country's 34 provincial capitals. The United States increased troop presence to aid in evacuations of U.S. personnel and U.S. "allies."

But who were these allies? And what of Afghan women activists whose work was funded by the United States, fueled by the rhetoric of "liberation," build from promises of equality, bolstered by the global feminist movement, and—worryingly—in direct opposition to the Taliban.

I began to receive alarming emails from old contacts in the country who explained that their work on women's rights was now a direct threat to their safety. They had heard of U.S. visas for allies and human rights defenders—did they not qualify? Their lives were at risk. *What should they do?*, they called out to feminists worldwide.

A fellow feminist with a long history of work in Afghanistan had this to say about the evacuation of selected women from Afghanistan:

> Which women? Important women? Who decides which women are "important"? What about the ordinary women? You need a name to be determined important. A name that is meaningful to foreigners. What happens to the woman whose name is not known? Is she not important?! What of the 15 year old girl who is left behind—whose life will be destroyed? Was she not important? The international community stratifies women—determining a hierarchy based on who the international system thinks is important....

Another one added:

Who is thinking of the common woman? People are thinking of the best interests of the warlords—not the women. And meanwhile she is there, stuck. She
has been raped and has no escape. And the warlords are protected. And they
are the rapists. What are we saying? It is this: we value the rapists first. At the
expense of women. This is true in Afghanistan. It is true everywhere.

Also on 14 August, Afghan president Ashraf Ghani delivered an address
stating that consultations were underway to end the fighting. The next day,
he fled the country.

On 15 August, the Taliban had reached Kabul. By the end of that fateful day, Mullah Abdul Ghani Baradar, a leader and co-founder of the Taliban, issued this announcement to all Afghans: "We are responsible for your
lives and all that pertain to everyday living, and to convince you that we
will provide everything to make your lives better."

I wrote to Aziza. She said:

The situation is so uncertain in Afghanistan. Most of us are on the brink of
escape from the country but we are stuck as there is no way to get out. My fellow women activists believe that their voices were silenced when the government was negotiating with the Taliban. We women warned the government that
if Taliban came, history will repeat itself. The 20 years of democracy that Americans promised for women will go in vain, but no one listened to us.

The next day, President Biden delivered a speech justifying the withdrawal. That day, thousands of civilians swarmed Hamid Karzai International Airport in Kabul, running across the tarmac, clinging to airplanes,
desperate to escape.

I wrote to Aziza. As a women's rights activist, as a well-known figure,
as someone who had been outspoken against the Taliban, shouldn't she try
to leave, I asked? True to her spirit, her anger for all Afghan women trumped
her fear for her own life.

The talk of Taliban wanting to marry young girls is on the streets and even
among little girls as young as six and seven. My granddaughters and her friends,
they are twelve and thirteen. They speak of suicide if Taliban came to their
houses demanding to take them as brides.

The Americans showed women how freedom looks when they came in 2001,
they introduced us to their Western democracy, freedom of speech, freedoms to
go to school, and to understand our rights. After twenty years, the new generation
of women are now journalists, artists, entrepreneurs and human rights activists.
Little did they know that they would be abandoned by the same people who
helped them progress. Now what? Just drop it all and leave them to the barbaric
Taliban?

The question then rises: why all the efforts in the first place? Why were these
women empowered only to see their fate in hands of Taliban? Women are questioning the rhetoric of the Americans, and the world.

On 17 August, the Taliban stated that it will respect women's rights as long as it is "within Islamic law." Violence continues. The airport remained a scene of desperation.

That day, Aziza said:

> The government has fallen now, as you know. Everyone is told to stay home. I am quarantined at home like the rest.
>
> The local media says that there will be an announcement tonight if there will be negotiation with Taliban and if a new government will be formed.

And later that day, together with Aziza, I drafted a call to action and posted this:

> Afghanistan has been taken over by the Taliban, and Afghan women's lives are at risk. They will lose the freedom they've gained in these last two decades—access to school, work, and all aspects of public life. Afghan women activists are under threat. I'm helping to get one woman out, she's a known activist and women's rights defender. I worked with her when I lived in Afghanistan (2002–2006). She has been advocating for Afghan women for 50 years as a member of Parliament in the 1970s and as a leader of various women's rights organizations. Her work has taken her all around Afghanistan and Pakistan (where she was a refugee for many years). And she has spoken about Afghan women's rights around the world. While working on the very complicated process of getting her out—ideally to her family in Canada—we need to raise money to help cover her costs. This includes travel to a third country, refugee case processing, waiting time (up to fourteen months), and basic living expenses. ANYTHING HELPS. We aren't releasing any additional information about her for her protection, but please contact me if you have questions/leads/ideas.

Indeed, those leads and ideas came, thanks to the strength of the international feminist network. I pursued all of these, under the direction of Aziza.

I tried to set up a GoFundMe, to receive donations more easily. They rejected my request, removed my fundraiser, and thanked me for supporting "those affected by the ongoing crisis in Afghanistan." GoFundMe reinforced their commitment to deliver funds "safely and securely" and urged me to instead deliver funds through their centralized hub of "verified fundraisers"—none of which were Afghan. Even two decades later, the irony that those on the outside knew best what Afghan women might need was still as powerful as ever.

In August, the Women's Collective of Muslims issued a statement, offering a counter-narrative to those who excuse the Taliban of its past crimes while also rejecting "the alarmist and Islamophobic narratives of media outlets that reproduce tired tropes suggesting that Muslim women everywhere are oppressed and require 'saviours.'"[24] The letter ended with this: "Should there be any attempts to suppress or oppress [Afghan women], as a collective, we pledge that we will not stand idly by and allow their voices and their dreams to be silenced."[25]

I Hope It Will Be Enough...

Aziza and I carried on, remaining in close contact, examining options.

The airport is surrounded by Taliban and a huge blockage behind it as hundreds of people are stuck outside and Taliban is using guns to send people back home. Taliban has assured they won't go inside people's homes. It is not safe to go to the airport right now.

I asked if women's organizations are at particular risk.

They haven't entered the NGO buildings or offices yet. They may do it once they have full access to the system.

Meanwhile, Taliban have asked people to go back to their works but everyone is scared to, including the high ranking government officials. People believe that this is another way for them to mark everyone. But their spokesperson has assured people that they won't enter homes forcefully. Not yet.

She continued, angrily:

But, they aren't letting people leave the country. And people don't trust them anymore. Women have not gone outside—they don't have proper outfit to go outside! So far they haven't announced their dress code for women, but women fear being beaten if they go without bourka.

Have women been hurt yet? Beaten? I was afraid to ask.

The only shots that happened were at the airport. They shot people who were rushing to the planes.

So everyone is waiting in fear...?

People are using their past experience to anticipate things this time. People are obviously disappointed in U.S. and the president that left. People believe the U.S. paved the way for Taliban and handed over to them because they failed the war. And right now we have nothing—access to little internet, for some of us. There is no calling card in the market. Stores are closed.

At least the older women remember this—the young ones never saw it. There is no school and girls are traumatized with what is happening. No TV channel broadcasts anything in fear.

It is a waiting game....

And women, I asked? What will happen to the women?

Women are in fear right now. With Americans gone they are terrified. No one is going to school, university. All women NGOs shut as of now. No woman appears on TV.

People of Afghanistan feel abandoned and left alone with their worst nightmare. There is no hope of support from the international community. I think the world should raise their voices so Taliban understand that they won't be able to carry on with their crimes like the past.

The international community let Afghanistan down. They left people in the dark about their peace negotiations or their plan to exit. It all happened overnight. People did not predict that things will move this fast. It was all con-

A girl completes a cultural performance to celebrate the opening of a new NGO, Kabul.

nected. They leave one night and in the morning Taliban enter Afghanistan from all borders. People think they have moved back in time. Twenty years of constructing a new Afghanistan is reversed in one week!

What happened to the democracy that the Americans had promised? Your U.S. President said "it was never about nation-building." What about the Bonn Agreement in 2001 when they came up with a new constitution to build a new country? That was supposed to be the foundation. Of a nation.

What could I say?

On 18 August, I asked how she was. What could she say? Her messages were becoming more brief.

I am ok. I have not left the house in five days. I have enough food for one month. I hope it will be enough.

And the next day, this came:

We remember you, Lina. Your time in Afghanistan. Those were the golden days. Everything changed after.

On 20 August, I wrote again to check in.

I am in a safe house, out of imminent danger. At least for a short time.

I gave her the options I had found to get her out of the country, mostly to neighboring countries.

If I go, I will need to stay longer than expected. There will be visas and paperwork and legal challenges. I don't speak the language. I cannot work. I will be alone. Will I be able to return? Will I be able to get out?

On 22 August, she sent this update:

Things are getting worse. Taliban are searching homes of those who may have weapons. They have access to biometric database so they can identify people. I have changed my name on my social media accounts.

And two days later:

I heard the news that they want all evacuations to be done by end of this month. No news for me. I am getting worried.

They may close the roads to the airport. Only those who are approved to get to the airport and escorted by a foreigner can go in.

I asked if she was safe, at least?

Yes, right now. I am safe. Flights are ending, we hear. Banks are closed and we cannot get our money out. My passport is stuck in the office for renewal. I cannot get out if I do not have it.

And later, she sent this update, following the explosion at Kabul airport.

Did you hear of the explosion? Piles and piles of people just dead.

Afghans are saying America did this to justify the end of evacuations and blamed it on ISIS. Lots of talks going on … it is just horrible.

What more can I do? Please tell me how I can help you, I asked in desperation.

I am a survivor, Lina. I am strong. I will take care of myself until there is a way out. I know what I need to do—the new passport, a visa to move to a third country. Now everything is still closed. Once they reopen, I will look for a route. I will find a way out.

On 28 August, I posted this update:

For those who donated and who are concerned about the Afghan woman activist, she remains stuck in Kabul. Recent events have made her exit even more challenging. The family thanks those who have already donated. We are still collecting donations—money will be used to secure safe passage and to cover transit costs. Further updates as we have them. Until then … we can only hope.

The next day, she wrote to me:

I begin to be fearful. So much uncertainty. I fear I may stay here longer than expected….

On 31 August, I received this:

I am disappointed. A lifetime of work for a cause that will now be undone.

It was now September, and the news continued to worsen. Sima Samar argued that women's rights are not just "Western values," and that peace and security cannot be possible without women. She refuted the notion that women's rights were "doomed to fail" because of Afghanistan's culture and traditions, adding that they absolutely cannot be "negotiated away" but should be a key condition for future aid.[26]

I wrote to Aziza, asking if she was ok—at least if she was safe and not in immediate danger.

> I feel safe for now, but for how long we don't know. No women are on the streets unless they are essential workers like doctors or nurses who are summoned to go back to work. Female health workers are needed to treat female patients, that is why they are back to work. They received a special letter demanding this.
> They have no choice. No woman has any choice anymore.

On 2 September, she said that many women activists had left, or were in hiding.

> They are keeping a low profile. There are no gatherings. They have even deleted their social media. Burned their certificates. Erased their work. Their history.

On 3 September I checked in again.

> Everyone is in survival mode. We do not know what will come of this.

On 4 September, Afghan women started to fight back. They marched in Kabul, demanding their rights. The Taliban responded with whips and lashes. I checked in with Aziza.

> Some women especially the younger generation have actually stepped out of homes taking the risk and doing protests! There are women-led uprisings all over the city!

On that day, and for the days that followed, her tone had regained its power.

Women were on the streets with placards and chanting, "Long live the women of Afghanistan." "I will sing freedom over and over," one read.

Women were detained, beaten and told to go home, and to recognize and respect the Emirate. Afghan women refused. "Why should we accept the Emirate while no inclusion or rights have been given to us?" Protests grew to 500 women. The Taliban responded with more brute force.

A *New York Times* video on 30 August highlighted the voices of Afghan women, and how their lives have changed since the Taliban re-occupied the country. One young woman's words broke my heart:

> I had a world full of hope. I had a world full of goals. I had a world full of plans for my future. Now that I think about it, I should have breathed it in more. Right now I'm just trying to stay alive.

Women dance and play music to celebrate their graduation from a vocational training program, Kabul.

No woman should have to say this about her future. Meanwhile, Afghan women continued to take to the streets, calling on the international community, asking those who called for women's rights for two decades where they were today. They are needed now more than ever.

Liberating Ourselves

A conversation with a group of aid workers reinforced Aziza's concerns.

KN: The trillion-dollar question is ... what did the U.S. get in return for all those years while purporting to train the military in Afghanistan? That's the reason they went there ... not for the women or anyone else ... never for the women. The false savior mentality at play!

SI: It was never the intent of Americans to "liberate" ... they only play a geopolitical game, and women are pawns.

PA: There's an African saying: When elephants fight, it is the grass that suffers. But the women's movement will not be silenced!

SI: That was quick. China is already on board with the new terrorist gang. The rest rush now to catch up. Pure exploitation. Mineral rich Afghanistan. So much for 20 years of … what was it again?

KN: Women have to liberate themselves … and hold their own government to account. What did that government do, anyway? Stolen money, corruption, billions of aid to the government—did it reach the people? No! It filled political pockets. Claiming to fund women's movements is pure rhetoric. Public relations!

PA: Women's lives are always about survival, one has even to survive the man who sleeps beside you, survive your family, survive your environment, survive your children, survive everything!

SI: But parachuting women out is not the answer. It helps those few, but is also dangerously elitist. Millions of Afghan women whose names we don't even know—they remain in the country. They should be our utmost concern.

KN: Afghan women will do what they have always done—continue their underground operations of setting schools for young girls which they did during the Taliban. The bottom line is about local solutions—those are the ones that last. Our job now is to support them, their organizations, their resilience, and their resistance!

But did we have to put Afghan women's legendary "resilience" to the test yet again? Afghan women—and *all* women—are only resilient when we have to be. When we have no choice.

So-called women's empowerment in Afghanistan needs to be detached from the Western-imposed or the UN-enforced notion of empowerment. Their main cause is survival—now more than ever. They want to live. They have shown that they will do whatever it takes to do so.

Women's organizations have always survived day by day. But they do survive. In the early days of the intervention, they told us to support them in strengthening their access to healthcare, to employment, to education. They told the international community what was important, what they wanted. They still tell us. At last let us give Afghan women the leadership they have long deserved.

Today we speak about getting the few Afghan women out of the country, women leaders who can galvanize strong movements outside the country to support their Afghan sisters. Women whose lives are at risk if they remain. This is still a critical operation. We can do this, while also focusing our efforts on those who have no choice but to remain.

And if we succeed in evacuating those who are at risk, we are draining the country of its capacity. We are extracting the strongest women, the fiercest fighters, the most outspoken feminists. An activist-brain-drain.

On 10 September, Aziza wrote:

> Yes, I must leave. I might die if I stay. But what happens if I leave? If all the women with voices, with strength, with experience leave the country, how will

the rest fight this war for them? Who will lead the women's uprisings when the women leaders are gone?

Afghan women said they knew this would happen. But under such circumstances, feminist fires cannot be put out. Even more women leaders emerge, fueled by the will to survive. Now women's rights activists outside of the country must prepare. Afghan women are already prepared. They always have been.

One week later, Aziza wrote:

Currently the situation for women is deteriorating. There is no place for women in this government. Taliban have resumed schools and universities classes for men only. All girls starting from elementary to higher education have to stay at home. At the time most of the well-known women activists are either in hiding or have left the country. I have no contact with any of them. The women I stood side by side with for years.

Women who used to be the sole income earner in their families have lost their jobs. Around 3000 women civil servants are unemployed, those who used to work at the Former Ministry of Women Affairs. The ministry have been abolished and replaced with the Ministry of Virtue and Vice. There is no room for women to work there. But those women, they are the ones on the streets doing protests against Taliban.

And then a few days later, on 20 September, Aziza wrote to tell me about a woman who worked with her, when women had been allowed to work:

Amina, she was the only breadwinner in the family. She lost her job. She won't be able to feed her children and will soon become homeless. "Women have been the victim of these politics behind the scenes between the government, the U.S. and the Taliban," she said. "They decide our fate and our lives." With nothing to look forward to, we are told to just deal with it, to try to live.

But trying to live is different from living....

I wrote to Aziza again and again. What can I do, I kept asking? She responded:

We will rise again, on our own terms. We have done so before. The situation is unraveling day by day. Our worry is survival, security.

Aziza emphasized that the international community now must take their cue from Afghan women on what they need, and what approach to take, particularly as the situation unravels rapidly. The global women's movement must now rally at a distance, providing a collective response in support of Afghan women. We can advocate for security and greater access to resources. But first, security. Women's security above all. This is the barometer by which our new role should be judged.

In an article on 31 August, author and activist Rita Manchanda wrote that Afghanistan's unraveling was a moment of reckoning for many global agendas, for causes and campaigns that we held onto, touted, and sold to others:[27] The War on Terror, efforts to globalize liberal values, the western "savior" trope and the attempt to "liberate" Afghan women, and the UN's Women, Peace and Security Agenda.

"Afghan women will work out their own equation with the Taliban," she said, "but they need the moral pressure of the world to be watching. The alternative dystopia is too dark to reimagine."

Meanwhile, on the 20th anniversary of September 11, the Arab-American Anti-Discrimination Committee (ADC) issued a message of commemoration, as well as a harsh reminder of what has happened since. And an equally harsh reminder that wars don't stay neatly confined within their borders. What happens in Afghanistan does not stay in Afghanistan. Ultimately, we are all responsible.

The commemoration message honored the 3000 innocent victims that perished on that fateful day, and the hundreds of thousands more who went on to lose their lives in the senseless wars that followed. And in the United States, the message said, hate crimes against individuals who looked Arab experienced a wave of anger. This backlash targeted not only Arabs, but also any Muslims, Sikhs, and South Asians.

The United States became polarized in ways it has yet to undo. This discrimination continues nearly unabated, moving from the fringes of political discourse to the front row for political candidates and xenophobic movements. Civil rights were undone, government surveillance grew exponentially, fueled by blatant racial profiling. These practices continue, and have led to unjust wars not only in Afghanistan, but also Iraq, and the violence in Guantanamo Bay.

Now is the time to recognize these interconnections and acknowledge that change is long overdue. We may have come full circle in Afghanistan, but let us ensure that further mistakes of the past two decades do not continue.

The Passage to Freedom

Where does the quest for equality for Afghan women go from here?

Afghan women have always made gains, despite the forces working against them. Despite patriarchy, religious fundamentalism, conflict and insecurity, they raise their voices. Do they now risk losing it all? I believe that they would never allow this to happen. Yes, gains made in these last two decades risk being lost. The pain is real—they tasted greater freedom and possibility and could be worse off than they were before.

But their fight is stronger than ever.

The United States and international partners have spent 20 years encouraging women to come out, to study, to work, to vote, to run for office. Women were told they could now be visible—present, public, powerful. Now these changes hang in the balance. Women's rights in Afghanistan—or anywhere—are not a light switch to be flicked on or off based on who is in power. They are permanent and non-negotiable—in Afghanistan and everywhere.

What is our role now, as allies and advocates and supporters? As global feminists?

Afghan women will lead us. They will articulate exactly what they need—and we must listen. We must be ready to rise to this occasion. Our role is limited, but it remains important. We can support them and also work to transform the systems that continue to hold them back, giving them greater access to what they need to lead this new revolution. We can advocate for political and diplomatic efforts to help bring peace, security, and stability to the country. To help build a stronger foundation on which women's rights can anchor. I will listen to Aziza, and to women like her.

Afghan women have agency and have always fought for their rights— they will continue to do so now.

I recently came across a report summarizing a 2005 conference on Afghan women. Their voices were clear. They repeatedly urged the international community to better understand Afghan culture in order to intervene in ways that would be of use to Afghans. Aid groups should not leave the country before their work is done, they argued. And, most important, they urged the international community not to abandon the country to warlords, as happened in 1992. Most of all, they called for security, reminding us all that, even in times of suppressed conflict, that is not peace. Peace must be won—for women.

I still believe that Afghan women are the face and the force of their country's future. The research says the same[28]; a country's chances of peace, prosperity, and progress rest not on the fiscal or legislative but on the way in which it treats its women. But Afghanistan's women will continue to need support—resources, tools, access to opportunities—in order to build the Afghanistan that they deserve. The United States might be withdrawing, but direct funding for frontline women's groups must continue. In fact, it must increase. And women must be included in every aspect of leadership and decision-making at every level. It is the best chance Afghanistan has.

My 2009 book was about "liberation"—what it means, and on whose terms it is, told from the perspective of aid interventions. This book builds from decades of data and experience to bring to light an understanding of "liberation" on Afghan women's terms. This is more important now than ever.

At the time of writing these final pages, Aziza was still in Kabul. On 6 October 2021, she sent me this:

Masooda, Sarah, and Khatera celebrate International Women's Day, wearing traditional clothing made by a small women's business, Kabul.

I am fine—do not worry about me! There are bigger things I want to say. This is much bigger than me. Don't let the world forget Afghan women. Don't let the Taliban decide their fate. My whole life has been this one thing, this one story, this one fight. A woman should have the right to an education, the right to work alongside men, the right to be in politics. Afghan mothers, we have lived through generations. We have seen this before. We have lived through all the wars, but we are the real fighters in Afghanistan. And today we will lead the path to success for the next generation.

In revisiting this 2009 book in 2021, I set out to firstly do justice to the voices and stories of Afghan women that I was privileged to hear during my time in the country in 2002–2006. What I heard then still rings true today. Now we can tell the full story of what happened to the project of "liberating" Afghan women—while they were already out liberating themselves, in spite of it all.

In 2006, at the end of my four years in Afghanistan, I asked a young Afghan man what he thought of all this work with women. He answered: "The world thought they could bring freedom to Afghan women, but freedom is only won from the inside."

In the end, who will define that freedom? Afghan women.

Sarah Ahmadi—Afghan woman leader, Aziza's daughter, and my friend and sister—told me this:

Sunset on the hills overlooking Kabul.

Freedom can not be brought from outsiders, it has to be won by the people themselves. Afghan women's freedom can only be won if the entire nation is free.

The Dari word for transition, *gozargah*, represents a place people pass through, a point of transition, and an historic location in Kabul where nomads sought respite. Afghanistan's *gozargah* is neither the beginning of the journey nor the end. Afghanistan has endured—suffered—through a series of transitions, and they do so again today. Women *are* the transition.

It is through the voices of Afghan women that this *gozargah*, this juncture in Afghanistan's transition, is understood. It is also through these voices that understandings of freedom are imagined. Listen to them, and build from there.

And only then will we understand that freedom is won from the inside.

Dari Terminology

Afghaniyat. Afghan national identity

Baad. Offering women as brides in reparation for offenses

Badal. Offering women as brides in exchange for another bride

Be-ghayrati-i. Dishonor

Bey-namoos. Without chastity

Bourka. Full body covering for women

Chaddari. Full body covering for women

Dar be dar. Door to door

Dari. Persian dialect spoken in Afghanistan

Ghayrat. Right to defend one's honor by force

Gozargah. Transition, juncture

Hijab. Women's veil

Imam. One who leads prayers, also head of Islamic community

Inja Afghanistan ast. This is Afghanistan

Jihad. Holy war

Jinsiyat. Sexuality

Jinsiyat ejtemai. Social sex

Jirga. Tribal council

Kash-ma-kash. Conflict

Kharab. Bad

Khariji. Foreigner

Khshoonat aley-he zanaan. Domestic violence

Khub Musselman ast. He's a good Muslim

Landay. Short poem

Loya Jirga. Grand Assembly

Mahram. Male guardian

Maida. Slowly

Mamus. Men's duty to protect and respect women

Marda ra qawl. Men of honor.

Mardumdar. Having people, belonging

Ma'sulyat. Responsibility

Mujahideen. Fighters in the holy war (plural)

Mullah. Religious official of small community

Naan. Afghan bread

Namoos. Pride

Nang. Honor

Nar-shedza. Man-woman

Nezaa. Fighting

Pashto. Language spoken in Afghanistan

Pashtun. Afghan ethnic group, Pashto speakers

Pashtunwali. Pashtun tribal code

Purdah. Restricted movements for women

Sandalee. A low table covered with a blanket, used for warmth in winter

Shabnama. Night letters

Talib Student of religion

Taliban (plural)

Tarsidah. Fear

Tashadud. Violence

Tashadud aley-he zanaan. Violence against women

Wasita. Having special contacts and access

Wolesi Jirga. House of the People

Zan. Woman

Zanaan. Women

Zina. Adultery

Acronyms and Abbreviations

ACBAR—Agency Coordinating Body for Afghan Relief
AIHRC—Afghanistan Independent Human Rights Commission
ANDS—Afghanistan National Development Strategy
CEDAW—Convention on the Elimination of All Forms of Discrimination
   Against Women
EVAW—Elimination of Violence Against Women
GDP—Gross Domestic Product
MoWA—Ministry of Women's Affairs
NAP—National Action Plan
NAPWA—National Action Plan for Women of Afghanistan
NDF—National Development Framework
NGO—Non-Governmental Organization
NSP—National Security Programme
RAWA—Revolutionary Association of the Women of Afghanistan
UN—United Nations
UNAMA—United Nations Assistance Mission in Afghanistan
UNDP—United Nations Development Programme
UNIFEM—United Nations Development Fund for Women
UNSC—United Nations Security Council
UNSCR—United Nations Security Council Resolution
USAID—United States Agency for International Development
WPS—Women, Peace and Security

Chapter Notes

CHAPTER 1

1. N.H. Dupree. (1985). Women in Afghanistan: A brief 1985 update. In F. Rahimi (Ed.). *Women in Afghanistan.* Kabul: Paul Bucherer-Dietschi, 14.

2. F. Rahimi. (1977). *Women in Afghanistan.* Kabul: Paul Bucherer-Dietschi, 36.

3. A. Hans. (2004). Escaping conflict: Afghan women in transit. In W. Giles and J. Hyndman (Eds.). *Sites of violence: Gender and conflict zones.* Berkeley: University of California Press.

4. N. Amini. (2018). Education in the Era of Shah Amanullah Khan. *Afghanistan Quarterly Journal* 32 and 33(01 and 02), 88–102.

5. Canadian Women for Women in Afghanistan. (2011). *Afghan Women in History: The 20th Century,* 1–3.

6. For further information, see H. Emadi. (2002). *Repression, resistance, and women in Afghanistan.* Westport, CT: Praeger.

7. D. Ellis. (2000). *Women of the Afghan War.* Westport, CT: Greenwood; P. McAllister. (1991). *This River of Courage: Generations of women's resistance and action.* Philadelphia: New Society Publishers.

8. S.K. Burki. (2011). The Politics of Zan from Amanullah to Karzai. In Jennifer Heath and Ashraf Zahedi (Eds.). *Land of the Unconquerable: The Lives of Contemporary Afghan Women.* Berkeley: University of California Press, 45–50.

9. P. McAllister. (1991). *This River of Courage: Generations of women's resistance and action.* Philadelphia: New Society Publishers.

10. Bureau of Democracy, Human Rights and Labor. (2001). *Report on the Taliban's War Against Women.* 2001–2009.

state.gov. Available at https://2001–2009. state.gov/g/drl/rls/6185.htm.

11. Human Rights Watch. (2004). *Between Hope and Fear: Intimidation and Attacks against Women in Public Life in Afghanistan.* www.hrw.org. Available at https://www.hrw.org/legacy/backgrounder/asia/afghanistan1004/index.htm.

12. N.H. Dupree. (1985). Women in Afghanistan: A brief 1985 update. In F. Rahimi (Ed.). *Women in Afghanistan.* Kabul: Paul Bucherer-Dietschi.

13. R. Skaine. (2002). *The women of Afghanistan under the Taliban.* Jefferson, NC: McFarland and Co., 18–19.

14. D.B. Edwards. (2003). *Before Taliban: Genealogies of the Afghan Jihad.* Berkeley: University of California Press.

15. A. Hans. (2004). Escaping conflict: Afghan women in transit. In W. Giles and J. Hyndman (Eds.). *Sites of violence: Gender and conflict zones.* Berkeley: University of California Press, 235.

16. N.H. Dupree. (2004). Cultural heritage and national identity in Afghanistan. In S. Barakat (Ed.). *Reconstructing war-torn societies: Afghanistan.* Hampshire, Eng.: Palgrave Macmillan, 317.

17. R. Skaine. (2002). *The women of Afghanistan under the Taliban.* Jefferson, NC: McFarland and Co., 17.

18. M. Weiner and A. Banuazizi (Eds.). (1994). *The politics of social transformation in Afghanistan, Iran, and Pakistan.* Syracuse: Syracuse University Press, 25.

19. H. Ahmed-Ghosh. (2003). A History of Women in Afghanistan: Lessons Learnt for the Future or Yesterdays and Tomorrow. *Journal of International Women's Studies* 4(3), 1–14. Available at https://vc.bridgew.edu/jiws/vol4/iss3/1/.

20. *Ibid.*

21. The United States viewed the conflict in Afghanistan as an integral part of the Cold War struggle, and the CIA provided assistance to anti–Soviet mujahideen rebels to fuel their fight.

22. R. Skaine. (2002). *The women of Afghanistan under the Taliban.* Jefferson, NC: McFarland and Co., 30.

23. V.M. Moghadam. (1999). Revolution, religion, and gender politics: Iran and Afghanistan compared. *Journal of Women's History* 10(4), 172–195.

24. D. Kandiyoti (Ed.). (1991). *Women, Islam and the state.* Philadelphia: Temple University Press, 8.

25. A.E. Brodsky. (2011). Centuries of Threat, Centuries of Resistance: The Lessons of Afghan Women's Resilience. In Jennifer Heath and Ashraf Zahedi (Eds.). *Women of Afghanistan in the Post-9/11 Era: Paths to Empowerment.* Berkeley: University of California Press.

26. *Ibid.*

27. *Ibid.*

28. CNN Editorial Research. (2021). *Taliban Fast Facts.* CNN. Available at https://edition.cnn.com/2013/09/20/world/taliban-fast-facts/index.html.

29. Bureau of Democracy, Human Rights and Labor. (2001). *Report on the Taliban's War Against Women.* 2001–2009. state.gov. Available at https://2001–2009.state.gov/g/drl/rls/6185.htm.

30. A. Besant. (2012). *Some Taliban sent their daughters to school, new report claims.* The World from PRX. Available at https://www.pri.org/stories/2012-12-11/some-taliban-sent-their-daughters-school-new-report-claims.

31. LandInfo. (2011). *Report Afghanistan: Marriage.* Available at https://www.landinfo.no/asset/1852/1/1852_1.pdf.

32. J. Burke. (1998). Taliban prepare for civilian rule. *The Independent.* Available at https://www.independent.co.uk/news/taliban-prepare-for-civilian-rule-1173015.html.

33. Bureau of Democracy, Human Rights and Labor. (2001). *Report on the Taliban's War Against Women.* 2001–2009. state.gov. Available at https://2001–2009.state.gov/g/drl/rls/6185.htm.

34. Revolutionary Association of the Women of Afghanistan. (2018). *Some of the restrictions imposed by Taliban in Afghanistan.* Rawa.org. Available at http://www.rawa.org/rules.htm.

35. S. Samar. (2019). Feminism, Peace, and Afghanistan. *Journal of International Affairs.* Available at https://jia.sipa.columbia.edu/feminism-peace-and-afghanistan.

36. E. Bonino. (1998). Afghanistan: A Flower for the Women of Kabul. *The Guardian.*

37. S. Samar. (2019). Feminism, Peace, and Afghanistan. *Journal of International Affairs.* Available at https://jia.sipa.columbia.edu/feminism-peace-and-afghanistan.

38. *Ibid.*

39. J. Boone. (2010). Afghan feminists fighting from under the burqa. *The Guardian.* 30 Apr. Available at https://www.theguardian.com/world/2010/apr/30/afghanistan-women-feminists-burqa.

40. *Ibid.*

41. S. Miglani. (2008). Taliban executions still haunt Afghan soccer field. *Reuters.* 12 Sep. Available at https://www.reuters.com/article/us-afghan-stadium/taliban-executions-still-haunt-afghan-soccer-field-idUSSP12564220080913.

42. H. Hadid and J. Dell. (2013). Summary amputations: Taliban justice in Afghanistan. *BBC News.* 27 Apr. Available at https://www.bbc.com/news/world-asia-22311036.

43. CBS News. (2012). Taliban attacks on Afghan women worsening. www.youtube.com. Available at https://www.youtube.com/watch?v=Wb2Gm2Q0MV8.

44. S. George and A. Tassal (2020). How life under Taliban rule in Afghanistan has changed—and how it hasn't. *Washington Post.* Available at https://www.washingtonpost.com/graphics/2020/world/asia/afghanistan-taliban-rule-territory/.

45. H. Ahmed-Ghosh. (2003). A History of Women in Afghanistan: Lessons Learnt for the Future *or* Yesterdays and Tomorrow. *Journal of International Women's Studies* 4(3), 1–14. Available at https://vc.bridgew.edu/jiws/vol4/iss3/1/.

46. R. Skaine. (2002). *The women of Afghanistan under the Taliban.* Jefferson, NC: McFarland and Co., 30.

47. For these purposes, the "international community" refers to the aid apparatus. I limit use of the term in that it appears to be a misnomer, assuming uniformity

of opinion and behavior, in the way one might imagine of a community. Regarding Afghanistan's official entry into the international community, the country gained membership to the United Nations on 19 November 1946.

48. Bureau of Democracy, Human Rights and Labor. (2001). *Report on the Taliban's War Against Women.* 2001–2009. state.gov. Available at https://2001–2009. state.gov/g/drl/rls/6185.htm.

49. J. Benjamin. (2000). Afghanistan: Women survivors of war under the Taliban. In J. Mertus (Ed.). *War's offensive on women: The humanitarian challenge in Bosnia, Kosovo, and Afghanistan.* West Hartford, Eng.: Kumarian Press.

50. S. Barakat and G. Wardell. (2004). Exploited by whom? An alternative perspective on humanitarian assistance to Afghan women. In S. Barakat (Ed.). *Reconstructing war-torn societies: Afghanistan.* Hampshire, Eng.: Palgrave Macmillan.

51. A. Russo. (2006). The Feminist Majority Foundation's Campaign to Stop Gender Apartheid. *International Feminist Journal of Politics* 8(4), 557–580.

52. A.M. Jaggar. (1998). Globalizing feminist ethics. *Hypatia* 13(2), 8–9.

53. S. Kolhatkar. (2021). "Saving" Afghan Women. *RAWA.* Available at http://www.rawa.org/znet.htm.

54. B. Ehrenreich. (2003). Veiled threat. In A. Joseph and K. Sharma (Eds.). *Terror, counter-terror: Women speak out.* London: Zed Books, p. 77.

55. For more information, please see http://urbanlegends.about.com/library/blafghan.htm.

56. R. Zakaria. (2021). White Feminists Wanted to Invade. www.thenation.com. Available at https://www.thenation.com/article/world/white-feminists-wanted-to-invade/.

57. J. Benjamin. (2000). Afghanistan: Women survivors of war under the Taliban. In J. Mertus (Ed.). *War's offensive on women: The humanitarian challenge in Bosnia, Kosovo, and Afghanistan.* West Hartford, Eng.: Kumarian Press.

58. S. Wali. (2002). Afghanistan: Truth and mythology. In S. Mehta (Ed.). *Women for Afghan women: Shattering myths and claiming the future.* New York: Palgrave Macmillan, 1.

59. R. Zakaria. (2021). White Feminists Wanted to Invade. www.thenation.com. Available at https://www.thenation.com/article/world/white-feminists-wanted-to-invade/.

60. J. Abrahams. (2021). Towards a Real Feminist Foreign Policy. *Prospect Magazine.* Available at https://www.prospectmagazine.co.uk/world/towards-a-real-feminist-foreign-policy?mc_cid=693e3d4a93&mc_eid=399e3547f7.

61. M. Ferguson. (2005). "W" Stands for Women: Feminism and Security Rhetoric in the Post-9/11 Bush Administration. *Politics & Gender* 1(1), 9–38.

62. N. Niland. (2004). Justice postponed: The marginalization of human rights in Afghanistan. In A. Donini, N. Niland, and K. Wermester (Eds.). *Nation-building unraveled? Aid, peace and justice in Afghanistan.* Bloomfield, CT: Kumarian Press, 79.

63. Afghanistan Independent Human Rights Commission (AIHRC). (2007). *Afghanistan Independent Human Rights Commission Annual Report 1 January 2006–31 December 2006.* Refworld. Available at https://www.refworld.org/docid/471f4a540.html.

64. W. Byrd. (2007). *Responding to Afghanistan's development challenges: An assessment of experience during 2002–2007 and issues and priorities for the future.* Kabul: World Bank.

65. *Ibid.*

66. Georgetown Institute for Women, Peace and Security. (2019). *Women, Peace and Security Index 2019/2020.* Washington, D.C. Available at https://giwps.georgetown.edu/wp-content/uploads/2019/12/WPS-Index-2019-20-Report.pdf.

67. United Nations. (2005). *World population prospects: The 2004 revision—Highlights.* New York: Department of Economic and Social Affairs of the UN Secretariat.

68. Estimate made for 2020 available in: United Nations. (2019). *World population prospects: The 2019 revision.* Department of Economic and Social Affairs of the UN Secretariat.

69. *Ibid.*

70. Z. Nader and A. Ferris-Rotman. (2021). What Afghanistan's Women Stand to Lose. *Time.* Available at https://time.com/6091712/aghanistan-women-loss/.

71. United Nations Population Fund (UNFPA). (2005). The promise of equality: Gender equity, reproductive health and the

millennium development goals. *The state of world population report.* New York: United Nations Population Fund.

72. The World Bank. (2017). *Maternal mortality ratio (modeled estimate, per 100,000 live births)—Afghanistan | Data.* Worldbank.org. Available at https://data.worldbank.org/indicator/SH.STA.MMRT?locations=AF.

73. CIA. (2021). *Afghanistan—The World Factbook.* www.cia.gov. Available at https://www.cia.gov/the-world-factbook/countries/afghanistan/#people-and-society.

74. Human Rights Watch. (2021). *"I Would Like Four Kids—If We Stay Alive."* Human Rights Watch. Available at https://www.hrw.org/report/2021/05/06/i-would-four-kids-if-we-stay-alive/womens-access-health-care-afghanistan#4460.

75. S. Devi. (2020). Access to health care under threat in Afghanistan. *The Lancet* 395(10242), 1962.

76. L. Crawfurd and S. Hares. (2021). *Girls' Education: A Casualty of the Disastrous Withdrawal from Afghanistan?* Center for Global Development. Available at https://www.cgdev.org/blog/girls-education-casualty-disastrous-withdrawal-afghanistan.

77. *Ibid.*

78. Human Rights Watch. (2020). *Gender Alert on Covid-19 Afghanistan.* Human Rights Watch. Available at https://www.hrw.org/news/2020/10/14/gender-alert-covid-19-afghanistan#.

79. UN Office for the Coordination of Humanitarian Affairs and REACH Initiative. (2018). *Afghanistan: Hard to Reach Assessment Report, June 2018—Afghanistan.* ReliefWeb. Available at https://reliefweb.int/report/afghanistan/afghanistan-hard-reach-assessment-report-june-2018.

80. Human Rights Watch. (2020). *Gender Alert on Covid-19 Afghanistan.* Human Rights Watch. Available at https://www.hrw.org/news/2020/10/14/gender-alert-covid-19-afghanistan#.

81. *Ibid.*

82. CIA. (2021). *Afghanistan—The World Factbook.* www.cia.gov. Available at https://www.cia.gov/the-world-factbook/countries/afghanistan/#people-and-society.

83. UNESCO. (2021). *Afghanistan: Education and Literacy.* uis.unesco.org. Available at http://uis.unesco.org/en/country/af?theme=education-and-literacy.

84. CIA. (2021). *Afghanistan—The World Factbook.* www.cia.gov. Available at https://www.cia.gov/the-world-factbook/countries/afghanistan/#people-and-society.

85. S. Gollob and M. O'Hanlon. (2020). *Afghanistan Index: Tracking Variables of Reconstruction and Security in Post-9/11 Afghanistan.* Brookings. Available at https://www.brookings.edu/wp-content/uploads/2020/08/FP_20200825_afganistan_index.pdf.

86. R. Stone. (2021). Resignations Follow Taliban Pick to Run Top Afghan University. *Science.* Available at https://www.science.org/content/article/resignations-follow-taliban-pick-run-top-afghan-university.

87. UN Office for the Coordination of Humanitarian Affairs and REACH Initiative. (2018). *Afghanistan: Hard to Reach Assessment Report, June 2018—Afghanistan.* ReliefWeb. Available at https://reliefweb.int/report/afghanistan/afghanistan-hard-reach-assessment-report-june-2018.

88. Human Rights Watch. (2020). *Gender Alert on Covid-19 Afghanistan.* Human Rights Watch. Available at https://www.hrw.org/news/2020/10/14/gender-alert-covid-19-afghanistan#.

89. K. Forde. (2021). What Sources of Cash Will the Taliban Have? *Aljazeera.* Available at https://www.aljazeera.com/economy/2021/8/19/what-will-happen-to-afghanistans-economy-under-taliban-rule.

90. United Nations Development Programme. (2005). *Vision 2020—Afghanistan millennium development goals report 2005.* Kabul: United Nations Development Programme.

91. S. Gollob and M. O'Hanlon. (2020). *Afghanistan Index: Tracking Variables of Reconstruction and Security in Post-9/11 Afghanistan.* Brookings. Available at https://www.brookings.edu/wp-content/uploads/2020/08/FP_20200825_afganistan_index.pdf.

92. UN Women. (2021). *Country Fact Sheet | UN Women Data Hub.* data.unwomen.org. Available at https://data.unwomen.org/country/afghanistan.

93. *Ibid.*

94. International Rescue Committee. (2021). IRC Warns of Invisible Crisis in Afghanistan, as 50% of Those in Need of Humanitarian Assistance Are Women and Girls. [Press Release] Available at https://

www.rescue.org/press-release/irc-warns-invisible-crisis-afghanistan-50-those-need-humanitarian-assistance-are-women.

95. M. Kelemen. (2021). The Future Is Unclear for Foreign Aid Work in Afghanistan Under the Taliban. *NPR*. Available at https://www.npr.org/2021/08/26/1031412042/the-future-is-unclear-for-foreign-aid-work-in-afghanistan-under-the-taliban.

96. J. Abrahams. (2021). Towards a Real Feminist Foreign Policy. *Prospect Magazine*. Available at https://www.prospectmagazine.co.uk/world/towards-a-real-feminist-foreign-policy?mc_cid=693e3d4a93&mc_eid=399e3547f7.

97. S. Gollob and M. O'Hanlon. (2020). *Afghanistan Index: Tracking Variables of Reconstruction and Security in Post-9/11 Afghanistan*. Brookings. Available at https://www.brookings.edu/wp-content/uploads/2020/08/FP_20200825_afganistan_index.pdf.

98. F. Nawa. (2011). *Opium Nation: Child Brides, Drug Lords, and One Woman's Journey Through Afghanistan*. New York: HarperCollins.

99. S. Gollob and M. O'Hanlon. (2020). *Afghanistan Index: Tracking Variables of Reconstruction and Security in Post-9/11 Afghanistan*. Brookings. Available at https://www.brookings.edu/wp-content/uploads/2020/08/FP_20200825_afganistan_index.pdf.

100. Information on urban livelihoods in this section is taken from J. Beall and S. Schutte. (2006). Urban livelihoods in Afghanistan. Issues Paper Series. Kabul: Afghanistan Research and Evaluation Unit.

101. United Nations Development Programme. (2021). *Gender Inequality Index (GII) | Human Development Reports*. Undp.org. Available at http://hdr.undp.org/en/content/gender-inequality-index-gii.

102. UN Women. (2021). *Country Fact Sheet | UN Women Data Hub*. data.unwomen.org. Available at https://data.unwomen.org/country/afghanistan.

103. *Ibid.*

104. *Ibid.*

105. UN Office of the High Commissioner for Human Rights. (2018). *Injustice and Impunity Mediation of Criminal Offences of Violence against Women*. Available at https://unama.unmissions.org/sites/default/files/unama_ohchr_evaw_report_2018_injustice_and_impunity_29_may_2018.pdf.

106. UN Women. (2021b). *Global Database on Violence against Women: Afghanistan*. evaw-global-database.unwomen.org. Available at https://evaw-global-database.unwomen.org/en/countries/asia/afghanistan#1.

107. UN Office of the High Commissioner for Human Rights. (2018). *Injustice and Impunity Mediation of Criminal Offences of Violence against Women*. Available at https://unama.unmissions.org/sites/default/files/unama_ohchr_evaw_report_2018_injustice_and_impunity_29_may_2018.pdf.

108. UNICEF. (2018). *The situation of children and women in Afghanistan*. Unicef.org. Available at https://www.unicef.org/afghanistan/situation-children-and-women-afghanistan.

109. F.A. Khan. (2018). *2018 Survey of Afghan People Shows Women's Rights are Complicated—The Asia Foundation*. The Asia Foundation. Available at https://asiafoundation.org/2018/12/05/2018-survey-of-afghan-people-shows-womens-rights-are-complicated/.

110. S. Safi. (2018). Why female suicide in Afghanistan is so prevalent. *BBC News*. 30 Jun. Available at https://www.bbc.com/news/world-asia-44370711.

111. S. Saif. (2021). Afghanistan: 47,600 Civilians Killed in 20 Years of Deadly War. *Anadolu Agency*. Available at https://www.aa.com.tr/en/asia-pacific/afghanistan-47-600-civilians-killed-in-20-years-of-deadly-war/2219156.

112. N. Crawford and C. Lutz. (2019). *Human Cost of Post-9/11 Wars: Direct War Deaths in Major War Zones*. Watson Institute for International and Public Affairs. Available at https://watson.brown.edu/costsofwar/figures/2019/direct-war-death-toll-2001-801000.

113. United Nations Assistance Mission of Afghanistan. (2013). *Protection of Civilians in Armed Conflict*. Kabul. Available at https://unama.unmissions.org/sites/default/files/2012_annual_report_eng_0.pdf.

114. UN News. (2021). Afghanistan: Record Number of Women and Children Killed or Wounded. *UN News*. Available at https://news.un.org/en/story/2021/07/1096382.

115. S. Gollob and M. O'Hanlon. (2020). *Afghanistan Index: Tracking Variables of Reconstruction and Security in Post-9/11 Afghanistan.* Brookings. Available at https://www.brookings.edu/wp-content/uploads/2020/08/FP_20200825_afganistan_index.pdf.

116. Institute for Economics and Peace. (2021). *Global Peace Index 2021.* Sydney. Available at https://www.visionofhumanity.org/wp-content/uploads/2021/06/GPI-2021-web-1.pdf.

117. *Ibid.*

118. United Nations Development Programme & Islamic Republic of Afghanistan. (2004). *Afghanistan national human development report 2004: Security with a human face: Challenges and responsibilities.* Kabul: United Nations Development Programme.

119. United Nations Development Programme. (2020). *Human Development Data (1990–2017) Human Development Reports.* Undp.org. Available at http://hdr.undp.org/en/data.

120. World Economic Forum. (2021). *Global Gender Gap Report: 2021.* World Economic Forum. Available at http://www3.weforum.org/docs/WEF_GGGR_2021.pdf.

121. Georgetown Institute for Women, Peace and Security. (2019). *Tracking sustainable peace through inclusion, justice, and security for women Women Peace and Security Index.* Available at https://giwps.georgetown.edu/wp-content/uploads/2019/12/WPS-Index-2019–20-Report.pdf.

122. S. Gollob and M. O'Hanlon. (2020). *Afghanistan Index: Tracking Variables of Reconstruction and Security in Post-9/11 Afghanistan.* Brookings. Available at https://www.brookings.edu/wp-content/uploads/2020/08/FP_20200825_afganistan_index.pdf.

123. L. Bohn. (2018). "We're All Handcuffed in This Country." Why Afghanistan Is Still the Worst Place in the World to Be a Woman. *Time Magazine.* Available at https://time.com/5472411/afghanistan-women-justice-war/.

124. J. Goodwin. (2003). *Price of honor: Muslim women lift the veil of silence on the Islamic world.* New York: Plume.

125. Orientalism is a term coined by Edward Said and elaborated in his 1978 book, *Orientalism.* He defines this term as acceptance in the West of "the basic distinction between East and West as the starting point for elaborate theories, epics, novels, social descriptions, and political accounts concerning the Orient, its people, customs, 'mind,' destiny and so on."

126. United Nations Secretary General. (1997). *The situation in Afghanistan and its implications for international peace and security.* New York: United Nations General Assembly Security Council.

127. G. Whitlock. (2005). The skin of the *bourka*: Recent life narratives from Afghanistan. *Biography* 28(1), 57.

128. Nancy Hatch Dupree is one of the foremost authorities on Afghanistan. She has directed the ACBAR (Agency Coordinating Body for Afghan Relief) Resource and Information Centre in Peshawar since 1989. She is the author of six guidebooks on Afghanistan and has published over 150 articles on Afghanistan. Her husband, the late Louis Dupree, was a prominent anthropologist and Afghanistan specialist. No research on Afghanistan is complete without referencing the Duprees' work. N.H. Dupree. (1985). Women in Afghanistan: A brief 1985 update. In F. Rahimi (Ed.). *Women in Afghanistan.* Kabul: Paul Bucherer-Dietschi, 14.

129. It should be noted that the Taliban also did their part to pit men against women by requiring that men enforce the edict that "their women" wear the *chaddari*. Failure to do this would result in severe punishment. "In this way, the Taliban accomplish control over both men and women. They not only obliterate women's presence but also by usurping what was the purview of the family, they put to shame the men of the family, thus rendering them disempowered." N. Gross. (2000). The messy side of globalization: Women in Afghanistan. *Symposium on Globalization and Women in Muslim Societies.* Washington, D.C.: Library of Congress.

130. L. Abirafeh. (2004, October). Burqa politics: The plights of women in Afghanistan. *Chronogram,* http://www.chronogram.com/issue/2004/10/news/burqa.php.

131. J. Boone. (2010). Afghan feminists fighting from under the burqa. *The Guardian.* Available at https://www.theguardian.com/world/2010/apr/30/afghanistan-women-feminists-burqa.

132. U. Narayan. (1997). *Dislocating cultures: Identities, traditions, and third world feminism.* New York: Routledge.

133. M. Hannun. (2021). *"Saving" Afghan Women, Now*. The American Prospect. Available at https://prospect.org/world/saving-afghan-women-now/.

134. G. Dorronsoro. (2005). *Revolution unending: Afghanistan: 1979 to the present*. New York: Columbia University Press, 291–292.

135. M. Sultan. (2005). *From rhetoric to reality: Afghan women on the agenda for peace*. Washington, D.C.: Women Waging Peace Policy Commission, 31.

136. I was invited to speak on the issue of Afghan women at the Women as Global Leaders Conference in Dubai, United Arab Emirates. At that point I had already been working in Afghanistan for nearly three years. I used the conference as an opportunity to gauge public opinion on the situation of Afghan women more than three years after their "liberation" and their virtual disappearance from the media. The audience was comprised of 40 female participants, mostly American. They were conference participants who elected to attend my session on Afghanistan. Ages ranged from 15 to 68 and included students, academics, and development practitioners. At the beginning of the two-hour session, I circulated a questionnaire to the participants and asked that they complete it immediately. The answers then served as the starting point for the discussion on images of Afghan women.

137. While most of the participants mentioned the *chaddari*, it is important to note that all of them used the word *bourka*. In fact, none of them were familiar at all with the word *chaddari*.

138. A.M. Jaggar. (1998). Globalizing feminist ethics. *Hypatia* 13(2), 10.

139. *Bourka* was the preferred spelling of the publisher. *Chaddari* was not a well-known term and would not illicit the same response in the article.

140. A. Ferris-Rotman. (2021). "What About My Dreams?" How the U.S. Abandoned Women in Afghanistan. *Vanity Fair*. Available at https://www.vanityfair.com/news/2021/08/how-the-us-abandoned-women-in-afghanistan.

141. T.K. Beck. (2018). "Liberating the Women of Afghanistan." *Socio* (11), 57–75.

142. *Ibid.*

143. G.C. Spivak. (1993). "Can the Subaltern Speak?" in P. Williams and L. Chisman (Eds.). *Colonial Discourse and Post-Colonial Theory: A Reader*. Harvester, 93.

144. M. Yam. (2021). As Afghans try to figure out Taliban's new rules, burqas are barometer of sorts. *Los Angeles Times*. Available at https://www.latimes.com/world-nation/story/2021-08-23/as-afghans-try-to-figure-out-talibans-new-rules-burqas-serve-as-a-barometer.

Chapter 2

1. K. Staudt. (2002). Dismantling the master's house with the master's tools? Gender work in and with powerful bureaucracies. In K. Saunders (Ed.). *Feminist post-development thought: Rethinking modernity, post-colonialism and representation*. London: Zed Books, 57.

2. C. Johnson and J. Leslie. (2004). *Afghanistan: The mirage of peace*. London: Zed Books, 77.

3. E. Rostami-Povey. (2007). *Afghan women: Identity and invasion*. London: Zed Books.

4. N.H. Dupree. (2004). The family during crisis in Afghanistan. *Journal of Comparative Family Studies* 32(2), 311–332.

5. The rationale behind this exercise was to come to a better understanding of how Afghans value particular aspects of their identities. Asking respondents to prioritize one identity as the most important does not intend to negate the existence of multiple identities simultaneously, nor does it ignore the fact that identities and affiliations change in time and in different contexts. This aspect of the research simply demonstrates that the artificial divisions in programming based on sex might not have been valid for some participants. It might have, in fact, extracted women and men from their social roles and challenged their other, perhaps stronger, affiliations.

6. S. Walby. (1997). *Gender transformations*. London: Routledge.

7. M.H. Kamali. (2003). *Islam, pernicious custom, and women's rights in Afghanistan*. Malaysia: International Islamic University.

8. D. Kandiyoti (Ed.). (1991). *Women, Islam and the state*. Philadelphia: Temple University Press 14.

9. It is generally assumed that Pashtuns are the more conservative ethnic group. This leads to facile analyses assuming that

all things "traditional" emanate from this particular group. Such an example reinforces the importance of not taking ethnic identity at face value. For more information, see C. Johnson and J. Leslie. (2004). *Afghanistan: The mirage of peace.* London: Zed Books.

10. Segments of this section were previously published. L. Abirafeh. (2003). The role of religion in the lives of women in the new Afghanistan. *Critical Half* 1(1), 36–37.

11. W.G. Azoy. (2003). *Buzkashi: Game and power in Afghanistan* (2nd ed.). Prospect Heights, Ill: Waveland Press.

12. Allusions to the "other culture" that has altered Islam generally refer to the Wahhabi version of Islam, originating in Saudi Arabia.

13. The majority ethnicities are Pashtun (42 percent) and Tajik (27 percent).

14. United Nations Development Programme & Islamic Republic of Afghanistan. (2004). *Afghanistan national human development report 2004: Security with a human face: Challenges and responsibilities.* Kabul: United Nations Development Programme, 11.

15. C. Johnson and J. Leslie (2004). *Afghanistan: The mirage of peace.* London: Zed Books, 52.

16. A. Sen. (2006). *Identity and violence: The illusion of destiny.* London: Penguin.

17. S. Shah. (2003). *The storyteller's daughter.* London: Penguin.

18. N.H. Dupree. (2004). The family during crisis in Afghanistan. *Journal of Comparative Family Studies* 32(2), 311–332.

19. United Nations Development Programme & Islamic Republic of Afghanistan. (2004). *Afghanistan national human development report 2004: Security with a human face: Challenges and responsibilities.* Kabul: United Nations Development Programme, 216–217.

20. R. Khan. (2021). *Afghanistan and the colonial project of feminism: dismantling the binary lens. London School of Economics.* Available at https://blogs.lse.ac.uk/medialse/2021/09/02/afghanistan-and-the-colonial-project-of-feminism-dismantling-the-binary-lens/?fbclid=IwAR3894i-1zYAdFymtBbwK91WceRzYYPSFZtfcAC-N7ONZEHvoIdm9wK1-m7BI.

21. The concept of "do no harm" expands on this, arguing in favor of a contextualized understanding so that aid interventions

avoid additional damage to those they are trying to assist. M.B. Anderson. (1999). *Do no harm: How aid can support peace— or war.* Boulder: Lynne Rienner Publishers.

22. L. AbiRafeh (2008). *Women of Afghanistan in the Post-Taliban Era: How Lives Have Changed and Where They Stand Today.* In R. Skaine. Jefferson, NC: McFarland and Co, 123–150.

23. By this he means Frozan is confronting her husband, or facing him with new confidence.

24. Akram Osman's (2005) short stories provide a good definition of the use of the proverb: "In colloquial Dari, Turkestan is often used as the place where someone who is misdirected ends up" (p. 39).

25. These women's stories were previously published in R. Skaine. (2008). *Women of Afghanistan in the post–Taliban era: How lives have changed and where they stand today.* Jefferson: McFarland and Co.

CHAPTER 3

1. S. Shah. (2003). *The storyteller's daughter.* London: Penguin, 8.

2. For more information, see A. Osman and A. Loewen. (2005). *Real men keep their word: Tales from Kabul, Afghanistan: A selection of Akram Osman's Dari short stories.* Oxford: Oxford University Press; S.B. Majrouh. (1994). Songs of love and war: Afghan women's poetry. New York: Other Press.

3. A. Osman and A. Loewen. (2005). *Real men keep their word: Tales from Kabul, Afghanistan: A selection of Akram Osman's Dari short stories.* Oxford: Oxford University Press, xxxi.

4. S. Shah. (2003). *The storyteller's daughter.* London: Penguin.

5. C. Echavez, S. Mosawi, and L. Echavez-Pilongo. (2016). *The Other Side of Gender Inequality: Men and Masculinities in Afghanistan.* Kabul: Afghanistan Research and Evaluation Unit. Available at https://www.refworld.org/pdfid/577b5ae04.pdf.

6. A. Osman and A. Loewen. (2005). *Real men keep their word: Tales from Kabul, Afghanistan: A selection of Akram Osman's Dari short stories.* Oxford: Oxford University Press, 101.

7. *Ibid.,* 173.

8. *Ibid.,* 140.

9. *Ibid.,* 204.

10. Afghan literature, particularly the short stories of Akram Osman, can be used as social comment. Following Muhammad Daud Khan, Osman employed the symbol of the eagle as a metaphor to criticize foreign influence in Afghanistan. An excerpt from his story titled "The Blind Eagle" expresses this sentiment: "Here, immersed in a realm free from the dictates of the East and the West, the eagle lost himself in a burning desire of unknown love" (Osman, 2005, 201). A. Osman and A. Loewen. (2005). *Real men keep their word: Tales from Kabul, Afghanistan: A selection of Akram Osman's Dari short stories*. Oxford: Oxford University Press.

11. *Ibid.*, xiii.

12. S.B. Majrouh. (1994). *Songs of love and war: Afghan women's poetry*. New York: Other Press, xi.

13. N.H. Dupree. (1990). A sociocultural dimension: Afghan women refugees in Pakistan. In E.W. Anderson and N.H. Dupree. *The cultural basis of Afghan nationalism*. London: Pinter Publishers, 128.

14. S.B. Majrouh. (1994). *Songs of love and war: Afghan women's poetry*. New York: Other Press, xvi.

15. *Ibid.*

16. N.H. Dupree. (1990). A sociocultural dimension: Afghan women refugees in Pakistan. In E.W. Anderson and N.H. Dupree. *The cultural basis of Afghan nationalism*. London: Pinter Publishers.

17. *Ibid.*

18. W.G. Azoy. (2003). *Buzkashi: Game and power in Afghanistan* (2nd ed.). Prospect Heights, Ill: Waveland Press, 30.

19. World Bank. (2004). *Afghanistan: State building, sustaining growth, and reducing poverty: A country economic report*. Kabul: World Bank, 80.

20. *Purdah* refers to the Islamic practice of seclusion of women. More information can be found in P. Marsden. (1998). *The Taliban: War, religion, and the new order in Afghanistan*. London: Zed Books.

21. S. Shah. (2003). *The storyteller's daughter*. London: Penguin, 118.

22. R. Skaine. (2002). *The women of Afghanistan under the Taliban*. Jefferson: McFarland and Co., 142.

23. N.H. Dupree. (2004). The family during crisis in Afghanistan. *Journal of Comparative Family Studies* 32(2), 311–332.

24. S. Shah. (2003). *The storyteller's daughter*. London: Penguin, 29.

25. A. Osman and A. Loewen. (2005). *Real men keep their word: Tales from Kabul, Afghanistan: A selection of Akram Osman's Dari short stories*. Oxford: Oxford University Press, 85.

26. World Bank. (2005). *National reconstruction and poverty reduction: The role of women in Afghanistan's future*. Kabul: World Bank, 80.

27. H. Ahmed-Ghosh. (2003). A History of Women in Afghanistan: Lessons Learnt for the Future or Yesterdays and Tomorrow. *Journal of International Women's Studies* 4(3), 1–14. Available at https://vc.bridgew.edu/jiws/vol4/iss3/1/.

28. S. Azarbaijani-Moghaddam. (2004). Afghan women on the margins of the twenty-first century. In A. Donini, N. Niland, and K. Wermester (Eds.). *Nation-building unraveled? Aid, peace and justice in Afghanistan*. Bloomfield, CT: Kumarian Press, 103.

29. G.C. Spivak. (1993). "Can the Subaltern Speak?" in P. Williams and L. Chisman (Eds.). *Colonial Discourse and Post-Colonial Theory: A Reader*. Harvester, 93.

30. K. Hunt. (2002). The strategic co-optation of women's rights: Discourse in the "war on terrorism." *International Feminist Journal of Politics* 4(1), 116–121.

31. F. Cleaver (Ed.). (2002). *Masculinities matter! Men, gender and development*. London: Zed Books, 24.

32. In this case, the UN is used to represent the international community as a whole.

33. B. Francis. (2018). *The Local Level Implementation of Afghanistan's National Action Plan on UNSCR 1325 — Women, Peace and Security*. International Alert. Available at https://www.international-alert.org/sites/default/files/Afghanistan_NationalActionPlanUNSCR1325_EN_2018.pdf.

34. M. Centlivres-Demont. (1994). Afghan women in peace, war, and exile. In M. Weiner and A. Banuazizi (Eds.). *The politics of social transformation in Afghanistan, Iran, and Pakistan*. Syracuse: Syracuse University Press, 358.

35. H. Ahmed-Ghosh. (2003). A History of Women in Afghanistan: Lessons Learnt for the Future or Yesterdays and Tomorrow. *Journal of International Women's Studies*

4(3), 1–14. Available at https://vc.bridgew.
edu/jiws/vol4/iss3/1/.

36. M. Sultan. (2002). Hope in Afghani-
stan. In S. Mehta. *Women for Afghan women:
Shattering myths and claiming the future.*
New York: Palgrave Macmillan, 202.

37. Women and Children Legal Research Foundation. (2005). *Report on
women political participation in Afghanistan.* Kabul: Open Society Institute.

38. S. Azarbaijani-Moghaddam.
(2009). Manly Honor and the Gendered
Male in Afghanistan. *Middle East Institute.* Available at https://www.mei.edu/
publications/manly-honor-and-gendered-
male-afghanistan.

39. C. Echavez, S. Mosawi, and L.
Echavez-Pilongo. (2016). *The Other Side of
Gender Inequality: Men and Masculinities in
Afghanistan.* Kabul: Afghanistan Research
and Evaluation Unit. Available at https://
www.refworld.org/pdfid/577b5ae04.pdf.

40. A. Kleinman. (2021). Afghan Women
on What's at Stake for Women in Afghanistan. *1A.* Available at https://the1a.org/
segments/afghan-women-on-whats-at-
stake-for-women-in-afghanistan/.

Chapter 4

1. Quote from village leader, Kunar
Province, in *Human Rights and Reconstruction in Afghanistan.* (2002). Center
for Economic and Social Rights. Available
at https://www.cesr.org/sites/default/files/
Human_Rights_and_Reconstructions_in_
Afghanistan.pdf.

2. N. Turak. (2021). Donors pledging billions in aid to Afghanistan face a challenge
navigating the Taliban. *CNBC.* Available
at https://www.cnbc.com/2021/09/17/aid-
funding-for-afghanistan-at-risk-of-taliban-
misuse-corruption.html.

3. Special Inspector General for Afghanistan Reconstruction. (2021). *Reconstruction Update: April 30, 2021 Quarterly
Report to Congress.* Available at https://
www.sigar.mil/pdf/quarterlyreports/2021–
04–30qr-section2-funding.pdf.

4. United Nations Development Programme. (2021). *97 percent of Afghans could
plunge into poverty by mid-2022, says UNDP.*
Available at https://www.undp.org/press-
releases/97-percent-afghans-could-plunge-
poverty-mid-2022-says-undp.

5. United States Agency for International
Development. (2021). *U.S. Overseas Loans
and Grants (Greenbook) Data.* Available
at https://data.usaid.gov/Administration-
and-Oversight/U-S-Overseas-Loans-and-
Grants-Greenbook-Data/7cnw-pw8v.

6. J. Ferguson. (1994). *The anti-politics
machine: "Development," depoliticization,
and bureaucratic power in Lesotho.* Minneapolis: University of Minnesota Press.

7. Foreign Assistance. (2021). *Country File: Afghanistan.* Available at https://
foreignassistance.gov./.

8. Congressional Research Service.
(2021). *Afghan Women and Girls: Status and
Congressional Action.* Available at https://
crsreports.congress.gov/product/pdf/IF/
IF11646.

9. Special Inspector General for Afghanistan Reconstruction. (2021). *Reconstruction Update: April 30, 2021 Quarterly
Report to Congress.* Available at https://
www.sigar.mil/pdf/quarterlyreports/2021–
04–30qr-section2-funding.pdf.

10. C. Whitlock. (2019). At War with the
Truth. *Washington Post.* Available at https://
www.washingtonpost.com/graphics/2019/
investigations/afghanistan-papers/
afghanistan-war-confidential-documents/.

11. Special Inspector General for
Afghanistan Reconstruction. (2021). *What
We Need to Learn: Lessons from Twenty Years
of Afghanistan Reconstruction.* Virginia:
SIGAR. Available at https://www.sigar.mil/
pdf/lessonslearned/SIGAR-21–46-LL.pdf.

12. A. Ferris-Rotman. (2021). "What
About My Dreams?": How the U.S. Abandoned Women in Afghanistan. *Vanity Fair.*
Available at https://www.vanityfair.com/
news/2021/08/how-the-us-abandoned-
women-in-afghanistan.

13. Feminist Majority Foundation.
(2003). Bush Administration's Rhetoric
Does Not Match Reality on Global Women's
Rights Issues. *Feminist Majority Foundation.* Available at https://feminist.org/news/
press/bush-administrations-rhetoric-does-
not-match-reality-on-global-womens-
rights-issues/.

14. Feminist Majority Foundation.
(2004). Bush Policies on Iraq and Afghanistan Fail Women. *Feminist Majority
Foundation.* Available at https://feminist.
org/news/bush-policies-on-iraq-and-
afghanistan-fail-women/.

15. H. Ruiz. (2002). *Afghanistan: conflict and displacement 1978 to 2001.* Forced

Migration Review. Available at https://www.fmreview.org/september-11th-has-anything-changed/ruiz.

16. D. Mitchell. (2017). NGO Presence and Activity in Afghanistan, 2000–2014: A Provincial-Level Dataset. *Stability: International Journal of Security and Development* 6(1), 5.

17. H. Ruiz. (2002). *Afghanistan: conflict and displacement 1978 to 2001*. Forced Migration Review. Available at https://www.fmreview.org/september-11th-has-anything-changed/ruiz.

18. United Nations Security Council. (1996). *Resolution 1076: The Situation in Afghanistan*. Available at http://unscr.com/en/resolutions/doc/1076.

19. United Nations. (2002). Security Council adopts humanitarian exemptions to sanctions against Al-Qaida. *UN News*. Available at https://news.un.org/en/story/2002/12/54972-security-council-adopts-humanitarian-exemptions-sanctions-against-al-qaida.

20. M. Fielden and S. Azarbaijani-Moghadam. (2001). *Female Employment in Afghanistan: A Study of Decree #8*. Inter-Agency Taliban Edict Task Force. Available at https://www.refworld.org/pdfid/48aa82df0.pdf.

21. Ibid.

22. *The Times of India*. (2000). Taliban arrest U.S. aid worker for employing women. Available at http://www.rawa.org/ban-wo.htm.

23. M. Fielden and S. Azarbaijani-Moghadam. (2001). *Female Employment in Afghanistan: A Study of Decree #8*. Inter-Agency Taliban Edict Task Force. Available at https://www.refworld.org/pdfid/48aa82df0.pdf.

24. Ibid.

25. D. Mitchell. (2017). NGO Presence and Activity in Afghanistan, 2000–2014: A Provincial-Level Dataset. *Stability: International Journal of Security and Development* 6(1), 5.

26. M. Fielden and S. Azarbaijani-Moghadam. (2001). *Female Employment in Afghanistan: A Study of Decree #8*. Inter-Agency Taliban Edict Task Force. Available at https://www.refworld.org/pdfid/48aa82df0.pdf.

27. CBS. (2001). Taliban Uses Food as a Weapon. *CBS News*. Available at https://www.cbsnews.com/news/taliban-uses-food-as-weapon/.

28. Breakdown of aid disbursement as follows: $6.5 million by International Committee of the Red Cross (ICRC), $4 million by the World Food Program (WFP), $3 million by the International Federation of the Red Cross and Red Crescent Societies (IFRC), $2 million by the International Organization for Migration (IOM), $2 million by the United Nations Organization for the Coordination of Humanitarian Affairs (OCHA), and $600,000 by the United Nations Population Fund (UNFPA). Source: U.S. Department of State Available at https://2001-2009.state.gov/r/pa/prs/ps/2001/5766.htm.

29. O. Oliker; R. Kauzlarich; J. Dobbins; K. Basseuner; D. Sampler; J. McGinn; M. Dziedzic; A. Grissom; B. Pirnie; N. Bensahel; and A. Guven. (2004). *Aid during conflict: interaction between military and civilian assistance providers in Afghanistan, September 2001–June 2002*. Santa Monica, CA: RAND Corporation.

30. CNN. (2001). Afghanistan wakes after night of intense bombings. *CNN*. Available at https://edition.cnn.com/2001/U.S./10/07/gen.america.under.attack/.

31. Bureau of Democracy, Human Rights and Labor. (2001). *Report on the Taliban's War Against Women*. U.S. Department of State. Available at https://2001-2009.state.gov/g/drl/rls/6185.htm.

32. The New Humanitarian (2001). Women welcome U.S. relief law. *The New Humanitarian*. Available at https://www.thenewhumanitarian.org/fr/node/183112.

33. Ibid.

34. *The Bonn Agreement (S/2001/1154)*. (2001). Bonn: United Nations Security Council. https://peacemaker.un.org/sites/peacemaker.un.org/files/AF_011205_AgreementProvisionalArrangementsinAfghanistan%28en%29.pdf.

35. OECD/DAC Network on Gender Equality, et al. (2003). *Gender and Post-Conflict Reconstruction: Lessons Learned from Afghanistan*. Paris. Available at https://www.un.org/womenwatch/ianwge/taskforces/ParisJoint_Workshop_Report_final.pdf.

36. A. Nijat and J. Murtazashvili. (2015). *Special Report: Women's Leadership Roles in Afghanistan*. Washington, D.C.: United States Institute of Peace. Available at https://www.usip.org/sites/default/files/SR380-Women-s-Leadership-Roles-in-Afghanistan.pdf.

37. A. Larson. (2008). *A Mandate to Mainstream: Promoting Gender Equality in Afghanistan*. Kabul: Afghanistan Research and Evaluation Unit. https://genderand security.org/sites/default/files/Larson_-_A_Mandate_to_Mainstream.pdf.

38. A. Nijat and J. Murtazashvili. (2015). *Special Report: Women's Leadership Roles in Afghanistan*. Washington, D.C.: United States Institute of Peace. Available at https://www.usip.org/sites/default/files/SR380-Women-s-Leadership-Roles-in-Afghanistan.pdf.

39. An estimated $3,317,500 million out of $6.645 billion national budget as cited in N. Birtsh and A. Hedayat. (2016). *Gender-Responsive Budgeting in Afghanistan: A Work in Progress*. Kabul: AREU. Available at https://www.acbar.org/upload/147737128796.pdf.

40. U.S. Department of State. (2002). *USAID funds rebuilding of Afghan Women's Affairs Ministry*. Available at https://reliefweb.int/report/afghanistan/usaid-funds-rebuilding-afghan-womens-affairs-ministry.

41. Afghanistan Reconstruction Trust Fund. (2021). About us | Afghanistan Reconstruction Trust Fund. www.artf.af. Available at https://www.artf.af/who-we-are/about-us.

42. The World Bank. (2020). Afghanistan Reconstruction Trust Fund (ARTF) Steering Committee Meets. *World Bank*. Available at https://www.worldbank.org/en/news/press-release/2020/09/02/afghanistan-reconstruction-trust-fund-artf-steering-committee-meets.

43. Center for Economic and Social Rights. (2002). *Human Rights and Reconstruction in Afghanistan*. Available at https://www.cesr.org/sites/default/files/Human_Rights_and_Reconstructions_in_Afghanistan.pdf.

44. *Ibid.*

45. United Nations Development Programme. (2002). *Afghanistan: Donors Pledge $4.5 Billion in Tokyo*. [Press Release] Available at https://reliefweb.int/report/afghanistan/afghanistan-donors-pledge-45-billion-tokyo.

46. Afghan Authority for the Coordination of Assistance. (2002). *The National Development Framework: A Summary*. Kabul. Available at http://www.kabul-reconstructions.net/images/ndf.pdf.

47. Islamic Republic of Afghanistan. (2002). *National development framework: Draft: Version 2*. Kabul: Islamic Republic of Afghanistan.

48. Center for Economic and Social Rights. (2002). *Human Rights and Reconstruction in Afghanistan*. Available at https://www.cesr.org/sites/default/files/Human_Rights_and_Reconstructions_in_Afghanistan.pdf.

49. *Ibid.*

50. Institute for the Study of War. (2007). Provincial Reconstruction Teams (PRTS). *Institute for the Study of War*. Available at https://www.understandingwar.org/provincial-reconstruction-teams-prts.

51. *Ibid.*

52. Special Inspector General for Afghanistan Reconstruction. (2021). *What We Need to Learn: Lessons from Twenty Years of Afghanistan Reconstruction*. Available at https://www.sigar.mil/pdf/lessonslearned/SIGAR-21-46-LL.pdf.

53. L. Abirafeh. (2004, October). Burqa politics: The plights of women in Afghanistan. *Chronogram*, http://www.chronogram.com/issue/2004/10/news/burqa.php.

54. Islamic Republic of Afghanistan. (2004). *Securing Afghanistan's future: Accomplishments and the strategic path forward*. Kabul: A Government/International Agency Report: Islamic Republic of Afghanistan, Asian Development Bank, United Nations Assistance Mission to Afghanistan, United Nations Development Program, The World Bank Group. Available at https://reliefweb.int/sites/reliefweb.int/files/resources/7E32C513FD03CA1349256E6900208A3F-govafg-afg-17mar.pdf.

55. *Ibid.*

56. This statement is problematic as women were in fact harassed at the Loya Jirga.

57. A. Beath, F. Christia, and R. Enikolopov. (2015). The National Solidarity Programme: Assessing the Effects of Community-Driven Development in Afghanistan. *International Peacekeeping* 22(4), 302–320.

58. *Ibid.*

59. *Ibid.*, 302.

60. *Ibid.*, 303.

61. *Ibid.*

62. S. Azarbaijani-Moghaddam. (2021). *A Study of Gender Equity Through the*

National Solidarity Programme's Community Development Councils. Kabul: Danish Committee for Aid to Afghan Refugees (DACAAR).

63. *Ibid.*

64. *Ibid.*

65. *Ibid.*

66. A. Beath, F. Christia, and R. Enikolopov. (2015). The National Solidarity Programme: Assessing the Effects of Community-Driven Development in Afghanistan. *International Peacekeeping* 22(4), 302–320.

67. *Ibid.*

68. *Ibid.*, 315.

69. Australian Government Department of Foreign Affairs and Trade. (2017). *Independent Review of the World Bank's Afghanistan Reconstruction Trust Fund (ARTF) 2017.* Available at https://www.dfat.gov.au/about-us/publications/Pages/afghanistan-reconstruction-trust-fund-review.

70. S.G. Jones. (2006). Averting failure in Afghanistan. *Survival* 48, 111–128.

71. CARE International in Afghanistan: Policy brief. (2003). Kabul, CARE International.

72. Prices adjusted for comparison. M. O'Hanlan. (2001). *The Aid and Reconstruction Agenda for Afghanistan.* Brookings. Available at https://www.brookings.edu/research/the-aid-and-reconstruction-agenda-for-afghanistan/.

73. C. Robichaud. (2006). Remember Afghanistan? A glass half full, on the *Titanic. World Policy Journal* 23(1), 17.

74. *Ibid.*

75. CARE International in Afghanistan: Policy brief. (2003). Kabul, CARE International, 4.

76. S. Gollob and M. O'Hanlon. (2020). *Afghanistan Index: Tracking variables of reconstruction and security in post-9/11 Afghanistan.* Brookings Institute. Available at https://www.brookings.edu/wp-content/uploads/2020/08/FP_20200825_afganistan_index.pdf.

77. *Ibid.*

78. *Ibid.*

79. *Ibid.*

80. For more information, see http://www.oneworld.net and http://democracyinaction.org.

81. Afghan Women, Security and Freedom Act of 2004. (2004). *Congress.gov.* Available at https://www.congress.gov/bill/108th-congress/house-bill/4117/text?r=60&s=1.

82. For more information, see www.boxer.senate.gov.

83. Afghan Women, Security and Freedom Act of 2004 (2004). *Congress.gov.* Available at https://www.congress.gov/bill/108th-congress/house-bill/4117/text?r=60&s=1.

84. Initiated in 2007, adopted in 2008.

85. "NAPWA Final Assessment." Ministry of Women's Affairs (MoWA). 2018. Available: https://mowa.gov.af/sites/default/files/2019–08/NAPWA%20Assessment%20Final%20and%20Approved.pdf.

86. *PBS NewsHour.* (2021). A Historical Timeline of Afghanistan. Available at https://www.pbs.org/newshour/politics/asia-jan-june11-timeline-afghanistan.

87. B. Jones. (2010). The Afghanistan Donor Conference: Timetables and Theatrics in Kabul. *Brookings Institute.* Available at https://www.brookings.edu/blog/up-front/2010/07/20/the-afghanistan-donor-conference-timetables-and-theatrics-in-kabul/.

88. C. Whitlock. (2019). At War with the Truth. *Washington Post.* Available at https://www.washingtonpost.com/graphics/2019/investigations/afghanistan-papers/afghanistan-war-confidential-documents/.

89. Women's International League for Peace & Freedom. (2010). Afghanistan-2010 Commitments—1325 National Action Plans. *1325 National Action Plans (NAPs).* Available at http://1325naps.peacewomen.org/index.php/2010-committments/afghanistam-2010-commitments/.

90. *Ibid.*

91. International Crisis Group. (2013). *Women and Conflict in Afghanistan.* International Crisis Group. Available at https://www.crisisgroup.org/asia/south-asia/afghanistan/women-and-conflict-afghanistan.

92. R. Nordland. (2018). U.S. Aid Program Vowed to Help 75,000 Afghan Women. Watchdog Says It's a Flop. *New York Times.* Available at https://www.nytimes.com/2018/09/13/world/asia/afghanistan-women-usaid.html.

93. *Ibid.*

94. USAID. (2021). Promote. *USAID* Available at https://www.usaid.gov/afghanistan/promote.

95. Special Inspector General for Afghanistan Reconstruction. (2016b). *Quarterly Report to the United States Congress.* Available at https://www.sigar.mil/pdf/quarterlyreports/2016-10-30qr.pdf.

96. C. Whitlock. (2019). At War with the Truth. *Washington Post.* Available at https://www.washingtonpost.com/graphics/2019/investigations/afghanistan-papers/afghanistan-war-confidential-documents/.

97. *Ibid.*

98. *Ibid.*

99. R. Nordland. (2018). U.S. Aid Program Vowed to Help 75,000 Afghan Women. Watchdog Says It's a Flop. *New York Times.* Available at https://www.nytimes.com/2018/09/13/world/asia/afghanistan-women-usaid.html.

100. *Ibid.*

101. Women's International League for Peace & Freedom. (2015). Afghanistan-2015 Commitments—1325 National Action Plans. Women's International League for Peace & Freedom. Available at http://1325naps.peacewomen.org/index.php/2015-committments/afghanistan-2015-committments/.

102. Australian Government Department of Foreign Affairs and Trade (2017). *Independent Review of the World Bank's Afghanistan Reconstruction Trust Fund (ARTF) 2017.* Available at https://www.dfat.gov.au/sites/default/files/afghanistan-reconstruction-trust-fund-review.pdf.

103. United Nations. (2011). Security Council Presidential Statement Welcomes Bonn Declaration of "Transition Process," "Transformation Decade" for Afghanistan. *Un.org.* Available at https://www.un.org/press/en/2011/sc10494.doc.htm.

104. PBS NewsHour. (2021). A Historical Timeline of Afghanistan. *PBS.* Available at https://www.pbs.org/newshour/politics/asia-jan-june11-timeline-afghanistan.

105. *Ibid.*

106. Special Inspector General for Afghanistan Reconstruction. (2021). *What We Need to Learn: Lessons from Twenty Years of Afghanistan Reconstruction.* Virginia: SIGAR. Available at https://www.sigar.mil/pdf/lessonslearned/SIGAR-21-46-LL.pdf.

107. REACH. (2018). *Hard to Reach Assessment.* Available at https://reliefweb.int/sites/reliefweb.int/files/resources/reach_afg_report_hard_to_reach_assessment_june_2018_0.pdf.

108. Advanced Training Program on Humanitarian Action (ATHA). (2018). *Fragile Future: The Human Cost of Conflict in Afghanistan.* Humanitarian Action at the Frontlines: Field Analysis Series. Available at https://reliefweb.int/sites/reliefweb.int/files/resources/SSRN-id3291982.pdf.

109. Women's International League for Peace & Freedom (2019). Afghanistan-2019 Commitments—1325 National Action Plans. Women's International League for Peace & Freedom. Available at http://1325naps.peacewomen.org/index.php/afghanistan-2019-commitments/.

110. Foreign Assistance. (2020). *Country File: Afghanistan.* Available at https://foreignassistance.gov./.

111. Women's International League for Peace and Freedom. (2020). *Women, Peace and Security in Afghanistan.* Kabul. Available at https://www.wilpf.org/wp-content/uploads/2020/02/Submission_Afghanistan_CEDAW_Feb2020.pdf.

112. Global Affairs Canada. (2020). *Evaluation of International Assistance Programming in Afghanistan Final Report—June 2020 2014/15 to 2019/20.* Available at https://www.oecd.org/derec/canada/afghanistan-evaluation-report.pdf.

113. *Ibid.*

114. *Ibid.*

115. A. McGrail. (2021). Facts on Foreign Aid Efforts in Afghanistan. *The Borgen Project.* Available at https://borgenproject.org/foreign-aid-efforts-in-afghanistan/.

116. A. Rappeport. (2021). Afghanistan Faces Economic Shock as Sanctions Replace Foreign Aid. *New York Times.* Available at https://www.nytimes.com/2021/08/21/business/afghanistan-economy.html.

117. A. McGrail. (2021). Facts on Foreign Aid Efforts in Afghanistan. *The Borgen Project.* Available at https://borgenproject.org/foreign-aid-efforts-in-afghanistan/.

118. Special Inspector General for Afghanistan Reconstruction. (2020). *Support for Gender Equality: Lessons from the U.S. Experience in Afghanistan.* Virginia: SIGAR. Available at https://www.sigar.mil/pdf/lessonslearned/SIGAR-21-18-LL.pdf.

119. The World Bank. (2012). Afghanistan in Transition: Looking Beyond 2014. *The World Bank.* Available at https://www.worldbank.org/en/news/feature/2012/05/09/afghanistan-in-transition-looking-beyond-2014.

120. A. Zahedi. (2014). Afghan Women's Hopes for the Future. *E-International Relations*. Available at https://www.e-ir.info/2014/03/23/afghan-womens-hopes-for-the-future/.

121. *Ibid.*

122. *Ibid.*

123. Sippi Azarbaijani-Moghaddam has worked in Afghanistan since 1995 with civil society, government, donor and military institutions, addressing issues from gender and social exclusion to land reform.

124. S. Azarbaijani-Moghaddam. (2021). Progress was always fitful. Many Afghan women felt unsafe before the Taliban's arrival. *The Guardian*. Available at https://www.theguardian.com/commentisfree/2021/aug/22/p-was-always-fitful-many-afghan-women-felt-unsafe-before-the-talibans-arrival.

125. Afghanistan Public Policy Research Organization. (2017). *Gender Programming in Afghanistan: Critical Analysis of National Action Plans on Women, Peace and Security*. Kabul: APPRO. Available at https://tile.loc.gov/storage-services/service/gdc/gdcovop/2018306331/2018306331.pdf.

126. Localization is one of the nine work streams that emerged from the Grand Bargain of the 2016 World Humanitarian Summit in Istanbul with the goal of improving responsiveness and accountability to humanitarian action.

127. UN Women. (2019). Technical Guidance Note: Gender and the Localization Agenda. *Gblocalisation.ifrc.org*. Available at https://gblocalisation.ifrc.org/wp-content/uploads/2019/08/13082019-FV-UN-Women-Guidance-Note-Summary-Localisation.pdf.

128. Human Rights Watch. (2006). *Lessons in terror: Attacks on education in Afghanistan*. Kabul: Human Rights Watch, 9–10.

129. Congressional Research Service. (2021). *Afghan Women and Girls: Status and Congressional Action*. Available at https://crsreports.congress.gov/product/pdf/IF/IF11646.

130. *Ibid.*

131. C. Whitlock. (2019). At War with the Truth. *Washington Post*. Available at https://www.washingtonpost.com/graphics/2019/investigations/afghanistan-papers/afghanistan-war-confidential-documents/.

132. S. Azarbaijani-Moghaddam. (2004). Afghan women on the margins of the twenty-first century. In A. Donini, N. Niland, and K. Wermester (Eds.). *Nationbuilding unraveled? Aid, peace and justice in Afghanistan*. Bloomfield, CT: Kumarian Press, 101.

133. *Ibid.* p. 104.

134. D. Mosse. (2005). *Cultivating development: An ethnography of aid policy and practice*. London: Pluto Press, 91.

135. J. Stamm. (2009). Poultry Project Empowers Afghan Women. *DVIDS*. Available at https://www.dvidshub.net/news/37788/poultry-project-empowers-afghan-women.

136. U.S. Department of Defense. (2006). Afghanistan: Five Years Later. *Archive.defense.gov*. Available at https://archive.defense.gov/home/dodupdate/For-the-record/documents/afghanfactsheet20061019.pdf.

137. Watkins explains that "only poorer classes, usually Hazaras, ever permitted their women to work as maids, so servants were and to a large extent still are males," thus it is not even appropriate for most Afghan women to work in houses. For more information, see M.B. Watkins. (1963). *Afghanistan: Land in transition*. Princeton: D. Van Nostrand Co.

138. Women's International League for Peace & Freedom. (2010). Afghanistan-2010 Commitments—1325 National Action Plans. *1325 National Action Plans (NAPs)*. Available at http://1325naps.peacewomen.org/index.php/2010-committments/afghanistan-2010-commitments/.

139. *Ibid.*

140. Women's International League for Peace & Freedom. (2015). Afghanistan-2015 Commitments—1325 National Action Plans. Women's International League for Peace & Freedom. Available at http://1325naps.peacewomen.org/index.php/2015-committments/afghanistan-2015-committments/.

141. B. Francis. (2018). *The Local Level Implementation of Afghanistan's National Action Plan on UNSCR 1325—Women, Peace and Security*. International Alert. Available at https://www.international-alert.org/sites/default/files/Afghanistan_NationalActionPlanUNSCR1325_EN_2018.pdf.

142. Women's International League for

Peace and Freedom. (2020). *Women, Peace and Security in Afghanistan*. p. 2. Kabul. Available at https://www.wilpf.org/wp-content/uploads/2020/02/Submission_Afghanistan_CEDAW_Feb2020.pdf.

143. D. Dijkzeul and D. Salomons. (2021). *International Organizations Revisited: Agency and Pathology in a Multipolar World*. Berghahn Books.

144. *Ibid.*

145. B. Francis. (2018). *The Local Level Implementation of Afghanistan's National Action Plan on UNSCR 1325—Women, Peace and Security*. International Alert. Available at https://www.international-alert.org/sites/default/files/Afghanistan_NationalActionPlanUNSCR1325_EN_2018.pdf.

146. D. Dijkzeul and D. Salomons. (2021). *International Organizations Revisited: Agency and Pathology in a Multipolar World*. Berghahn Books.

147. *Ibid.*

148. B. Francis. (2018). *The Local Level Implementation of Afghanistan's National Action Plan on UNSCR 1325—Women, Peace and Security*. International Alert. Available at https://www.international-alert.org/sites/default/files/Afghanistan_NationalActionPlanUNSCR1325_EN_2018.pdf.

149. Women's International League for Peace and Freedom. (2020). *Women, Peace and Security in Afghanistan*. p. 2. Kabul. Available at https://www.wilpf.org/wp-content/uploads/2020/02/Submission_Afghanistan_CEDAW_Feb2020.pdf.

150. Stockholm International Peace Research Institute (SIPRI). (2021). *Trends in International Arms Transfers, 2020*. Available at https://sipri.org/sites/default/files/2021–03/fs_2103_at_2020.pdf.

151. B. Francis. (2018). *The Local Level Implementation of Afghanistan's National Action Plan on UNSCR 1325—Women, Peace and Security*. International Alert. Available at https://www.international-alert.org/sites/default/files/Afghanistan_NationalActionPlanUNSCR1325_EN_2018.pdf.

152. *Ibid.*

153. W. Frogh. (2017). *Afghanistan's National Action Plan: "A Wish List of Many Dreams."* LSE Centre for Women Peace and Security. Available at http://eprints.lse.ac.uk/104030/1/Frogh_afghanistans_national_action_plan_published.pdf.

154. *Ibid.*

155. *Ibid.*

156. Women's International League for Peace and Freedom. (2020). *Women, Peace and Security in Afghanistan*. p. 2. Kabul. Available at https://www.wilpf.org/wp-content/uploads/2020/02/Submission_Afghanistan_CEDAW_Feb2020.pdf.

157. Transparency International. (2021). What Is Corruption? *Transparency.org*. Available at https://www.transparency.org/en/what-is-corruption.

158. Special Inspector General for Afghanistan Reconstruction. (2016). Corruption in Conflict. *Sigar.mil*. Available at https://www.sigar.mil/interactive-reports/corruption-in-conflict/part1.html.

159. S. Gollob and M. O'Hanlon. (2020). *Afghanistan Index: Tracking Variables of Reconstruction and Security in Post-9/11 Afghanistan*. Brookings. Available at https://www.brookings.edu/wp-content/uploads/2020/08/FP_20200825_afganistan_index.pdf.

160. Transparency International. (2020). Corruption Perceptions Index 2020. *Transparency.org*. Available at https://www.transparency.org/en/cpi/2020/index/afg.

161. S. Gollob and M. O'Hanlon. (2020). *Afghanistan Index: Tracking Variables of Reconstruction and Security in Post-9/11 Afghanistan*. Brookings. Available at https://www.brookings.edu/wp-content/uploads/2020/08/FP_20200825_afganistan_index.pdf.

162. S. Barakat. (2020). A peace deal alone cannot solve Afghanistan's myriad problems. *Aljazeera*. Available at https://www.aljazeera.com/opinions/2020/11/6/a-peace-deal-alone-cannot-solve-afghanistans-myriad-problems/.

163. C. Whitlock. (2019). Consumed by Corruption. *Washington Post*. Available at https://www.washingtonpost.com/graphics/2019/investigations/afghanistan-papers/afghanistan-war-corruption-government/.

164. C. Wilkie. (2021). "9/11 Millionaires" and Mass Corruption: How American Money Helped Break Afghanistan. *CNBC*. Available at https://www.cnbc.com/2021/09/10/9/11-millionaires-and-how-us-money-helped-break-afghanistan.html.

165. C. Whitlock. (2019). Consumed by Corruption. *Washington Post*. Available

at https://www.washingtonpost.com/graphics/2019/investigations/afghanistan-papers/afghanistan-war-corruption-government/.

166. F. Nawa. (2011). *Opium Nation: Child Brides, Drug Lords, and One Woman's Journey Through Afghanistan*. New York: HarperCollins.

167. *Frontline*. (2012). *Opium Brides*. [Video]. Transcript available at https://www.pbs.org/wgbh/frontline/film/opium-brides/transcript/.

168. *Ibid.*

169. M. Hoonsuwan. (2012). Afghanistan's Opium Child Brides. *The Atlantic*. Available at https://www.theatlantic.com/international/archive/2012/02/afghanistans-opium-child-brides/252638/.

170. USAID. (2019). Incentives Driving Economic Alternatives for the North, East and West (IDEA-NEW). *Usaid.gov*. Available at https://www.usaid.gov/news-information/fact-sheets/incentives-driving-economic-alternatives-north-east-and-west-idea-new.

171. *Ibid.*

172. United Nations Office on Drugs and Crime. (2019). *Afghanistan Opium Survey 2019*. Kabul. Available at https://www.drugsandalcohol.ie/33801/1/Afganistan_opium_report_2021.pdf.

173. M. Hoonsuwan. (2012). Afghanistan's Opium Child Brides. *The Atlantic*. Available at https://www.theatlantic.com/international/archive/2012/02/afghanistans-opium-child-brides/252638/.

174. C. Wilkie. (2021). "9/11 Millionaires" and Mass Corruption: How American Money Helped Break Afghanistan. *CNBC*. Available at https://www.cnbc.com/2021/09/10/9/11-millionaires-and-corruption-how-us-money-helped-break-afghanistan.html.

175. *Ibid.*

176. *Ibid.*

177. Special Inspector General for Afghanistan Reconstruction (2021). *What We Need to Learn: Lessons from Twenty Years of Afghanistan Reconstruction*. Available at https://www.sigar.mil/pdf/lessonslearned/SIGAR-21-46-LL.pdf.

178. S. Samar. (2013). Corruption Is a Brutal Enemy of Afghan Women. *Thomson Reuters Foundation*. Available at https://news.trust.org/item/20130502130716-v16ht/?source=hpblogs.

179. A. Habershon. (2021). Gender and Corruption: The Time Is Now. *World Bank Blogs*. Available at https://blogs.worldbank.org/governance/gender-and-corruption-time-now.

180. A. Fuentes Téllez. (2021). The Link Between Corruption and Gender Inequality: A Heavy Burden for Development and Democracy. *Wilson Center*. Available at https://www.wilsoncenter.org/publication/the-link-between-corruption-and-gender-inequality-heavy-burden-for-development-and.

181. *Ibid.*

182. BBC News. (2021). *Afghanistan: World Bank halts aid after Taliban takeover*. Available at https://www.bbc.com/news/business-58325545.

183. A. Rappeport. (2021). Afghanistan Faces Economic Shock as Sanctions Replace Foreign Aid. *New York Times*. Available at https://www.nytimes.com/2021/08/21/business/afghanistan-economy.html.

184. Letter addressed to the President of the United Nations Security Council. (2011). Available at https://www.undocs.org/pdf?symbol=en/S/2021/486.

185. K. Watkins. (2021). The Taliban are not the only threat to Afghanistan. Aid cuts could undo 20 years of progress. *The Guardian*. Available: https://www.theguardian.com/global-development/2021/sep/11/the-taliban-are-not-the-only-threat-to-afghanistan-aid-cuts-could-undo-20-years-of-progress.

186. United Nations Office for the Coordination of Humanitarian Affairs. (2021). *Daily Noon Briefing Highlights: Afghanistan—Syria*. Available at https://www.unocha.org/story/daily-noon-briefing-highlights-afghanistan-syria.

187. Congressional Research Service. (2021). *Afghan Women and Girls: Status and Congressional Action*. Available at https://crsreports.congress.gov/product/pdf/IF/IF11646.

188. Heather Barr in J. Brinkely. (2012). Afghanistan: How Not to Give Aid. *POLITICO*. Available at https://www.politico.com/story/2012/07/afghanistan-example-of-how-not-to-give-aid-079000.

189. Special Inspector General for Afghanistan Reconstruction (2021). *What We Need to Learn: Lessons from Twenty Years of Afghanistan Reconstruction*. Available at https://www.sigar.mil/pdf/lessonslearned/SIGAR-21-46-LL.pdf.

190. *Ibid.*

191. *Ibid.*

192. *Ibid.*

193. UCLA Asia Pacific Center. (2021). *Afghanistan: An Evolving Situation.* [Webinar] Available at https://www.international. ucla.edu/apc/event/15193.

194. A. Merelli. (2021). Don't Pity the Women of Afghanistan, Support Them. *Quartz.* Available at https://qz.com/2048632/women-in-afghanistan-need-your-help-not-pity/.

195. *Ibid.*

196. The Astraea Foundation. (2021). Feminist Funding Principles. *Astraea foundation.org.* Available at https://astraea foundation.org/microsites/feminist-funding-principles/.

197. L. AbiRafeh. (2021). Opinion: For Afghan Women, the U.S. Rhetoric of Liberation Has Fallen Short. *CNN.* Available at https://edition.cnn.com/2021/06/16/opinions/afghan-women-us-liberation-promise-abirafeh/index.html.

CHAPTER 5

1. E. Rostami-Povey. (2007a). *Afghan women: Identity and Invasion.* London: Zed Books, 138.

2. C. Johnson and J. Leslie. (2004). *Afghanistan: The mirage of peace.* London: Zed Books.

3. *Ibid.,* 63.

4. United Nations. (2021). *Global Issues: Democracy.* United Nations. Available at https://www.un.org/en/global-issues/democracy.

5. Women and Children Legal Research Foundation. (2004). *Impact of traditional practices on women.* Kabul: Afghan Women Leaders Connect, 60.

6. R.H. Magnus and E. Naby. (1998). *Afghanistan: Mullah, Marx, and Mujahid.* Boulder: Westview Press, 22–23.

7. A. Wieland-Karimi. (2005). *Afghanistan: Looking back on 2004, looking forward to 2005.* Kabul: Friedrich-Ebert-Stiftung, 6.

8. H. Ahmed-Ghosh. (2003). A History of Women in Afghanistan: Lessons Learnt for the Future or Yesterdays and Tomorrow. *Journal of International Women's Studies* 4(3), 1–14. Available at https://vc.bridgew. edu/jiws/vol4/iss3/1/.

9. Mohammed Daud Khan served as president of Afghanistan from 1973 to 1978.

10. H. Ahmed-Ghosh. (2003). A History of Women in Afghanistan: Lessons Learnt for the Future or Yesterdays and Tomorrow. *Journal of International Women's Studies* 4(3), 1–14. Available at https://vc.bridgew. edu/jiws/vol4/iss3/1/.

11. *Ibid.*

12. *Ibid.*

13. Defense Committee for Malai Joya. (2007). *The Brave and Historical Speech of Malai Joya in the LJ* [Video]. YouTube. https://www.youtube.com/watch?v= iLC1KBrwbck.

14. T. Coghlan. (2006). Afghan MP Says She Will Not Be Silenced. *BBC News South Asia.* Available at http://news.bbc.co.uk/2/hi/south_asia/4606174.stm.

15. L. Grenfell. (2004). The Participation of Afghan Women in the Reconstruction Process. *Human Rights Brief* 12(1), 22–25.

16. *Ibid.*

17. Gender Quotas Database. (2021). *International IDEA.* Available at https://www.idea.int/data-tools/data/gender-quotas/country-view/44/35.

18. M. Ibrahim and R Mussarat. (2014). Women Participation in Politics: A Case Study of Afghan Women. *Journal of Public Administration and Governance.* 4(3), 433–447.

19. C. Charney, R. Nanda, and N. Yakatan. (2004). *Voter Education Planning Survey: Afghanistan 2004 National Elections.* Kabul: The Asia Foundation. Available at https://www.charneyresearch.com/wp-content/uploads/2014/03/Voter-Education-Planning-Survey-Afghanistan-2004-National-Elections-.pdf.

20. Human Rights Watch. (2004). *Afghanistan: Between Hope and Fear: IV. Obstacles to Women's Participation in the Presidential Election.* www.hrw.org. Available at https://www.hrw.org/legacy/backgrounder/asia/afghanistan1004/4.htm#_Toc84582646.

21. L. Abirafeh. (2004, October). Burqa politics: The plights of women in Afghanistan. *Chronogram.* Available at http://www.chronogram.com/issue/2004/10/news/burqa.php.

22. Consortium on Gender, Security & Human Rights. (2021). Frontrunner: The Afghan Woman Who Surprised the World. Available at https://genderandsecurity.org/projects-resources/filmography/frontrunner-afghan-woman-who-surprised-world.

23. A. Ferris-Rotman. (2017). Sima Wali Obituary. *The Guardian.* Available at https://www.theguardian.com/world/2017/nov/05/sima-wali-obituary.

24. M.E. Greenberg and E. Zuckerman. (2006). *The gender dimensions of post-conflict reconstruction: The challenges of development aid.* Helsinki: UNU-WIDER, 3.

25. T. Bouta, G. Frerks and I. Bannon. (2005). Gender, conflict, and development. Washington, D.C.: International Bank for Reconstruction and Development, 131–132.

26. C. Johnson and J. Leslie. (2004). *Afghanistan: The mirage of peace.* London: Zed Books.

27. United Nations Development Programme. (2004). *Electoral Systems and Processes: Practice Note.* Available at http://aceproject.org/ero-en/misc/undp-electoral-systems-and-processes-practice-note, 9.

28. Human Rights Watch. (2004). *Between Hope and Fear Intimidation and Attacks against Women in Public Life in Afghanistan.* www.hrw.org. Available at https://www.hrw.org/legacy/backgrounder/asia/afghanistan1004/index.htm.

29. C. Johnson and J. Leslie. (2004). *Afghanistan: The mirage of peace.* London: Zed Books, 174.

30. A.B. Saeed. (2005). *Dangers of running for office in Afghanistan.* Kabul: Institute for War and Peace Reporting.

31. Afghan Independent Human Rights Commission–United Nations Assistance Mission in Afghanistan. (2005a). *Joint verification of political rights, first report, 19 April–3 June 2005.* Kabul: Afghan Independent Human Rights Commission.

32. Afghan Independent Human Rights Commission–United Nations Assistance Mission in Afghanistan. (2005b). *Joint verification of political rights, second report, 4 June–16 August 2005.* Kabul: Afghan Independent Human Rights Commission.

33. Sharia is the Islamic code of law, based on the Koran.

34. Afghan Independent Human Rights Commission–United Nations Assistance Mission in Afghanistan. (2005c). *Joint verification of political rights, third report, 17 August–13 September 2005.* Kabul: Afghan Independent Human Rights Commission.

35. Human Rights Watch. (2005). *Cam-paigning against fear: Women's participation in Afghanistan's 2005 elections.* New York: Human Rights Watch, 15.

36. E. Rubin. (2005). Women's work. *New York Times Magazine,* 6.

37. J.G. Swank, Jr. (2005). Success for females in Afghanistan. Canada Free Press, http://www.canadafreepress.com/2005/swank090205.htm.

38. Women and Children Legal Research Foundation. (2005). *Report on women political participation in Afghanistan.* Kabul: Open Society Institute, 52.

39. T. Coghlan. (2005). Election hopes of Afghan women. *BBC News.* Qalat.

40. *Ibid.*

41. S. Biswas. (2005). Campaign climax in Afghanistan. *BBC News.* Kabul.

42. A. Wilder. (2005). *A house divided? Analysing the 2005 Afghan elections.* Kabul: Afghanistan Research and Evaluation Unit, 35.

43. L. Dupree. (1980). *Afghanistan* (3rd ed.). Princeton: Princeton University Press, 587.

44. Human Rights Watch. (2006). *Lessons in terror: Attacks on education in Afghanistan.* Kabul: Human Rights Watch, 14.

45. L.S. Noory. (2006). Where have all the women gone? *The Examiner.* Retrieved 23 June 2006, from http://www.examiner.com/a-158037~Lida_Sahar_Noory__Where_have_all_the_women_gone_.html.

46. Communication from distribution list to select members, 28 March 2006.

47. Human Rights Watch. (2009). "Afghanistan: Law Curbing Women's Rights Takes Effect." Available at https://www.hrw.org/news/2009/08/13/afghanistan-law-curbing-womens-rights-takes-effect.

48. *Ibid.*

49. M. Schramm. (2019). Do Quotas Actually Help Women in Politics? *Georgetown Institute of Women Peace and Security.* Available at https://giwps.georgetown.edu/do-quotas-actually-help-women-in-politics/.

50. International Crisis Group. (2013). *Women and Conflict in Afghanistan.* International Crisis Group. Available at https://www.crisisgroup.org/asia/south-asia/afghanistan/women-and-conflict-afghanistan.

51. *Ibid.*

52. M. Jalal. (2013). Karzai: A Legacy

of Failure on Afghan Women's Rights? *Opendemocracy*. Available at https://www. opendemocracy.net/en/5050/karzai-legacy-of-failure-on-afghan-womens-rights/.

53. A. Shaheed. (2019). Ghani Stresses Preserving Women's Rights in Peace Process. *Tolonews*. Available at https://tolonews.com/afghanistan/ghani-stresses-preserving-women%E2%80%99s-rights-peace-process.

54. S. Saif. (2020). Afghanistan Forms New Women's Council Ahead of Taliban Talks. *Reuters*. Available at https://www.reuters.com/article/us-afghanistan-taliban-women/afghanistan-forms-new-womens-council-ahead-of-taliban-talks-idUSKCN25A25D.

55. M. Alam. (2015). Equality for Afghan Women Remains a Critical Goal for President Ghani. *The World*. Available at https://www.pri.org/stories/equality-afghan-women-remains-critical-goal-president-ghani.

56. S. Azadmanesh and I. Ghafoori. (2020). *Women's Participation in the Afghan Peace Process: A Case Study*. Kabul: Afghan Research and Evaluation Unit. Available at https://reliefweb.int/sites/reliefweb.int/files/resources/2012E-Womens-Participation-in-the-Afghan-Peace-Process.pdf.

57. N. Coburn and M.H. Wafaey. (2019). *Violence against Women in Afghanistan's 2018 Parliamentary Elections*. Afghanistan Research and Evaluation Unit Organization. Available at https://areu.org.af/publication/violence-against-women-in-afghanistans-2018-parliamentary-elections/, 5.

58. *Ibid.*

59. Human Rights Watch. (2019). *Afghanistan: Events of 2018*. Human Rights Watch. Available at https://www.hrw.org/world-report/2019/country-chapters/afghanistan#.

60. Women's International League for Peace and Freedom. (2020). *Women, Peace and Security in Afghanistan*. Kabul. Available at https://www.wilpf.org/wp-content/uploads/2020/02/Submission_Afghanistan_CEDAW_Feb2020.pdf.

61. *Ibid.*

62. S. Saif. (2018). Voting for Landmark Afghan Parliament Polls Concludes. *Anadolu Agency*. Available at https://www.aa.com.tr/en/asia-pacific/voting-for-landmark-afghan-parliament-polls-concludes/1288710.

63. Women's International League for Peace and Freedom. (2020). *Women, Peace and Security in Afghanistan*. Kabul. Available at https://www.wilpf.org/wp-content/uploads/2020/02/Submission_Afghanistan_CEDAW_Feb2020.pdf.

64. Inter-Parliamentary Union. (2021). *Women in Politics: 2021*. Inter-Parliamentary Union. Available at https://www.ipu.org/women-in-politics-2021.

65. K. Fox. (2021). Afghanistan is now one of very few countries with no women in top government ranks. CNN. Available at https://edition.cnn.com/2021/09/09/asia/taliban-government-women-global-comparison-intl/index.html.

66. The World Bank. (2019). Proportion of Seats Held by Women in National Parliaments (%) *Data.worldbank.org*. Available at https://data.worldbank.org/indicator/SG.GEN.PARL.ZS?end=2019&name_desc=false&start=1997.

67. H. Bahesh and H. Subh. (2021). How Afghan Women Conquered a 27% Share in Parliament After Decades of War. *8Am Newspaper*. Available at https://8am.af/eng/how-afghan-women-conquered-a-27-share-in-parliament-after-decades-of-war/.

68. The World Bank. (2019). Proportion of Seats Held by Women in National Parliaments (%) *Data.worldbank.org*. Available at https://data.worldbank.org/indicator/SG.GEN.PARL.ZS?end=2019&name_desc=false&start=1997.

69. The World Bank. (2020). Proportion of Seats Held by Women in National Parliaments (%) *Data.worldbank.org*. Available at https://data.worldbank.org/indicator/SG.GEN.PARL.ZS?end=2020&name_desc=false&start=199.

70. Human Rights Watch. (2005). *Blood-Stained Hands Past Atrocities in Kabul and Afghanistan's Legacy of Impunity Human Rights Watch*. Available at https://www.hrw.org/reports/2005/afghanistan0605/afghanistan0605.pdf, 7.

71. V. Narain. (2021). *Women negotiators in Afghan/Taliban peace talks could spur global change*. The Conversation. Available at https://theconversation.com/women-negotiators-in-afghan-taliban-peace-talks-could-spur-global-change-159033.

72. S. Samar. (2019). Feminism, Peace,

and Afghanistan. *Journal of International Affairs*. Available at https://jia.sipa.columbia.edu/feminism-peace-and-afghanistan.

73. PeaceWomen. (2021). Resolution 1325 Is Not About Rescuing Women. *Peacewomen: Women's International League for Peace and Freedom*. Available at https://www.peacewomen.org/content/resolution-1325-not-about-rescuing-women-it-not-only-about-helping-wom.

74. Ministry of Foreign Affairs. (2015). *Afghanistan's National Action Plan on UNSCR 1325—Women, Peace and Security*. Kabul. Available at https://www.lse.ac.uk/women-peace-security/assets/documents/2019/NAP/NAPAfghanistan 2015.pdf.

75. *Ibid.*

76. B. Francis. (2018). *The local level implementation of Afghanistan's National Action Plan on UNSCR 1325—Women, peace and security*. International Alert. Available at https://www.internationalalert.org/sites/default/files/Afghanistan_NationalActionPlanUNSCR1325_EN_2018.pdf.

77. Ministry of Foreign Affairs. (2015). *Afghanistan's National Action Plan on UNSCR 1325—Women, Peace and Security*. Kabul. Available at https://www.lse.ac.uk/women-peace-security/assets/documents/2019/NAP/NAPAfghanistan 2015.pdf.

78. PeaceWomen. (2021). Afghanistan—1325 National Action Plans. *WILPF*. Available at http://1325naps.peacewomen.org/index.php/afghanistan/.

79. H. Malikyar. (2015). Women's Gains and a Taliban Peace Deal. *Aljazeera.com*. Available at https://www.aljazeera.com/opinions/2015/3/9/will-womens-gains-be-sold-out-in-taliban-peace-deal.

80. P. Hassan. (2010). *The Afghan Peace Jirga: Ensuring That Women Are at the Peace Table*. Washington, D.C.: United States Institute of Peace. https://www.usip.org/sites/default/files/PB%2029%20Afghan%20 Peace%20Jirga.pdf.

81. Ministry of Foreign Affairs. (2015). *Afghanistan's National Action Plan on UNSCR 1325—Women, Peace and Security*. Kabul. Available at https://www.lse.ac.uk/women-peace-security/assets/documents/2019/NAP/NAPAfghanistan 2015.pdf.

82. B. Francis. (2018). *The local level implementation of Afghanistan's National Action Plan on UNSCR 1325—Women, peace and security*. International Alert. Available at https://www.internationalalert.org/sites/default/files/Afghanistan_NationalActionPlanUNSCR1325_EN_2018.pdf.

83. S. Azadmanesh and I. Ghafoori. (2020). *Women's Participation in the Afghan Peace Process: A Case Study*. Kabul: Afghan Research and Evaluation Unit. Available at https://reliefweb.int/sites/reliefweb.int/files/resources/2012E-Womens-Participation-in-the-Afghan-Peace-Process.pdf.

84. Q. Ludin. (2019). *How Peace Was Made: An Inside Account of Talks Between the Afghan Government and Hezb-E Islami*. United States Institute of Peace. Available at https://www.usip.org/sites/default/files/2019-03/sr_444-how_peace_was_made_an_inside_account_of_talks_between_the_afghan_government_and_hezb-e_islami.pdf.

85. *Ibid.*

86. D. Steinberg. (2009). Beyond Victimhood: Protection and Participation of Women in the Pursuit of Peace. *Crisis Group*. Available at https://www.crisisgroup.org/global/beyond-victimhood-protection-and-participation-women-pursuit-peace.

87. M. Kelemen. (2019). U.S. Trying to Get the Taliban and Afghan Government to Start Negotiations. *NPR*. Available at https://www.npr.org/2019/07/12/741237631/u-s-trying-to-get-the-taliban-and-afghan-government-to-start-negotiations.

88. PeaceWomen. (2021). Afghanistan—1325 National Action Plans. *WILPF*. Available at http://1325naps.peacewomen.org/index.php/afghanistan/.

89. F. Faizi and D. Zucchino. (2019). "You Should Be in the Kitchen": At Afghan Assembly, Women Are Told They Don't Belong. *New York Times*. Available at https://www.nytimes.com/2019/05/03/world/asia/afghanistan-women-assembly-loya-jirga.html.

90. W. Frogh. (2019). *Women and the Afghan Peace Process: A Conversation with Wazhma Frogh*. Council on Foreign Relations. Available at https://www.cfr.org/blog/women-and-afghan-peace-process-conversation-wazhma-frogh.

91. International Civil Society Action Network. (2021). *Sanam Naraghi Anderlini Interview with WRHU-FM on the Situation in Afghanistan*. ICAN. Available at https://icanpeacework.org/2021/08/19/sanam-naraghi-anderlini-interview-wrhu-afghanistan/.

92. L. Halima-Ahmad. (2020). The U.S. and Taliban Are Partners Now: What About the Afghan Women? *International Peace Research Initiative*. Available at http://conflictreader.org/view_ipri_articles.php?ArticleNo=5&url=Afghanistan&record No=60.

93. H. Malikyar. (2015). Women's Gains and a Taliban Peace Deal. *Aljazeera.com*. Available at https://www.aljazeera.com/opinions/2015/3/9/will-womens-gains-be-sold-out-in-taliban-peace-deal.

94. *Ibid.*

95. State Ministry for Peace. (2019). *Peace Negotiation Team of the Islamic Republic of Afghanistan*. Available at https://smp.gov.af/en/peace-negotiation-team-islamic-republic-afghanistan.

96. S. Qazi. (2020). Who are the Afghan women negotiating peace with the Taliban? *Aljazeera*. Available at https://www.aljazeera.com/features/2020/10/7/who-are-the-afghan-women-negotiating-peace-with-taliban.

97. A.M. Makoii and M. Safi. (2021). "Terrible days ahead": Afghan women fear the return of the Taliban. *The Guardian*. Available at https://www.theguardian.com/world/2021/apr/14/afghan-women-fear-the-return-of-the-taliban.

98. Georgetown Institute for Women, Peace and Security. (2020). *An Open Letter from World Leaders Calling for Afghan Women's Meaningful Participation in the Peace Process*. Available at https://giwps.georgetown.edu/an-open-letter-from-world-leaders-calling-for-afghan-womens-meaningful-participation-in-the-peace-process/.

99. *Ibid.*

100. M. Rahmaty. (2021). "The Exclusion of Women's Voices from Afghan Peace Talks Remains the Norm." *IPI Global Observatory*. Available at https://theglobalobservatory.org/2021/03/exclusion-womens-voices-afghan-peace-talks-remains-norm/.

101. *Ibid.*

102. S. Qazi. (2020). Who are the Afghan women negotiating peace with the Taliban? *Aljazeera*. Available at https://www.aljazeera.com/features/2020/10/7/who-are-the-afghan-women-negotiating-peace-with-taliban.

103. United Nations Assistance Mission in Afghanistan. (2021). *Afghanistan Protection of Civilians in Armed Conflict Midyear Update: 1 January to 30 June 2021*. Available at https://unama.unmissions.org/sites/default/files/unama_poc_midyear_report_2021_26_july.pdf.

104. *The Guardian*. (2021). Afghan Peace Summit Includes Just One Female Delegate. *The Guardian*. Available at https://www.theguardian.com/world/2021/mar/18/afghan-activists-warn-over-absence-of-women-in-peace-process.

105. R. Kobia. (2021). [Twitter]. March 18 2021. Available at https://twitter.com/RolandKobia/status/1372515217268166658?s=20.

106. UNAMA. (2021). *Protection of Civilians in Armed Conflict Midyear Report*. Available at https://unama.unmissions.org/sites/default/files/unama_poc_midyear_report_2021_26_july.pdf.

107. R. Kumar and H. Noori. (2021). Shock as Two Female Afghan Supreme Court Judges Gunned Down in Kabul Ambush. *The National News*. Available at https://www.thenationalnews.com/world/asia/shock-as-two-female-afghan-supreme-court-judges-gunned-down-in-kabul-ambush-1.1147550.

108. S. Akbar. (2021a). Afghans are living in terror. That must change for peace. *Washington Post*. Available at https://www.washingtonpost.com/opinions/2021/02/26/afghans-are-living-terror-that-must-change-peace/.

109. My Red Line. (2021). *Press Release: MyRedLine Opposes AWN's Statement*. MyRedLine. Available at https://myredline.af/press-release-03/.

110. *Ibid.*

111. Islamic Republic of Afghanistan Central Statistics Organization. (2018). *Afghanistan Living Conditions Survey 2016–17*. Available at https://washdata.org/sites/default/files/documents/reports/2018–07/Afghanistan%20ALCS%202016–17%20Analysis%20report.pdf.

112. International Crisis Group. (2020). *What Will Peace Talks Bode for Afghan Women?* International Crisis Group. Avail-

able at https://www.crisisgroup.org/asia/south-asia/afghanistan/what-will-peace-talks-bode-afghan-women.

113. A. Jackson. (2018). *Life under the Taliban shadow government.* Overseas Development Institute. Available at https://cdn.odi.org/media/documents/12269.pdf.

114. International Civil Society Action Network. (2021). *Sanam Naraghi Anderlini Interview with WRHU-FM on the Situation in Afghanistan.* ICAN. Available at https://icanpeacework.org/2021/08/19/sanam-naraghi-anderlini-interview-wrhu-afghanistan/.

115. *Ibid.*

116. R. Manchanda. (2021). The Afghanistan Catastrophe Is a Moment of Reckoning for the "Women, Peace and Security" Agenda. *The Wire.* Available at https://thewire.in/south-asia/the-afghan-catastrophe-is-a-moment-of-reckoning-for-the-women-peace-and-security-agenda.

117. *Ibid.*

118. N. Jamshidi. (2021). The Freedom of Afghan Women Depends on Education and Empowerment. *Ms. Magazine.* Available at https://msmagazine.com/2021/07/07/afghanistan-troop-withdrawal-afghan-women-freedom-education/.

119. J. Abrahams. (2021). Towards a Real Feminist Foreign Policy. *Prospect Magazine.* Available at https://www.prospectmagazine.co.uk/world/towards-a-real-feminist-foreign-policy?mc_cid=693e3d4a93&mc_eid=399e3547f7.

120. *Ibid.*

121. *Ibid.*

122. Council on Foreign Relations. (2020). Including Women at the Peace Table Produces Better Outcomes. Available at https://www.cfr.org/womens-participation-in-peace-processes/.

123. S. Qazi. (2020). Who are the Afghan women negotiating peace with the Taliban? www.aljazeera.com. Available at https://www.aljazeera.com/features/2020/10/7/who-are-the-afghan-women-negotiating-peace-with-taliban.

124. S. Samar. (2019). Feminism, Peace, and Afghanistan. *Journal of International Affairs.* Available at https://jia.sipa.columbia.edu/feminism-peace-and-afghanistan.

125. L. AbiRafeh. (2020). "There Is No P and No S Without W…". *UN Peacekeeping.* Available at https://unpeacekeeping.

medium.com/there-is-no-p-and-no-s-without-w-6ce74e610a8d.

Chapter 6

1. M. Safa. (2005). Women, defense and security. *Deputy Minister for Technical and Policy Concerns.* Afghanistan: Ministry of Women's Affairs.

2. Intimate partner violence is violence (sexual, physical, emotional, economic) that takes place in the context of an intimate relationship, i.e., a former/current spouse or partner, who inflicts violence against the other spouse or partner.

3. M. Hussain Saramad and L. Sultani. (2013). *Violence Against Women in Afghanistan.* Kabul: Refworld. Available at https://www.refworld.org/pdfid/5297436c4.pdf.

4. United Nations Assistance Mission in Afghanistan and Office of the United Nations High Commissioner for Human Rights. (2009). *Silence Is Violence: End the Abuse of Women in Afghanistan.* Kabul. Available at https://www.ohchr.org/documents/press/vaw_report_7july09.pdf.

5. *Ibid.*

6. *Ibid.*

7. Human Rights Watch (2021). I Thought Our Life Might Get Better. *Human Rights Watch.* Available at https://www.hrw.org/report/2021/08/05/i-thought-our-life-might-get-better/implementing-afghanistans-elimination.

8. M. Hussain Saramad and L. Sultani. (2013). *Violence Against Women in Afghanistan.* Kabul: Refworld. Available at https://www.refworld.org/pdfid/5297436c4.pdf.

9. *Ibid.*

10. Women's Commission for Refugee Women and Children. (2005). *Masculinities: Male roles and male involvement in the promotion of gender equality.* New York: Women's Commission for Refugee Women and Children.

11. United Nations Assistance Mission in Afghanistan and Office of the United Nations High Commissioner for Human Rights. (2009). *Silence Is Violence: End the Abuse of Women in Afghanistan.* Kabul. Available at https://www.ohchr.org/documents/press/vaw_report_7july09.pdf.

12. Women's Commission for Refugee Women and Children. (2006). *Displaced women and girls at risk: Risk factors, protection solutions and resource tools.* New York:

Women's Commission for Refugee Women and Children, 16.

13. U. Narayan. (1997). *Dislocating cultures: Identities, traditions, and third world feminism.* New York: Routledge.

14. *Ibid.*

15. United Nations Security Council. (2002). *Report of the Secretary-General on Women, Peace and Security.* Available at https://undocs.org/S/2002/1154.

16. J. Barry. (2005). *Rising up in response: Women's rights activism in conflict.* Boulder, CO: Urgent Action Fund for Women's Human Rights, 70.

17. Institute for Economics and Peace. (2021). *Global Peace Index 2021.* Sydney. Available at https://www.visionofhumanity.org/wp-content/uploads/2021/06/GPI-2021-web-1.pdf.

18. *Ibid.*

19. C. Moser and C. McIlwaine. (2001). *Violence in a post-conflict context: Urban poor perceptions from Guatemala.* Washington, D.C.: The World Bank, 41.

20. United Nations Development Programme & Islamic Republic of Afghanistan. (2004). *Afghanistan national human development report 2004: Security with a human face: Challenges and responsibilities.* Kabul: United Nations Development Programme, 56.

21. IRIN (2004). Our bodies—Their battle ground: Gender-based violence in conflict zones. *IRIN web special.* From http://www.irinnews.org, 18.

22. S. Turner. (2000). Vindicating masculinity: The fate of promoting gender equality. *Forced Migration Review* (9), 8.

23. *Ibid.*

24. R. Perez. (2002). Practising theory through women's bodies: Public violence and women's strategies of power and place. In K. Saunders (Ed.). *Feminist post-development thought: Rethinking modernity, post-colonialism and representation.* London: Zed Books, 32.

25. E. Enarson. (2005). Women and girls last? Averting the second post–Katrina disaster. *Affilia: Journal of Women and Social Work* 22(1), 2.

26. Islamic Republic of Afghanistan. (2006). *Afghanistan national development strategy.* Kabul: Islamic Republic of Afghanistan.

27. M. Safa. (2005). Women, defense and security. *Deputy Minister for Technical and Policy Concerns.* Afghanistan: Ministry of Women's Affairs.

28. UN Human Rights Office of the High Commissioner (2015). *Statement by the Special Rapporteur on violence against women finalizes country mission to Afghanistan and calls for sustainable measures to address the causes and consequences of violence against women, including at the individual, institutional and structural level.* www.ohchr.org. Available at https://www.ohchr.org/EN/NewsEvents/Pages/DisplayNews.aspx?NewsID=15284&LangID=E.

29. United Nations. (2003). *The situation of women and girls in Afghanistan: Report of the secretary-general.* Commission on the Status of Women. New York: United Nations Economic and Social Council.

30. M. Jalal. (2005, June 27). *Accelerating national peace and reconstruction by safeguarding women's rights and security.* Afghanistan: Ministry of Women's Affairs.

31. C. Johnson and J. Leslie. (2004). *Afghanistan: The mirage of peace.* London: Zed Books, 23.

32. N.H. Dupree. (2004). The family during crisis in Afghanistan. *Journal of Comparative Family Studie* 32(2), 311–332.

33. Ministry of Women's Affairs. (2005). *Statistical compilation on gender issues in Afghanistan: Background study for a gender policy framework.* Kabul: Ministry of Women's Affairs, UNIFEM.

34. Amnesty International. (2005). Afghanistan: Women still under attack—A systematic failure to protect. Available at http://web.amnesty.org/library/print/ENGASA110072005.

35. Women's International League for Peace and Freedom. (2020). *Women, Peace and Security in Afghanistan: Submission to the UN Committee of the Elimination of Discrimination Against Women.* Kabul. Available at https://www.wilpf.org/wp-content/uploads/2020/02/Submission_Afghanistan_CEDAW_Feb2020.pdf.

36. *Ibid.*

37. RAWA, the Revolutionary Association of the Women of Afghanistan, is an oft-cited example of an Afghan feminist movement documenting such abuses.

38. Ministry of Women's Affairs. (2005). *Statistical compilation on gender issues in Afghanistan: Background study for a gender policy framework.* Kabul: Ministry of Women's Affairs, UNIFEM.

39. See www.rawa.org/temp/runews/2007/03/08/afghanistan-women-s-hopes-for-equality-fade.htm.

40. S. Samar. (2013). Corruption Is a Brutal Enemy of Afghan Women. *Thomson Reuters Foundation*. Available at https://news.trust.org/item/20130502130716-v16ht/?source=hpblogs.

41. Y. Erturk. (2005). Integration of the human rights of women and a gender perspective: Violence against women. New York: United Nations, 2.

42. Islamic Republic of Afghanistan and UNDP. (2005). *Millennium development goals: Islamic Republic of Afghanistan country report 2005: Vision 2020*. Kabul: Islamic Republic of Afghanistan and UNDP.

43. Amnesty International. (2005). Afghanistan: Women still under attack—A systematic failure to protect. Available at http://web.amnesty.org/library/print/ENGASA110072005.

44. C. Alexander. (2021). As the Taliban Return, a History of Afghan Women's Rights. *Washington Post*. Available at https://www.washingtonpost.com/enterprise/as-taliban-return-a-history-of-afghan-womens-rights/2021/09/13/593dd980-14a3-11ec-a019-cb193b28aa73_story.html.

45. F. Hayward. (2017). *Progress on gender equity in Afghan higher education*. University World News. Available at https://www.universityworldnews.com/post.php?story=20170111130351745.

46. P. Gossman and F. Abbasi. (2021). *Interview: Why Now Is the Time to Support Women's Rights in Afghanistan*. Human Rights Watch. Available at https://www.hrw.org/news/2021/08/05/interview-why-now-time-support-womens-rights-afghanistan#.

47. J. Allen and V. Felbab-Brown. (2020). The Fate of Women's Rights in Afghanistan. *Brookings*. Available at https://www.brookings.edu/essay/the-fate-of-womens-rights-in-afghanistan/.

48. P. Gossman and F. Abbasi. (2021). *Interview: Why Now Is the Time to Support Women's Rights in Afghanistan*. Human Rights Watch. Available at https://www.hrw.org/news/2021/08/05/interview-why-now-time-support-womens-rights-afghanistan#.

49. International Crisis Group (2013). *Women and Conflict in Afghanistan*. International Crisis Group. Available at https://www.crisisgroup.org/asia/south-asia/afghanistan/women-and-conflict-afghanistan.

50. Women's International League for Peace and Freedom. (2020). *Women, Peace and Security in Afghanistan: Submission to the UN Committee on the Elimination of Discrimination Against Women*. Kabul. Available at https://www.wilpf.org/wp-content/uploads/2020/02/Submission_Afghanistan_CEDAW_Feb2020.pdf.

51. J. Allen and V. Felbab-Brown. (2020). The Fate of Women's Rights in Afghanistan. *Brookings*. Available at https://www.brookings.edu/essay/the-fate-of-womens-rights-in-afghanistan/.

52. Human Rights Watch. (2021). I Thought Our Life Might Get Better. *Human Rights Watch*. Available at https://www.hrw.org/report/2021/08/05/i-thought-our-life-might-get-better/implementing-afghanistans-elimination.

53. United Nations Assistance Mission in Afghanistan. (2018). *Injustice and Impunity Mediation of Criminal Offences of Violence against Women*. Available at https://www.ohchr.org/Documents/Countries/AF/UNAMA_OHCHR_EVAW_Report2018_InjusticeImpunity29May2018.pdf.

54. Women's International League for Peace and Freedom. (2020). *Women, Peace and Security in Afghanistan: Submission to the UN Committee on the Elimination of Discrimination Against Women*. Kabul. Available at https://www.wilpf.org/wp-content/uploads/2020/02/Submission_Afghanistan_CEDAW_Feb2020.pdf.

55. Afghanistan Independent Human Rights Commission. (2018). *Summary of the Report on Violence Against Women: The causes, context, and situation of violence against women in Afghanistan*. Refworld. Available at https://www.refworld.org/docid/5ab132774.html.

56. Asia Foundation. (2018). *2018 Survey of Afghan People Shows Women's Rights are Complicated—The Asia Foundation*. Asia Foundation. Available at https://asiafoundation.org/2018/12/05/2018-survey-of-afghan-people-shows-womens-rights-are-complicated/.

57. *Ibid*.

58. Ministry of Economy. (2017). *HLPF—A2017 Voluntary National Review at the High Level Political Forum SDGs' Progress Report Afghanistan*. Available at

https://sustainabledevelopment.un.org/content/documents/16277Afghanistan.pdf.

59. Women's International League for Peace and Freedom. (2020). *Women, Peace and Security in Afghanistan: Submission to the UN Committee on the Elimination of Discrimination Against Women*. Kabul. Available at https://www.wilpf.org/wp-content/uploads/2020/02/Submission_Afghanistan_CEDAW_Feb2020.pdf.

60. Georgetown Institute for Women, Peace and Security. (2019). *Afghanistan's Performance on the Women, Peace, and Security Index*. Georgetown Institute of Women Peace and Security. Available at https://giwps.georgetown.edu/country/afghanistan/.

61. Asia Foundation. (2018). *2018 Survey of Afghan People Shows Women's Rights are Complicated—The Asia Foundation*. Asia Foundation. Available at https://asiafoundation.org/2018/12/05/2018-survey-of-afghan-people-shows-womens-rights-are-complicated/.

62. S.K. Saif. (2017). *Around 3,000 Afghans commit suicide every year*. www.aa.com.tr. Available at https://www.aa.com.tr/en/asia-pacific/around-3-000-afghans-commit-suicide-every-year/912627.

63. *Ibid.*

64. L. Bohn. (2018). *"We're All Handcuffed in This Country." Why Afghanistan Is Still the Worst Place in the World to Be a Woman*. Time Magazine. Available at https://time.com/5472411/afghanistan-women-justice-war/.

65. United Nations Assistance Mission in Afghanistan. (2018). *Injustice and Impunity Mediation of Criminal Offences of Violence against Women*. Available at https://www.ohchr.org/Documents/Countries/AF/UNAMA_OHCHR_EVAW_Report2018_InjusticeImpunity29May2018.pdf.

66. International Crisis Group. (2013). *Women and Conflict in Afghanistan*. International Crisis Group. Available at https://www.crisisgroup.org/asia/south-asia/afghanistan/women-and-conflict-afghanistan.

67. Women's International League for Peace & Freedom. (2010). *Afghanistan-2010 Commitments—1325 National Action Plans*. 1325 National Action Plans (NAPs). Available at http://1325naps.peacewomen.org/index.php/2010-committments/afghanistam-2010-commitments/.

68. M. Jardine. (2021). The world must evacuate women police in Afghanistan. *Lowy Institute*. Available at https://www.lowyinstitute.org/the-interpreter/world-must-evacuate-women-police-afghanistan #:~:text=In%20early%202021%2C%20women%20police.

69. United Nations Security Council. (2020). *Women and peace and security, Report of the Secretary-General*. Available at https://www.securitycouncilreport.org/atf/cf/%7B65BFCF9B-6D27-4E9C-8CD3-CF6E4FF96FF9%7D/s_2020_946.pdf.

70. United Nations Office of the Special Representative of the Secretary-General on Sexual Violence in Conflict. (2021). *Afghanistan*. Available at https://www.un.org/sexualviolenceinconflict/countries/afghanistan/.

71. Human Rights Watch. (2021a). *"I Thought Our Life Might Get Better."* Human Rights Watch. Available at https://www.hrw.org/report/2021/08/05/i-thought-our-life-might-get-better/implementing-afghanistans-elimination.

72. A. Pal. (2021). Taliban replaces women's ministry with ministry of virtue and vice. *Reuters*. 17 Sep. Available at https://www.reuters.com/world/asia-pacific/taliban-replaces-womens-ministry-with-ministry-virtue-vice-2021-09-17/.

73. R. Manchanda. (2021). The Afghanistan Catastrophe is a Moment of Reckoning for the "Women, Peace and Security" agenda. *The Wire*. Available at https://thewire.in/south-asia/the-afghan-catastrophe-is-a-moment-of-reckoning-for-the-women-peace-and-security-agenda.

74. United Nations Research Institute for Social Development. (2005). *Gender equality: Striving for justice in an unequal world*. Geneva: United Nations Research Institute for Social Development, 233.

75. S. Schutte. (2004). Urban vulnerability in Afghanistan: Case studies from three cities. *Working Paper Series*. Kabul: Afghanistan Research and Evaluation Unit, 23.

76. N.H. Dupree. (1996). *The women of Afghanistan*. Stockholm: Swedish Committee for Afghanistan, 6.

77. C. Jancke. (2021). *Living in a Taliban-controlled Afghanistan as an Afghan Female Aid Worker*. Global Interagency Security Forum. Available at https://gisf.ngo/blogs/living-in-a-taliban-controlled-afghanistan-as-an-afghan-female-aid-worker/.

78. This email was sent to a select distribution list, of which I am a member, on 6 May 2005.

79. *Daily Outlook: Afghanistan's Leading Independent Newspaper.* (2005, May 11). 53.

80. *Soundless Cries* by Nadia Anjuman was translated by Abdul S. Shayek and can be found at http://www.pulpmovies.com/gagwatch/2005/11/lethal-poetry/.

81. Sippi Azarbaijani-Moghaddam has worked in Afghanistan since 1995 with civil society, government, donor and military institutions, addressing issues from gender and social exclusion to land reform.

82. S. Azarbaijani-Moghaddam. (2021). Progress was always fitful. Many Afghan women felt unsafe before the Taliban's arrival. *The Guardian.* Available at https://www.theguardian.com/commentisfree/2021/aug/22/p-was-always-fitful-many-afghan-women-felt-unsafe-before-the-talibans-arrival.

83. *Ibid.*

84. *Ibid.*

85. F. Marofi. (2015). Farkhunda belongs to all of the women of Kabul, of Afghanistan *The Guardian.* Available at https://www.theguardian.com/global-development/2015/mar/28/farkhunda-women-kabul-afghanistan-mob-killing.

86. *Ibid.*

87. Associated Press in Kabul. (2015). Thousands march in Kabul demanding justice for woman killed by mob. *The Guardian.* Available at https://www.theguardian.com/world/2015/mar/24/farkhunda-thousands-march-in-kabul-demanding-justice-for-woman-killed-by-mob.

88. Reuters. (2021). U.S. considers visas for vulnerable Afghan women after military exit. *Reuters.* Available at https://www.reuters.com/world/us-considers-visas-vulnerable-afghan-women-after-military-exit-2021-07-08/.

CHAPTER 7

1. N. Long. (2000). Exploring local/global transformations: A view from anthropology. In N. Long and A. Acre (Eds.). *Anthropology, development and modernities: Exploring discourses, counter-tendencies and violence.* London: Routledge, 191.

2. D. Hilhorst. (2003). *The real world of NGOs: Discourses, diversity and development.* London: Zed Books.

3. N. Kabeer. (1994). *Reversed realities: Gender hierarchies in development thought.* London: Verso, 224.

4. A. Cornwall and K. Brock. (2005). Beyond Buzzwords: "Poverty reduction," "participation" and "empowerment" in development policy. Overarching Concerns Programme Paper Number 10. Geneva: United Nations Research Institute for Social Development, iii.

5. M. Molyneux and S. Lazar. (2003). *Doing the rights thing: Rights-based development and Latin American NGOs.* London: ITDG Publishing, 2.

6. V. Ware. (2006). *Info-war and the politics of feminist curiosity: Exploring new frameworks for feminist intercultural studies.* London: Gender Institute, London School of Economics.

7. J. Ferguson. (1994). *The anti-politics machine: "Development," depoliticization, and bureaucratic power in Lesotho.* Minneapolis: University of Minnesota Press, 281.

8. The Human Development Report explains that aid strategies for Afghanistan were presented to Afghans as a *fait accompli.* United Nations Development Programme & Islamic Republic of Afghanistan. (2004). *Afghanistan national human development report 2004: Security with a human face: Challenges and responsibilities.* Kabul: United Nations Development Programme.

9. D. Kandiyoti. (2005). The politics of gender and reconstruction in Afghanistan. *Occasional Paper.* Geneva: United Nations Research Institute for Social Development, vii.

10. F. Pickup, S. Williams, and C. Sweetman. (2001). *Ending violence against women: A challenge for development and humanitarian work.* Oxford: Oxfam Great Britain.

11. For example, in the 1980s, aid to Afghanistan was tied to Cold War alliances, and in the mid-1990s the agenda switched to promote peace. For more information, see C. Johnson and J. Leslie. (2004). *Afghanistan: The mirage of peace.* London: Zed Books.

12. I. Smillie and L. Minear. (2004). *The charity of nations: Humanitarian action in a calculating world.* Bloomfield: Kumarian Press, 102.

13. N.H. Dupree. (1990). A socio-cultural dimension: Afghan women refugees in Pakistan. In E.W. Anderson and N.H. Dupree. *The cultural basis of Afghan nationalism.* London: Pinter Publishers, 131.

14. S. Walby. (1997). *Gender transformations*. London: Routledge.

15. J. Ferguson. (1994). *The anti-politics machine: "Development," depoliticization, and bureaucratic power in Lesotho*. Minneapolis: University of Minnesota Press, 58.

16. C. Johnson and J. Leslie (2004). *Afghanistan: The mirage of peace*. London: Zed Books., 157.

17. The nickname for U.S. operations, "sex, drugs, and rock 'n' roll" referred to gender, poppy, and terrorism, as previously mentioned in Chapter 4.

18. R. Hassan. (2002). Muslim women's rights: A contemporary debate. In S. Mehta (Ed.). *Women for Afghan women: Shattering myths and claiming the future*. New York: Palgrave Macmillan, 137.

19. B. McCaffrey. (2006). *Academic report—Trip to Afghanistan and Pakistan*. New York: United States Military Academy, West Point.

20. For further information, see L. Abirafeh. (2005, November). From Afghanistan to Sudan: How peace risks marginalizing women. *Forced Migration Review* 24, 46–47.

21. D. Kandiyoti (Ed.). (1991). *Women, Islam and the state*. Philadelphia: Temple University Press.

22. This term was first coined by Edward Said. E.W. Said. (1979). *Orientalism*. New York: Vintage.

23. S. Mehta (Ed.). (2002). *Women for Afghan women: Shattering myths and claiming the future*. New York: Palgrave Macmillan. p. 142.

24. United Nations Development Programme & Islamic Republic of Afghanistan. (2004). *Afghanistan national human development report 2004: Security with a human face: Challenges and responsibilities*. Kabul: United Nations Development Programme, 218.

25. M. Weiner and A. Banuazizi (Eds.). (1994). *The politics of social transformation in Afghanistan, Iran, and Pakistan*. Syracuse: Syracuse University Press, 24–25.

26. C. Johnson and J. Leslie. (2004). *Afghanistan: The mirage of peace*. London: Zed Books, 25.

27. E. Rostami-Povey. (2005). Women and work in Iran. *State of Nature*, Autumn, 75.

28. E. Rostami-Povey. (2007). *Afghan women: Identity and invasion*. London: Zed Books.

29. Women's Commission for Refugee Women and Children. (2005). *Masculinities: Male roles and male involvement in the promotion of gender equality*. New York: Women's Commission for Refugee Women and Children.

30. C. Johnson and J. Leslie (2004). *Afghanistan: The mirage of peace*. London: Zed Books, 23.

31. www.rawa.org/temp/runews/2007/03/03/afghanistan-no-gender-equality-under-occupation.htm.

32. International Crisis Group (2003). Afghanistan: Women and reconstruction. *ICG Asia Report No 48*. Kabul: International Crisis Group, 23.

33. R. Skaine. (2002). *The women of Afghanistan under the Taliban*. Jefferson: McFarland and Co., 102.

34. D. Kandiyoti. (2003). *Integrating gender analysis into socio-economic needs assessment in Afghanistan*. Kabul: United Nations Development Fund for Women, 4–5.

35. United Nations Development Programme & Islamic Republic of Afghanistan. (2004). *Afghanistan national human development report 2004: Security with a human face: Challenges and responsibilities*. Kabul: United Nations Development Programme, 18.

36. Rabbani is a Tajik leader who founded Jamiat-i-Islami as an offshoot of the Muslim Brotherhood in the late 1960s and played a key role in the Afghan *jihad*, or holy war.

37. M. Bhadrakumar. (2006, 3 June). Kabul riots a turning point for Afghanistan, Karzai. *Asia Times Online*. Retrieved 3 June 2006, from http://www.atimes.com/atimes/South_Asia/HF03Df04.html.

38. B.J. Stapleton. (2006). *Security and reconstruction in Afghanistan: Shortcomings and mid-term prospects*. Karachi: University of Karachi, 6.

39. Afghanistan in print. (2005, May 11–17). *Kabul Weekly*, 168.

40. *Ibid.*

41. R. Morarjee. (2006, May 30). Riots breach Kabul "Island." *Christian Science Monitor*.

42. R. Morarjee. What has Afghans so angry. *Time World: Web Exclusive*. Retrieved 30 May 2006, from http://www.time.com/time/world/article/0,8599,1199254,00.html.

43. This information was compiled through Human Rights Watch, the Afghanistan NGO Security Office, and Patronus Analytical.

44. A. Stoddard, M. Czwarno, and M. Breckenridge. (2021). *Figures at a Glance.* Humanitarian Outcomes. Available at https://www.humanitarianoutcomes.org/figures_at_a_glance_2021.

45. J. Beall and D. Esser. (2005). Shaping urban futures: Challenges to governing and managing Afghan cities. Issues Paper Series. Kabul: Afghanistan Research and Evaluation Unit (AREU), 27.

46. This is particularly relevant in the battle between the Northern Alliance (various ethnic groups) and the Taliban (largely Pashtun).

47. History documents the Afghan legacy of abandonment following the end of Soviet occupation. The country fell into civil war and plunged into international anonymity. All this changed with the Taliban and 11 September 2001.

48. A full analysis of lessons learned—or not—can be found in L Abirafeh. (2005). Lessons from gender-focused international aid in post-conflict Afghanistan ... learned? In A. Wieland-Karimi. *Gender in international cooperation.* Bonn: Friedrich-Ebert-Stiftung.

49. M.A. Nawabi. (2003). Women's rights in the new constitution of Afghanistan, 7. Retrieved from http://www.cic.nyu.edu/peacebuilding/oldpdfs/E22Womens%20RightsFullVersionNawabi.pdf.

50. B.R. Rubin. (1994). Redistribution and the state in Afghanistan: The red revolution turns green. In M. Weiner and A. Banuazizi. *The politics of social transformation in Afghanistan, Iran, and Pakistan.* Syracuse: Syracuse University Press, 216–217.

51. Unpublished quote from B. Rubin in 2021.

52. L. AbiRafeh. (2021). Opinion: For Afghan Women, the U.S. Rhetoric of Liberation Has Fallen Short. CNN. Available at https://edition.cnn.com/2021/06/16/opinions/afghan-women-us-liberation-promise-abirafeh/index.html.

53. D. Loyn (Director). (2006). Afghanistan: Losing the aid game [Television broadcast]. *BBC Special Report,* 35 minutes.

54. S. Shah. (2003). *The storyteller's daughter.* London: Penguin, 200.

55. Friends Committee on National Legislation. (2016). *Costs of War: By the Numbers.* Available at https://www.fcnl.org/updates/2016-10/costs-war-numbers.

56. N. Biji Ahuja. (2021). An Afghan NGO Is Determined to Educate Girls Despite Taliban's Return. *The Week.* Available at https://www.theweek.in/news/world/2021/08/20/an-afghan-ngo-determined-to-educate-girls-depite-taliban-return.html.

57. *Ibid.*

58. The magazine is named after the famed heroine Malalai, who is known for securing an Afghan victory in the Battle of Maiwand in 1880 during the second Anglo-Afghan war. Malalai used her veil as a banner to encourage Afghan soldiers. Her name has become part of Afghan legend and is used for many schools, hospitals, and so on.

59. J. Mujahed. (2002). Freedom for women: Only words. *Malalai,* 1.

60. Afghan Women's Resource Center, Afghan Women's Network, and Women for Women International (2003). *International Women's Day Statement: 8 March 2003.* Kabul: AWRC, AWN, WWI.

Chapter 8

1. R. Ali. (2014). Empowerment beyond resistance: Cultural ways of negotiating power relations. *Women's Studies International Forum* 45, 119–126.

2. *Ibid.,* 367.

3. L. Abu-Lughod. (2002). Do Muslim women really need saving? Anthropological reflections on cultural relativism and its others. *American Anthropologist* 104(3), 783–790.

4. M. Centlivres-Demont. (1994). Afghan women in peace, war, and exile. In M. Weiner and A. Banuazizi (Eds.). *The politics of social transformation in Afghanistan, Iran, and Pakistan.* Syracuse: Syracuse University Press.

5. I. Delloye. (2003). *Women of Afghanistan.* Saint Paul: Ruminator Books, 158.

6. L. Addario. (2021). The Taliban's Return Is Catastrophic for Women. *The Atlantic.* Available at https://www.theatlantic.com/international/archive/2021/08/the-talibans-return-is-awful-for-women-in-afghanistan/619765/.

7. *Ibid.*

8. Aljazeera. (2021). Fawzia Koofi:

Afghan Women Pay Highest Price for What Goes Wrong. [Video] *Aljazeera*. Available at https://www.aljazeera.com/program/talk-to-al-jazeera/2021/9/4/fawzia-koofi-afghan-women-pay-highest-price-for-what-goes-wrong.

9. *Ibid.*

10. N. Ghulam. (2017). Nadia Ghulam Web Official. *Nadiaghulam.com*. Available at http://www.nadiaghulam.com/en/.

11. R. Parsons. (2019). *The Interview—Being a Man Was "The Only Way to Survive" Under the Taliban*. [Video] France 24. Available at https://www.france24.com/en/20190218-interview-nadia-ghulam-women-afghanistan-taliban-secret-turban-survive.

12. Women and Peace Studies Organization. (2021). Current Projects. *Women and Peace Studies Organization*. Available at http://wpso-afg.org/current-projects/.

13. Part of the conversation published in L. AbiRafeh. (2021). What Does It Mean to Keep Your Children Safe? *Romper*. Available at https://www.romper.com/life/girls-of-afghanistan-taliban.

14. B. Swails, C. Ward, and S. McWhinnie. (2021). Women in Kabul Return to Work, School and the Streets, in Defiance of the Taliban. *CNN*. Available at https://edition.cnn.com/2021/10/04/asia/kabul-women-work-school-defiance-taliban-intl/index.html.

15. L. Addario. (2021). The Taliban's Return Is Catastrophic for Women. *The Atlantic*. Available at https://www.theatlantic.com/international/archive/2021/08/the-talibans-return-is-awful-for-women-in-afghanistan/619765/.

16. D. Kumar. (2021). Afghan Women's Voices on Peace Heard with UN Mission's Backing. *In Depth News*. Available at https://www.indepthnews.net/index.php/sustainability/gender-equality/4297-afghan-women-s-voices-on-peace-heard-with-un-mission-s-backing.

17. Further biographical information published by the Afghan Women Skills Development Center. Available at https://awsdc.org.af/biography-of-mahbouba-seraj/.

18. E. Johnson, M. Elbardicy, and A. Rezvani. (2021). She Is Staying in Afghanistan to Ensure Women's Gains Aren't Lost Under Taliban Rule. *NPR*. Available at https://www.npr.org/2021/08/17/10284 22817/afghanistan-women-taliban-afghan-womens-network-mahbooba-seraj.

19. R. Manchanda. (2021). The Afghanistan Catastrophe is a Moment of Reckoning for the "Women, Peace and Security" agenda. *The Wire*. Available at https://thewire.in/south-asia/the-afghan-catastrophe-is-a-moment-of-reckoning-for-the-women-peace-and-security-agenda.

20. Revolutionary Association of the Women of Afghanistan. Available at http://www.rawa.org/index.php.

21. J. Fluri. (2008). Feminist-nation building in Afghanistan: an examination of the Revolutionary Association of the Women of Afghanistan (RAWA) *Feminist Review* 89, 34–54.

22. RAWA. *Biography of Martyred Meena, RAWA's Founding Leader*. Available at http://www.rawa.org/meena.html.

23. M. Chavis. (2013). *Meena, Heroine of Afghanistan: The Martyr Who Founded RAWA, the Revolutionary Association of the Women of Afghanistan*. New York: St. Martin's Press.

24. Revolutionary Association of the Women of Afghanistan. Available at http://www.rawa.org/index.php.

25. MyRedLine. (2019). The Voice of Afghanistan for Sustainable Peace. *Myredline*. Available at https://myredline.af/.

26. G. Tzemach Lemmon. (2021). These Women fought for Afghanistan's Future. Now They Don't Want to Leave It Behind. *Time Magazine*. Available at https://time.com/6087101/women-afghanistan-what-comes-next/?utm_source=twitter&utm_medium=social&utm_campaign=editorial&utm_term=ideas_&linkId=126640601.

27. United Nations Assistance Mission in Afghanistan. (2021). *Special report: Killing of human rights defenders, journalists and media workers in Afghanistan 2018–2021—Afghanistan*. Available at https://reliefweb.int/report/afghanistan/special-report-killing-human-rights-defenders-journalists-and-media-workers.

28. A. Kelly. (2021). Zahra Joya: The Afghan Reporter Who Fled the Taliban—and Kept Telling the Truth About Women. *The Guardian*. Available at https://www.theguardian.com/society/2021/sep/22/zahra-joya-the-afghan-reporter-who-fled-the-taliban-and-kept-telling-the-truth-about-women?CMP=Share_iOSApp_Other.

29. *Ibid.*

30. Further information on Sahar Speaks. Available at http://www.saharspeaks.org/our-story.

31. A. Ferris-Rotman. (2021). *"What About My Dreams?": How the U.S. Abandoned Women in Afghanistan. Vanity Fair.* Available at https://www.vanityfair.com/news/2021/08/how-the-us-abandoned-women-in-afghanistan.

32. Afghanistan After America. (2020). *Leading the Charge, with Farahnaz Forotan.* Afghanistan After America. Available at https://www.afghanistanafteramerica.com/.

33. F. Forotan. (2021). I Met a Taliban Leader and Lost Hope for My Country. *New York Times.* 21 Apr. Available at https://www.nytimes.com/2021/04/21/opinion/Afghanistan-Taliban-Women.html.

34. Human rights Watch. (2021). *Afghanistan: Taliban Target Journalists, Women in Media.* Available at https://www.hrw.org/news/2021/04/01/afghanistan-taliban-target-journalists-women-media#.

35. *Ibid.*

36. Afghan Journalists Safety Committee. (2021). *AJSC 2020 Annual Report.* https://ajsc.af/211/ajsc-2020-annual-report. Available at https://ajsc.af/211/ajsc-2020-annual-report, 9.

37. *Ibid.*, 10.

38. Y. Serhan. (2021). The Women Burning Their Degree Certificates. *The Atlantic.* Available at https://www.theatlantic.com/international/archive/2021/09/afghanistan-brain-drain/619959/.

39. A. Kelly. (2021). Zahra Joya: The Afghan Reporter Who Fled the Taliban—and Kept Telling the Truth About Women. *The Guardian.* Available at https://www.theguardian.com/society/2021/sep/22/zahra-joya-the-afghan-reporter-who-fled-the-taliban-and-kept-telling-the-truth-about-women?CMP=Share_iOSApp_Other.

40. L. Addario. (2021). The Taliban's Return Is Catastrophic for Women. *The Atlantic.* Available at https://www.theatlantic.com/international/archive/2021/08/the-talibans-return-is-awful-for-women-in-afghanistan/619765/.

41. S. Qazi. (2020). Who are the Afghan women negotiating peace with the Taliban? *Aljazeera.* www.aljazeera.com. Available at https://www.aljazeera.com/features/2020/10/7/who-are-the-afghan-women-negotiating-peace-with-taliban.

42. E. Graham-Harrison. (2021). Taliban Ban Girls from Secondary Education in Afghanistan. *The Guardian.* Available at https://www.theguardian.com/world/2021/sep/17/taliban-ban-girls-from-secondary-education-in-afghanistan.

43. *Ibid.*

44. L. Zirack. (2021). Women's Education: Afghanistan's Biggest Success Story Now At Risk. *The Diplomat.* Available at https://thediplomat.com/2021/09/womens-education-afghanistans-biggest-success-story-now-at-risk/.

45. Human Rights Watch (2020). *Gender Alert on Covid-19 Afghanistan.* Human Rights Watch. Available at https://www.hrw.org/news/2020/10/14/gender-alert-covid-19-afghanistan#.

46. T. Pherali. (2021). Education in Afghanistan Was a Battlefield Long Before the Taliban Returned. *The Conversation.* Available at https://theconversation.com/education-in-afghanistan-was-a-battlefield-long-before-the-taliban-returned-167204.

47. Human Rights Watch. (2006). *Lessons in terror: Attacks on education in Afghanistan.* Kabul: Human Rights Watch, 50.

48. *Ibid.*, 46.

49. A. Gopal. (2021). The Other Afghan Women. *The New Yorker.* Available at https://www.newyorker.com/magazine/2021/09/13/the-other-afghan-women.

50. Human Rights Watch. (2006). *Lessons in terror: Attacks on education in Afghanistan.* Kabul: Human Rights Watch, 79.

51. *Ibid.*, 98.

52. UNICEF and the Ministry of Education. (2018). *All in School and Learning: Global Initiative on Out-Of-School Children—Afghanistan Country Study.* Kabul. Available at https://www.unicef.org/afghanistan/media/2471/file/afg-report-oocs2018.pdf%20.pdf.

53. Human Rights Watch. (2006). *Lessons in terror: Attacks on education in Afghanistan.* Kabul: Human Rights Watch, 125.

54. The Global Coalition to Protect Education from Attack. (2021). *The Impact of Explosive Weapons on Education: A Case Study of Afghanistan.* Kabul. Available at https://protectingeducation.org/wp-content/uploads/EWIPA-Afghanistan-2021.pdf.

55. Global Coalition to Protect Education from Attack (2020). *Education Under Attack 2020—A Global Study of Attacks on Schools, Universities, their Students and Staff, 2019–2017*. Kabul.

56. B. Johnson. (2017). Boris Johnson: The World Would Be Better If All Girls Went to School. *Evening Standard*. Available at https://www.standard.co.uk/comment/comment/boris-johnson-the-world-would-be-a-better-place-if-all-girls-went-to-school-a3477121.html.

57. E. Graham-Harrison. (2021). Taliban Ban Girls from Secondary Education in Afghanistan. *The Guardian*. Available at https://www.theguardian.com/world/2021/sep/17/taliban-ban-girls-from-secondary-education-in-afghanistan.

58. T. Lister and R. Gigova. (2021). Curtains Separate Male and Female Afghan Students as New Term Begins Under Taliban Rule. *CNN*. Available at https://edition.cnn.com/2021/09/07/asia/afghan-university-male-female-segregation-curtain-intl/index.html.

59. N. Biji Ahuja. (2021). An Afghan NGO Is Determined to Educate Girls Despite Taliban's Return. *The Week*. Available at https://www.theweek.in/news/world/2021/08/20/an-afghan-ngo-determined-to-educate-girls-depite-taliban-return.html.

60. The Asia Foundation. (2019). *A Survey of the Afghan People—Afghanistan in 2019*. Kabul. Available at https://reliefweb.int/report/afghanistan/survey-afghan-people-afghanistan-2019.

61. *Ibid.*

62. Human Rights Watch (2020). *Gender Alert on Covid-19 Afghanistan*. Human Rights Watch. Available at https://www.hrw.org/news/2020/10/14/gender-alert-covid-19-afghanistan#.

63. B. Swails, C. Ward, and S. McWhinnie. (2021). Women in Kabul Return to Work, School and the Streets, in Defiance of the Taliban. *CNN*. Available at https://edition.cnn.com/2021/10/04/asia/kabul-women-work-school-defiance-taliban-intl/index.html.

64. R. Wright, A. Coren, and A. Basir Bina. (2021). Afghanistan's Women Judges Are in Hiding, Fearing Reprisal Attacks from Men They Jailed. *CNN*. Available at https://edition.cnn.com/2021/09/19/asia/afghanistan-women-judges-hnk-dst-intl/index.html.

65. C. Jancke. (2021). Living in a Taliban-Controlled Afghanistan as an Afghan Female Aid Worker. *Global Interagency Security Forum*. Available at https://gisf.ngo/blogs/living-in-a-taliban-controlled-afghanistan-as-an-afghan-female-aid-worker/.

66. Anonymous. (2021). I Am an Afghan Woman Working for a Western NGO in Kabul. I Feel Forgotten. *The Guardian*. Available at https://www.theguardian.com/commentisfree/2021/aug/18/afghan-woman-working-western-ngo-kabul-forgotten.

67. L. AbiRafeh. (2021). Opinion: For Afghan Women, the U.S. Rhetoric of Liberation Has Fallen Short. *CNN*. Available at https://edition.cnn.com/2021/06/16/opinions/afghan-women-us-liberation-promise-abirafeh/index.html.

CHAPTER 9

1. N. Robertson. (2021). *"What Are They Going to Do? Kill All of Us?": Hear from Female Activist in Kabul*. [Video]. CNN. Available at https://www.cnn.com/videos/world/2021/09/16/afghanistan-taliban-mahbouba-seraj-robertson-intl-ldn-vpx.cnn.

2. Revolutionary Association of the Women of Afghanistan. (2021). Let Us No Longer Mourn But Make the Enemy Weep! *Rawa.org*. Available at http://www.rawa.org/rawa/2021/03/08/let-us-no-longer-mourn-but-make-the-enemy-weep.htm.

3. K. Gannon. (2021). As U.S. Mulls Afghan Exit, Activist Sees Long Fight for Women. *AP NEWS*. Available at https://apnews.com/article/afghanistan-activists-women-rights-e7a746817fb24f45e1ff702ca269ccc5.

4. Special Inspector General for Afghanistan Reconstruction. (2021). *What We Need to Learn: Lessons from Twenty Years of Afghanistan Reconstruction*. Virginia: SIGAR. Available at https://www.sigar.mil/pdf/lessonslearned/SIGAR-21-46-LL.pdf.

5. VOA News. (2021). Women's Groups Call for UN Peacekeeping Force in Afghanistan. *VOA*. Available at https://www.voanews.com/a/us-afghanistan-troop-withdrawal_womens-groups-call-un-peacekeeping-force-afghanistan/6208324.html.

6. *Ibid.*

7. L. AbiRafeh. (2021). Opinion: For Afghan Women, the U.S. Rhetoric of Liberation Has Fallen Short. *CNN*. Available at https://edition.cnn.com/2021/06/16/opinions/afghan-women-us-liberation-promise-abirafeh/index.html.

8. L. Abirafeh. (2009). *Gender and International Aid in Afghanistan: The Politics and Effects of Intervention*. Jefferson, NC: McFarland.

9. World Bank Afghanistan. (2018). Making Higher Education Accessible to Afghan Women. *World Bank Blogs*. Available at https://blogs.worldbank.org/endpovertyinsouthasia/making-higher-education-accessible-afghan-women.

10. L. Garcia-Navarro. (2021). All Female Flight Crew in Afghanistan Makes History. *NPR*. Available at https://www.npr.org/2021/02/28/972217774/all-female-flight-crew-in-afghanistan-makes-history.

11. S. Jones. (2018). The Many Dangers of Being an Afghan Woman in Uniform. *New York Times Magazine*. Available at https://www.nytimes.com/2018/10/05/magazine/afghanistan-women-security-forces.html.

12. F. Bezhan and S. Furogh. (2021). Acceptance Is First Challenge for Afghanistan's First Female in a Senior Security Post. *Radiofreeeurope/Radioliberty*. Available at https://www.rferl.org/a/acceptance-is-first-challenge-for-afghanistan-s-first-female-in-a-senior-security-post/29641506.html.

13. A. Torgan. (2016). Acid Attacks, Poison: What Afghan Girls Risk by Going to School. *CNN*. Available at https://edition.cnn.com/2012/08/02/world/meast/cnnheroes-jan-afghan-school/index.html.

14. J. Boone. (2010). Afghan feminists fighting from under the burqa. *The Guardian*. 30 Apr. Available at https://www.theguardian.com/world/2010/apr/30/afghanistan-women-feminists-burqa.

15. S. Engel Rasmussen. (2021). The Taliban Say They've Changed. On the Ground, They're Just as Brutal. *Wall Street Journal*. Available at https://www.wsj.com/articles/the-taliban-say-theyve-changed-on-the-ground-theyre-just-as-brutal-afghanistan-us-troops-11622487148.

16. A. Agha and G. Davies. (2021). Recent Killings in Afghanistan Highlight Ongoing Issue of Violence Against Women. *ABC News*. Available at https://abcnews.go.com/International/recent-killings-afghanistan-highlight-ongoing-issue-violence-women/story?id=76251017.

17. N. Paton Walsh. (2021). "No One Can Dare Ask Why": What It's Like to Live in a Town Where Everything Is Controlled by the Taliban. *CNN*. Available at https://edition.cnn.com/2021/04/14/middleeast/afghanistan-life-under-the-taliban-musa-qala-intl/index.html.

18. F. Bashari. (2016). *Women Empowerment in Rural Areas in Afghanistan*. [Press Release] Available at https://reliefweb.int/report/afghanistan/women-empowerment-rural-areas-afghanistan.

19. Human Rights Watch. (2021). *I Would Like Four Kids—If We Stay Alive*. HRW. Available at https://www.hrw.org/report/2021/05/06/i-would-four-kids-if-we-stay-alive/womens-access-health-care-afghanistan.

20. Human Rights Watch. (2017). Afghanistan: Girls Struggle for an Education. *HRW*. Available at https://www.hrw.org/news/2017/10/17/afghanistan-girls-struggle-education.

21. AP News. (2021). Bush Criticizes Afghanistan Withdrawal, Fears for Women. *AP NEWS*. Available at https://apnews.com/article/joe-biden-afghanistan-7d6d9ef298bc24fea43086ebbe4d7c17.

22. S. Samar. (2021). If the U.S. Doesn't Learn from the Past, Afghan Women and Girls Will Pay the Price. *Ms. Magazine*. Available at https://msmagazine.com/2021/08/12/afghanistan-taliban-violence-women-children-minorities/.

23. Middle East Matters. (2021). Interview with Mahbooba Seraj. [Video]. Available at https://www.instagram.com/p/CSbjZtBHCql/.

24. Statement by Women's Collective Re Taliban Take-Over of Afghanistan. (2021). Available at https://docs.google.com/forms/d/e/1FAIpQLScFT5wcg-B-1lCMi1SJjmAHODllbnH-gfpEvC3Ta-_WwXYGlg/viewform?fbclid=IwAR3Edms5EkEEBGqt5XlLk20l9ogVXZYF9jzhRM-Ugvupw T4fGfGJ5u1E55A.

25. *Ibid.*

26. S. Samar. (2021). Women's Rights Are Not Just "Western Values": A Warning Not to Learn the Wrong Lessons from Afghanistan. *Ms. Magazine*. Available at https://msmagazine.com/2021/09/22/womens-rights-western-values-afghanistan-feminism/?omhide=

true&emci=d2ba0ad2-ac1c-ec11–
981f-0050f271a1a2&emdi=37f31d9d-
b91c-ec11–981f-0050f271a1a2&c
eid=345743.

27. R. Manchanda. (2021). The Afghanistan Catastrophe Is a Moment of Reckoning for the "Women, Peace and Security"
Agenda. The Wire. Available at https://
thewire.in/south-asia/the-afghan-
catastrophe-is-a-moment-of-reckoning-
for-the-women-peace-and-security-
agenda.

28. The World Bank Group. (2014).
Voice and Agency: Empowering Women
and Girls for Shared Prosperity. Available at
https://www.worldbank.org/content/dam/
Worldbank/document/Gender/Voice_and_
agency_LOWRES.pdf.

Bibliography

AbiRafeh, L. (2003). The role of religion in the lives of women in the new Afghanistan. *Critical Half* 1(1), 36–37.

AbiRafeh, L. (2004, October). Burqa politics: The plights of women in Afghanistan. *Chronogram*. http://www.chronogram.com/issue/2004/10/news/burqa.php.

AbiRafeh, L. (2005). Lessons from gender-focused international aid in post-conflict Afghanistan ... learned? In A. Wieland-Karimi (Ed.). *Gender in international cooperation*. Bonn: Friedrich-Ebert-Stiftung.

AbiRafeh, L. (2005, November). From Afghanistan to Sudan: How peace risks marginalizing women. *Forced Migration Review* 24, 46–47.

AbiRafeh, L. (2007a). Freedom is only won from the inside: Domestic violence in post-conflict Afghanistan. In M. Alkhateeb and S.E. Abugideiri (Eds.). *Change from within: Diverse perspectives on domestic violence in Muslim communities*. Washington, D.C.: Peaceful Families Project.

AbiRafeh, L. (2007b). An opportunity lost? Engaging men in gendered interventions: Voices from Afghanistan. *Journal of Peacebuilding and Development* 3(3).

AbiRafeh, L. (2009a). Afghanistan: Gendered interventions, identity, and the liberation agenda. In F. Shirazi (Ed.). *Images vs. realities: Muslim women in war and crisis: From reality to representation*. Austin: University of Texas Press.

AbiRafeh, L. (2009b). *Gender And International Aid in Afghanistan: The Politics and Effects of Intervention*. Jefferson, NC: McFarland.

AbiRafeh, L. (2020). "There Is No P and No S Without W..." *UN Peacekeeping*. Available at https://unpeacekeeping.medium.com/there-is-no-p-and-no-s-without-w-6ce74e610a8d.

AbiRafeh, L. (2021a). Opinion: For Afghan Women, The US Rhetoric of Liberation Has Fallen Short. *CNN*. Available at https://edition.cnn.com/2021/06/16/opinions/afghan-women-us-liberation-promise-abirafeh/index.html.

AbiRafeh, L. (2021b). What Does It Mean to Keep Your Children Safe? *Romper*. Available at https://www.romper.com/life/girls-of-afghanistan-taliban.

AbiRafeh, L. (2011). *Chadari Politics: Translating Perceptions into Policy and Practice*. In J. Heath and A. Zahedi (Eds.) *Land of the Unconquerable: The Lives of Contemporary Afghan Women*. Berkeley: University of California Press.

AbiRafeh, L., and Skaine, R. (2008). Voices and images of Afghan people. In R. Skaine. *Women of Afghanistan in the Post-Taliban Era: How Lives Have Changed and Where They Stand Today*. Jefferson, NC: McFarland, 123–150.

Abrahams, J. (2021). Towards a Real Feminist Foreign Policy. *Prospect Magazine*.

Abu-Lughod, L. (1989). Women as political actors. In L. Abu-Lughod (Ed.). *Remaking women: Feminism and modernity in the Middle East*. Princeton: Princeton University Press.

Abu-Lughod, L. (2002). Do Muslim women really need saving? Anthropological reflections on cultural relativism and its others. *American Anthropologist* 104(3), 783–790.

Acre, A. (2000). Creating or regulating development: Representing modernities through language and discourse. In A. Acre and N. Long (Eds.). *Anthropology, development and modernities: Exploring discourses, counter-tendencies and violence*. London: Routledge.

Addario, L. (2021). The Taliban's Return Is Catastrophic for Women. *The Atlantic*.

Advanced Training Program on Humanitarian Action (ATHA). (2018). *Fragile Future: The Human Cost of Conflict in Afghanistan*. Humanitarian Action at the Frontlines: Field Analysis Series.

Afary, J., and Anderson, K.B. (2005). *Foucault and the Iranian revolution: Gender and the seductions of Islamism*. Chicago: University of Chicago Press.

Afghan Authority for the Coordination of Assistance. (2002). *The National Development Framework: A Summary*. Kabul.

Afghan Journalists Safety Committee. (2021). *AJSC 2020 Annual Report*. Available at https://ajsc.af/211/ajsc-2020-annual-report.

Afghan Lipstick Liberation. (2002). *BBC News Online: World Edition*. Available at http://news.bbc.co.uk/2/hi/south_asia/2336303.stm.

Afghan Women, Security and Freedom Act of 2004 (2004). *Congress.gov*. Available at https://www.congress.gov/bill/108th-congress/house-bill/4117/text?r=60&s=1.

Afghan Women's Resource Center, Afghan Women's Network and Women for Women International. (2003). *International Women's Day Statement: 8 March 2003*. Kabul: AWRC, AWN, WWI.

Afghanistan After America. (2020). *Leading the Charge, with Farahnaz Forotan*. Available at https://www.afghanistanafteramerica.com/.

Afghanistan in Print. (2005, May 11-17). *Kabul Weekly*, 168.

Afghanistan Independent Human Rights Commission. (2006) *Report on economic and social rights in Afghanistan*. Kabul: Afghanistan Independent Human Rights Commission.

Afghanistan Independent Human Rights Commission. (2007). *Afghanistan Independent Human Rights Commission Annual Report 1 January 2006-31 December 2006*. Kabul: Afghanistan Independent Human Rights Commission.

Afghanistan Independent Human Rights Commission (2018). *Summary of the Report on Violence Against Women The causes, context, and situation of violence against women in Afghanistan*. Available at https://www.refworld.org/docid/5ab132774.html.

Afghanistan Independent Human Rights Commission–United Nations Assistance Mission in Afghanistan (2005a). *Joint verification of political rights, first report, 19 April-3 June 2005*. Kabul: Afghanistan Independent Human Rights Commission.

Afghanistan Independent Human Rights Commission–United Nations Assistance Mission in Afghanistan (2005b). *Joint verification of political rights, second report, 4 June-16 August 2005*. Kabul: Afghanistan Independent Human Rights Commission.

Afghanistan Independent Human Rights Commission–United Nations Assistance Mission in Afghanistan (2005c). *Joint verification of political rights, third report, 17 August-13 September 2005*. Kabul: Afghanistan Independent Human Rights Commission.

Afghanistan National Human Development Report 2004. (2004). Kabul: United Nations Development Programme Afghanistan, Islamic Republic of Afghanistan.

Afghanistan Public Policy Research Organization. (2017). *Gender Programming In Afghanistan: Critical Analysis Of National Action Plans On Women, Peace And Security*. Kabul: APPRO.

Afghanistan Reconstruction Trust Fund. (2021). About us | Afghanistan Reconstruction Trust Fund. www.artf.af.

Afshar, H. (2004). Introduction: War and peace: What do women contribute? In H. Afshar and D. Eade (Eds.). *Development, women and war: Feminist perspectives*. Oxford: Oxfam.

Afshar, H., and Eade, D. (Eds.). (2004). *Development, women and war: Feminist perspectives*. Oxford: Oxfam.

Agha, A. and Davies, G. (2021). Recent Killings in Afghanistan Highlight Ongoing Issue of Violence Against Women. *ABC News*.

Ahmed-Ghosh, H. (2003). A history of women in Afghanistan: Lessons learnt for the future or yesterdays and tomorrow: Women in Afghanistan. *Journal of International Women's Studies* 4(3).

Ahmedi, F., and Ansary, T. (2005). *The story of my life: An Afghan girl on the other side of the sky*. New York: Simon & Schuster.

Akbar, S. (2021). Afghans are living in terror. That must change for peace. *Washington Post*.

Alam, M. (2015). Equality for Afghan Women Remains a Critical Goal for President Ghani. *The World*.

Alexander, C. (2021). As The Taliban Return, a History of Afghan Women's Rights. *Washington Post*.

Ali, R. (2014). Empowerment beyond resistance: Cultural ways of negotiating power relations. *Women's Studies International Forum* 45, 119–126.

Aljazeera. (2021). *Fawzia Koofi: Afghan Women Pay Highest Price for What Goes Wrong*. [Video] Available at https://www.aljazeera.com/program/talk-to-aljazeera/2021/9/4/fawzia-koofi-afghan-women-pay-highest-price-for-what-goes-wrong.

Allen, J., and Felbab-Brown, V. (2020). The Fate of Women's Rights in Afghanistan. *The Brookings Institute*.

Alvarez, S.E. (1990). *Engendering democracy in Brazil: Women's movements in politics*. Princeton: Princeton University Press.

Amini, N. (2018). Education in the Era of Shah Amanullah Khan. *Afghanistan Quarterly Journal* 32 and 33(01 and 02), 88–102.

Amnesty International (2005). *Afghanistan: Women still under attack—A systematic failure to protect*. Available at http://web.amnesty.org/library/print/ENGASA110072005.

Anderson, M.B. (1999). *Do no harm: How aid can support peace—or war*. Boulder: Lynne Rienner Publishers.

Anderson, M.B., and Woodrow, P.J. (1998). *Rising from the ashes: Development strategies in times of disaster*. Paris: UNESCO.

AP News. (2021). Bush Criticizes Afghanistan Withdrawal, Fears for Women. *AP News*.

Appadurai, A. (1990). Disjuncture and difference in the global cultural economy. *Public Culture* 2(2).

Asia Foundation. (2018). *2018 Survey of Afghan People Shows Women's Rights are Complicated*. Kabul: Asia Foundation.

Asia Foundation. (2019). *A Survey of the Afghan People—Afghanistan in 2019*. Kabul: Asia Foundation.

Associated Press in Kabul. (2015). Thousands march in Kabul demanding justice for woman killed by mob. *The Guardian*.

The Astraea Foundation. (2021). Feminist Funding Principles. Available at https://astraeafoundation.org/microsites/feminist-funding-principles/.

Australian Government Department of Foreign Affairs and Trade. (2017). *Independent Review of the World Bank's Afghanistan Reconstruction Trust Fund (ARTF) 2017*. Available at https://www.dfat.gov.au/about-us/publications/Pages/afghanistan-reconstruction-trust-fund-review.

Azadmanesh, S., and Ghafoori, I. (2020). *Women's Participation in the Afghan Peace Process: A Case Study*. Kabul: Afghan Research and Evaluation Unit.

Azarbaijani-Moghaddam, S. (2004). Afghan women on the margins of the twenty-first century. In A. Donini, N. Niland, and K. Wermester (Eds.). *Nation-building unraveled? Aid, peace and justice in Afghanistan*. Bloomfield, CT: Kumarian Press.

Azarbaijani-Moghaddam, S. (2009). Manly Honor and the Gendered Male in Afghanistan. *Middle East Institute*.

Azarbaijani-Moghaddam, S. (2021a). *A Study of Gender Equity Through The National Solidarity Programme's Community Development Councils*. Kabul: Danish Committee for Aid to Afghan Refugees (DACAAR).

Azarbaijani-Moghaddam, S. (2021b). Progress was always fitful. Many Afghan women felt unsafe before the Taliban's arrival. *The Guardian*.

Azoy, W.G. (2003). *Buzkashi: Game and power in Afghanistan* (2nd ed.). Prospect Heights, Ill: Waveland Press.

Bahesh, H., and Subh, H. (2021). How Afghan Women Conquered A 27% Share in Parliament After Decades of War. *8Am Newspaper*.

Barakat, S. (2004). Setting the scene for Afghanistan's reconstruction: The challenges and critical dilemmas. In S. Barakat (Ed.). *Reconstructing war-torn societies: Afghanistan*. Hampshire, Eng.: Palgrave Macmillan.

Barakat, S. (2020). A peace deal alone cannot solve Afghanistan's myriad problems. *Aljazeera*.

Barakat, S., and Chard, M. (2004). Theories,

rhetoric and practice: Recovering the capacities of war-torn societies. In S. Barakat (Ed.). *Reconstructing war-torn societies: Afghanistan*. Hampshire, Eng.: Palgrave Macmillan.

Barakat, S., and Wardell, G. (2001). Capitalizing on capacities of Afghan women: Women's role in Afghanistan's reconstruction and development. Infocus Programme on Crisis Response and Reconstruction series. Geneva: International Labour Organization.

Barakat, S., and Wardell, G. (2004). Exploited by whom? An alternative perspective on humanitarian assistance to Afghan women. In S. Barakat (Ed.). *Reconstructing war-torn societies: Afghanistan*. Hampshire, Eng.: Palgrave Macmillan.

Barr, H. (2012) in J. Brinkely. Afghanistan: How Not to Give Aid. *Politico*. Available at https://www.politico.com/story/2012/07/afghanistan-example-of-how-not-to-give-aid-079000.

Barry, J. (2005). *Rising up in response: Women's rights activism in conflict*. Boulder, CO: Urgent Action Fund for Women's Human Rights.

Bashari, F. (2016). *Press Release: Women Empowerment In Rural Areas In Afghanistan*. Available at https://reliefweb.int/report/afghanistan/women-empowerment-rural-areas-afghanistan.

BBC News. (2021). *Afghanistan: World Bank halts aid after Taliban takeover*. Available at https://www.bbc.com/news/business-58325545.

Beall, J. (1996). Urban governance: Why gender matters. *Gender in Development Monographs series*. New York: United Nations Development Programme (UNDP).

Beall, J. (1998a). The gender and poverty nexus in the DFID White Paper: Opportunity or constraint? *Journal of International Development* 10, 235–246.

Beall, J. (1998b). Trickle-down or rising tide? Lessons on mainstreaming gender policy from Colombia and South Africa. *Social Policy and Administration* 32(5), 513–534.

Beall, J., and Esser, D. (2005). Shaping urban futures: Challenges to governing and managing Afghan cities. Issues Paper Series. Kabul: Afghanistan Research and Evaluation Unit (AREU).

Beall, J., and Schutte, S. (2006). Urban livelihoods in Afghanistan. Issues Paper Series. Kabul: Afghanistan Research and Evaluation Unit.

Beath, A., Christia, F., and Enikolopov, R. (2015). The National Solidarity Programme: Assessing the Effects of Community-Driven Development in Afghanistan. *International Peacekeeping* 22(4), 302–320.

Beck, T.K. (2018). "Liberating the Women of Afghanistan." *Socio* 11, 57–75.

Beneria, L. (2003). *Gender, development, and globalization: Economics as if people mattered*. New York: Routledge.

Benjamin, J. (2000). Afghanistan: Women survivors of war under the Taliban. In J. Mertus (Ed.). *War's offensive on women: The humanitarian challenge in Bosnia, Kosovo, and Afghanistan*. West Hartford, Eng.: Kumarian Press.

Besant, A. (2012). Some Taliban sent their daughters to school, new report claims. *The World from PRX*. Available at https://www.pri.org/stories/2012-12-11/some-taliban-sent-their-daughters-school-new-report-claims.

Bezhan, F., and Furogh, S. (2021.) Acceptance Is First Challenge for Afghanistan's First Female in a Senior Security Post. *Radiofreeeurope/Radioliberty*.

Bhadrakumar, M. (2006, June 3). Kabul riots a turning point for Afghanistan, Karzai. *Asia Times Online*. Available at http://www.atimes.com/atimes/South_Asia/HF03Df04.html.

Biji Ahuja, N. (2021). An Afghan NGO Is Determined to Educate Girls Despite Taliban's Return. *The Week*.

Bill, H. (2002). Country without a state—Does it really make a difference for the women? In C. Noelle-Karimi, C. Schetter, and R. Schlangintweit (Eds.). *Afghanistan—A Country Without a State*. Frankfurt: IKO.

Birtsh, N., and Hedayat, A. (2016) *Gender-Responsive Budgeting in Afghanistan: A Work in Progress*. Kabul: AREU.

Biswas, S. (2005). Campaign climax in Afghanistan. *BBC News*. Kabul.

Boege, F. (2004). *Women and politics in Afghanistan: How to use the chance of the 25% quota for women*. Kabul: Friedrich-Ebert-Stiftung.

Boesen, I. (2004). *From subjects to citizens: Local participation in the national solidarity program (NSP)*. Kabul: Afghanistan Research and Evaluation Unit (AREU).

Boesen, I.W. (1990). Honour in exile: Continuity and change among Afghan refugees. In E.W. Anderson and N.H. Dupree (Eds.). *The Cultural Basis of Afghan Nationalism*. London: Pinter Publishers.

Bohn, L. (2018). "We're All Handcuffed in This Country." Why Afghanistan Is Still the Worst Place in the World to Be a Woman. *Time Magazine*.

Bonino, E. (1998). Afghanistan: A Flower for the Women of Kabul. *The Guardian*.

The Bonn Agreement (S/2001/1154). (2001). Bonn: United Nations Security Council. https://peacemaker.un.org/sites/peacemaker.un.org/files/AF_011205_AgreementProvisionalArrangementsinAfghanistan%28en%29.pdf.

Boone, J. (2010). Afghan feminists fighting from under the burqa. *The Guardian*.

Boserup, E. (1970). *Woman's role in economic development*. New York: St. Martin's Press.

Bouta, T., Frerks, G., and Bannon, I. (2005). *Gender, conflict, and development*. Washington, D.C.: International Bank for Reconstruction and Development.

Brittain, V. (2002). Women in war and crisis zones: One key to Africa's wars of underdevelopment. Crisis States Programme Working Papers. London: London School of Economics Development Research Centre.

Brodsky, A.E. (2011). Centuries of Threat, Centuries of Resistance: The Lessons of Afghan Women's Resilience. In Jennifer Heath and Ashraf Zahedi (Eds.) *Women of Afghanistan in the Post-9/11 Era: Paths to Empowerment*. Berkeley: University of California Press.

Bryer, J. (2006). Those Heady Days—But Just Look at Us Now, Afghan Links.

Bureau of Democracy, Human Rights and Labor. (2001). *Report on the Taliban's War Against Women*. Available at https://2001-2009.state.gov/g/drl/rls/6185.htm.

Burke, J. (1998). Taliban prepare for civilian rule. *The Independent*. Available at https://www.independent.co.uk/news/taliban-prepare-for-civilian-rule-1173015.html.

Burke, J. (2006, June 25). Fear battles hope on the road to Kandahar. *Guardian Unlimited*. Available at http://observer.

guardian.co.uk/world/story/0,,1805334,00.html.

Burki, S.K. (2011). The Politics of Zan from Amanullah to Karzai. In Jennifer Heath and Ashraf Zahedi (Eds.). *Land of the Unconquerable: The Lives of Contemporary Afghan Women*. Berkeley: University of California Press, 45–50.

Burman, M.J., Batchelor, S.A., and Brown, J.A. (2001). Researching girls and violence: Facing the dilemmas of fieldwork. *British Journal of Criminology* 41, 443–459.

Byrd, W. (2007). *Responding to Afghanistan's development challenges: An assessment of experience during 2002–2007 and issues and priorities for the future*. Kabul: World Bank.

Canadian Women for Women in Afghanistan (2011). *Afghan Women in History: The 20th Century*. 1–3.

CARE International in Afghanistan: Policy brief. (2003). Kabul: CARE International.

Carlin, A. (2005). *OTI Afghanistan program evaluation: Gender initiatives and impacts: October 2001 to June 2005*. Kabul: PACT/DevTech Systems.

CBS News. (2001). Taliban Uses Food as a Weapon. Available at https://www.cbsnews.com/news/taliban-uses-food-as-weapon/.

CBS News (2012). *Taliban attacks on Afghan women worsening*. YouTube. Available at https://www.youtube.com/watch?v=Wb2Gm2Q0MV8.

Center For Economic and Social Rights (2002). *Human Rights and Reconstruction in Afghanistan*. New York: CESR.

Centlivres-Demont, M. (1994). Afghan women in peace, war, and exile. In M. Weiner and A. Banuazizi (Eds.). *The politics of social transformation in Afghanistan, Iran, and Pakistan*. Syracuse: Syracuse University Press.

Charlesworth, H., and Chinkin, C. (2002). Sex, gender and September 11. *American Journal of International Law* 96(3), 600–605.

Charney, C., Nanda, R., and Yakatan, N. (2004). *Voter Education Planning Survey: Afghanistan 2004 National Elections*. Kabul: The Asia Foundation.

Chavis, M. (2013). *Meena, Heroine of Afghanistan: The Martyr Who Founded RAWA, the Revolutionary Association of the Women of Afghanistan*. New York: St. Martin's Press.

CIA (2021). *Afghanistan—The World Fact-book*. Available at https://www.cia.gov/the-world-factbook/countries/afghanistan/#people-and-society.

Clark, K. (2004). The struggle for hearts and minds: The military, aid, and the media. In A. Donini, N. Niland, and K. Wermester (Eds.). *Nation-building unraveled? Aid, peace and justice in Afghanistan*. Bloomfield, CT: Kumarian Press.

Cleaver, F. (Ed.). (2002). *Masculinities matter! Men, gender and development*. London: Zed Books.

CNN. (2001). Afghanistan wakes after night of intense bombings. *CNN*. Available at https://edition.cnn.com/2001/US/10/07/gen.america.under.attack/.

CNN Editorial Research. (2021). Taliban Fast Facts. *CNN*. Available at https://edition.cnn.com/2013/09/20/world/taliban-fast-facts/index.html.

Coburn, N., and Wafaey, M.H. (2019). *Violence against Women in Afghanistan's 2018 Parliamentary Elections*. Kabul: Afghanistan Research and Evaluation Unit Organization.

Cockburn, C. (2004). *The line: Women, partition and the gender order in Cyprus*. London: Zed Books.

Coghlan, T. (2005). Election hopes of Afghan women. *BBC News*. Qalat.

Coghlan, T. (2006). Afghan MP Says She Will Not Be Silenced. *BBC News South Asia*.

Congressional Research Service. (2021). *Afghan Women and Girls: Status and Congressional Action*. Available at https://crsreports.congress.gov/product/pdf/IF/IF11646.

Consortium on Gender, Security & Human Rights. (2021). *Frontrunner: The Afghan Woman Who Surprised the World*. Available at https://genderandsecurity.org/projects-resources/filmography/frontrunner-afghan-woman-who-surprised-world.

Cornwall, A., and Brock, K. (2005). Beyond buzzwords: "Poverty reduction," "participation" and "empowerment" in development policy. Overarching Concerns Programme Paper Number 10. Geneva: United Nations Research Institute for Social Development.

Cornwall, A., Harrison, E., and Whitehead, A. (Eds.). (2007). *Feminisms in development: Contradictions, contestations and challenges*. London: Zed Books.

Corrin, C. (2004). International and local interventions to reduce gender-based violence against women in post-conflict situations. Available at http://www.wider.unu.edu/conference/conference-2004-1/conference%202004-1-papers/Corrin-3105.pdf.

Costy, A. (2004). The dilemma of humanitarianism in the post–Taliban transition. In A. Donini, N. Niland, and K. Wermester (Eds.). *Nation-building unraveled? Aid, peace and justice in Afghanistan*. Bloomfield, CT: Kumarian Press.

Council on Foreign Relations. (2020). *Including Women at the Peace Table Produces Better Outcomes*. Available at https://www.cfr.org/womens-participation-in-peace-processes/.

Crawford, N., and Lutz, C. (2019). *Human Cost of Post-9/11 Wars: Direct War Deaths in Major War Zones*. Watson Institute for International and Public Affairs.

Crawfurd, L., and Hares, S. (2021). *Girls' Education: A Casualty of the Disastrous Withdrawal from Afghanistan?* Center for Global Development.

Crisis States Programme (2001). *Crisis States Programme concepts and research agenda*. London: London School of Economics Development Research Center.

Daily Outlook: Afghanistan's Leading Independent Newspape. (2005, May 11). 53.

Defense Committee for Malai Joya. (2007). *The Brave and Historical Speech of Malai Joya in the LJ*. [YouTube Video]. https://www.youtube.com/watch?v=iLC1KBrwbck.

Delloye, I. (2003). *Women of Afghanistan*. Saint Paul: Ruminator Books.

Development Initiatives. (2003). Afghanistan: How pledges are being turned into spending. *Afghanistan Update*. Somerset: Development Initiatives.

Devi, S. (2020). Access to health care under threat in Afghanistan. *The Lancet* 395(10242), 1962.

de Vries, P. (1992). A research journey: On actors, concepts and the text. In A. Long and N. Long (Eds.). *Battlefields of knowledge: The interlocking of theory and practice in social research and development*. London: Routledge.

Dijkzeul, D., and Salomons, D. (2021).

International Organizations Revisited: Agency and Pathology in a Multipolar World. New York: Berghahn Books.

Donini, A. (2004). Principles, politics, and pragmatism in the international response to the Afghan crisis. In A. Donini, N. Niland, and K. Wermester (Eds.). *Nation-building unraveled? Aid, peace and justice in Afghanistan*. Bloomfield, CT: Kumarian Press.

Donini, A., Niland, N., and Wermester, K. (Eds.). *Nation-building unraveled? Aid, peace and justice in Afghanistan*. Bloomfield, CT: Kumarian Press.

Dorronsoro, G. (2005). *Revolution unending: Afghanistan: 1979 to the present*. New York: Columbia University Press.

Doubleday, V. (2006). *Three women of Herat: A memoir of life, love and friendship in Afghanistan*. London: Tauris Parke.

Drinan, R.F., and Drinan, R.J. (2001). *The mobilization of shame: A world view of human rights*. New Haven: Yale University Press.

Duffield, M. (2001a). *Global governance and the new wars: The merging of development and security*. London: Zed Books.

Duffield, M. (2001b). Governing the borderlands: Decoding the power of aid. *Disaster* 25(4), 308–320.

Duffield, M. (2002). Politics vs. aid. *Insights*, 39.

Duffield, M. (2005). Human security: Linking development and security in an age of terror. *General Conference of the EADI*. Bonn.

Dupree, L. (1980). *Afghanistan* (3rd ed.). Princeton: Princeton University Press.

Dupree, N.H. (1985). Women in Afghanistan: A brief 1985 update. In F. Rahimi (Ed.). *Women in Afghanistan*. Kabul: Paul Bucherer-Dietschi.

Dupree, N.H. (1990). A socio-cultural dimension: Afghan women refugees in Pakistan. In E.W. Anderson and N.H. Dupree. *The cultural basis of Afghan nationalism*. London: Pinter Publishers.

Dupree, N.H. (1996). *The women of Afghanistan*. Stockholm: Swedish Committee for Afghanistan.

Dupree, N.H. (1998). Afghan women under the Taliban. In W. Maley (Ed.). *Fundamentalism reborn? Afghanistan and the Taliban*. London: Hurst and Co.

Dupree, N.H. (2004). Cultural heritage and national identity in Afghanistan. In S.

Barakat (Ed.). *Reconstructing war-torn societies: Afghanistan*. Hampshire, Eng.: Palgrave Macmillan.

Dupree, N.H. (2004). The family during crisis in Afghanistan. *Journal of Comparative Family Studies* 32(2), 311–332.

Eade, D. (2004). Introduction: Peace and reconstruction: Agency and agencies. In H. Afshar and D. Eade (Ed.). *Development, women and war: Feminist perspectives*. Oxford: Oxfam.

Echavez, C., Mosawi, S., and Echavez-Pilongo, L. (2016). *The Other Side of Gender Inequality: Men and Masculinities in Afghanistan*. Kabul: Afghanistan Research and Evaluation Unit.

Edwards, R., and Ribbens, J. (1998). Living on the edges: Public knowledge, private lives, personal experience. In J. Ribbens and E. Rosalind (Eds.). *Feminist dilemmas in qualitative research: Public knowledge and private lives*. London: Sage.

Ehrenreich, B. (2003). Veiled threat. In A. Joseph and K. Sharma (Eds.). *Terror, counter-terror: Women speak out*. London: Zed Books.

Ellis, D. (2000). *Women of the Afghan war*. Westport, CT: Greenwood Press.

Emadi, H. (2002). *Repression, resistance, and women in Afghanistan*. Westport, CT: Praeger.

Enarson, E. (2007). Women and girls last? Averting the second post–Katrina disaster. *Affilia: Journal of Women and Social Work* 22(1), 5–8.

Engel Rasmussen, S. (2021). The Taliban Say They've Changed. On the Ground, They're Just as Brutal. *Wall Street Journal*.

Erturk, Y. (2005). Integration of the human rights of women and a gender perspective: Violence against women. New York: United Nations.

Evaluation report on general situation of women in Afghanistan. (2007). Kabul: Afghanistan Independent Human Rights Commission.

Faguet, J.-P. (2004). Democracy in the desert: Civil society, nation-building and empire. *Crisis States Programme Discussion Paper*. London: London School of Economics Development Research Centre.

Faizi, F., and Zucchino, D. (2019). "You Should Be in the Kitchen": At Afghan Assembly, Women Are Told They Don't Belong. *New York Times*.

Feminist Majority Foundation. (2003). Bush Administration's Rhetoric Does Not Match Reality on Global Women's Rights Issues. *Feminist Majority Foundation*.

Feminist Majority Foundation. (2004). Bush Policies on Iraq and Afghanistan Fail Women. *Feminist Majority Foundation*.

Ferguson, J. (1994). *The anti-politics machine: "Development," depoliticization, and bureaucratic power in Lesotho*. Minneapolis: University of Minnesota Press.

Ferguson, M. (2005). "W" Stands for Women: Feminism and Security Rhetoric in the Post-9/11 Bush Administration. *Politics & Gender* 1(1), 9–38.

Ferris-Rotman, A. (2017). Sima Wali Obituary. *The Guardian*. Available at https://www.theguardian.com/world/2017/nov/05/sima-wali-obituary.

Ferris-Rotman, A. (2021). "What About My Dreams?": How the U.S. Abandoned Women in Afghanistan. *Vanity Fair*. Available at https://www.vanityfair.com/news/2021/08/how-the-us-abandoned-women-in-afghanistan.

Fielden, M., and Azarbaijani-Moghadam, S. (2001). *Female Employment in Afghanistan: A Study of Decree #8*. Inter-Agency Taliban Edict Task Force.

Fluri, J. (2008). Feminist-nation building in Afghanistan: an examination of the Revolutionary Association of the Women of Afghanistan (RAWA). *Feminist Review* 89, 34–54.

Follain, J., and Cristofari, R. (2002). *Zoya's story: An Afghan woman's struggle for freedom*. New York: HarperCollins.

Forde, K. (2021). What Sources of Cash Will the Taliban Have? *Aljazeera*.

Foreign Assistance. (2021). *Country File: Afghanistan*. Available at https://foreignassistance.gov/.

Forotan, F. (2021). I Met a Taliban Leader and Lost Hope for My Country. *New York Times*.

Fox, K. (2021). Afghanistan is now one of very few countries with no women in top government ranks. *CNN*.

Francis, B. (2018). *The Local Level Implementation of Afghanistan's National Action Plan on UNSCR 1325—Women, Peace And Security*. International Alert.

Friends Committee on National Legislation. (2016). *Costs of War: By the Numbers*. Available at https://www.fcnl.org/updates/2016–10/costs-war-numbers.

Frogh, W. (2017). Afghanistan's National Action Plan: "A Wish List of Many Dreams." *LSE Centre for Women Peace and Security*. Available at https://blogs.lse.ac.uk/wps/2017/11/28/afghanistans-national-action-plan-a-wish-list-of-many-dreams-wazhma-frogh-102017/.

Frogh, W. (2019). *Women and the Afghan Peace Process: A Conversation with Wazhma Frogh*. Council on Foreign Relations.

Frontline. (2012). *Opium Brides*. Transcript available at https://www.pbs.org/wgbh/frontline/film/opium-brides/transcript/.

Fuentes Téllez, A. (2021). The Link Between Corruption and Gender Inequality: A Heavy Burden for Development and Democracy. *Wilson Center*.

Gall, C. (2005). Afghan poet dies after beating by husband. *New York Times*, 4.

Gannon, K. (2021). As US Mulls Afghan Exit, Activist Sees Long Fight for Women. *AP News*.

Garcia-Navarro, L. (2021). All Female Flight Crew in Afghanistan Makes History. *NPR*.

Gardner, K., and Lewis, D. (2000). Dominant paradigms overturned or "business as usual"? Development discourse and the White Paper on international development. *Critique of Anthropology* 20(1), 15–29.

Gasper, D., and Apthorpe, R. (1996). Discourse analysis and policy discourse. In D. Gasper and R. Apthorpe (Eds.). *Arguing development policy: Frames and discourses*. London: Frank Cass.

Geertz, C. (1983). *Local knowledge: Further essays in interpretive anthropology*. New York: Basic Books.

Gender Quotas Database. (2021). *International IDEA*. Available at https://www.idea.int/data-tools/data/gender-quotas/country-view/44/35.

George, S., and Tassal, A. (2020). How life under Taliban rule in Afghanistan has changed—and how it hasn't. *Washington Post*. Available at https://www.washingtonpost.com/graphics/2020/world/asia/afghanistan-taliban-rule-territory/.

Georgetown Institute for Women, Peace and Security. (2019a). *Afghanistan's Performance on the Women, Peace, and Security Index*. Washington, D.C.: Georgetown Institute of Women Peace and Security.

Georgetown Institute for Women, Peace and Security. (2019b). *Women, Peace and Security Index 2019/2020.* Washington, D.C.: Georgetown Institute of Women Peace and Security.

Georgetown Institute for Women, Peace and Security. (2020). *An Open Letter from World Leaders Calling for Afghan Women's Meaningful Participation in the Peace Process.* Available at https://giwps.georgetown.edu/an-open-letter-from-world-leaders-calling-for-afghan-womens-meaningful-participation-in-the-peace-process/.

Ghulam, N. (2017). Nadia Ghulam Web Oficial. *Nadiaghulam.com.* Available at http://www.nadiaghulam.com/en/.

Giles, W., and Hyndman, J. (Eds.). (2004). *Sites of violence: Gender and conflict zones.* Berkeley: University of California Press.

Glatzer, B. (2002). *Conflict analysis: Afghanistan.* Kabul: Friedrich-Ebert-Stiftung, Gesellschaft fur Technische Zusammenarbeit (GTZ).

Global Affairs Canada. (2020). *Evaluation Of International Assistance Programming in Afghanistan Final Report—June 2020 2014/15 To 2019/20.* Global Affairs Canada.

Global Coalition to Protect Education from Attack (2020). *Education Under Attack 2020—A Global Study of Attacks on Schools, Universities, their Students and Staff, 2019–2017.* Kabul: GCPEA.

Global Coalition to Protect Education from Attack. (2021) *The Impact of Explosive Weapons on Education: A Case Study Of Afghanistan.* Kabul: GCPEA. Available at https://protectingeducation.org/wp-content/uploads/EWIPA-Afghanistan-2021.pdf.

Goetz, A.M. (1997). Local heroes: Patterns of fieldwork discretion in implementing GAD policy in Bangladesh. In A.M. Goetz (Ed.). *Getting institutions right for women in development.* London: Zed Books.

Gollob, S., and O'Hanlon, M. (2020). *Afghanistan Index: Tracking Variables of Reconstruction and Security in Post-9/11 Afghanistan.* The Brookings Institute.

Goodhand, J. (2002). Aiding violence or building peace? The role of international aid in Afghanistan. *Third World Quarterly* 23(5), 837–859.

Goodhand, J., and Cramer, C. (2002). Try again, fail again, fail better? War, the state, and the "post-conflict" challenge in Afghanistan. *Development and Change* 33(5), 885–909.

Goodwin, J. (2003). *Price of honor: Muslim women lift the veil of silence on the Islamic world.* New York: Plume.

Gopal, A. (2021). The Other Afghan Women. *The New Yorker.*

Gossman, P., and Abbasi, F. (2021). *Interview: Why Now Is the Time to Support Women's Rights in Afghanistan.* Human Rights Watch.

Graham-Harrison, E. (2021). Taliban Ban Girls from Secondary Education in Afghanistan. *The Guardian.*

Greenberg, M.E., and Zuckerman, E. (2006). The gender dimensions of post-conflict reconstruction: The challenges of development aid. Helsinki: UNU-WIDER.

Grenfell, L. (2004). The Participation of Afghan Women in the Reconstruction Process. *Human Rights Brief* 12(1), 22–25.

Grillo, R., and Stirrat, R. (1997). *Discourses of development: Anthropological perspectives.* Oxford: Berg.

Gross, N. (2000a). Problems of the evolution of our Afghan national identity. In N. Gross (Ed.). *Steps of peace and our responsibility as Afghans.* Falls Church: Kabultec.

Gross, N. (2000b). The messy side of globalization: Women in Afghanistan. *Symposium on Globalization and Women in Muslim Societies.* Washington, D.C.: Library of Congress.

The Guardian. (2021a). Afghan Peace Summit Includes Just One Female Delegate. *The Guardian.* Available at https://www.theguardian.com/world/2021/mar/18/afghan-activists-warn-over-absence-of-women-in-peace-process.

The Guardian. (2021b). I Am an Afghan Woman Working for a Western NGO in Kabul. I Feel Forgotten. *The Guardian.* Available at https://www.theguardian.com/commentisfree/2021/aug/18/afghan-woman-working-western-ngo-kabul-forgotten.

Gupta, A. (1995). Blurred boundaries: The discourse of corruption, the culture of politics, and the imagined state. *American Ethnologist* 22(2), 375–402.

Habershon, A. (2021). Gender And Corruption: The Time Is Now. *World Bank Blogs*. Available at https://blogs.worldbank.org/governance/gender-and-corruption-time-now.

Hadid, H., and Dell, J. (2013). Summary amputations: Taliban justice in Afghanistan. *BBC News*. Available at https://www.bbc.com/news/world-asia-22311036.

Halima-Ahmad, L. (2020). The US And Taliban Are Partners Now: What About the Afghan Women? *International Peace Research Initiative*.

Hannun, M. (2021). "Saving" Afghan Women, Now. *The American Prospect*. Available at https://prospect.org/world/saving-afghan-women-now/.

Hans, A. (2004). Escaping conflict: Afghan women in transit. In W. Giles and J. Hyndman (Eds.). *Sites of violence: Gender and conflict zones*. Berkeley: University of California Press.

Harcourt, W. (2005). The body politic in global development discourse: A woman and the politics of place perspective. In W. Harcourt and A. Escobar (Eds.). *Women and the politics of place*. Bloomfield, CT: Kumarian Press.

Hassan, P. (2010). *The Afghan Peace Jirga: Ensuring That Women Are at the Peace Table*. Washington, D.C.: United States Institute of Peace.

Hassan, R. (2002). Muslim women's rights: A contemporary debate. In S. Mehta (Ed.). *Women for Afghan women: Shattering myths and claiming the future*. New York: Palgrave Macmillan.

Hayward, F. (2017). Progress on gender equity in Afghan higher education. *University World News*.

Hensher, P. (2006, July 6). It's deja vu in Afghanistan. Available at http://www.SeattlePI.com.

Herold, M.W. (2006, June 4). Afghanistan as an empty space. *Cursor*. Available at http://www.cursor.org/stories/empty space.html.

Heuvel, K.V. (2002). *A just response: The nation on terrorism, democracy, and September 11, 2001*. New York: Avalon Publishing Group, Inc.

Hilhorst, D. (2003). *The real world of NGOs: Discourses, diversity and development*. London: Zed Books.

Hoonsuwan, M. (2012). Afghanistan's Opium Child Brides. *The Atlantic*. Available at https://www.theatlantic.com/international/archive/2012/02/afghanistans-opium-child-brides/252638/.

Hosseini, K. (2003). *The kite runner*. New York: Riverhead Books.

Human Rights Watch. (1999). *World report 1999*. New York: Human Rights Watch.

Human Rights Watch. (2004). *Between hope and fear: Intimidation and attacks against women in public life in Afghanistan*. New York: Human Rights Watch.

Human Rights Watch. (2005a). *Blood-Stained Hands Past Atrocities in Kabul and Afghanistan's Legacy of Impunity Human Rights Watch*. New York: Human Rights Watch.

Human Rights Watch. (2005b). *Campaigning against fear: Women's participation in Afghanistan's 2005 elections*. New York: Human Rights Watch.

Human Rights Watch. (2006). *Lessons in terror: Attacks on education in Afghanistan*. Kabul: Human Rights Watch.

Human Rights Watch. (2009). *Afghanistan: Law Curbing Women's Rights Takes Effect*. Available at https://www.hrw.org/news/2009/08/13/afghanistan-law-curbing-womens-rights-takes-effect.

Human Rights Watch. (2017). *Afghanistan: Girls Struggle for an Education*. Available at https://www.hrw.org/news/2017/10/17/afghanistan-girls-struggle-education.

Human Rights Watch. (2019). *Afghanistan: Events of 2018*. Available at https://www.hrw.org/world-report/2019/country-chapters/afghanistan#.

Human Rights Watch. (2020). *Gender Alert on Covid-19 Afghanistan*. Available at https://www.hrw.org/news/2020/10/14/gender-alert-covid-19-afghanistan#.

Human Rights Watch. (2021a). *Afghanistan: Taliban Target Journalists, Women in Media*. Available at https://www.hrw.org/news/2021/04/01/afghanistan-taliban-target-journalists-women-media#.

Human Rights Watch. (2021b). *I Thought Our Life Might Get Better*. Available at https://www.hrw.org/report/2021/08/05/i-thought-our-life-might-get-better/implementing-afghanistans-elimination.

Human Rights Watch. (2021c). *"I Would Like Four Kids—If We Stay Alive."* Available at https://www.hrw.org/report/2021/05/06/i-would-four-kids-if-we-stay-alive/womens-access-health-care-afghanistan#4460.

Hunt, K. (2002). The strategic co-optation of women's rights: Discourse in the "war on terrorism." *International Feminist Journal of Politics* 4(1), 116–121.

Hunte, P. (2004). *Some notes on the livelihoods of the urban poor in Kabul, Afghanistan.* Kabul: Afghanistan Research and Evaluation Unit.

Hussain Saramad, M., and Sultani, L. (2013). *Violence Against Women in Afghanistan.* Kabul: Refworld.

Hymowitz, K.S. (2003). Why feminism is AWOL on Islam. *City Journal.*

Ibrahim, M., and Mussarat, R. (2014). Women Participation in Politics: A Case Study of Afghan Women. *Journal of Public Administration and Governance* 4(3), 433–447.

Institute for Economics and Peace. (2021). *Global Peace Index 2021.* Sydney: IEP.

Institute for the Study of War. (2007). Provincial Reconstruction Teams (PRTS). *Institute for the Study of War.*

Inter-Parliamentary Union. (2021). *Women in Politics: 2021.* Inter-Parliamentary Union.

International Civil Society Action Network. (2021). *Sanam Naraghi Anderlini Interview with WRHU-FM on the Situation in Afghanistan.* ICAN. Available at https://icanpeacework.org/2021/08/19/sanam-naraghi-anderlini-interview-wrhu-afghanistan/.

International Crisis Group. (2003). Afghanistan: Women and reconstruction. *ICG Asia Report No 48.* Kabul: International Crisis Group.

International Crisis Group. (2013). *Women and Conflict in Afghanistan.* Available at https://www.crisisgroup.org/asia/south-asia/afghanistan/women-and-conflict-afghanistan.

International Crisis Group. (2020). *What Will Peace Talks Bode for Afghan Women?* Available at https://www.crisisgroup.org/asia/south-asia/afghanistan/what-will-peace-talks-bode-afghan-women.

International Rescue Committee. (2021). *IRC Warns of Invisible Crisis in Afghanistan, as 50% of Those in Need of Humanitarian Assistance Are Women and Girls.* [Press Release]. Available at https://www.rescue.org/press-release/irc-warns-invisible-crisis-afghanistan-50-those-need-humanitarian-assistance-are-women.

IRIN. (2004). Our bodies—Their battle ground: Gender-based violence in conflict zones. *IRIN web special.* http://www.irinnews.org.

Islamic Republic of Afghanistan. (2002). *National development framework: Draft: Version 2.* Kabul: Islamic Republic of Afghanistan.

Islamic Republic of Afghanistan. (2004). *Securing Afghanistan's future: Accomplishments and the strategic path forward.* Kabul: A Government/International Agency Report: Islamic Republic of Afghanistan, Asian Development Bank, United Nations Assistance Mission to Afghanistan, United Nations Development Program, the World Bank Group.

Islamic Republic of Afghanistan. (2005). *National development strategy FAQ.* Kabul: Islamic Republic of Afghanistan.

Islamic Republic of Afghanistan. (2005). *Vision 2020—Afghanistan millennium development goals report 2005.* Kabul: United Nations Development Programme.

Islamic Republic of Afghanistan. (2006a). *Afghanistan national development strategy.* Kabul: Islamic Republic of Afghanistan.

Islamic Republic of Afghanistan. (2006b). *Interim national action plan for the women of Afghanistan: Executive summary.* Kabul: Islamic Republic of Afghanistan.

Islamic Republic of Afghanistan. (2006c). *The Afghanistan compact: Building on success.* The London Conference on Afghanistan. London: Islamic Republic of Afghanistan.

Islamic Republic of Afghanistan and United Nations Development Programme. (2005). *Millennium development goals: Islamic Republic of Afghanistan country report 2005: Vision 2020.* Kabul: Islamic Republic of Afghanistan and UNDP.

Islamic Republic of Afghanistan Central Statistics Organization. (2018). *Afghanistan Living Conditions Survey 2016–17.*

Jackson, A. (2018). Life under the Taliban shadow government. *Overseas Development Institute.*

Jacobson, R. (2000). Women and peace in Northern Ireland: A complicated relationship. In S. Jacobs, R. Jacobson, and J.

Marchbank (Eds.). *States of conflict: Gender, violence and resistance*. London: Zed Books.

Jaggar, A. (1988). *Feminist politics and human nature*. Totowa: Rowman and Littlefield.

Jaggar, A.M. (1998). Globalizing feminist ethics. *Hypatia* 13(2), 7–31.

Jaggar, A.M. (2004). Saving Amina. In *Global justice for women and intercultural dialogue*. Boulder: University of Colorado.

Jaggar, A.M. (2005). Arenas of citizenship: Civil society, state and the global order. *International Feminist Journal of Politics* 7(1).

Jalal, M. (2005). *Accelerating national peace and reconstruction by safeguarding women's rights and security*. Afghanistan: Ministry of Women's Affairs.

Jalal, M. (2013). Karzai: A Legacy of Failure on Afghan Women's Rights? *Open Democracy*. Available at https://www.opendemocracy.net/en/5050/karzai-legacy-of-failure-on-afghan-womens-rights/.

Jamshidi, N. (2021). The Freedom of Afghan Women Depends on Education and Empowerment. *Ms. Magazine*.

Jancke, C. (2021). Living in a Taliban-controlled Afghanistan as an Afghan Female Aid Worker. *Global Interagency Security Forum*.

Jardine, M. (2021). The world must evacuate women police in Afghanistan. *Lowy Institute*.

Johnson, B. (2017). Boris Johnson: The World Would Be Better If All Girls Went to School. *Evening Standard*.

Johnson, C., and Leslie, J. (2004). *Afghanistan: The mirage of peace*. London: Zed Books.

Johnson, E., Elbardicy, M., and Rezvani, A. (2021). She Is Staying in Afghanistan to Ensure Women's Gains Aren't Lost Under Taliban Rule. *NPR*.

Jonasdottir, A.G. (1988). On the concept of interest, women's interests, and the limitations of interest theory. In K.B. Jones and A.G. Jonasdottir (Eds.). *The political interests of gender: Developing theory and research with a feminist face*. London: Sage.

Jones, B. (2004). Aid, peace, and justice in a reordered world. In A. Donini, N. Niland, and K. Wermester. *Nation-Building Unraveled? Aid, Peace and Justice in Afghanistan*. Bloomfield, CT: Kumarian Press.

Jones, B. (2010). The Afghanistan Donor Conference: Timetables and Theatrics in Kabul. *The Brookings Institute*.

Jones, S. (2018). The Many Dangers of Being an Afghan Woman in Uniform. *New York Times Magazine*.

Jones, S.G. (2006). Averting failure in Afghanistan. *Survival* 48, 111–128.

Kabeer, N. (1994). *Reversed realities: Gender hierarchies in development thought*. London: Verso.

Kamal, S. (2006). *Development communications strategies and domestic violence in Afghanistan*. Retrieved from Peaceful Families Project, http://www.peacefulfamilies.org/kamal.html.

Kamali, M.H. (2003). *Islam, pernicious custom, and women's rights in Afghanistan*. Malaysia: International Islamic University.

Kandiyoti, D. (1988). Bargaining with patriarchy. *Gender and society* 2(3), 274–290.

Kandiyoti, D. (1998). Gender, power and contestation: Rethinking bargaining with patriarchy. In C. Jackson and R. Pearson (Ed.). *Feminist visions of development: Gender analysis and policy*. London: Routledge.

Kandiyoti, D. (2003). *Integrating gender analysis into socio-economic needs assessment in Afghanistan*. Kabul: United Nations Development Fund for Women.

Kandiyoti, D. (2005). The politics of gender and reconstruction in Afghanistan. *Occasional Paper*. Geneva: United Nations Research Institute for Social Development.

Kandiyoti, D. (2007). Political fiction meets gender myth: Post-conflict reconstruction, "democratization" and women's rights. In A. Cornwall, E. Harrison, and A. Whitehead (Eds.). *Feminisms in Development: Contradictions, Contestations and Challenges*. London: Zed Books.

Kandiyoti, D. (Ed.). (1991). *Women, Islam and the state*. Philadelphia: Temple University Press.

Karam, A.M. (2000). Islamisms and the decivilising processes of globalisation. In A. Acre and N. Long (Ed.). *Anthropology, development and modernities: Exploring discourses, counter-tendencies and violence*. London: Routledge.

Karzai, H., Japan, United States, European Union, & Saudi Arabia. (2002, January 21–22). Co-chairs' Summary of conclusions: The international conference on reconstruction assistance to Afghanistan. *Bonn agreement*. Tokyo, Japan.

Kazem, H. (2005). Afghans decry violence against women. *Los Angeles Times*.

Kelemen, M. (2019). U.S. Trying to Get the Taliban and Afghan Government to Start Negotiations. *NPR*.

Kelemen, M. (2021). The Future Is Unclear for Foreign Aid Work In Afghanistan Under the Taliban. *NPR*.

Kelly, A. (2021). Zahra Joya: The Afghan Reporter Who Fled the Taliban—and Kept Telling the Truth About Women. *The Guardian*.

Kelly, L. (2000). Wars against women: Sexual violence, sexual politics and the militarized State. In S. Jacobs, R. Jacobson, and J. Marchbank. *States of conflict: Gender, violence and resistance*. London: Zed Books.

Kensinger, L. (2003). Plugged in praxis: Critical reflections on U.S. feminism, internet activism, and solidarity with women in Afghanistan. *Journal of International Women's Studies* 5(1).

Khadra, Y. (2004). *The swallows of Kabul*. New York: Anchor Books.

Khan, F.A. (2018). 2018 Survey of Afghan People Shows Women's Rights are Complicated. *The Asia Foundation*.

Khan, R. (2021). Afghanistan and the colonial project of feminism: dismantling the binary lens. *London School of Economics*.

Khan, S. (2001). Between here and there: Feminist solidarity and Afghan women. *Genders* 33.

Kleinman, A. (2021). Afghan Women on What's at Stake for Women in Afghanistan. *IA*.

Kobia, R. (2021). March 18 2021. Available at https://twitter.com/RolandKobia/status/1372515217268166658?s=20.

Kolhatkar, S. (2021). "Saving" Afghan Women. *RAWA*. Available at http://www.rawa.org/znet.htm.

Kumar, D. (2021). Afghan Women's Voices on Peace Heard with UN Mission's Backing. *In Depth News*.

Kumar, R., and Noori, H. (2021). Shock as Two Female Afghan Supreme Court Judges Gunned Down in Kabul Ambush. *The National News*.

Kunder, J.P. (2006). *USAID's progress in helping the people of Afghanistan: Statement to committee on armed services at the US House of Representatives*. Washington, D.C.: United States Agency for International Development.

LandInfo. (2011). Report Afghanistan: Marriage. Available at https://www.landinfo.no/asset/1852/1/1852_1.pdf.

Larson, A. (2008). *A Mandate to Mainstream: Promoting Gender Equality in Afghanistan*. Kabul: Afghanistan Research and Evaluation Unit.

Latifa. (2001). *My forbidden face: Growing up under the Taliban: A young woman's story*. New York: Hyperion.

Leader, N., and Atmar, M.H. (2004). Political projects: Reform, aid, and the state in Afghanistan. In A. Donini, N. Niland, and K. Wermester (Eds.). *Nation-Building Unraveled? Aid, Peace and Justice in Afghanistan*. Bloomfield, CT: Kumarian Press.

Lederach, J.P. (1997). *Building peace: Sustainable reconciliation in divided societies*. Washington, D.C.: United States Institute of Peace Press.

LeVine, M., Mortensen, V., and Evans, J. (2003). *Twilight of empire: Responses to occupation*. Santa Monica, CA: Perceval Press.

Lister, T., and Gigova, R. (2021). Curtains Separate Male and Female Afghan Students as New Term Begins Under Taliban Rule. *CNN*.

Logan, H. (2002). *Unveiled: Voices of women in Afghanistan*. New York: Regan Books.

Long, N. (1977). *An introduction to the sociology of rural development*. London: Tavistock Publications.

Long, N. (1984). Creating space for change: A perspective on the sociology of development. *Sociologia Ruralis* 24(3/4), 168–184.

Long, N. (2000). Exploring local/global transformations: A view from anthropology. In N. Long and A. Acre (Eds.). *Anthropology, development and modernities: Exploring discourses, countertendencies and violence*. London: Routledge.

Long, N., and Long, A. (Eds.). (1992). *Battlefields of knowledge: The interlocking of theory and practice in social research and development*. London: Routledge.

Loyn, D. (Director). (2006). Afghanistan:

Losing the aid game. *BBC Special Report*, 35 minutes.

Ludin, Q. (2019). *How Peace Was Made: An Inside Account of Talks Between the Afghan Government and Hezb-E Islami.* Washington, D.C.: United States Institute of Peace.

Macrae, J. (2002). Politics vs. aid: Is coherence the answer? *Insights* 39.

Magnus, R.H., and Naby, E. (1998). *Afghanistan: Mullah, Marx, and Mujahid.* Boulder: Westview Press.

Majrouh, S.B. (1994). *Songs of love and war: Afghan women's poetry.* New York: Other Press.

Makoii, A.M., and Safi, M. (2021). "Terrible days ahead": Afghan women fear the return of the Taliban. *The Guardian.*

Malikyar, H. (2015). Women's Gains and a Taliban Peace Deal. *Aljazeera.*

Manchanda, R. (2021). The Afghanistan Catastrophe Is a Moment of Reckoning for the "Women, Peace And Security" Agenda. *The Wire.* https://thewire.in/south-asia/the-afghan-catastrophe-is-a-moment-of-reckoning-for-the-women-peace-and-security-agenda.

Margesson, R. (2002). Afghanistan's path to reconstruction: Obstacles, challenges, and issues for Congress. Washington, D.C.: Congressional Research Service.

Marofi, F. (2015). Farkhunda belongs to all of the women of Kabul, of Afghanistan. *The Guardian.*

Marsden, P. (1998). *The Taliban: War, religion, and the new order in Afghanistan.* London: Zed Books.

McAllister, P. (1991). *This river of courage: Generations of women's resistance and action.* Philadelphia: New Society Publishers.

McCaffrey, B. (2006). *Academic report—Trip to Afghanistan and Pakistan.* New York: United States Military Academy, West Point.

McGrail, A. (2021). Facts on Foreign Aid Efforts in Afghanistan. *The Borgen Project.* Available at https://borgenproject.org/foreign-aid-efforts-in-afghanistan/.

Mehta, S., and Mamoor, H. (2002). Building community across difference. In S. Mehta (Ed.). *Women for Afghan women: Shattering myths and claiming the future.* New York: Palgrave Macmillan.

Mehta, S. (Ed.). (2002). *Women for Afghan women: Shattering myths and claiming the future.* New York: Palgrave Macmillan.

Meintjes, S., Turshen, M., and Pillay, A. (Eds.). (2001). *The aftermath: Women in post-conflict transformation.* London: Zed Books.

Merelli, A. (2021). Don't Pity the Women of Afghanistan, Support Them. *Quartz.*

Mernissi, F. (1975). *Beyond the veil: Male-female dynamics in a modern Muslim society.* New York: John Wiley & Sons.

Mertus, J. (2000). *War's offensive on women: The humanitarian challenge in Bosnia, Kosovo, and Afghanistan.* West Hartford, CT: Kumarian Press.

Middle East Matters. (2021). Interview with Mahbooba Seraj. Available at https://www.instagram.com/p/CSbjZtBHCql/.

Miglani, S. (2008). Taliban executions still haunt Afghan soccer field. *Reuters.* Available at https://www.reuters.com/article/us-afghan-stadium/taliban-executions-still-haunt-afghan-soccer-field-idUSSP12564220080913.

Miller, R.L., and Brewer, J.D. (Eds.). (2003). *The A-Z of social research.* London: Sage.

Ministry of Economy (2017). *HLPF—2017 Voluntary National Review at the High Level Political Forum SDGs' Progress Report Afghanistan.* Available at https://sustainabledevelopment.un.org/content/documents/16277Afghanistan.pdf.

Ministry of Foreign Affairs. (2015). *Afghanistan's National Action Plan on UNSCR 1325 Women, Peace and Security.* Kabul: Ministry of Women's Affairs.

Ministry of Women's Affairs. (2005). *Statistical compilation on gender issues in Afghanistan: Background study for a gender policy framework.* Kabul: Ministry of Women's Affairs, UNIFEM.

Ministry of Women's Affairs. (2018). *NAPWA Final Assessment.* Available at https://mowa.gov.af/sites/default/files/2019-08/NAPWA%20Assessment%20Final%20and%20Approved.pdf.

Ministry of Women's Affairs. *Ministry of Women's Affairs Proposed Framework for the Work of the CG Advisory Group on Gender.* Kabul: Ministry of Women's Affairs.

Miraki, D.M.D. (2006, April 30). Death made in America. *Rense.* Available at http://www.rense.com/general70/death mde.htm.

Mitchell, D. (2017). NGO Presence and Activity in Afghanistan, 2000–2014: A Provincial-Level Dataset. *Stability: International Journal of Security and Development* 6(1), p.5.

Moghadam, V.M. (1992). Patriarchy and the politics of gender in modernising societies: Iran, Pakistan and Afghanistan. *International Sociology* 7(1), 35–53.

Moghadam, V.M. (1994). Reform, revolution, and reaction: The trajectory of the "woman question" in Afghanistan. In V.M. Moghadam (Ed.). *Gender and National Identity: Women and Politics in Muslim Societies.* London: Zed Books.

Moghadam, V.M. (1999). Revolution, religion, and gender politics: Iran and Afghanistan compared. *Journal of Women's History* 10(4), 172–195.

Mohanty, C.T. (2003). *Feminism without borders: Decolonizing theory, practicing solidarity.* Durham: Duke University Press.

Molyneux, M. (1985). Mobilization without emancipation? Women's interests, the state, and revolution in Nicaragua. *Feminist Studies* 11(2), 227–254.

Molyneux, M. (1991). The law, the state and socialist policies with regard to women; the case of the People's Democratic Republic of Yemen, 1967–1990. In D. Kandiyoti (Ed.). *Women, Islam and the state.* Philadelphia: Temple University Press.

Molyneux, M. (1998). Analysing women's movements. In C. Jackson and R. Pearson (Eds.). *Feminist visions of development: Gender analysis and policy.* London: Routledge.

Molyneux, M. (2007). The chimera of success: Gender ennui and the changed international policy environment. In A. Cornwall, E. Harrison, and A. Whitehead (Eds.). *Feminisms in development: Contradictions, contestations and challenges.* London: Zed Books.

Molyneux, M., and Lazar, S. (2003). *Doing the rights thing: Rights-based development and Latin American NGOs.* London: ITDG Publishing.

Molyneux, M., and Razavi, S. (Eds.). (2002). *Gender justice, development, and rights.* Oxford Studies in Democratization. Oxford: Oxford University Press.

Morarjee, R. (2006, May 30). Riots breach Kabul "Island." *Christian Science Monitor.*

Morarjee, R. (2006). What has Afghans so angry. *Time World: Web Exclusive.* Available at http://www.time.com/time/world/article/0,8599,1199254,00.html.

Morris, D. (2004). *Off with their heads: Traitors, crooks, and obstructionists in American politics, media, and business.* New York: Regan Books.

Mosadiq, H. (2005). The new Afghan constitution: How women succeeded in ensuring certain rights and what challenges remain. *Critical Half,* summer.

Moser, C., and McIlwaine, C. (2001). *Violence in a post-conflict context: Urban poor perceptions from Guatemala.* Washington, D.C.: The World Bank.

Moser, C.O.N. (1993). *Gender planning and development: Theory, practice and training.* London: Routledge.

Moser, C.O.N., and Clark, F.C. (Eds.). (2001). *Victims, perpetrators or actors? Gender, armed conflict and political violence.* London: Zed Books.

Mosse, D. (2005). *Cultivating development: An ethnography of aid policy and practice.* London: Pluto Press.

Mujahed, J. (2002). Freedom for women: Only words. *Malalai,* 1.

My Red Line. (2021). *MyRedLine Opposes AWN's Statement.* [Press Release] MyRedLine. Available at https://myredline.af/press-release-03/.

Nader, Z., and Ferris-Rotman, A. (2021). What Afghanistan's Women Stand to Lose. *Time Magazine.*

Narain, V. (2021). Women negotiators in Afghan/Taliban peace talks could spur global change. *The Conversation.*

Narayan, U. (1997). *Dislocating cultures: Identities, traditions, and third world feminism.* New York: Routledge.

Nassery, H. (2004). *The gender issue in Afghanistan.* Kabul: United Nations Development Programme.

National Center for Policy Research. (2004). *The database of women's projects in Afghanistan: December 2001 to August 2003.* Kabul: Kabul University, Department of Social Sciences.

Nawa, F. (2011). Opium Nation: *Child Brides, Drug Lords, And One Woman's Journey Through Afghanistan.* New York: HarperCollins.

Nawabi, M.A. (2003). Women's rights in the new constitution of Afghanistan. Available at http://www.cic.nyu.edu/

peacebuilding/oldpdfs/E22Womens%20 RightsFullVersionNawabi.pdf.

The New Humanitarian (2001). Women welcome US relief law. *The New Humanitarian.* Available at https://www.the newhumanitarian.org/fr/node/183112.

Nijat, A., and Murtazashvili, J. (2015) *Special Report: Women's Leadership Roles in Afghanistan.* Washington, D.C.: United States Institute of Peace.

Niland, N. (2004). Justice postponed: The marginalization of human rights in Afghanistan. In A. Donini, N. Niland, and K. Wermester (Eds.). *Nation-building unraveled? Aid, peace and justice in Afghanistan.* Bloomfield, CT: Kumarian Press.

Noory, L.S. (2006). Where have all the women gone? *The Examiner.* Available at http://www.examiner.com/a-158037~ Lida_Sahar_Noory_Where_have_all_ the_women_gone_.html.

Nordland, R. (2018). U.S. Aid Program Vowed to Help 75,000 Afghan Women. Watchdog Says It's a Flop. *New York Times.*

Nussbaum, B. (2001). Commentary: Liberation. *BusinessWeek.* Available at http:// www.businessweek.com/magazine/ content/01_49/b3760701.htm.

O'Hanlan, M. (2001) *The Aid and Reconstruction Agenda for Afghanistan.* The Brookings Institute.

Oliker, O.; Kauzlarich, R.; Dobbins, J.; Basseuner, K.; Sampler, D.; McGinn, J.; Dziedzic, M.; Grissom, A.; Pirnie, B.; Bensahel, N.; and Guven, A. (2004). *Aid during conflict: interaction between military and civilian assistance providers in Afghanistan, September 2001–June 2002.* Santa Monica, CA: RAND Corporation.

Osman, A., and Loewen, A. (2005). *Real men keep their word: Tales from Kabul, Afghanistan: A selection of Akram Osman's Dari short stories.* Oxford: Oxford University Press.

OTI Afghanistan. (2005). *Evaluation of OTI's program in Afghanistan: Focus on gender: Scope of work, OTI.*

Oxfam. (2008). Afghanistan: Development and humanitarian priorities. Kabul: Oxfam International, Afghanistan.

Paci, P. (2002). *Gender in transition.* Washington, D.C.: World Bank.

Pal, A. (2021). Taliban replaces women's ministry with ministry of virtue and vice. *Reuters.*

Pankhurst, D. (1998). *Mainstreaming gender in peacebuilding: A framework for action.* London: International Alert.

Pankhurst, D. (2000). Women, gender and peacebuilding. *Department of Peace Studies Working Paper.* Bradford: University of Bradford.

Pankhurst, D. (2007). Gender issues in post-war contexts: A review of analysis and experience, and implications for policies. *Peace Studies Papers.* Bradford: United Nations Research Institute for Social Development and University of Bradford.

Parpart, J. (2002). Lessons from the field: Rethinking empowerment, gender and development from a post-(post?)-development perspective. In K. Saunders (Ed.). *Feminist post-development thought: Rethinking modernity, post-colonialism and representation.* London: Zed Books.

Parsons, R. (2019). *The Interview—Being a Man Was "The Only Way to Survive" Under the Taliban.* France 24. Available at https://www.france24.com/ en/20190218-interview-nadia-ghulam-women-afghanistan-taliban-secret-turban-survive.

Paton Walsh, N. (2021). "No One Can Dare Ask Why": What It's Like to Live in a Town Where Everything Is Controlled By The Taliban. *CNN.*

PBS NewsHour. (2021). *A Historical Timeline of Afghanistan.* Available at https:// www.pbs.org/newshour/politics/asia-jan-june11-timeline-afghanistan.

Perez, R. (2002). Practising theory through women's bodies: Public violence and women's strategies of power and place. In K. Saunders (Ed.). *Feminist post-development thought: Rethinking modernity, post-colonialism and representation.* London: Zed Books.

Pherali, T. (2021). Education In Afghanistan Was a Battlefield Long Before the Taliban Returned. *The Conversation.*

Pickup, F., Williams, S., and Sweetman, C. (2001). *Ending violence against women: A challenge for development and humanitarian work.* Oxford: Oxfam Great Britain.

Pugh, M. (1998). Post-conflict rehabilitation: The humanitarian dimension. *Networking the Security Community in the Information Age.* Zurich: Swiss Interdepartmental Coordination Committee for Partnership for Peace.

Qazi, S. (2020). Who are the Afghan women negotiating peace with the Taliban? *Aljazeera.*

Rahimi, F. (1977). *Women in Afghanistan.* Kabul: Paul Bucherer-Dietschi.

Rahmaty, M. (2021). "The Exclusion of Women's Voices from Afghan Peace Talks Remains the Norm." *IPI Global Observatory.*

Ramachandra, V. (1999). *Faith in conflict: Christian integrity in a multicultural world.* Downers Grove, Ill.: InterVarsity Press.

Range, M. (2005, June 20). Gender equality as a driving force for achieving the MDGs. *Monday Developments.*

Rappeport, A. (2021) Afghanistan Faces Economic Shock as Sanctions Replace Foreign Aid. *New York Times.*

RAWA. *Biography of Martyred Meena, RAWA's Founding Leader.* Available at http://www.rawa.org/meena.html.

Rawi, M. (2004). Rule of the rapists. *The Guardian.* London.

REACH. (2018). *Hard To Reach Assessment.* Available at https://reliefweb.int/sites/reliefweb.int/files/resources/reach_afg_report_hard_to_reach_assessment_june_2018_0.pdf.

Reuters. (2021). U.S. considers visas for vulnerable Afghan women after military exit. *Reuters.* Available at https://www.reuters.com/world/us-considers-visas-vulnerable-afghan-women-after-military-exit-2021-07-08/.

Revolutionary Association of the Women of Afghanistan (2018). *Some of the restrictions imposed by Taliban in Afghanistan.*

Revolutionary Association of the Women of Afghanistan. (2021) Let Us No Longer Mourn but Make the Enemy Weep! Available at http://www.rawa.org/rawa/2021/03/08/let-us-no-longer-mourn-but-make-the-enemy-weep.htm.

Revolutionary Association of the Women of Afghanistan. (2021). Available at http://www.rawa.org/index.php.

Reynolds, A., Jones, L., and Wilder, A. (2005). *A guide to the parliamentary elections in Afghanistan.* Kabul: Afghanistan Research and Evaluation Unit.

Rist, R.C. (1994). Influencing the policy process with qualitative research. In N. Denzin and Y. Lincoln. *Handbook of qualitative research.* Thousand Oaks, CA: Sage Publications.

Roashan, R.G. (2006, May 4). The compact is a contract with a conscience. *Institute for Afghan Studies.* Available at http://www.institute-for-afghan-studies.org/Contributions/Commentaries/DRRoashanArch/2006/020406.htm.

Robertson, N. (2021). "*What Are They Going to Do? Kill All of Us?*': Hear from Female Activist In Kabul. CNN. Available at https://www.cnn.com/videos/world/2021/09/16/afghanistan-taliban-mahbouba-seraj-robertson-intl-ldn-vpx.cnn.

Robichaud, C. (2006). Remember Afghanistan? A glass half full, on the *Titanic.* *World Policy Journal* 23(1).

Robinson, J. (2002). *Development and Displacement.* Oxford: Oxford University Press.

Ross, J., Maxwell, S., and Buchanan-Smith, M. (1994). *Linking relief and development.* Brighton: Institute of Development Studies.

Rostami-Povey, E. (2004). Women in Afghanistan: Passive victims of the *borga* or active social participants? In H. Afshar and D. Eade (Eds.). *Development, women and war: Feminist perspectives.* Oxford: Oxfam.

Rostami-Povey, E. (2005). Women and work in Iran. *State of Nature,* Autumn.

Rostami-Povey, E. (2006). The reality of life in Afghanistan since the fall of the Taliban. *State of Nature,* Spring.

Rostami-Povey, E. (2007a). *Afghan women: Identity and invasion.* London: Zed Books.

Rostami-Povey, E. (2007b). Gender, agency and identity, the case of Afghan women in Afghanistan, Pakistan and Iran. *Journal of Development Studies* 43(2), 294–311.

Rowlands, J. (1998). A word of the times, but what does it mean? Empowerment in the discourse and practice of development. In H. Afshar (Ed.). *Women and empowerment: Illustrations from the third world.* London: Macmillan.

Roy, O. (1994). The new political elite of Afghanistan. In M. Weiner and A. Banuazizi (Eds.). *The politics of social transformation in Afghanistan, Iran, and Pakistan.* Syracuse: Syracuse University Press.

Rubin, B.R. (1994). Redistribution and the state in Afghanistan: The red revolution turns green. In M. Weiner and A.

Banuazizi. *The politics of social transformation in Afghanistan, Iran, and Pakistan.* Syracuse: Syracuse University Press.

Rubin, E. (2005). Women's work. *New York Times Magazine.*

Ruiz, H. (2002). *Afghanistan: Conflict and displacement 1978 to 2001.* Forced Migration Review.

Russo, A. (2006). The Feminist Majority Foundation's Campaign to Stop Gender Apartheid. *International Feminist Journal of Politics* 8(4), 557–580.

Saeed, A.B. (2005). *Dangers of running for office in Afghanistan.* Kabul: Institute for War and Peace Reporting.

Safa, M. (2005, September 13). Women, defense and security. *Deputy Minister for Technical and Policy Concerns.* Afghanistan: Ministry of Women's Affairs.

Safi, S. (2018). Why female suicide in Afghanistan is so prevalent. *BBC News.*

Said, E.W. (1979). *Orientalism.* New York: Vintage.

Saif, S. (2017). Around 3,000 Afghans commit suicide every year. Available at https://www.aa.com.tr/en/asia-pacific/around-3-000-afghans-commit-suicide-every-year/912627.

Saif, S. (2018). Voting For Landmark Afghan Parliament Polls Concludes. *Anadolu Agency.*

Saif, S. (2020). Afghanistan Forms New Women's Council Ahead of Taliban Talks. *Reuters.*

Saif, S. (2021). Afghanistan: 47,600 Civilians Killed in 20 Years of Deadly War. *Anadolu Agency.*

Samar, S. (2013). Corruption Is a Brutal Enemy of Afghan Women. *Thomson Reuters Foundation.*

Samar, S. (2019). Feminism, Peace, and Afghanistan. *Journal of International Affairs.*

Samar, S. (2021a). If the U.S. Doesn't Learn from the Past, Afghan Women and Girls Will Pay the Price. *Ms. Magazine.*

Samar, S. (2021b). Women's Rights Are Not Just "Western Values": A Warning Not to Learn the Wrong Lessons from Afghanistan. *Ms. Magazine.*

Sayigh, R. (1996). Researching gender in a Palestinian camp: Political, theoretical and methodological issues. In D. Kandiyoti (Ed.). *Gendering the Middle East: Emerging perspectives.* London: I.B. Tauris & Co.

Schramm, M. (2019). *Do Quotas Actually Help Women in Politics?* Washington, D.C.: Georgetown Institute of Women Peace And Security.

Schutte, S. (2004). Urban vulnerability in Afghanistan: Case studies from three cities. *Working Paper Series.* Kabul: Afghanistan Research and Evaluation Unit.

Schutte, S. (2006). Searching for security: Urban livelihoods in Kabul. *Case Study Series.* Kabul: Afghanistan Research and Evaluation Unit.

Security and Peace Initiative (2005). *American attitudes toward national security, foreign policy and the war on terror.* Washington, D.C.: Security and Peace Initiative.

Sen, A. (2006). *Identity and violence: The illusion of destiny.* London: Penguin.

Sen, P. (2002). In women's name? *Trouble and Strife,* 43 (Summer).

Serhan, Y. (2021). The Women Burning Their Degree Certificates. *The Atlantic.* Available at https://www.theatlantic.com/international/archive/2021/09/afghanistan-brain-drain/619959/.

Shah, S. (2003). *The storyteller's daughter.* London: Penguin.

Shaheed, A. (2019). Ghani Stresses Preserving Women's Rights in Peace Process. *Tolonews.*

Shapiro, A. (2004). *Gender and the war on terror: Partnerships, security and women in Afghanistan.* Symposium conducted at the 9th International Interdisciplinary Congress on Women, American University, Washington, D.C.

Sharoni, S. (2001). Rethinking women's struggles in Israel-Palestine and in the north of Ireland. In C.O.N. Moser and F.C. Clark (Eds.). *Victims, perpetrators or actors? Gender, armed conflict and political violence.* London: Zed Books.

Skaine, R. (2002). *The women of Afghanistan under the Taliban.* Jefferson, NC: McFarland.

Skaine, R. (2008). *Women of Afghanistan in the post–Taliban era: How lives have changed and where they stand today.* Jefferson, NC: McFarland.

Skjelsbæk, I., Barth, E.F., and Hostens, K. (2004). Gender aspects of conflict interventions: Intended and unintended consequences. *Report to the Norwegian Ministry of Foreign Affairs.* PRIO. Oslo: International Peace Research Institute.

Smillie, I., and Minear, L. (2004). *The charity of nations: Humanitarian action in a calculating world*. Bloomfield: Kumarian Press.

Special Inspector General for Afghanistan Reconstruction. (2016a). *Corruption in Conflict*. Available at https://www.sigar.mil/interactive-reports/corruption-in-conflict/part1.html.

Special Inspector General for Afghanistan Reconstruction (2016b). *Quarterly Report to the United States Congress*. Available at https://www.sigar.mil/pdf/quarterlyreports/2016-10-30qr.pdf.

Special Inspector General for Afghanistan Reconstruction. (2020). *Support for Gender Equality: Lessons from the US Experience in Afghanistan*. Virginia: SIGAR.

Special Inspector General for Afghanistan Reconstruction. (2021a) *Reconstruction Update: April 30, 2021 Quarterly Report to Congress*. Virginia: SIGAR.

Special Inspector General for Afghanistan Reconstruction. (2021b). *What We Need to Learn: Lessons from Twenty Years of Afghanistan Reconstruction*. Virginia: SIGAR.

Spivak, G.C. (1993). "Can the Subaltern Speak?" P. Williams and L. Chisman. *Colonial Discourse and Post-Colonial Theory: A Reader*. Harvester, 93.

Stamm, J. (2009). Poultry Project Empowers Afghan Women. *DVIDS*. Available at https://www.dvidshub.net/news/37788/poultry-project-empowers-afghan-women.

Stapleton, B.J. (2006). Security and reconstruction in Afghanistan: Shortcomings and mid-term prospects. Karachi: University of Karachi.

State Ministry for Peace. (2019). *Peace Negotiation Team of the Islamic Republic of Afghanistan*. Available at https://smp.gov.af/en/peace-negotiation-team-islamic-republic-afghanistan.

Staudt, K. (2002). Dismantling the master's house with the master's tools? Gender work in and with powerful bureaucracies. In K. Saunders (Ed.). *Feminist post-development thought: Rethinking modernity, post-colonialism and representation*. London: Zed Books.

Steinberg, D. (2009). Beyond Victimhood: Protection and Participation of Women in the Pursuit of Peace. *Crisis Group*.

Stockholm International Peace Research Institute. (SIPRI). (2021) *Trends in International Arms Transfers, 2020*. SIPRI.

Stockton, N. (2004). Afghanistan, war, aid, and international order. In A. Donini, N. Niland, and K. Wermester (Eds.). *Nation-building unraveled? Aid, peace and justice in Afghanistan*. Bloomfield: Kumarian Press.

Stoddard, A., Czwarno, M., and Breckenridge, M. (2021). *Figures at a Glance*. Humanitarian Outcomes.

Stone, R. (2021). Resignations Follow Taliban Pick to Run Top Afghan University. *Science*.

Sultan, M. (2002). Hope in Afghanistan. In S. Mehta. *Women for Afghan women: Shattering myths and claiming the future*. New York: Palgrave Macmillan.

Sultan, M. (2005). *From rhetoric to reality: Afghan women on the agenda for peace*. Washington, D.C.: Women Waging Peace Policy Commission.

Swails, B., Ward, C., and McWhinnie, S. (2021). Women in Kabul Return to Work, School and the Streets, in Defiance of the Taliban. *CNN*.

Swank, Jr., J.G. (2005). Success for females in Afghanistan. *Canada Free Press*. Available at http://www.canadafreepress.com/2005/swank090205.htm.

Sweetman, C., Gell, F., et al. (2001). Editorial. In C. Sweetman (Ed.). *Gender, development, and humanitarian work*. Oxford: Oxfam Great Britain.

Tapper, N. (1991). *Bartered brides: Politics, gender and marriage in an Afghan tribal society*. Cambridge: Cambridge University Press.

Tarzi, A. (2006). Afghan president gets key cabinet picks, but at what price? Available at http://www.rferl.org/content/article/1067838.html.

Terre des Hommes (2003). *The nutrition capitalization report: TDH projects in Afghanistan*. Kabul: Terre des Hommes.

The Times of India. (2000). Taliban arrest US aid worker for employing women. Available at http://www.rawa.org/ban-wo.htm.

Tonkiss, F. (1988). Analysing discourse. In C. Seale (Ed.). *Researching society and culture*. Thousand Oaks, CA: Sage Publications.

Torgan, A. (2016). Acid Attacks, Poison: What Afghan Girls Risk by Going to School. *CNN*.

Tortajada, A. (2004). *The silenced cry: One woman's diary of a journey to Afghanistan.* New York: St. Martin's Press.

Transparency International. (2020). *Corruption Perceptions Index 2020.* Available at https://www.transparency.org/en/cpi/2020/index/afg.

Transparency International. (2021). *What Is Corruption?* Available at https://www.transparency.org/en/what-is-corruption.

Turak, N. (2021). Donors pledging billions in aid to Afghanistan face a challenge navigating the Taliban. *CNBC.*

Turner, S. (2000). Vindicating masculinity: The fate of promoting gender equality. *Forced Migration Review, 9.*

Tzemach Lemmon, G. (2021). These Women Fought for Afghanistan's Future. Now They Don't Want to Leave it Behind. *Time Magazine.*

UCLA Asia Pacific Center. (2021). *Afghanistan: An Evolving Situation.* [Webinar] Available at https://www.international.ucla.edu/apc/event/15193.

UN Women (2021). *Global Database on Violence against Women: Afghanistan.* Available at https://evaw-global-database.unwomen.org/en/countries/asia/afghanistan#1.

United Nation Assistance Mission in Afghanistan. (2021b). *Protection Of Civilians in Armed Conflict Midyear Report.* Kabul: UNAMA.

United Nations. (2003). *The situation of women and girls in Afghanistan: Report of the secretary-general.* Commission on the Status of Women. New York: United Nations Economic and Social Council.

United Nations. (2005a). *The situation of women and girls in Afghanistan: Commission on the status of women.* New York: United Nations Economic and Social Council.

United Nations. (2005b). *World population prospects: The 2004 revision—Highlights.* New York: Department of Economic and Social Affairs of the UN Secretariat.

United Nations. (2006). *The situation in Afghanistan and its implications for international peace and security: Emergency international assistance for peace, normalcy and reconstruction in war-stricken Afghanistan.* New York: United Nations General Assembly Security Council.

United Nations. (2011). Security Council Presidential Statement Welcomes Bonn Declaration of "Transition Process," "Transformation Decade" for Afghanistan. Available at https://www.un.org/press/en/2011/scl0494.doc.htm.

United Nations. (2019). *World population prospects: The 2019 revision.* Department of Economic and Social Affairs of the UN Secretariat.

United Nations. (2021). *Global Issues: Democracy.* Available at https://www.un.org/en/global-issues/democracy.

United Nations Agency for International Development. (2004). *Afghanistan reborn: Building Afghan democracy.* Kabul: United Nations Agency for International Development Afghanistan.

United Nations Agency for International Development. (2006). *International women's day special report.* Kabul: United Nations Agency for International Development Afghanistan.

United Nations Agency for International Development/OTI/Afghanistan. (2005). *OTI grants benefitting women and girls, October 2001–April 2005.* OTI.

United Nations Assistance Mission in Afghanistan. (2009). *Silence Is Violence: End the Abuse of Women in Afghanistan.* Kabul: Office of the United Nations High Commissioner for Human Rights.

United Nations Assistance Mission in Afghanistan (2018). *Injustice and Impunity Mediation of Criminal Offences of Violence against Women.* Kabul: UNAMA.

United Nations Assistance Mission in Afghanistan. (2021a). *Afghanistan Protection of Civilians in Armed Conflict Midyear Update: 1 January to 30 June 2021.* Kabul: UNAMA.

United Nations Assistance Mission in Afghanistan. (2021c). *Special report: Killing of human rights defenders, journalists and media workers in Afghanistan 2018–202.* Kabul: UNAMA.

United Nations Assistance Mission in Afghanistan. (2013). *Protection of Civilians in Armed Conflict.* Kabul: UNAMA.

United Nations Development Fund for Women (UNIFEM). (2004). *Promoting women's empowerment and gender equality in Afghanistan: Strategic plan 2004–2007* (Draft: 28 April 2004). Kabul: United Nations Development Fund for Women.

United Nations Development Programme.

(2002). *Afghanistan: Donors Pledge $4.5 Billion in Tokyo*. [Press Release] Available at https://reliefweb.int/report/afghanistan/afghanistan-donors-pledge-45-billion-tokyo.

United Nations Development Programme. (2003). *Executive board of the United Nations Development Programme and of the United Nations population fund, assistance to Afghanistan (2004–2005), note by administrator*. Kabul: United Nations Development Programme.

United Nations Development Programme. (2004). *Electoral Systems and Processes: Practice Note*. New York: United Nations Development Programme.

United Nations Development Programme. (2005a). *Afghanistan: A country on the move*. Kabul: United Nations Development Programme.

United Nations Development Programme. (2005b). *Human Development Report 2005: International cooperation at a crossroads: Aid, trade and security in an unequal world*. New York: United Nations Development Programme.

United Nations Development Programme. (2005c). *Vision 2020—Afghanistan millennium development goals report 2005*. Kabul: United Nations Development Programme.

United Nations Development Programme. (2020). *Human Development Data (1990–2017) Human Development Reports*. Available at http://hdr.undp.org/en/data.

United Nations Development Programme (2021a). *Gender Inequality Index (GII) | Human Development Reports*. Available at http://hdr.undp.org/en/content/gender-inequality-index-gii.

United Nations Development Programme. (2021b). 97 percent of Afghans could plunge into poverty by mid-2022, says UNDP. Available at https://www.undp.org/press-releases/97-percent-afghans-could-plunge-poverty-mid-2022-says-undp.

United Nations Development Programme & Islamic Republic of Afghanistan. (2004). *Afghanistan national human development report 2004: Security with a human face: Challenges and responsibilities*. Kabul: United Nations Development Programme.

United Nations Economic and Social Council. (2004). The situation of women and girls in Afghanistan: Report of the secretary-general. *Women 2000: Gender equality, development and peace for the twenty-first century*. Commission on the Status of Women. New York: United Nations.

United Nations Educational Scientific and Cultural Organization. (2021). *Afghanistan: Education and Literacy*. Available at http://uis.unesco.org/en/country/af?theme=education-and-literacy.

United Nations Inter-Agency Network on Women and Gender Equality. (2003). *Collaboration with OECD/DAC Network on Gender Equality*. Retrieved from http://www.un.org/womenwatch/ianwge/collaboration.htm.

United Nations International Children's Emergency Fund. (2018a). *All in School and Learning: Global Initiative on Out-of-School Children—Afghanistan Country Study*. Kabul: Ministry of Education.

United Nations International Children's Emergency Fund (2018b). *The situation of children and women in Afghanistan*. Available at https://www.unicef.org/afghanistan/situation-children-and-women-afghanistan.

United Nations News. (2002). Security Council adopts humanitarian exemptions to sanctions against Al-Qaida. *UN News*. Available at https://news.un.org/en/story/2002/12/54972-security-council-adopts-humanitarian-exemptions-sanctions-against-al-qaida.

United Nations News. (2021). Afghanistan: Record Number of Women and Children Killed or Wounded. *UN News*. Available at https://news.un.org/en/story/2021/07/1096382.

United Nations Office for the Coordination of Humanitarian Affairs. (2021). *Daily Noon Briefing Highlights: Afghanistan—Syria*. Available at https://www.unocha.org/story/daily-noon-briefing-highlights-afghanistan-syria.

United Nations Office for the Coordination of Humanitarian Affairs and REACH Initiative. (2018). *Afghanistan: Hard to Reach Assessment Report, June 2018 - Afghanistan*. Available at https://reliefweb.int/report/afghanistan/afghanistan-hard-reach-assessment-report-june-2018.

United Nations Office of the High Commissioner for Human Rights. (2018).

Injustice and Impunity Mediation of Criminal Offences of Violence against Women. UNAMA.

United Nations Office of the Special Representative of the Secretary-General on Sexual Violence in Conflict. (2021). *Afghanistan*. Available at https://www.un.org/sexualviolenceinconflict/countries/afghanistan/.

United Nations Office on Drugs and Crime. (2019). *Afghanistan Opium Survey 2019*. Kabul: UNODC.

United Nations Population Fund (UNFPA). (2005). The promise of equality: Gender equity, reproductive health and the millennium development goals. *The state of world population report*. New York: United Nations Population Fund.

United Nations Research Institute for Social Development. (2005). Gender equality: Striving for justice in an unequal world. Geneva: United Nations Research Institute for Social Development.

United Nations Secretary General. (1997). *The situation in Afghanistan and its implications for international peace and security*. General Assembly Security Council. New York: United Nations.

United Nations Secretary General. (2002). *The situation in Afghanistan and its implications for international peace and security*. New York: United Nations General Assembly Security Council.

United Nations Security Council. (1996). *Resolution 1076: The Situation in Afghanistan*.

United Nations Security Council. (2002). *Report of the Secretary-General on Women, Peace and Security*. Available at https://undocs.org/S/2002/1154.

United Nations Security Council. (2011). *Letter addressed to the President of the United Nations Security Council*. Available at https://www.undocs.org/pdf?symbol=en/S/2021/486.

United Nations Security Council. (2020). *Women and peace and security Report of the Secretary-General*. Available at https://www.securitycouncilreport.org/atf/cf/%7B65BFCF9B-6D27-4E9C-8CD3-CF6E4FF96FF9%7D/s_2020_946.pdf.

United Nations Women. (2019). *Technical Guidance Note: Gender and the Localization Agenda*. Available at https://gblocalisation.ifrc.org/wp-content/uploads/2019/08/13082019-FV-UN-Women-Guidance-Note-Summary-Localisation.pdf.

United Nations Women (2021). Country Fact Sheet. *UN Women Data Hub*. Available at https://data.unwomen.org/country/afghanistan.

United States Agency for International Development. (2019). *Incentives Driving Economic Alternatives for the North, East and West (IDEA-NEW)*. Available at https://www.usaid.gov/news-information/fact-sheets/incentives-driving-economic-alternatives-north-east-and-west-idea-new.

United States Agency for International Development. (2021). *Promote*. Available at https://www.usaid.gov/afghanistan/promote.

United States Agency for International Development. (2021). *U.S. Overseas Loans and Grants (Greenbook) Data*. Available at https://data.usaid.gov/Administration-and-Oversight/U-S-Overseas-Loans-and-Grants-Greenbook-Data/7cnw-pw8v.

United States Department of Defense. (2006) Afghanistan: Five Years Later. *Archive.defense.gov*.

United States Department of State. (2002). *USAID funds rebuilding of Afghan Women's Affairs Ministry*. Available at https://reliefweb.int/report/afghanistan/usaid-funds-rebuilding-afghan-womens-affairs-ministry.

Villarreal, M. (1992). The Poverty of practice: Power, gender and intervention from an actor-oriented perspective. In A. Long and N. Long (Eds.). *Battlefields of knowledge: The interlocking of theory and practice in social research and development*. London: Routledge.

VOA News. (2021) Women's Groups Call for UN Peacekeeping Force in Afghanistan. *VOA*.

Wakefield, S., and Bauer, B. (2005). A place at the table: Afghan women, men and decision-making authority. *AREU Briefing Paper*. Kabul: Afghanistan Research and Evaluation Unit.

Walby, S. (1988). Gender politics and social theory. *Sociology* 22(2), 215–232.

Walby, S. (1990). *Theorizing patriarchy*. Oxford: Blackwell.

Walby, S. (1997). *Gender transformations*. London: Routledge.

Walby, S. (2000). Analyzing social inequality in the twenty-first century: Globalization and modernity restructure inequality. *Contemporary Sociology* 29(6), 813–818.

Walczak, L., Crock, S., and Balfour, F. (2001, December 3). Winning the peace. *Business Week*.

Wali, S. (2002). Afghanistan: Truth and mythology. In S. Mehta (Ed.). *Women for Afghan women: Shattering myths and claiming the future*. New York: Palgrave Macmillan.

Ward, J. (2002). *If not now, when? Addressing gender-based violence in refugee, internally displaced, and post-conflict settings: A global overview*. New York: The Reproductive Health for Refugees Consortium.

Ware, V. (2006). *Info-war and the politics of feminist curiosity: Exploring new frameworks for feminist intercultural studies*. London: Gender Institute, London School of Economics.

Watkins, K. (2021). The Taliban are not the only threat to Afghanistan. Aid cuts could undo 20 years of progress. *The Guardian*.

Watkins, M.B. (1963). *Afghanistan: Land in transition*. Princeton: D. Van Nostrand Co.

Weiner, M., and Banuazizi, A. (Eds.). (1994). *The politics of social transformation in Afghanistan, Iran, and Pakistan*. Syracuse: Syracuse University Press.

Weiss, T.G., and Collins, C. (2000). *Humanitarian challenges and intervention: World politics and the dilemmas of help*. Boulder: Westview Press.

Whitlock, C. (2019a). At War with the Truth. *Washington Post*.

Whitlock, C. (2019b). Consumed by Corruption. *Washington Post*.

Whitlock, G. (2005). The skin of the *bourka*: Recent life narratives from Afghanistan. *Biography* 28(1).

Wieland-Karimi, A. (2005). *Afghanistan: Looking back on 2004, looking forward to 2005*. Kabul: Friedrich-Ebert-Stiftung.

Wieringa, S. (1994). Women's interests and empowerment: Gender planning reconsidered. *Development and change* 25, 829–848.

Wilder, A. (2005). *A house divided? Analysing the 2005 Afghan elections*. Kabul: Afghanistan Research and Evaluation Unit.

Wilkie, C. (2021). "9/11 Millionaires" and Mass Corruption: How American Money Helped Break Afghanistan. *CNBC*.

Winthrop, R. (2003). Reflections on working in post-conflict Afghanistan: Local vs. international perspectives on gender relations. *Women's Studies Quarterly* 31(3–4).

Women and Children Legal Research Foundation. (2004). *Impact of traditional practices on women*. Kabul: Afghan Women Leaders Connect.

Women and Children Legal Research Foundation. (2005). *Report on women political participation in Afghanistan*. Kabul: Open Society Institute.

Women and Peace Studies Organization. (2021). Current Projects. Available at http://wpso-afg.org/current-projects/.

Women in Afghanistan: Challenges and opportunities for women's organizations in Afghan civil society. (2005). Washington, D.C.: ActionAid International USA.

Women's Collective Re Taliban Take-Over of Afghanistan. (2021). *Statement*. Available at https://docs.google.com/forms/d/e/1FAIpQLScFT5wcg-B-1lCMi1SJjmAHODllbnH-gfpEvC3Ta-_WwXYGlg/viewform?fbclid=IwAR3Edms5EkEEBGqt5XlLk20l9ogVXZYF9jzhRM-UgvupwT4fGfGJ5u1E55A.

Women's Commission for Refugee Women and Children. (2005). *Masculinities: Male roles and male involvement in the promotion of gender equality*. New York: Women's Commission for Refugee Women and Children.

Women's Commission for Refugee Women and Children. (2006). *Displaced women and girls at risk: Risk factors, protection solutions and resource tools*. New York: Women's Commission for Refugee Women and Children.

Women's International League for Peace & Freedom. (2010). Afghanistan-2010 Commitments—1325 National Action Plans. *1325 National Action Plans (NAPs)*. Available at http://1325naps.peacewomen.org/index.php/2010-committ ments/afghanistam-2010-commitments/.

Women's International League for Peace & Freedom. (2015). Afghanistan-2015 Commitments—1325 National Action Plans. *1325 National Action Plans (NAPs)*. Available at http://1325naps.peacewomen.org/index.php/2015-committ ments/afghanistan-2015-committments/.

Women's International League for Peace & Freedom (2019). Afghanistan-2019 Commitments—1325 National Action Plans. *1325 National Action Plans (NAPs)*. Available at http://1325naps.peacewomen.org/index.php/2019-committments/afghanistan-2019-commitments/.

Women's International League for Peace and Freedom. (2020). *Women, Peace and Security in Afghanistan: Submission to the UN Committee on the Elimination of Discrimination Against Women*. Kabul: CEDAW.

Women's International League for Peace and Freedom. (2021a). Afghanistan—1325 National Action Plans. *Peace Women*. Available at http://1325naps.peacewomen.org/index.php/afghanistan/.

Women's International League for Peace and Freedom. (2021b). Resolution 1325 Is Not About Rescuing Women. *Peace Women*.

World Bank. (2002a). The conflict analysis framework (CAF): Identifying conflict-related obstacles to development. *Dissemination notes*. Social Development Department: Conflict Prevention and Reconstruction Unit. Washington, D.C.: World Bank.

World Bank. (2002b). *Transitional support strategy: Afghanistan*. Washington, D.C.: World Bank.

World Bank. (2004). *Afghanistan: State building, sustaining growth, and reducing poverty: A country economic report*. Kabul: World Bank.

World Bank. (2005). *National reconstruction and poverty reduction: The role of women in Afghanistan's future*. Kabul: World Bank.

World Bank. (2012). Afghanistan In Transition: Looking Beyond 2014. *Worldbank.org*.

World Bank. (2017). Maternal mortality ratio (modeled estimate, per 100,000 live births) – Afghanistan. *Data.worldbank.org*.

World Bank. (2019). Proportion of Seats Held by Women in National Parliaments (%). *Data.worldbank.org*. Available at https://data.worldbank.org/indicator/SG.GEN.PARL.ZS?end=2019&start=1997.

World Bank. (2020a). Afghanistan Reconstruction Trust Fund (ARTF) Steering Committee Meets.

World Bank. (2020b). Proportion Of Seats Held by Women in National Parliaments (%). *Data.worldbank.org*. Available at https://data.worldbank.org/indicator/SG.GEN.PARL.ZS.

World Bank Afghanistan. (2018). Making Higher Education Accessible to Afghan Women. *World Bank Blogs*. Available at https://blogs.worldbank.org/endpovertyinsouthasia/making-higher-education-accessible-afghan-women.

The World Bank Group. (2014). *Voice And Agency: Empowering Women and Girls for Shared Prosperity*. Available at https://www.worldbank.org/content/dam/Worldbank/document/Gender/Voice_and_agency_LOWRES.pdf.

World Economic Forum. (2021). *Global Gender Gap Report: 2021*. World Economic Forum.

Wright, R., Coren, A., and Basir Bina, A. (2021). Afghanistan's Women Judges Are in Hiding, Fearing Reprisal Attacks from Men They Jailed. *CNN*.

Yam, M. (2021). As Afghans try to figure out Taliban's new rules, burqas are barometer of sorts. *Los Angeles Times*.

Yin, R.K. (1994). *Case study research: Design and methods*. London: Sage.

Young, K. (1993). *Planning development with women: Making a world of difference*. London: Macmillan.

Zahedi, A. (2014). Afghan Women's Hopes for the Future. *E-International Relations*.

Zakaria, R. (2021). *White Feminists Wanted to Invade*. Available at https://www.thenation.com/article/world/white-feminists-wanted-to-invade/.

Zirack, L. (2021). Women's Education: Afghanistan's Biggest Success Story Now at Risk. *The Diplomat*.

Index